Multicultural Psychology

Second Edition

Gordon C. Nagayama Hall
University of Oregon

Prentice Hall

Boston   Columbus   Indianapolis   New York   San Francisco   Upper Saddle River
Amsterdam   Cape Town   Dubai   London   Madrid   Milan   Munich   Paris   Montreal   Toronto
Delhi   Mexico City   Sao Paulo   Sydney   Hong Kong   Seoul   Singapore   Taipei   Tokyo

Editorial Director: Leah Jewell
Editor in Chief: Susan Hartman
Acquisitions Editor: Jeff Marshall
Editorial Project Manager: LeeAnn Doherty
Editorial Assistant: Amy Trudell
Director of Marketing: Brandy Dawson
Marketing Manager: Nicole Kunzmann
Marketing Assistant: Jen Lang
Project Manager: Renata Butera
Operations Specialist: Renata Butera
Cover Designer: Bruce Kenselaar
Cover Art: Jane Sterrett/Images.com/Corbis

**Manager, Cover Visual Research &
Permissions:** Karen Sanatar
Full-Service Project Management:
Nitin Agarwal/Aptara®, Inc.
Composition: Aptara®, Inc.
Printer/Binder: Bind-Rite/Command Web
Cover Printer: Bind-Rite/Command Web
Text Font: Minion
Back Cover Image Credits (left to right):
© JupiterImages, © Veer, © Monkey Business
Images/Shutterstock, © Value RF/Corbis

Library of Congress Cataloging-in-Publication Data
Hall, Gordon C. Nagayama.
   Multicultural psychology / Gordon C. Nagayama Hall.—2nd ed.
      p. cm.
   ISBN-13: 978-0-205-63235-0
   ISBN-10: 0-205-63235-1
   1. Ethnopsychology—United States.   2. Minorities—United States—Psychology.
I. Title.
   GN502.H335 2010
   155.8'20973—dc22

                                        2009019001

10 9 8 7 6 5 4 3   16 15 14 13 12

Prentice Hall
is an imprint of

www.pearsonhighered.com

ISBN 10:   0-205-63235-1
ISBN 13: 978-0-205-63235-0

In memory of my parents, Charlie and Olive Tetsuko Hall,
who envisioned a multicultural world

CONTENTS

PREFACE

Much has changed since the publication of the first edition of *Multicultural Psychology* in 2002. At that time, I did not believe that I would see a non–European American, nonmale president of the United States during my lifetime. Now the president is a biracial African American man, and the runner-up for the Democratic Party presidential nomination was a woman. At the time Barack Obama was born in Hawaii, there were 16 U.S. states in which his parents could not legally have been married. Although racism has not ended and the United States has a long way to go in becoming a multicultural society in which its citizens are competent in multiple cultures, the election of Obama was a huge step forward.

The multicultural psychology literature has also changed since 2002. There is much more empirical research that is theoretically informed. Sophisticated methodologies, in which culture is conceptualized and measured, have helped identify cultural bases of behavior. No longer do we need to infer a cultural difference when culture is not directly investigated in studies in which ethnic or racial groups are compared. People of color are also no longer an afterthought in studies that seek to test the generalizability of theories that have been developed outside of communities of color. Culture-specific models of the unique qualities of people of color have been developed and validated with empirical research.

Most of the studies and literature reviewed in this second edition have been published since 2002. The same framework from the first edition is retained, with the first half of the book considering multicultural issues in the context of psychology and the second half considering psychology in the context of multicultural issues. The first chapter offers a rationale for the study of multicultural psychology and an overview of models of racial/ethnic identity and acculturation, which provide the context for the research in subsequent chapters. The second chapter focuses on quantitative multicultural research methods, including theory-based conceptualization, sampling, assessment, data analysis, and communication and dissemination of findings. Chapter 3 covers an emerging multicultural literature in biological psychology, with a focus on genetic, evolutionary, and health issues. Developmental research on persons of color is the topic of Chapter 4. The effects on development of racial and ethnic identity, acculturation, and discrimination are considered. Multicultural literature in social psychology is reviewed in Chapter 5. Unlike the traditional focus in social psychology on European Americans as perpetrators of racism and discrimination, this chapter focuses on the impact of racism and discrimination on people of color, interethnic group relations, and reducing prejudice and increasing organizational diversity.

The second half of the book goes into greater depth on the experiences of African Americans, Asian Pacific Americans, Latino/a Americans, American Indians/Alaska Natives, and multiracial Americans. Each of these chapters begins with an historical overview, which has been updated for each group since the last edition of *Multicultural Psychology* to reflect the recent history of each group. Each chapter on these groups also reviews literature on cultural values and identity, family issues, mental health, and academic achievement and career development. Unlike the previous edition, this book devotes a full chapter to multiracial Americans because of literature on multiracial Americans that has recently developed.

Those familiar with the first edition of *Multicultural Psychology* will notice that my colleague and former student Christy Barongan is not a coauthor of the second edition. This reflects my moving to the West Coast and having much less contact with Dr. Barongan since we wrote the first edition of the book together. I continue to be proud of her and her accomplishments, but recently we have not had opportunities to collaborate. Anything about the second edition that is not as good as the first is my responsibility!

The University of Oregon provided a sabbatical during which I completed much of the work on this book. This work was also supported in part by the Asian American Center on Disparities Research (National Institute of Mental Health grant: 1P50MH073511-01A2). I am grateful to Janet Ng, Jessica Murakami, Jennifer Pfeifer, and Melanie Domenech-Rodriguez for their feedback on drafts of the first section of the book. My colleagues in the Department of Ethnic Studies at the University of Oregon provided references that were valuable in writing the history sections in the second half of the book. I also greatly appreciate Jeff Marshall's and Prentice Hall's support of this book revision project.

I am hopeful about societal changes and the growing literature in multicultural psychology since the publication of the first edition of this book. As I indicate in Chapter 10, I hope that the research reviewed in this book can help guide us on a path toward a more perfect, multicultural union.

I would also like to thank the following reviewers to this edition: Ana Ruiz, Ph.D., Alvernia College; Dorothy Abram, Ph.D., Johnson & Wales University; Ju Hui Park, Ph.D., California State University, Davis; Leslie C. Jackson, Ph.D., Georgia State University; Marcellene Watson-Derbigny, Ph.D., California State University, Sacramento; Jean Mennuti-Washburn, Georgia State University; Page Anderson, Ph.D., Georgia State University.

Gordon C. Nagayama Hall

Eugene, Oregon

Multicultural Issues in the Context of Psychology

CHAPTER 1

What Is Multicultural Psychology?

Multicultural psychology is American psychology, albeit a part of American psychology that has been neglected. For those who intend to live and work in North America, which includes most people reading this book, an understanding of the diverse groups in North America is critical. Yet, most of the American psychology literature does not address cultural diversity. I have joked with my students that most psychology courses and textbooks should include a disclaimer that the theories and research to be presented have not been adequately evaluated with people of color and that it is unknown whether these theories and research apply to groups other than European Americans. This book is about the issues and people that are omitted from or marginalized in most other psychology textbooks and courses.

This chapter will discuss why cultural diversity has been neglected in psychology, as well as the importance of multicultural issues. Definitions of multicultural psychology, race, ethnicity, culture, and minority status are presented and the influence of social class on groups of color is discussed. Historical and contemporary models of racial and ethnic identity are compared and contrasted.

Multicultural means multiple ways of knowing or multiple worldviews. By its very nature, a multicultural approach is complex and contextual. What applies in one context may not necessarily apply in another. *Multicultural psychology* is the study of the influences of multiple cultures in a single social context on human behavior (G. Hall & Barongan, 2002). Whereas the assumption in traditional psychology is that theories and research are generalizable, the assumption in multicultural psychology is that there are both universal and culture-specific phenomena, with an emphasis on the latter.

The focus of this textbook is on cultural diversity in groups of color in North America. There are other forms of diversity, such as gender, socioeconomic status, sexual identity, disability, and religiosity, that intersect with cultural diversity. However, cultural diversity in groups of color is important because these groups are rapidly growing and changing the culture of North America. Moreover, cultural diversity is often influential beyond other forms of diversity. For example, being a Latina American changes one's status within diverse identities and is as important as these other identities. Although Latina American and European American lesbians may have common gender and sexual identities, Latina American women may have a cultural identity that European American women are unlikely to have. Although cultural diversity is the focus of this textbook, there will also be discussions of how cultural diversity intersects with other forms of diversity.

CULTURAL DIVERSITY AND MAINSTREAM PSYCHOLOGY

The concept of multicultural psychology may appear to be an oxymoron. Theories and research in psychology traditionally have been assumed to be universal—one size fits all. For example, empirically supported treatment approaches in clinical psychology are assumed to work equally well for everyone, yet there is limited empirical support for these treatments for anyone other than European Americans (Zane, Hall, Sue, Young & Nunez, 2004). As in other sciences, the goal of psychological theories and research is parsimony: The simpler the better. Why propose a complex, multicultural model of behavior instead of a simple monocultural one? Animal and computer models of human behavior in psychology do not include culture. Is culture something that is uniquely human that complicates human existence?

The universality assumption in psychology is largely untested. Most psychological theory development and research has occurred in the West, particularly in the United States. Psychology's typical cutoff for statistical significance is $p < .05$, meaning that events that occur less than 5% of the time are dismissed as chance events or error. Yet, the U.S. population is less than 5% of the world's population. So why should psychology assume that its theories and findings apply to the other 95% of the world (Arnett, 2008)? Is it possible that much of what we know in psychology does not apply to the rest of the world and is a function of chance or error? Why not base theories and research on a country that is more representative of the world's population, such as China, which constitutes more than one-fifth of the world's population?

Mainstream psychology has overlooked culture (Segall, Lonner, & Berry, 1998; D. W. Sue, 2004). When culture has been studied in psychology, it has not often been studied very rigorously. A common method is to include a small group of ethnic minority individuals in a research sample and assume that the research findings are generalizable because minorities were included. Separate analyses of the data on ethnic minority individuals are usually not conducted because the ethnic minority sample is too small or the researcher is not interested. However, if the majority of the sample is not ethnic minority individuals, ethnic differences may be reduced or invisible because the influence of the majority of the sample is greater than that of the minority.

Members of ethnic minority groups are often combined in research to increase sample size. Although African Americans, American Indians, Asian Americans, and Latina/Latino Americans have some common experiences as persons of color, each group also has unique experiences. This is why the second part of this book addresses each of these groups individually. Moreover, there is diversity within each of these major ethnic groups in terms of gender, sexual identity, and socioeconomic status. To simply lump ethnic minority individuals into an ethnic minority category or even into one of the broad ethnic categories (African Americans, American Indians, Asian Americans, and Latina/Latino Americans) is to miss within-group diversity (Trimble & Dickson, 2005).

Another relatively common approach in psychology to culture is to compare two groups that ostensibly differ in culture. For example, there have been many studies comparing individuals in the United States with those in Japan. Any differences between the groups are assumed to have a cultural basis. However, if culture is not directly measured, there may be other reasons for the differences. Different experiences that are not necessarily culturally based, such as living in more versus less densely populated areas or living under different political systems, could account for such differences between groups. Research approaches that conceptualize, measure, and analyze culture will be discussed in detail in Chapter 2.

Why has culture been neglected in psychology? Perhaps it is because many psychologists do not have a "theory of mind" concerning culture. Theory of mind is the ability to understand that individuals may perceive a situation in varying ways—that different individuals have different minds (Carlson & Moses, 2001). Younger preschoolers frequently believe that there can be only one perspective on a situation, which is their own. By the time most children are about 5 years old, they understand that different perspectives exist. Psychologists certainly are capable of having theories of mind regarding culture. However, it is possible that the apparent lack of a cultural theory of mind among psychologists is based on their demographics. A recent survey indicated that 88% of psychology faculty in graduate programs are not ethnic minorities (Maton, Kohout, Wicherski, Leary, & Vinokurov, 2006). Although there is probably some cultural diversity within this 88%, many psychologists do not come into contact with "other minds" when it comes to culture.

A "culture-free" psychology will soon become obsolete (C. C. I. Hall, 1997; D. W. Sue, Bingham, Porche-Burke, & Vasquez, 1999). According to the U.S. Census Bureau (August, 2007), nearly 1 in every 10 of the nation's 3,141 counties has a population that is more than 50% minority. Los Angeles County had the largest number of ethnic minorities in the country at 7 million, which was 71% of the county's population. Among the nation's most populous counties, Miami-Dade County in Florida had the highest percentage of ethnic minorities at 82%.

Given the existing and increasing ethnic diversity in the United States, diversification of psychological theories and research might seem inevitable. Nevertheless, psychology as a field has been slow to diversify. Although African Americans and Latina/Latino Americans combined constitute 25% of the U.S. population, these two groups constitute only about 10–12% of students entering PhD programs in psychology (Maton et al., 2006). This percentage of African American and Latina/Latino American psychology graduate students has not changed, despite U.S. demographic changes, particularly among Latino/Latina Americans. Thus, many psychology faculty and students are typically not exposed to other cultural minds. Even a majority of ethnic minority students and faculty might not change the field. As in South Africa, where for many years Blacks were in the majority and Whites in the minority, demographic changes will not inherently change the power structure of psychology (G. C. N. Hall, 2006).

Of course, it is possible that attention to culture in psychology could occur without demographic changes. Many nonminority psychologists study culture and ethnic minority issues. Nevertheless, ethnic minority psychologists tend to be interested in ethnic minority issues, just as majority psychologists tend to be interested in majority issues (G. Hall & Maramba, 2001). Moreover, calls for the ethnic diversification of psychology have largely gone unheeded over the past 30 years (G. Hall, Iwamasa, & Smith, 2003). On the other hand, the percentage of European American women in psychology has dramatically increased over this same period, as has attention in psychology to gender issues. It would now be unthinkable not to include women in psychological theories and research. Perhaps an ethnic diversification of psychologists could have a similar effect in placing culture at the core of psychology.

The lack of demographic diversity in psychology is reflected in its literature. Figure 1.1 presents a count of all articles in PsycInfo from 1981 through 2006 that included the terms *African American* or *Black, American Indian* or *Native American, Asian* or *Asian Americans Latino/a* or *Hispanic, racial* and *ethnic groups, ethnic identity, minority groups,* or *racial* and *ethnic differences.* The data reveal a fivefold increase in the number of these articles over this 25-year period. Figure 1.2 tells another story that is not so encouraging. This figure presents the percentage of PsycInfo articles using the above terms relative to all articles in PsycInfo. During the 1980s, the percentage of articles in psychology on people of color remained at 3%. There was a percentage increase in the 1990s, but the percentage has remained at about 4.5% throughout the 2000s. It could be argued that a low percentage of articles in psychology on persons of color is to be expected, as only about 10% of doctoral-level psychologists are persons of color. Nevertheless, 4.5% is a miniscule percentage, given the existing and growing ethnic diversity in North America.

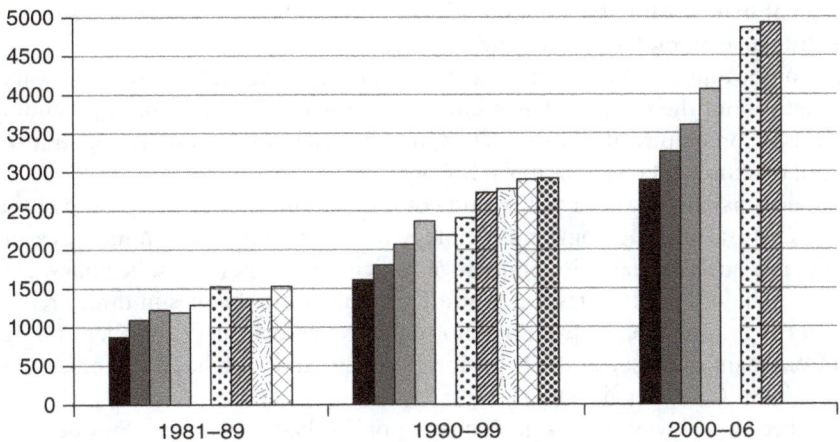

FIGURE 1.1 Number of Psychology Publications on People of Color

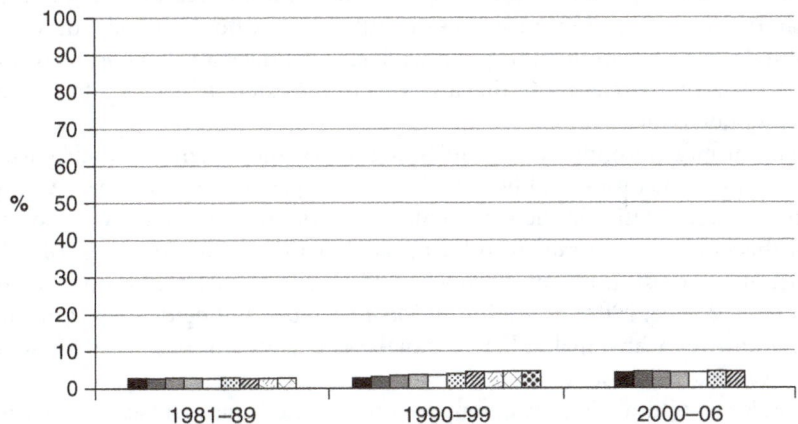

FIGURE 1.2 Percentage of All Psychology Publications on People of Color

In summary, mainstream psychological theories and research are typically assumed to be universal. Culture has been neglected in these theories and research. Psychology may not be culturally diverse because psychologists are not culturally diverse. Nevertheless, psychology needs to diversify if it is to remain relevant in the 21st century.

THE IMPORTANCE OF MULTICULTURAL ISSUES

Despite the relative neglect of culture in psychology, there is a growing and increasingly sophisticated literature within psychology on multicultural issues. This literature is not on the periphery of psychology. Much of this literature has been published in mainstream psychology journals, including *Cultural Diversity and Ethnic Minority Psychology*, which has been published by the American Psychological Association since 1999. The focus in this book will be on high-quality empirical research that is making psychology more relevant to our nation and world in the 21st century. Rather than ignoring, neglecting, or reacting to cultural diversity, as has been the tradition of mainstream psychology, multicultural psychology is proactive and is helping to shape the discourse on race, ethnicity, and culture.

Many of the topics addressed in this textbook are controversial, and there are varying opinions in society about these topics. The scholarly framework for this book is psychology, which bases knowledge on empirical research. Thus, the material in this book is not simply based on opinions but on empirical research in psychology.

What does psychology offer to the study of multicultural issues that other fields do not already offer? Cultural anthropology and sociology focus on culture in communities and groups. Social policy and social welfare disciplines focus on cultural issues in public policy. Unlike other disciplines, psychology contributes to the study of multicultural issues in three areas: (1) It addresses issues at a range of levels from the molecular to the societal, (2) its scientific rigor distinguishes it from many other social and behavioral sciences, and (3) it has direct or indirect benefits to human welfare (G. Hall et al., 2003).

I have been asked why there is not a chapter of this book devoted to European Americans, analogous to the chapters on African Americans, American Indians, Asian Americans, and Latina/o Americans. There actually is much discussion of European Americans in this book relative to groups of color. Moreover, psychological theory and research involving European Americans are thoroughly covered in most other psychology textbooks. Unlike these textbooks, in which cultural diversity is omitted or peripheral, cultural diversity is the focus of this textbook. European Americans are relevant in this textbook to the extent that they differ from the groups on which this book is focused.

When Europeans immigrate to the United States, they often lose their particular ethnic identities within a generation and become White and part of the European American culture that is considered normative in the United States (Spickard, 2007). Race, culture, and ethnicity, the foci of this book, are less salient to European Americans than to groups of color in North America because in most situations, European Americans do not have to confront what it means to be White (D. W. Sue, 2004). Attention to identity issues among dominant groups in society (e.g., European Americans, males, heterosexuals) is usually not necessary for social and economic survival (Harrell & Bond, 2006).

There also is cultural diversity among European Americans that has not been studied to the extent that cultural diversity has been studied in the groups of color that are the topic of this book (Trimble, 2007). The "melting pot" model of immigration assumes that immigrants come to North America, blend into the culture, and leave their cultures of origin behind. Because European cultures are relatively similar to dominant North American culture, becoming part of the melting pot may actually occur for many persons of European ancestry. Nevertheless, cultural and generational variability among North Americans of European ancestry have received less attention in psychology than even the relatively limited attention devoted to populations of color.

Another reason for the inattention to culture among European Americans is individualism. Many European Americans may perceive themselves as unique individuals who are not bound to the norms or traditions of cultural or other types of groups. Although European Americans may have common cultural characteristics, many European Americans, including psychologists, may not perceive culture as having a particularly important influence on their behavior as a group.

You may think that multicultural issues should be integrated into all psychology courses and textbooks, and that there should not be a need for this book (cf. Segall et al., 1998). I wholeheartedly agree with such sentiments. Nevertheless, multicultural issues are not integrated into most psychology courses and textbooks, and this state of affairs is unlikely to change soon. Books such as this one serve as a reminder to the field of the important aspects of the human experience that it overlooks.

At this point, you may still be thinking, "What's in this for me?" In addition to fostering cultural awareness and interest in social issues, the study of cultural diversity has been found to increase listening, critical thinking, and writing skills among college students of all ethnic backgrounds, including European Americans (Antonio et al., 2004; Gurin, Nagda, & Lopez, 2004; Hurtado, 2005). Thus, "thinking outside the box" can be beneficial for everyone.

In summary, there is a growing body of empirical research on multicultural issues that will be reviewed in this book. Psychology's contributions to the study of multicultural issues involve its broad focus from the molecular to society, its scientific rigor, and its application to human welfare. Whereas European Americans have been the focus of most of psychology, this textbook will focus on groups of color in North America. Such a focus on cultural diversity can benefit persons from all backgrounds.

Definitions of Multicultural Psychology, Race, Ethnicity, Culture, and Minority Status

North America is an excellent laboratory for the study of multicultural psychology because multiple groups having distinct cultures live together in single countries. Immigrants to the United States are influenced by the traditions and practices of their culture(s) of origin. They are also influenced by cultures within the United States, particularly by dominant European American cultures. One does not have to be an immigrant to be influenced by more than one culture in the United States. A person whose family has been in the United States for multiple generations but whose culture of origin differs from European American cultures can still be influenced by their culture of origin. For example, although African Americans have been in North America for centuries, individual African Americans may vary to the extent that they are influenced by African and United States cultures (Landrine & Klonoff, 1996a).

Navigating life in the United States for a person of color is not simply a matter of being influenced by or choosing more than one culture. Persons of color in the United States have minority status relative to European Americans in terms of numbers and societal power. Minority status may also be a new experience for persons who are leaving a country in which they are the majority. A major effect of minority status is discrimination. *Discrimination* involves harmful actions toward others because of their membership in a particular group (Fishbein, 1996). Racially or ethnically based discrimination is more commonly perceived among persons of color than among European Americans. For example, among fifth-graders through eighth-graders, 19% of African American males and 27% of African American females experienced discrimination within the past 6 months, whereas 7% of European American males and 11% of European American females had similar experiences (DuBois et al., 2002). Discrimination may limit social, educational, economic, professional, and political opportunities. Phenotypic salience (e.g., skin color, facial features, other physical characteristics) and cultural traditions that differ from those of European Americans may make it more difficult for persons of color to assimilate into American society than for persons of European backgrounds (C. L. Williams & Berry, 1991).

Another effect of minority status is a tendency by others to lump together persons having minority status, even when the persons are very different from one another. For example, new immigrants may be grouped with others with whom they have not previously been associated. Immigrants from China might not perceive themselves as having much in common with Koreans, yet in the United States, Chinese and Korean Americans are often grouped together as Asian Americans. Immigrant status may cause a person to be grouped with immigrants from other continents (e.g., Asia, Latin America). More broadly, persons of color may be lumped into a single non-White group. Although there are common issues across minority groups that will be addressed in the first part of this book, there are group-specific issues that will be addressed in the second part.

※ To summarize, <u>multicultural psychology is the study of cultural</u> (e.g., culture of origin, U.S. cultures) and sociocultural <u>influences</u> (e.g., minority status, discrimination) <u>on behavior</u>. This emphasis on both cultural and sociocultural influences distinguishes multicultural psychology from cultural psychology and cross-cultural psychology. *Cultural psychology* is the study of cultural influences on behavior within single cultural contexts (Shweder, 2000) without the consideration of sociocultural influences. Similarly, the focus of *cross-cultural psychology* is on cultural similarities and differences across different national contexts (Segall et al., 1998). However, because the nations studied in cross-cultural psychology typically do not share the same geographic space, sociocultural influences tend not to be emphasized. Moreover, cross-cultural psychology tends to use *etic* approaches, in which there is a search for the universality of behaviors observed in one culture, which usually is European American. In contrast, multicultural psychology includes etic approaches but emphasizes culture-specific, or *emic*, approaches that do not assume behaviors to be universal.

Cultural psychology and cross-cultural psychology tend to focus on cultural groups outside North America. The implicit assumption in these two approaches is that American culture is equivalent to European American culture. In contrast, multicultural psychology recognizes the existence and importance of multiple American cultural groups. While an understanding of global psychology is important, it is equally important to understand cultural diversity in North America, which is where most readers of this book live and probably will live in the future.

Important concepts in multicultural psychology include race, ethnicity, and culture. *Race* is a group of people with origins in a single geographic area who are more closely related biologically than are members of groups who live greater distances apart (Ota Wang & Sue, 2005). Perceptions of race are typically based on phenotypic characteristics (e.g., skin color, facial features, hair texture), and racial differences in psychological characteristics are often presumed to be biologically based (Ota Wang & Sue, 2005). Nevertheless, self- or other-perceived race does not directly correspond with genetic variation. For example, there is more genetic variation within than between racial groups, and no single gene is sufficient for classifying human populations into racial categories (Bonham, Warshaeuer-Baker, & Collins, 2005). Moreover, an increasing proportion of the world's population does not have recent ancestors from a single geographic region (Bonham et al., 2005). The meaning of race is socially constructed because it often serves as a proxy for culture or ethnicity, concepts that are of more interest in multicultural psychology than is race.

Culture involves shared attitudes, beliefs, norms, roles, and self-definitions (Triandis, 1996). Unlike the prevailing approach in psychology that assumes psychological characteristics reside within individuals (Bodas & Ollendick, 2005), culture resides neither in individuals or in society but in the interactions between individuals and society (Lopez & Guarnaccia, 2000). Thus, the development of culture is a reciprocal process. Cultural groups influence individuals while individuals influence social groups. For example, individual leaders, such as Rosa Parks, Martin Luther King, Jr., and Malcolm X, were influenced by the religion and politics in the African American communities in which they were raised but also changed African American religion and politics to become increasingly activist.

Ethnicity involves shared race, as well as a unique social and cultural heritage (Phinney, 1996; S. Sue, 1991). The term was originally used in the United States in the early 20th century to distinguish eastern and southern European immigrants from other European Americans and later was applied to immigrants from other parts of the world (Rees, 2007). Ethnicity may be relatively narrowly defined (e.g., Chinese American, German American) or defined more broadly (e.g., Asian American, European American). Ethnic groups may share particular cultural practices, such as language and food. They may also share psychological characteristics, such as relative emphasis on individuals versus the group and degree of emotional expression and restraint. Shared race is not always necessary for ethnic group membership. For example, Latina/o Americans may be from different racial backgrounds but may have common social and cultural backgrounds that unite them as an ethnic group.

To sum up, multicultural psychology focuses on both cultural and sociocultural influences on behavior. It is different from either cultural or cross-cultural psychology. The meaning of race is socially constructed and it often serves as a proxy for culture or ethnicity. Culture involves shared traditions, and ethnic groups share and practice culture.

SOCIAL CLASS

Persons of color are overrepresented among those near or below the poverty line. Poverty can be the result of restricted societal opportunities for persons of color as a function of discrimination. Much of the psychology literature on persons of color has focused on those who are poor (G. C. N. Hall, 2004). In this literature, ethnic minority status is synonymous with poverty (Nazroo, 2003). The relative absence of data on non-poor persons of color implies that research on poor persons of color generalizes to all persons of color.

It is important to note that the majority of persons of color are not poor. U.S. Census Bureau data indicate that one in four African Americans, (January, 2006), one in four American Indians (February, 2006), 1 in 10 Asian Pacific Americans (March, 2007), and 1 in five Latina/Latino Americans (July, 2007) is poor. These data compare with 1 in 10 European Americans who are poor (U.S. Bureau of the Census, 2007). Official records probably underestimate the number of persons affected by poverty. Nevertheless, poor persons of color do not represent the majority of persons of color. Moreover, there are almost as many poor European Americans in the United States (16 million) as African Americans (9.4 million), Asian Pacific Americans (1.4 million), and Latina/Latino Americans (9 million) combined (U.S. Bureau of the Census, 2007).

It is also important to note that socioeconomic status cannot explain all ethnic differences. Socioeconomic status and the cultures of groups of color often become conflated. There exists a culture of economic status in that persons with fewer economic resources may share attitudes and behaviors as a result of their life circumstances (Y. Jackson, 2003). Nevertheless, economic factors are not equivalent to cultural factors. In this book, we will examine research in which ethnicity and culture influence behavior beyond the influences of socioeconomic status. This is not to say that socioeconomic status is an unimportant consideration for persons of color. We will also examine research in which socioeconomic status is more influential than ethnicity and culture.

MODELS OF RACIAL/ETHNIC IDENTITY

Before the 1960s, cultural issues were virtually absent from psychological research (Ponterotto & Mallinckrodt, 2007). Initial research on culture during the 1960s and 1970s focused on race or ethnicity as a categorical variable (e.g., African American) and compared ethnic minority groups with European Americans. Although this categorical, comparative paradigm treats large groups of individuals as if they are all alike, some research using this paradigm continues at present. During the 1980s, theory and research began to focus on African American and European American identity and on Latina/o American and Asian American acculturation (Ponterotto & Mallinckrodt, 2007). Additional models of cultural identity were developed in the 1990s, and ethnic identity, which incorporates race and culture, was delineated from racial identity (Phinney, 1992).

Identities based on race, ethnicity, culture, and minority status will serve as the framework for this book. *Racial identity* focuses on the meaning and importance of race and responses to racism (Helms, 2007). *Racism* assumes that group differences are biologically based, that one's own race is superior, and that practices that formalize the domination of one racial group over another are justifiable (J. M. Jones, 1997). *Ethnic identity* involves the strength of identification with one's ethnic group (Phinney, 1996). Components of ethnic identity include self-labeling, a sense of belonging, positive evaluation, preference for the group, ethnic interest and knowledge, and involvement in activities associated with the group. There has been much recent research on racial/ethnic identity and its effects on behavior. In this section, I will highlight influential models.

Such a focus on racial/ethnic identity could be viewed as identity politics—the idea that such identity is politically motivated to garner special privileges for certain groups (Bernstein, 2005). Critics of multiculturalism contend that an emphasis on differences is not democratic. Some groups are provided special treatment while others are not. These critics may subscribe to a "color-blind" worldview. However, this color-blind approach is blind to colors except white (D. Sue, 2004). The world is evaluated by White, European American standards. Although those who advocate a color-blind society may eschew identity politics, they often practice an identity politics of their own: White identity politics. European Americans typically do not define themselves in terms of race or ethnicity (Phinney, 1996). Thus, they may not view a color-blind society in terms of race or ethnicity, although color-blind societies as they are typically construed impose standards in terms of the race and ethnicity of the dominant group. Such color-blind approaches often do not consider the merits of diverse cultural identities, which are valued by many members of both dominant and nondominant groups.

One reason to consider diverse cultures and not to be color-blind is a scientific one. It is good science to study and understand cultural differences rather than to deny that they exist. Moreover, it is good science to determine if theories and research developed in one group generalize to others (S. Sue, 1999). Overlooking cultural diversity in North America would be a failure of psychology to take advantage of a nascent multicultural laboratory in our own backyard.

Another reason to study cultural diversity is a psychological one. A strong racial/ethnic identity is often associated with psychological benefits (Ponterotto & Park-Taylor, 2007). To ignore cultural diversity could limit the capacities of individuals to reach their full potential. I will review the effects of racial/ethnic identity for specific ethnic groups in the second section of this book.

A third reason to consider cultural diversity involves social justice. Some have interpreted Martin Luther King, Jr.'s statement that people should not be judged by their skin but by the content of their character as advocating a color-blind society. However, the context of that statement was a society in which all groups have equal access and opportunity (D. W. Sue, 2004). Although some may believe that all groups in the United States currently do have equal access and opportunity and that discrimination is a thing of the past, individual and institutional barriers to success for persons of color continue to persist (Crosby, Iyer, Clayton, & Downing, 2003). Ignoring racial and ethnic identities lessens the ability to monitor inequities and may allow discrimination to go undetected (D. W. Sue, 2004).

Cross Model of Racial Identity

One of the earliest models of racial/ethnic identity that has influenced subsequent models was developed by William Cross (1971). Cross's (1971, 1991) model was developed in an African American context, but this model has implications for other ethnic groups. Cross conceptualized racial identity as a process involving four stages: Pre-Encounter, Encounter, Immersion/Emersion, and Internalization. The Cross Racial Identity Scale (Cross & Vandiver, 2001) assesses the stages of Cross's (1991) model of African American racial identity.

In the *Pre-Encounter* stage, African Americans view the world as non-Black or anti-Black. Because African Americans in this stage view European Americans as superior to African Americans, the goal is assimilation into European American society. African American identity is devalued. Such an assimilationist identity might be likely among African Americans who grow up isolated from other African Americans. Cross's (Cross & Vandiver, 2001) revised model includes three identity clusters in the Pre-Encounter stage. *Pre-encounter assimilation* identity involves a low salience of race and a strong identification with being American. *Pre-encounter miseducation* identity involves internalization of negative stereotypes of African Americans (e.g., lazy, criminal). *Pre-encounter self-hatred* identity involves negative views about African Americans and oneself. An example of an African American in the Pre-Encounter stage would be someone in a primarily European American organization who does not identify as African American and believes that she can fit in and succeed as well as anyone else. Such a person may not perceive any barriers to fitting in or to success as a result of her race or discrimination.

In the *Encounter* stage, African Americans become aware of what it means to be African American and begin to validate themselves in terms of that racial identity. Movement into this stage is often precipitated by some encounter with discrimination. For example, an African American who is attempting to succeed in a corporation realizes that there are no African Americans in upper management. Moreover, he may see himself passed over for an upper management position by a European American with the same credentials and seniority. Because the person cannot escape that his status as an African American makes him different from others, he actively searches for new and different interpretations of his identity.

African Americans in the *Immersion-Emersion* stage immerse themselves in African American culture and may reject all values that are not African American. Rejection of European American values may be viewed as necessary to prove that one is African American. Such a person on a college campus might be an activist in African American student organizations and be considered a "radical" or a "militant." A person emerges from this stage with a strong African American identity. Cross's (Cross & Vandiver, 2001) revised model includes two Immersion-Emersion identities. *Immersion-emersion intense Black involvement* identity views everything African American or Afrocentric as good. *Immersion-emersion anti-White* identity views everything European American or Eurocentric as bad.

In the final *Internalization* stage, African Americans develop a self-confident and secure African American identity and are also comfortable expressing interests and preferences for experiences from other cultures. Anti–European American feelings decline. Persons in the Internalization stage identify with the oppression of all people and often become involved in social activism. Malcolm X moved from the Immersion-Emersion state to the Internalization stage when he became a Muslim and began to accept and become involved in the struggles of persons of multiple ethnic backgrounds. Cross (Cross & Vandiver, 2001) proposed two internalization identities in his revised model. *Black nationalism* involves an Afrocentric identity that is not reactionary to other identities. *Multiculturalist inclusive* involves an African American identity as well as at least two other identities (e.g., gender, sexual identities).

Racial identity may be associated with other identities. The Pre-Encounter and Encounter stages were associated with traditional attitudes toward women among African American women in New York City (Martin & Hall, 1992). Although the Immersion-Emersion stage was not associated with attitudes toward women, the Internalization stage was associated with feminist attitudes.

TABLE 1.1   Comparison of the Cross Model of Racial Identity to Other Models

Cross	Pre-Encounter	Encounter	Immersion-Emersion	Internalization
Helms	Contact	Disintegration	Reintegration, Immersion/emersion	Autonomy
Sellers	Assimilationist, Humanist	Oppressed minority	Nationalist, Oppressed minority	Humanist
Phinney	Diffusion	Foreclosure	Moratorium	Achievement
Poston	Personal identity	Choice of group categorization	Enmeshment/Denial, Appreciation	Integration

Models similar to the Cross model have been developed for White racial identity, African American racial identity, ethnic identity, and biracial identity. These models are reviewed below. Table 1.1 compares the stages of these other models to the Cross model.

Helms Model of White Racial Identity

Do European Americans develop a racial identity? European Americans are typically taught, implicitly or explicitly, to ignore or minimize the meaning of their racial group membership (Ponterotto, Utsey, & Pedersen, 2006; D. W. Sue, 2004). Nevertheless, some European Americans do develop an identity in terms of their race or ethnicity. Helms (1990) developed a model of White racial identity that is analogous to the Cross (1971) model. As with the Cross model, there are a series of stages. The White Racial Identity Attitude Scale (Helms & Carter, 1990) is based on the Helms model of White racial identity.

The *Contact* stage in the Helms (1990) model is one in which race is not a distinguishing factor in psychological development. A person in this stage sees all people as having much in common. This stage is analogous to the Cross (1971, 1991) Pre-Encounter stage.

The second stage in the Helms model is *Disintegration* and involves a confusion and perplexity about being White. A European American in this stage may face moral dilemmas about what it means to be White in a society that denigrates persons who are not White. The Disintegration stage is analogous to the Cross (1971, 1991) Encounter stage. The Encounter stage for European Americans involves a recognition that European Americans perpetrate discrimination, rather than being victims of discrimination.

The third stage in the Helms model, *Reintegration*, is an attempt to deal with the sense of disintegration by asserting racial superiority. For persons in this stage, African Americans and other minorities are viewed as inferior. The Reintegration stage is similar to immersion in the Cross (1971, 1991) Immersion-Emersion stage.

Pseudo-independence is the fourth stage of the Helms model, in which a person gains a broader understanding of impact of race, ethnicity, and culture on psychological development. However, race issues become important only during interactions with persons of color. A person in the Pseudo-independence stage may develop generalized, sometimes stereotypic, assumptions about various ethnic groups.

The next stage, *Immersion/emersion*, is an attempt to develop a personal and moral definition of Whiteness. A person in this stage may also encourage other Whites to redefine Whiteness.

The Immersion/emersion stage is similar to emersion in the Cross (1971, 1991) Immersion-Emersion stage. This person realizes that European Americans have a culture that differs from that of other groups.

The final stage of the Helms model, *Autonomy*, involves the development of a nonracist White identity. A person in this stage gains an awareness of both the strengths and weaknesses of European American culture. This stage is analogous to the Cross (1971, 1991) Internalization stage. This person is comfortable with his or her own identity as well as with the identities of others who are not European Americans.

Sellers et al. Multidimensional Model of Racial Identity

A contemporary model of racial identity is the Multidimensional Model of Racial Identity (Sellers, Smith, Shelton, Rowley, & Chavous, 1998). Unlike the Cross (1971, 1991) model in which an individual is placed in sequential stages, the significance and meaning of racial identity in the Sellers et al., model may vary across time and situations. The Multidimensional Model of Racial Identity is assessed with the Multidimensional Inventory of Black Identity (Sellers, Rowley, Chavous, Shelton, & Smith 1997). Although the Multidimensional Model of Racial Identity focuses on race and was developed for African Americans, many aspects of the model are relevant to other ethnic groups (Phinney & Ong, 2007).

Racial identity in the Multidimensional Model of Racial Identity (Sellers et al., 1998) involves: (a) the importance of race in the individual's perception of self and (b) the meaning of being a member of a racial group. Race is considered one of many important identities, such as gender and occupational identity. Sellers and colleagues proposed four dimensions of racial identity: racial salience, the centrality of the identity, the regard in which the person holds the group associated with the identity, and the ideology associated with the identity.

Racial *salience* involves the relevance of race as part of one's self-concept in a particular situation. For example, race might become salient if one is the only member of a race in a social setting. It also might become salient if one witnesses racist comments or behavior. There are likely to be individual differences in salience within the same situation based on past experiences. In the case of being the only member of a race in a social setting, race might be less salient for a person if they have commonly been the only member of their race in a setting than for a person who is not used to having solo status. Racial salience is more relevant to people of color in North America than to European Americans, insofar as European Americans typically are the majority and race issues are not salient unless they are in situations in which they are the minority.

Racial *centrality* is the extent to which persons normatively identify themselves with race. Unlike racial salience, racial centrality is relatively stable across situations. Racial centrality also involves the importance of race relative to other identities, such as gender. Race would be the most important identity for someone for whom race is central. However, race is not the central identity for all members of a group. Thus, upon meeting an African American, it cannot be assumed that the person is strongly identified with her race. She may have other identities that are more central, such as gender, sexual identity, or occupational status.

Regard involves the positive and negative feelings a person has about his or her race. *Private regard* involves positive or negative feelings about one's race and positive or negative feelings about being a member of the racial group. *Public regard* involves perceptions of the positive or negative feelings of others in society toward African Americans. Private and public regard are not necessarily positively correlated. One could have positive private regard about one's race despite perceptions of negative public regard and vice versa.

Ideology involves a person's beliefs about the way African Americans should live and interact with society. A *nationalist* ideology emphasizes that African Americans should control their own destiny with minimal input from other groups. An *oppressed minority* ideology emphasizes the similarities between oppression faced by African Americans and oppression faced by other minority groups. The *assimilationist* ideology emphasizes similarities between African Americans and the rest of American society, particularly the mainstream, with a goal of becoming an indistinguishable part of American society. The *humanist* ideology is more global than the assimilationist ideology and emphasizes similarities among all humans, deemphasizing the importance of race and other distinguishing characteristics, such as gender.

These ideologies correspond to the Cross (1971, 1991) stages. A nationalist ideology is similar to the Immersion-Emersion stage. The oppressed minority ideology has similarities to the Encounter and Immersion-Emersion stages. The assimilationist ideology corresponds to the Pre-Encounter stage. The humanist ideology is similar to the Internalization stage but is also similar to the Pre-Encounter stage insofar as race is deemphasized.

Phinney Model of Ethnic Identity

Models of racial identity have primarily focused on African Americans and European Americans. Models of ethnic identity have focused on multiple ethnic groups. Phinney's (1989) influential model of ethnic identity is based on Marcia's (1980) model of personal identity, which did not focus on ethnic identity. Marcia conceptualized identity formation as involving: (a) exploration of identity issues; and (b) commitment, or a sense of belonging. Unlike personal identity, ethnic identity involves a shared sense of identity with others in one's ethnic group and is less determined by individual choice (Phinney & Ong, 2007). The development of ethnic identity moves from ethnic identity *diffusion* (a lack of a clear identity) to either *foreclosure* (commitment without exploration) or *moratorium* (exploration without commitment) to ethnic identity *achievement*, which involves a clear understanding of ethnicity based on exploration and commitment (Marcia, 1980; Phinney, 1989). The Phinney (1989) model spawned the Multigroup Ethnic Identity Measure (Phinney, 1992), the most widely used measure of ethnic identity.

The use of the terms *diffusion, foreclosure,* and *moratorium* in the Marcia (1980) and Phinney (1989) models is somewhat counterintuitive. Diffusion typically means that pieces of something that are dispersed or scattered, whereas diffusion in the Marcia and Phinney models means that identity is not yet developed. Foreclosure and moratorium typically mean inactivity, but in the Marcia and Phinney models, these stages involve activity with respect to identity.

The beginning and end points of the Phinney (1989) model are analogous to Cross's (1971, 1991) Pre-Encounter and Internalization stages. Foreclosure is somewhat similar to the Encounter stage, although the Encounter stage is characterized by exploration. Moratorium is also somewhat similar to the Immersion/Emersion stage, although the Immersion/Emersion stage is characterized by commitment. In a study of African American adolescents and adults using the Marcia (1980) and Sellers et al. (1998) identity models, Yip, Seaton, and Sellers (2006) found that racial centrality and private regard scores were higher for persons having achievement status than for persons having other statuses. However, public regard scores were lower for achievement status persons than for other groups, reflecting a realistic view of the public's perception of African Americans. Figure 1.3 illustrates racial centrality and public and private regard scores for persons having each of the Phinney ethnic identity statuses.

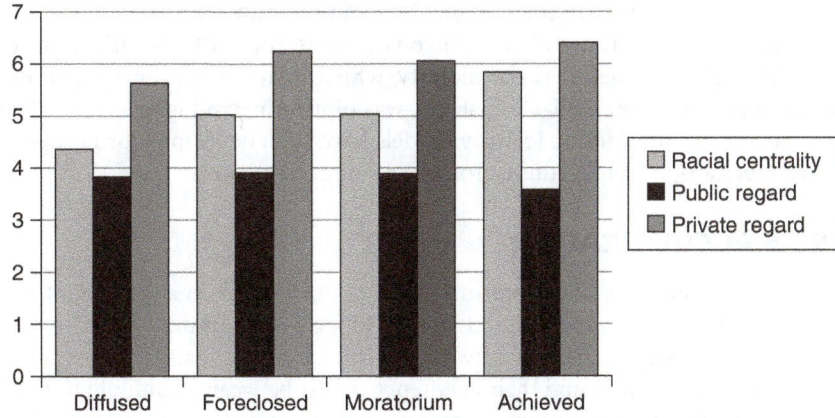

FIGURE 1.3 Racial Identity Content by Ethnic Identity Status

Poston Biracial Identity Development Model

The preceding models have focused on individuals of a single race or ethnicity. They do not account for the possibility of identifying with multiple racial or ethnic groups. There is an emerging literature on multiracial identity that will be discussed in detail in Chapter 9. However, there is much less empirical research on multiracial identity than there is on the monoracial models discussed above.

Poston (1990) proposed a stage model of biracial identity development to address identification with multiple groups. The *personal identity* stage involves a sense of self that is independent of racial or ethnic background, involving such factors as self-esteem or self-worth. Persons in this stage are often very young. The personal identity stage is analogous to the Cross (1971, 1991) Pre-Encounter stage.

Choice of group categorization is the second stage in which individuals usually choose one ethnic group (Poston, 1990). This choice is sometimes forced and influenced by the status of the ethnic groups to which one belongs, social support for acceptance and participation in a culture, and other factors, such as physical appearance and cultural knowledge. A choice of a multiethnic identity is unusual at this stage because it requires knowledge of multiple cultures and acceptance of multiple identities within a single individual. Choice of group categorization has some similarities to the Cross (1971, 1991) Encounter stage.

The third stage of the Poston (1990) model is *enmeshment/denial*. This stage involves confusion and guilt over choosing one identity over the other. Inherent in this stage is a sense of disloyalty and guilt over rejecting the identity of one parent. There may also be perceptions of a lack of acceptance from other groups. Enmeshment/denial is similar to the Immersion-Emersion stage of the Cross (1971, 1991) model.

The *appreciation* stage is when individuals begin to appreciate their multiple identities and to explore these identities (Poston, 1990). However, they still tend to identify with one group. Appreciation has some similarities to Cross's (1971, 1991) Immersion-Emersion stage.

In the *integration* stage, biracial persons recognize and value all their ethnic identities. Their identity is secure and integrated. This stage is similar to the Cross (1971, 1991) Internalization stage.

In summary, racial identity focuses on the meaning and importance of race, and responses to racism, whereas ethnic identity involves the strength of identification with one's ethnic group. The Cross model of racial identity, which includes Pre-Encounter, Encounter, Immersion-Emersion, and Internalization stages, was pioneering and is reflected in subsequent models of racial and ethnic identity. Identity models have been developed for European Americans, African Americans, multiple ethnic groups, and biracial persons.

MODELS OF ACCULTURATION

The previous models address issues of persons who presumably live in a single context in which there are multiple ethnic, racial, and cultural groups. Models of acculturation address movement from one culture to another. The balance between the culture of origin and the host culture is central to the identity of immigrants and their children. Contact between a cultural group and a host culture that changes either or both groups is known as *acculturation* (Berry, 2003). The host culture usually has more power than other cultural groups and exerts this power to change the other cultural groups. For example, there is strong pressure for immigrant groups in the United States to learn English, and some Americans want English to be the official language of the United States.

Acculturation is not necessarily a linear process in which a person smoothly transitions from one culture to another. Indeed, the acculturation process may be stressful (Berry, 2003; C. L. Williams & Berry, 1991). There are different strategies that individuals adopt in the process of acculturation.

Berry Model of Acculturation

Berry (1974) proposed *assimilation*, *separation*, *integration*, and *marginalization* as modes of acculturation that involve attitudes and behaviors in intercultural encounters. When a cultural group does not wish to maintain its cultural identity, it may seek to assimilate. This is the "melting pot" model of acculturation. The assimilation model may be more relevant for European immigrants, whose race and cultures are more similar to those of European Americans, than for immigrants of color. Moreover, some persons of color may seek to assimilate into the European American mainstream but may be prevented by the mainstream from doing so. In an international study of over 5,000 adolescent immigrants from 26 cultural backgrounds who immigrated into 13 White majority countries (U.S., Canada, Australia, New Zealand, European countries, Israel), less than one-fifth of the sample had an assimilation profile in which identity with the host nation (national identity) was strong and ethnic identity weak (Berry, Phinney, Sam, & Vedder, 2006). Assimilation corresponds to the Pre-Encounter stage in the Cross (1971, 1991) model of racial identity and to the assimilationist ideology of the Sellers et al. (1998) model.

Separation occurs when a group wishes to maintain its culture and does not wish to interact with others in the host culture. For example, sojourners who intend to return to their culture of origin may not wish to adopt the customs of the host country. Other separatists may believe that the host culture's values are detrimental or may be reacting to rejection by the host culture. Separatists are often segregated from the host culture, voluntarily (e.g., choosing to live in a particular community) or involuntarily (e.g., exclusion from a particular community). A separatist group would need to be relatively large and powerful to successfully maintain an identity. In the international study of adolescent immigration, about one-fourth of the respondents had a strong ethnic identification and weak national identification, which could be considered a separatist orientation (Berry et al., 2006). Separation generally corresponds to the Cross (1971, 1991) Immersion-Emersion stage and the Sellers et al. (1998) oppressed minority ideology.

The integration strategy involves maintaining one's culture while interacting with the host culture. Integrationists seek to participate in the host culture as members of their culture of origin. Integration can occur only when the dominant group is open to and inclusive of diverse groups. Such a multicultural society in which power is shared and in which integration is possible is difficult to achieve in practice (LaFromboise, Coleman, & Gerton, 1993). The United States has been characterized as relatively assimilationist and Canada as relatively integrationist (Berry, 2003). However, in both countries, persons of European ancestry are in power and there is limited evidence of willingness to share power at all levels of society. For example, until 2008, all the major political leaders of both countries had been men of exclusively European ancestry. In the international study of adolescent immigrants, ethnic identity and identity with the host country were positively associated among about one-third of the respondents (Berry et al., 2006). This was considered an integration strategy, but it is unclear how strongly the members of the host countries identified these immigrants as part of their country and culture. Integration corresponds to Cross's (1971, 1991) Internalization stage and the Sellers et al. (1998) humanist ideology.

Marginalization involves not being interested in maintaining one's culture of origin or in interacting with the host culture. As with separation, marginalization may be voluntary or involuntary. Those having low ethnic and national identities were the smallest group in the international adolescent immigration study (Berry et al., 2006). Marginalization does not exactly correspond with any of the Cross (1971, 1991) stages or Sellers et al. (1998) ideologies, although a person in the Encounter and Immersion-Emersion stages or having an oppressed minority ideology could feel marginalized.

LAFROMBOISE, COLEMAN, AND GERTON MODELS OF ACCULTURATION

LaFromboise and her colleagues (1993) have proposed models of acculturation that are applicable to American ethnic minority groups and offer alternatives in addition to the four acculturation strategies proposed by Berry (2003). LaFromboise and colleagues described five models of acculturation: assimilation, acculturation, fusion, alternation, and multicultural. Assimilation involves absorption into the dominant or more desirable culture. Immigrants who voluntarily come to the United States are more likely to desire to assimilate than those who have been forced to immigrate (e.g., slaves, refugees; Ogbu, 1986). Similarly, you are more likely to identify with a college that you are attending if you have chosen it than if your parents have chosen for you. In a sense you are an "involuntary immigrant" if your choice of college is restricted for economic or geographic reasons, whereas you are a "voluntary immigrant" if you are able to attend the college of your choice.

Not all who desire to assimilate into a culture are able to assimilate. The cultural distance between one's culture of origin and the second culture may affect one's ability to assimilate (C. L. Williams & Berry, 1991). For example, an Asian Indian who is a Hindu will probably have a more difficult time assimilating into mainstream American culture than a person from England who is a Christian. The dangers of assimilation involve loss of one's original cultural identity and rejection by the members of one's culture of origin (LaFromboise et al., 1993). Each ethnic group has its pejorative terms for persons of color who are White on the inside, including "oreo" (African Americans), "coconut" (Latinos), "banana" (Asian Americans), and "apple" (American Indians). The assimilation model is analogous to Berry's (2003) assimilation strategy.

A second model of acculturation is actually known as *acculturation* (LaFromboise et al., 1993). This involves a person who is competent in a second culture but always will be identified as a member of the minority culture. This person may be may be relegated to a lower status within the second culture and not completely accepted. An example is Asian Indian physicians who have had residency training in the United States and are competent in medicine. Yet, these physicians are viewed by many Americans as somehow "foreign." Such an experience may result in marginalization from both cultures. One reaction to such marginalization is separatism, which involves the formation of one's own group with the creation of the group's own standards. Rather than compete for acceptance in mainstream American culture, Asian Indian physicians might form their own group and associate exclusively with other Asian Indians. Difficulties with separatism are that some interaction with other groups is usually necessary unless one is in a large community of others similar to oneself. Another difficulty is that the mainstream can more easily ignore a separatist group than a group that attempts to interact with the mainstream. The acculturation model incorporates aspects of Berry's (2003) separation and marginalization strategies.

Another model of acculturation is *fusion* (LaFromboise et al., 1993). Fusion involves cultures sharing an economic, political, or geographic space, fusing together until they are indistinguishable and forming a new culture. This is the idea behind the melting pot theory. The fusion model differs from the assimilation model because aspects of multiple cultures are integrated into the new culture. It differs from the multicultural model because cultures of origin are not distinctively maintained. An example of fusion cuisine in sushi is the California roll. Sushi in Japan typically includes Japanese rice, seaweed (*nori*), vegetables, and seafood. The California roll includes Japanese rice and nori plus vegetables (avocado) and seafood (crab) from California. Thus, Japanese and American cuisines are fused to create something new. However, what typically occurs when multiple cultures share the same space is that the cultural minority groups become absorbed into the majority group at the price of their cultural identity (LaFromboise et al., 1993). Fusion is not clearly represented in Berry's (2003) model.

A fourth model of acculturation is *alternation*, which involves competence in two cultures (LaFromboise et al., 1993). The two cultures are regarded as equal, and a person maintains positive relationships with both cultures without having to choose between them. The biculturally competent individual alters his or her behavior to fit a particular sociocultural context. For example, if restraint is valued in one's cultural background, one is restrained in contexts where restraint is valued. In other settings where free expression is valued, such as in many European American settings, a biculturally competent person is able to shift to a more expressive mode. Alternation is regarded as an optimal mode of functioning by LaFromboise and her colleagues. However, American society does not equally value all cultures, and alternation may be difficult to maintain in practice. A truly biculturally competent person may have to overemphasize the non–European American culture in order to balance the emphasis of European American culture in society. In other words, an overemphasis on a minority culture may be required to actually regard the minority culture as equal to European culture and to achieve positive relationships with both cultures. Alternation incorporates aspects of Berry's (2003) integration strategy.

The *multicultural* model of acculturation involves distinct cultural identities that are maintained while cultures are tied together within a single multicultural social structure (LaFromboise et al., 1993). Individuals from one culture cooperate with those of other cultures to serve common needs. An example of this might be ethnic communities that have intergroup contact but at the same time maintain their culture of origin. A city might have Little Tokyo, Little Saigon, and Little Italy neighborhoods that are in geographic proximity and work cooperatively as part of the larger city structure. However, in real-life situations, separation of cultural groups is more common than interaction and cooperation. When there is interaction, there also tends to be mutual influence and cultures of origins tend not to be distinctly maintained. Thus, the multicultural model is difficult to achieve in practice (LaFromboise et al., 1993). The multicultural model is analogous to Berry's (2003) multicultural strategy.

In summary, acculturation involves contact between a cultural group and a host culture that changes either or both groups. Berry's classic model proposed assimilation, separation, integration, and marginalization as modes of acculturation. This model has parallels with racial identity models. LaFromboise and colleagues' theory of acculturation describes five models of acculturation: assimilation, acculturation, fusion, alternation, and multicultural. These models are alternatives to Berry's model.

Conclusion

Multicultural psychology is the study of multiple cultures within a single context. Psychology traditionally has not considered the influences of culture on behavior. Yet, a focus on culture is important for psychology if it is to be relevant in the 21st century in a rapidly diversifying North America.

There are common components across the models of racial/ethnic identity and acculturation. All include a component in which ethnic/racial identity or culture is not a critical consideration. There is also a component of exploration that is usually accompanied by conflict. Another common component is an integrated identity, in which there is an acceptance and understanding of multiple races, ethnicities, and cultures. In this book, we will learn how these racial, ethnic, and cultural identities influence behavior.

Discussion Questions

1. Did your parents teach you to be "color-blind"? Much of psychology is based on color-blind assumptions. How might a color-blind approach create difficulties in multicultural situations?

2. How might knowledge of one's own and another person's racial or ethnic identity be helpful in relationships?

3. Is bicultural competence, in which one is equally competent and accepted in two cultures, possible?

CHAPTER 2

Multicultural Research Methods

The purpose of this chapter is to review research design issues relevant to multicultural psychology. A consideration of these issues will allow you to critique the research of others and to conduct culturally competent research of your own. Unfortunately, much psychological research addresses few, if any, of these issues. No single study can address all the issues raised in this chapter. However, the more issues that are addressed, the more culturally competent the study will be.

This chapter begins with a discussion of issues in quantitative research. Most research in psychology, including multicultural psychology, is quantitative. The second section of the chapter is on qualitative research, which is particularly relevant when there are not existing theories or research on phenomena. The third section of the chapter is on communicating and disseminating research results, which is as important as designing and conducting research.

QUANTITATIVE RESEARCH METHODS

Theory-Guided Research

A scientific theory is a set of statements that is *explanatory* and *predictive*. A theory explains why a phenomenon occurs. This explanatory function involves the basis or mechanism of a phenomenon. For example, the Multidimensional Model of Racial Identity (Sellers et al., 1998) discussed in Chapter 1 explains how race affects self-perception. If race is salient in a particular situation and central to a person's identity, the person has positive regard for his racial group, he has a nationalist identity, then he is likely to have a positive self-perception.

A second function of a theory is prediction. Rather than simply describing a current phenomenon, a theory makes predictions concerning the future. Using the Multidimensional Model of Racial Identity as an example, the model would predict that a person with the characteristics described above would be politically active in causes that support the rights of African Americans to form their own identity and make their own decisions.

A good theory will lead to testable hypotheses and will guide the selection of measures, data analyses, and interpretation of data. A carefully designed study can provide support or lack of support for a particular theory. A single study does not prove or disprove a theory but may offer support or lack of support for the theory. However, a series of studies can provide evidence for the accuracy of a theory's predictions or may provide clues on how the theory should be modified.

As an example of how a theory can guide research, Smalls, White, Chavous, and Sellers (2007) used the Multidimensional Model of Racial Identity (MMRI) as a theoretical framework to predict academic engagement among African American adolescents. The theoretical model predicted that African American youth who endorsed an assimilationist ideology, which de-emphasized their uniqueness, would be less academically engaged than African American youth who endorsed a minority ideology, emphasizing pride in being African American and motivation to overcome discrimination. The Multidimensional Inventory of Black Identity, which is based on the MMRI, was used to assess the participants in the study. The predictions of the MMRI were supported. An assimilationist identity was associated with more fears of being viewed by peers as high achievers, less persistence with schoolwork, less interest and excitement in academic tasks, and more behavioral problems than was a minority identity.

Research without a theory often leads to post hoc speculation about the meaning of the results and may not advance science as far as providing support or lack of support for a scientific theory. Unfortunately, much research regarding racial and ethnic differences in psychology is athe-oretical. In my work as editor of two journals, I estimate that about one-third of manuscripts are rejected because of an inadequate theoretical framework. However, this does not mean that one-third of psychology research on race, ethnicity, and culture is atheoretical, as I have seen much atheoretical research on these topics published in journals that I do not edit. Thus, one-third is probably an underestimate of the amount of atheoretical research on race, ethnicity, and culture.

In summary, purposes of a theory are to explain and predict. A good theory leads to testable hypotheses and can guide the design of a study. Research without a theory leads to post hoc speculation.

Sampling Issues

Much of what we know in psychology is based on studies of college students. College students are readily available on the campuses where many psychology researchers do their work—college students are a convenience sample. Given that most psychological theories and research are as-sumed to generalize to all persons, the representativeness of college students either has not been addressed in studies or is addressed by a caveat about college students being not representative. The caveat about representativeness is often lip service, as subsequent research on many topics rarely ventures beyond college campuses.

U.S. census data indicate in 2005 that 43% of European Americans, 33% of African Amer-icans, 61% of Asian and Pacific Islander Americans, and 26% of Hispanic Americans aged 18 to 24 are enrolled in college (U.S. Bureau of the Census, October 2006). Data were not available for American Indians. Thus, non-college populations are more representative of young adults in the United States for ethnic groups other than Asian/Pacific Islander Americans.

Although college students are a convenience sample, they may be quite relevant for some research topics. Academic achievement studies would logically include college students. The col-lege environment also offers many opportunities for social and sexual interaction, some of which is aggressive. My colleagues and I have found that about one-third of college men admit to perpe-trating some form of sexual aggression and that there are not significant ethnic differences in this rate (G. C. N. Hall, Teten, DeGarmo, Sue, & Stephens 2005). College students may have more opportunities for sexually aggressive behavior than persons who are not in college. Nevertheless, college students are not representative of all members of any ethnic group.

Another convenience sample is persons of color who are of lower socioeconomic status. Access to these samples is often achieved via social service agencies, such as hospitals or community mental health clinics. However, persons of color who are of lower socioeconomic status are also not representative of most persons of color, who are not poor, as was discussed in Chapter 1. Research on persons of color who are of lower socioeconomic status is important because it could guide the development of useful interventions for these populations. Nevertheless, a disproportionate emphasis on these persons has left psychology with a dearth of information on persons of color who are not poor and the tendency to generalize from those who are poor to all members of ethnic groups (G. C. N. Hall, 2004).

Patients in mental health centers or psychiatric hospitals are another sample of convenience that is not representative of ethnic communities. It is obvious that persons with psychological disorders do not represent those in a community without disorders. However, psychiatric patients of color also may not be representative of persons of color with psychological disorders. For example, among Asian Americans and Mexican Americans with a probable psychological disorder in national community samples, only about one-third sought mental health services (Abe-Kim et al., 2007; Alegria et al., 2007). Nevertheless, patient populations are of interest because they may represent individuals having psychological disorders that are relatively severe, even if some community members with severe problems are not receiving services.

To summarize, convenience samples are typically studied in psychology research. These include college students, lower socioeconomic status populations, and clinical populations. Although none of these convenience samples is representative of populations of persons of color, each may be useful depending on the purpose of the research.

Recruitment of Participants

Once a population of interest is identified to study, how is a sample of the population recruited? The process of recruiting persons of color to psychology research may be analogous to how I choose a Japanese restaurant (cf. G. C. N. Hall & Eap, 2007). Authenticity of Japanese food is my criterion. If I am in an unfamiliar city, I may peek into the restaurant to see if the cook is Japanese and if the customers are Japanese. Recommendations of a restaurant from Japanese or Japanese American or other Asian friends might also get me to try it. Restaurant reviews by Japanese or Japanese American reviewers also could be persuasive. Of course, non-Japanese persons may be quite capable of cooking and evaluating the authenticity of Japanese food. Likewise, some Japanese or other Asian persons may be poor cooks and judges of the authenticity of Japanese food. Nevertheless, Japanese ethnicity suggests that the person is similar to me and is more likely to have similar tastes than someone who is not of the same ethnicity.

A process similar to that in my selection of Japanese restaurants may occur among persons of color who are deciding whether to participate in research. A researcher and participants in the project who are of the same ethnicity as the potential participants may be viewed as a rationale for participation. Also, word of mouth in an ethnic community may facilitate participation. If the researcher and participants are not ethnically similar, a potential participant could view the project as irrelevant. Even if the intent of the project is to recruit persons of color (e.g., African Americans), potential participants may be suspicious of the motives of a researcher who is not a person of color. For example, some members of ethnic communities may refuse or be reluctant to participate in research out of fear that the researchers will report their immigration status to government authorities. These issues of ethnic matching in research are analogous to ethnic matching in psychotherapy between therapist and client, which is associated with clients not dropping out of psychotherapy and showing greater improvements (Griner & Smith, 2006).

To the extent that researchers of color can attract persons of color to research projects, it is important for researchers of color to be represented on research teams (C. B. Fisher et al., 2002; G. C. N. Hall, 2001). This means that it is important to recruit students of color into the field of psychology. Persons of color may have expertise on ethnic communities and may have valuable contacts within ethnic communities that might facilitate community research participation. Ideally, persons of color should be co-investigators in research, not subordinates, and should be involved in the project from its inception. Of course, not all persons of color are identified with or connected to ethnic communities and may have no more expertise or contacts than someone who is not a person of color.

It has been recommended that culturally competent research teams be established to study communities of color (K. Chun, Morera, Andal, & Skewes, 2007). *Cultural competence* has been defined as (a) understanding one's own cultural background and how it shapes attitudes and beliefs, (b) knowledge of different worldviews of individuals and groups, and (c) skills in the use of culturally appropriate communication and intervention (D. W. Sue, 2001). In forming research teams, it has been suggested that formal measures of cultural competence, such as the Multicultural Awareness-Knowledge-Skills Survey (D'Andrea, Daniels, & Heck, 1991), be considered to stimulate self-assessment and team discussion and reflection (Chun et al., 2007). Culturally competent research involves the incorporation of culture at every stage of the research design, including its conceptualization (G. C. N. Hall, 2001; Yali & Revenson, 2004). Thus, the recruitment of a diverse sample in a project not designed to incorporate culture would not be culturally competent research.

A culturally competent researcher of color can serve as a culture broker between the psychology and ethnic communities. A *culture broker* is one who mediates between two or more cultural groups. A basic form of culture brokering involves language translation. Nevertheless, language skills do not necessarily ensure cultural competence. Culture brokering may involve other mediation, such as explaining cultural norms that differ between groups. For example, participation of persons from a collectivist community in a research project that is framed as a means of helping others in one's own community may be more appealing than a project framed as advancing scientific knowledge or as generally helping unspecified persons.

Even community "insiders" can experience ethnic community resistance to participation in research. American Indian psychologist Joseph Gone (2006) thoughtfully described his experience as an insider/outsider/hybrid in attempting to conduct research in a tribal community. Community members may be suspicious that those who have received training outside the community are no longer part of the community. Social class differences between researchers and participants may transcend ethnic similarity. Graduate education typically is a process of acculturation that may leave the trainee less competent in her ethnic community to the extent that the trainee has adopted the values of academia and left ethnic community values behind (G. C. N. Hall, Lopez, & Bansal, 2001). When a community perceives condescension, entitlement, assumptions of deviance, or self-absorbed career ambition on the part of a researcher, the community is unlikely to be fully cooperative (Harrell & Bond, 2006).

In addition to researchers of color, community leaders who are supportive of research can serve as culture brokers. In some contexts, such as with American Indian tribal groups, the approval of community leaders is mandatory for research to take place (P. A. Fisher & Ball, 2003). It is important to determine that those who appear to be leaders are actually considered leaders in the community. For example, researchers might consider persons in the community who are most educated to be leaders. Yet, the actual community leaders whose guidance is sought and who have decision-making authority may be others, such as elders, who do not necessarily have the most education. Also, leaders must have the cooperation of their community for their leadership to be effective. A leader could agree to have a community participate in research, but this agreement does not necessarily guarantee the community's interest and cooperation.

Is it possible for someone who is ethnically and culturally dissimilar to effectively gain entry into an ethnic community and recruit research participants? Les Whitbeck is a European American sociologist. Several years ago, he was interested in studying American Indian populations and made contact with a tribal leader. The leader took Les to a tribal meeting and instructed him not to speak. Les was introduced to the tribe by the leader as having a "good heart." Les attended these tribal meetings regularly for a year without speaking, and was introduced each time by the leader as having a good heart. After a year of silent participation, Les gained the tribe's trust and has been able to conduct extensive research with this and other American Indian communities in the Midwest. Rather than barging into the community while pushing his own agenda, Les was effective because he learned and respected the community's norms regarding trust of outsiders.

Community education can also be implemented in the recruitment of ethnic minority participants (C. B. Fisher et al., 2002). Researchers can educate communities about the research process and content via speakers' bureaus, mass media, schools, health centers, and religious organizations. Such previews of research allow potential participants to make informed decisions about participation.

There also may exist logistical barriers to ethnic minority research participation. These include work schedules, location of research projects, and transportation availability (K. M. Chun et al., 2007; C. B. Fisher et al., 2002). Offering monetary incentives and conducting research in familiar settings, such as the home, are strategies of increasing compliance (Burlew, 2003). However, monetary incentives may attract persons who need the money most, which could reduce the representativeness of a sample. Moreover, high payment levels could be considered coercive if no similar levels of payment are available for other activities. A culture broker may understand these logistical issues and may be able to create bridges from the research to the community that overcome these barriers to research participation.

One possible method of diversifying samples is Internet-based research (Gosling, Vazire, Srivastava, & John, 2004). However, the diversity of Internet samples is dependent upon access to and skills in using the Internet. There are ethnic differences in Internet use. Although a greater percentage of English-speaking Latino/a Americans (78%) than European Americans (73%) use the Internet, only 62% of African Americans use the Internet (Pew Internet & American Life Project, 2007). Moreover, representation of ethnic minorities in Internet research samples differs only slightly from traditional research samples. Gosling et al. (2004) reported that 77% of Internet-based research samples and 80% of traditional samples in social psychology research were European American. Nevertheless, Internet-based research samples tend to be quite large, and even small percentages of ethnic minority participants may constitute samples of 1,000 or more (Gosling et al., 2004).

In summary, ethnic similarity between researchers and research participants may facilitate recruitment of participants into research studies. Culture brokers from the community, cultural competence on the part of researchers, and offering benefits to a community, such as money or education, also facilitate the recruitment process. Internet-based research is an emerging method of recruiting samples of color.

Ethnic and Racial Identification

Once a diverse research sample is recruited, how is the race or ethnicity of the participants assessed? Perhaps the most common method of assessing race or ethnicity involves a single-item test in which a person chooses a category, such as White, Hispanic, Asian, African American, American Indian, or Other. Occasionally, a person is allowed to indicate more than one of these categories. However, these categories are not equivalent to any specific behaviors, traits, or biological or environmental conditions (C. B. Fisher et al., 2002; Helms, Jernigan, & Mascher, 2005). Moreover, self-designation of race or ethnicity may not correspond well with designations by others. In an analysis of more than 730,000 Veterans Administration files, there was only approximately 60% agreement between patients' self-designated ethnicities vs. their ethnicities determined by clinicians or registration clerks (Kressin, Chang, Hendricks, & Kazis, 2003). Agreement was particularly poor for patients who self-designated as American Indian or Asian Pacific Islander.

It has been contended that comparisons using racial and ethnic categories should not be used in empirical research (C. B. Fisher et al., 2002; Helms et al., 2005; Phinney, 1996). Such comparisons may unfairly portray non–European American groups as deviant, and some culture-specific constructs (e.g., loss of face, *familismo*) have different meanings across groups or little meaning at all for some groups. Conversely, other researchers have advocated ethnic group comparisons to test the cultural generalizability of theories (Heine & Norenzayan, 2006). Studies purely designed to determine the generalizability of a finding are atheoretical because they do not hypothesize reasons for possible cultural differences (van de Vijver & Leung, 2000). Broad racial/ethnic categories do not correspond with culture, and included within each racial/ethnic category is much variability. Therefore, if two ethnic groups differ from one another on some variable (e.g., extroversion), it cannot be concluded that race, ethnicity, or culture is the basis of the difference. The basis of a difference in such a simplistic contrast between ill-defined categories is unknown. Moreover, the absence of differences between two groups could also be a result of within-group variability. Individuals in both groups may vary on a dimension such that any between-groups differences are obscured.

The assessment of race and ethnicity is much more complex that endorsing one or a few categorical items. Trimble, Helms, and Root (2003) suggested that the assessment of race and ethnicity should address (a) natality, (b) subjective identification, (c) behavioral expressions of identity, and (d) situational or contextual influences. Natality includes where one and one's ancestors were born, which is objective information. However, one's subjective identification of ethnic or racial identity may or may not coincide with natality. A person could be born in the United States but identify with an ancestral ethnic or racial group. Behavioral expressions of identity may or may not correspond to natality and subjective identification. For example, a person may engage in ancestral cultural customs (e.g., religious ceremonies) because of family or peer pressure but not be subjectively identified with the group. Finally, opportunities for subjective identification and behavioral expressions of identity may depend on situational or contextual opportunities. For example, a person may not develop a subjective identification with a group in the absence of other members of the group. Similarly, one who has a strong subjective identification with a group may live in a situation in which there are not opportunities for behavioral expression (e.g., cultural festivals).

The most commonly used measures of ethnic and racial identity involve individual self-report (Cross & Vandiver, 1991; Helms & Carter, 1990; Phinney, 1992). However, self-report methods usually do not capture the fluid, contextual nature of ethnic and racial identity (Okazaki, 2002). One method of activating identity from the social cognition field is *priming*. Exposure to relevant cues activates an ethnic or racial meaning system in persons, which affects their social judgments and other behaviors. For example, ethnic identity primes (e.g., questionnaire about generational status, non–English language use) have been found to facilitate Asian American women's math performance relative to women who received gender identity primes (e.g., questionnaire about living in single sex vs. coed dorms) or no prime (Shih, Pittinsky, & Ambady, 1999;

Shih, Pittinsky, & Trahan, 2006). Priming ethnic identity boosted math performance because of stereotypes about good math performance among Asians, whereas priming gender identity decreased math performance because of stereotypes about poor math performance among women. A *stereotype* is a positive or negative set of beliefs about the characteristics of a group of people. However, seemingly positive stereotypes, such as Asian math skills, can backfire by creating undue performance pressure. Blatant ethnic primes (e.g., "I am a worthy member of the racial group I belong to"; "Overall, my race is considered good by others") created math performance decrements among Asian American women (Cheryan & Bodenhausen, 2000). Issues of stereotype threat will be discussed in more detail in Chapter 5.

To the extent that culture involves the interaction of individuals and the social environment (Lopez & Guarnaccia, 2000), it would appear informative to study how ethnic identity is expressed in group interactions. One method of eliciting interactional data on ethnic identity would be to have a group (e.g., family) discuss issues of race, ethnicity, and culture while being observed by a researcher. Although behavior observational methods have been shown to be valid for assessment of general behavior (e.g., parenting) in ethnic minority groups (e.g., Rodriguez, Davis, Rodriguez, & Bates, 2006), valid methods of observing expressions of ethnic identity have yet to be established. Structuring a discussion of race, ethnicity, and culture could create an artificial situation (e.g., forced discussion) that would not mirror how ethnic identity actually is expressed. Moreover, some cultural practices are not necessarily observable in brief samples of behavior. For example, parents may select "teachable moments" to convey their beliefs about race, ethnicity, and culture, and may not spontaneously do so during a behavioral observation. Moreover, a parent may silently transmit ethnic identity values, such as working hard and not complaining, by acting as a role model. Unless the parent were observed by researchers mentioning such cultural modeling in an interaction with her children, this modeling would not be detected.

Sociometric methods also assess the individual in the context of his peer group (Tsai, Chentsova-Dutton, & Wong, 2002). These methods are most commonly used with children. One method involves nominations of peers with whom they would most or least like to participate in an activity with. Another method involves rating characteristics of peers, such as who are "most Chinese" or "most American." However, sociometric methods have rarely been used in multicultural research.

In summary, the most common method of assessing race or ethnicity is with a single self-report item in which a person designates a category. However, race and ethnicity involve multiple components. Although the assessment of race and ethnicity typically involves self-report, other methods, such as priming as sociometric ratings, have been developed.

Cultural Equivalence of Constructs and Measures

A psychological *construct* is a variable of interest assessed (constructed) with multiple measures. For example, the construct of intelligence might be assessed via a combination of performance on a cognitive test, grades in school, a measure of verbal skills, and a measure of social skills. A critical issue in research with multiple racial, ethnic, or cultural groups is whether a construct and its measurement are valid for these groups (Trimble, 2007). *Conceptual equivalence* refers to whether the construct has the same meaning across groups (Berry, Poortinga, Segall, & Dasen, 2002). For example, the construct of alexithymia involves difficulty in identifying emotions and distinguishing them from bodily sensations in combination with difficulty in communicating emotions to others (G. J. Taylor, 1984). Asian Americans report greater levels of alexithymia than do European Americans (Le, Berenbaum, & Raghavan, 2002). Yet, if attention to emotions and emotional expression are viewed as maladaptive in East Asian cultural groups that value interpersonal harmony, then attending to and expressing emotions may not be valued (Yen, Robins, & Lin, 2000). Conversely, somatic symptoms may be a prescribed mode of communicating distress (Yen et al., 2000).

Linguistic equivalence involves whether a translated test of a construct has a similar meaning to the original test (Lonner & Ibrahim, 2002). An optimal approach to linguistic equivalence would be to simultaneously develop a measure in multiple cultures, but this approach is rare (van Widenfelt et al., 2005). To achieve linguistic equivalence, a test is translated from one language to a foreign language. Ideally, translation is conducted by a team that is bilingual, bicultural, and has expertise in psychology (van Widenfelt, Treffers, de Beurs, Siebelink, & Koudijs, 2005). Then, the foreign language version is translated into the original language, which is known as back translation. The back translation version of the test is compared with the original version of the test for accuracy. It is useful to have a review team independent of the translators react to the translation and back translation (Geisinger, 1994). This translation-back translation process can continue until an accurate version of the foreign language translation is achieved (Leong, Okazaki, & Tak, 2003). However, because some concepts are not equivalent across cultures, exact translations are sometimes difficult to achieve (Marsella & Leong, 1995). Moreover, the psychometric properties (e.g., reliability, validity) may not be equivalent for translated and nontranslated versions of a test. One method of testing the linguistic equivalence of a test translation is to have bilingual persons take both versions of the test and compare the results. However, even when a person speaks more than one language, it cannot be assumed that she is equally fluent in all languages that she speaks (Okazaki & Sue, 1995). Thus, test meaning may vary from language to language even for a bilingual person.

Metric equivalence involves whether the same score on a test has the same meaning for one ethnic group as it does for another (Trimble, 2007). Using the alexithymia example, differences in ability to read one's own emotions may be a function of measurement method. Although Asian Americans in the Le et al. (2002) study reported higher levels of alexithymia than did European Americans, in another study when directly asked, Chinese, Chinese Americans, and European Americans did not exhibit differences in emotional symptoms of depression (Yen et al., 2000). Other research suggests that Asian Americans express higher levels of unpleasant emotions (guilty, irritated, sad, worried) than European Americans, but they may express lower levels of pleasant emotions (happy, joyful; Scollon, Diener, Oishi, & Biswas-Diener, 2004). Thus, the construct of alexithymia may have a different meaning for Asian Americans versus European Americans, and group differences may be a function of the method of assessment. Conceptualizing alexithymia as a universal deficit may be biased because the validity of the construct and measurement of alexithymia are questionable across ethnic groups.

Another measurement issue pertinent to persons of color involves response style. Measures of social desirability have been developed to identify an impression management style in which a person tends not to admit to the presence of negative characteristics. There is evidence that African Americans, Latino/a Americans, and Asian Americans are more likely to make socially desirable responses that are European Americans (Dudley, McFarland, Goodman, Hunt, & Sydell, 2005). Such socially desirable responding may be a function of heightened skepticism about the testing situation and evaluation concerns among persons of color. Moreover, social desirability is assumed to compromise the validity of personality data. Yet, despite these differences in socially desirable responding, personality scores for ethnic minorities versus European Americans were not significantly different (Dudley et al., 2005). Thus, socially desirable responding may have a different meaning for groups of color than for European Americans. Moreover, a desire to maintain interpersonal harmony among persons having collectivist orientations may mitigate willingness to express responses that could be perceived as potentially disruptive. For example, persons in China tend not to make extreme responses in responding to tests (Hamid, Lai, & Cheng, 2001).

A common method of demonstrating metric equivalence is the use of factor analysis of the structure of the measure in two or more groups (Trimble, 2007). Factor analysis involves the identification of correlated test items that cluster into factors, or correlations of correlations. If the same test factors are found for multiple groups, the test is assumed to have metric equivalence for these groups. For example, Malcarne, Chavira, Fernandez, and Liu (2006) developed the 32-item Scale of Ethnic Experience. Ethnic Identity, Perceived Discrimination, Mainstream Comfort, and Social Affiliation were four factors that were replicated in separate factor analyses for African Americans, European Americans, Filipino Americans, and Mexican Americans. Thus, the Scale of Ethnic Experience has metric equivalence across these ethnic groups.

On the other hand, factor analyses of ethnic group data may mask within-group variability. In a factor-analytic study, Eap et al. (2008) found evidence of a five-factor personality structure in both European American and Asian American men on the Big Five Inventory (Benet-Martínez & John, 1998). The Big Five personality factors are Neuroticism, Extraversion, Openness to Experience, Agreeableness, and Conscientiousness. Asian Americans had significantly lower scores than European Americans on Extraversion, Conscientiousness, and Openness, and significantly higher scores on Neuroticism (Eap et al., 2008). The five-factor structure was weaker among Asian American men who were less acculturated to Western culture and more concerned about the East Asian value of loss of face. Although the five-factor structure on the Big Five Inventory was the same for both ethnic groups, there were important between-groups cultural differences in test means and in the strength of the factor structure, which casts doubt on the metric equivalence of the measure across ethnic groups.

Even when conceptual and metric equivalence exist for a construct, there is not necessarily *functional equivalence* (Dana, 1993; G. C. N. Hall, Bansal, & Lopez, 1999). Functional equivalence addresses whether the same behavior elicits the same reaction across groups. For example, verbal participation in classroom discussions and the ability to "think aloud" is valued by many professors and for some is equated with intelligence. Although talking while thinking has been found to facilitate the problem-solving performance of European Americans, it has been found to interfere with performance of Asian Americans (H. S. Kim, 2002). Asian Americans were found to perform better at problem-solving when they were silent. Asian Americans also have been found to attach less significance to verbal expression as a method of communicating about oneself than do European Americans (H. S. Kim & Sherman, 2007). Verbal expression may be less critical than actions in cultures that emphasize roles, social status, and relationships (H. S. Kim & Sherman, 2007). Thus, some Asian Americans may perceive performance on a formal written examination as more diagnostic of their intelligence than verbal participation in class discussion. Silence may not have functional equivalence across cultures, in that it could be interpreted as not being involved in one context and as thinking in another. Similarly, hearing the voices of dead relatives or religious figures might be common in some Latino American groups but could be misdiagnosed as symptoms of schizophrenia (Bravo, 2003). A key to differentially diagnosing culturally normative versus psychopathological behavior is whether the behavior is common in a cultural group and not maladaptive (e.g., harmful to self or others).

Summing up, equivalence of constructs, language, measures, and behaviors across groups is important in multicultural research. Ethnic group differences may be a result of a lack of equivalence, which does not necessarily mean that the differences are cultural differences. Nevertheless, there may be differences in normative behavior across ethnic groups.

Culture-Specific Constructs

Although the previous section addressed the cultural equivalence of constructs, there may be racial and ethnic group differences on some constructs, and other constructs may be culture specific and not exist across cultures. Western approaches to phenomena are likely to yield Western results (Bodas & Ollendick, 2005). For example, if one has a measure that assesses five personality factors, five personality factors are likely to be identified. When indigenous measures that assess personality factors in addition to the commonly assessed five factors, factors in addition to the Big Five may emerge (Katigbak, Church, Guanzon-Lapena, Carlota, & del Pilar, 2002).

A broad cultural construct along which ethnic groups differ is individualism–collectivism. Individualism assumes that individuals are independent of one another, whereas collectivism assumes that individuals are bound together and obligated by groups (Oyserman, Coon, & Kemmelmeier, 2002). It is often assumed that groups of color in North America are less individualistic and more collectivistic than are European Americans. Oyserman and colleagues conducted meta-analyses (summaries of effect sizes across studies) of studies that compared Asian Americans, Latino/a Americans, and African Americans with European Americans on measures of individualism and collectivism. Consistent with assumptions about groups of color in North America, Asian Americans were significantly less individualistic and more collectivistic than European Americans. Latino/a Americans were not significantly different than European Americans on individualism but significantly more collectivistic than European Americans. African Americans were significantly more individualistic than European Americans but not significantly different from European Americans on collectivism. This last finding may appear counterintuitive. However, J. M. Jones (1997) has explained African American individualism as functioning in service of the collective. This is similar to a jazz ensemble in which individual musicians are featured in solos but also blend back into the group. Soloists are part of the ensemble but strengthen it by displaying their individual musical skills.

Although individualism–collectivism has been the basis of many cross-cultural psychology studies, it is not a construct that is specific to particular cultural or ethnic groups. Individualists and collectivists exist in all ethnic groups. Moreover, the meaning of individualism–collectivism may differ across groups. For example, as discussed above, J. M. Jones (1997) suggested that individualism may have a different meaning in African American than in European American contexts. Although both Asian Americans and Latino/a Americans are more collectivistic than European Americans, it is also likely that Asian American and Latino/a American collectivism may not be equivalent. As such to the extent that these two groups differ in expressiveness, collectivism might be commonly expressed among Asian Americans by withholding criticism of others, whereas collectivism among Latino/a Americans might be commonly expressed by complimenting others.

Another cultural construct that is particularly relevant to immigrants is acculturation. Most measures of acculturation designed for ethnic groups in the United States assess language usage and may not assess identification with particular cultural groups (Zane & Mak, 2003). The majority of these measures assess acculturation as a linear phenomenon—one's orientation moves along a continuum from a culture of origin to a host culture. Yet, models of acculturation discussed in Chapter 1 conceptualize the possibility of bicultural acculturation (Berry 1974; LaFromboise et al., 1993). Moreover, acculturation is a relatively broad construct that does not necessarily account for specific behaviors (Zane & Mak, 2003).

More proximal to behavior are specific culture-specific elements of acculturation (Zane & Mak, 2003). One such culture-specific construct for Americans of East Asian ancestry is loss of face. In cultures that are collectivistic, individuals are obligated to preserve group harmony. If an individual's behavior interferes with group harmony, the individual experiences loss of face because he or she has not fulfilled his or her obligation to the group. Unlike shame that involves individual embarrassment and damage to self-image, loss of face occurs because of failed obligations to others. As might be expected, concern about loss of face is a deterrent against aggressive behavior among Asian Americans (G. C. N. Hall et al., 2005). This effect is culture specific insofar as concern about loss of face in the study was shown to be deterrent against Asian American men's sexual aggression but was not associated with European American men's sexual aggression. Loss of face concerns have also been found to deter Asian Americans' disclosure in psychotherapy, as discussing problems could result in face loss not only for oneself but for others in one's social network (Zane & Mak, 2003).

Other culture-specific constructs include African American and American Indian spirituality (e.g., Simon, Crowther, & Higgerson, 2007; Stone, Whitbeck, Chen, Johnson, & Olson, 2006) and *machismo* and *marianismo* in Latino/a American cultures (e.g., Casas, Turner, & Esparza, 2005; Moreno, 2007). Although a person in any culture might have some of these characteristics, these culture-specific constructs have a particular meaning in specific ethnic contexts. For example, spirituality in African American contexts is much more than attendance at religious services or even personal exploration of faith. African American spirituality is often rooted in participation in the African American community and may involve a sociopolitical emphasis. Similarly, gender roles prescribed by values of machismo for men and marianismo for women may appear sexist to outsiders. Machismo prescribes that males are strong and provide for their families. Marianismo prescribes that women should serve others and be submissive. Although there may be negative aspects to each of these constructs, positive aspects include a sense of responsibility to one's family and to the community and adherence to prosocial community norms.

In summary, culture-specific constructs are likely to be more informative about an ethnic group than constructs that are not sensitive to culture. Moreover, broad cultural constructs are likely to be less sensitive to the behaviors of a particular group than are constructs that are more specific to the particular group. There exist cultural constructs specific to ethnic groups that are likely to be predictive of behavior.

Data Analyses

The purpose of data analyses in multicultural research is to determine the possible cultural bases of behavior. Although I will not go into depth about data analytic strategies, two data analytic issues, moderation and mediation, are important in multicultural research. Moderator and mediator analyses can help in the determination of the psychological bases of ethnic differences.

A categorical variable that is associated with different outcomes based on one's status on the variable is known as a *moderator*. Racial or ethnic group membership (e.g, African American, European American) could be analyzed as a moderator. Moderator analyses can also be conducted within an ethnic group. For example, within Latino/a Americans, differences between Puerto Ricans and Mexican Americans could be examined. However, most researchers do not analyze possible ethnic group differences in their samples either because they are not interested, because of the small size of ethnic minority samples, or because that they believe it is controversial to do so.

Moderator analyses should be theoretically guided and not simply a "fishing expedition" for possible differences. Otherwise, the meaning of the presence or absence of group differences will be unknown. A good example of theoretically guided moderator analyses is a large study of the Los Angeles County mental health system by Stanley Sue and colleagues (1991). Sue and colleagues observed that ethnic minority clients often dropped out of treatment after only one treatment session and were rated by clinicians as having poorer outcomes even when they remained in

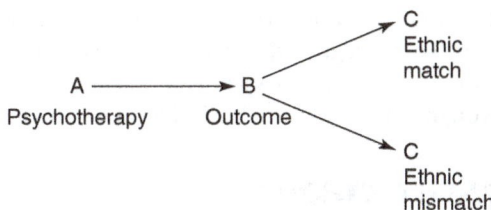

FIGURE 2.1 Moderation

treatment. They tested the hypothesis that ethnic match between therapist and client would be beneficial to clients in terms of preventing premature treatment termination and producing better treatment outcomes. Thus, ethnic match (therapist and client of same ethnicity vs. therapist and client of different ethnicities) was the potential moderator in the study. It was shown that African Americans, Asian Americans, European Americans, and Mexican Americans who were treated by therapists of their own ethnicity were less likely to drop out of treatment after one session and more likely to have better clinician rated outcomes than clients of these ethnicities who were treated by therapists of ethnicities other than their own. This moderator analysis is diagrammed in Figure 2.1.

A *mediator* is a third variable that serves as the vehicle through which one variable influences a second variable (Baron & Kenny, 1986). For mediation to occur, (a) Variable A must be associated with Variable C; (b) Variable B, the proposed mediator, must also be associated with Variable C; (c) and the association between Variables A and C is eliminated or substantially reduced when Variable B is accounted for. For example, S. Taylor and colleagues (2004) hypothesized that efforts to maintain group harmony might discourage persons of East Asian ancestry from using social support during times of stress. Indeed, Asian Americans reported using less social support to cope with stress than did European Americans. Thus, ethnicity (Variable A) was associated with use of social support (Variable C). However, those who perceived using social support as negatively affecting their social network were less likely to use social support in both ethnic groups. Thus, perceptions of the impact of using social support was a mediator (Variable B) of the association between ethnicity and use of social support. In other words, perceptions of the impact of using social support fully accounted for ethnic variation in the use of social support and was the basis of the apparent ethnic difference in use of social support. This mediator analysis is diagrammed in Figure 2.2. Although perceptions of the impact of using social support accounted for ethnic variation in use of social support, ethnicity still mattered in that Asian Americans perceived using social support as negatively affecting their social network more than did European Americans.

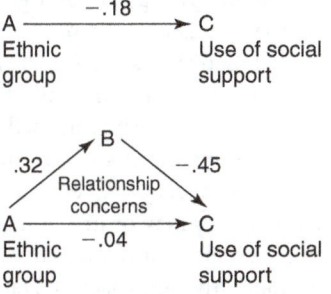

FIGURE 2.2 Mediation

In summary, moderator and mediator variables can help determine the basis of ethnic differences in behavior. Moderators are categorical variables, such as group membership, that are associated with different outcomes based on one's status on the variable. A mediator is a variable that serves as the vehicle through which one variable influences another.

QUALITATIVE RESEARCH METHODS

The approaches discussed up to this point in the chapter have been quantitative and normative, examining how individuals or groups vary on common constructs. In contrast to quantitative approaches, qualitative approaches are *exploratory* and *descriptive*. The goal is to explore and describe phenomena, often without a preexisting theoretical framework or other assumptions. Qualitative approaches are useful when theories and data on a phenomenon do not exist, which makes this approach particularly relevant to multicultural psychology.

Qualitative approaches are idiographic, examining individuals' unique perspectives via qualitative or quantitative data or both (D. Lee & Tracey, 2005). In-depth information about individuals is often lost in quantitative approaches. Moreover, qualitative approaches contextualize behavior, whereas quantitative approaches tend not to emphasize context and often assume that behavior is consistent across contexts (K. M. Chun et al., 2007). Unlike quantitative approaches in which hypotheses are developed a priori, hypotheses emerge in qualitative approaches during the research process. Qualitative approaches allow participants to structure the constructs, rather than having researchers impose structure that may be at odds with the participants' perspectives (D. Lee & Tracey, 2005). Of course, a limitation of qualitative approaches is that information from individuals is less generalizable than information from larger groups in quantitative approaches.

In addition to a focus on individuals, qualitative methods often involve small groups. Focus groups allow individuals to shape their own views via interactions with others (K. M. Chun et al., 2007). This process of individuals influencing the group and the group influencing the individual has been posited as the basis of culture (Lopez & Guarnaccia, 2000). Focus group members may be chosen because they are leaders in the community, have particular expertise or opinions, or represent a particular community group (e.g., adolescents). A group moderator who is of the same ethnicity and speaks the same language as the participants may be desirable for the same reasons that ethnic matching is desirable in psychotherapy (K. M. Chun et al., 2007). Participation in a focus group may be appealing to some persons of color because it is consistent with collectivist values of cooperation and group harmony (Iwamasa & Sorocco, 2002). Conversely, groups that are created for research or therapy are dissimilar to community groups in that research or therapy groups are contrived and temporary, which may result in a lack of commitment among people of color who value group involvement (Nagata, 1998).

Another qualitative method involving groups is ethnography. *Ethnography* involves a researcher entering a community or situation as a participant–observer. Data gathering may involve field notes, interviews, and archival material (K. M. Chun et al., 2007). These data tend to be detailed and comprehensive, as they may constitute the only data gathered. Understanding the perspectives of the community may result in a theory grounded in the community's experiences, or *grounded theory* (Charmaz, 2000). The researcher's involvement and participation in a community may vary, as does the researcher's objectivity. For example, community members may seek help from a researcher and the researcher may or may not become an advocate for the community. Nevertheless, the subjective experiences of the researcher and participants are valued as much as or more than objectivity in qualitative approaches. Data analyses involve the identification of themes across individuals or communities, if more than one community is studied.

Themes can emerge from the data or can be determined a priori. As an example of a priori structuring of questions in qualitative research, 18 African American women were specifically asked about the role of spirituality in their breast cancer treatment and health care, which was the focus of the study (Simon et al., 2007). Although the focus was on spirituality, the questions were broad enough to allow the women to describe their own perspectives.

Qualitative approaches are much less commonly used in psychology than quantitative approaches, but these approaches need not conflict. Qualitative work may form the basis of quantitative work (Berry, 2003). For example, focus groups may provide ideas for hypotheses that will be evaluated quantitatively.

To summarize, qualitative approaches offer rich descriptions of individuals or small groups of individuals. Although they are usually not guided by theory, theories may emerge from qualitative data. Data analyses involve extracting common themes across indviduals. Qualitative and quantitative approaches may complement one another.

COMMUNICATION AND DISSEMINATION OF FINDINGS

Just as cultural competence is important in designing and conducting research, it is critical in communicating and disseminating findings. Care must be taken not to negatively portray or stereotype groups of color. There is a particular danger of groups of color being negatively portrayed in comparative research involving European Americans. European American behavior is likely to be viewed as normative. So, if European Americans are found to be more assertive than another group, the other group is likely to be portrayed or at least perceived by the reader as overly passive. Conversely, if the other group is found to be more assertive than European Americans, the other group is likely to be perceived as overly aggressive. Thus, it is incumbent on the researcher to portray all ethnic groups in a fair manner.

Even when researchers take great pains to portray groups of color fairly, their work can be misinterpreted. Anita Bansal, Irene Lopez, and I (G. C. N. Hall et al., 1999) wrote a meta-analytic study that summarized 31 years of ethnic comparative research on the Minnesota Multiphasic Personality Inventory (MMPI). The MMPI is a true/false self-report inventory that is the most widely used measure of psychopathology worldwide. We did not find evidence that African Americans or Latino Americans are more pathological than European Americans. We also did not find evidence that the MMPI is biased against ethnic minority groups, although we emphasized that the test may not be sensitive to actual ethnic differences and that the same behavior (e.g., depression) may not be functionally equivalent across ethnic groups in that its community impact may differ.

When we submitted our meta-analytic study for publication, a reviewer recommended that we include a statement in the abstract that the MMPI does not unfairly portray African Americans and Latino Americans as pathological. We initially resisted this recommendation, fearing that some might read only the abstract and conclude that the MMPI can be used without concern for cultural issues. Eventually we relented and included the statement in the abstract. Unfortunately, our fears were realized in at least one instance. A colleague on a state psychology board told me of a case in which a psychologist used an English version of the MMPI with a bilingual person whose primary language was Spanish. The psychologist claimed that this practice was permissible based on the conclusion of the G. C. N. Hall et al. (1999) study that the MMPI is not biased against Latino Americans. This incident serves as a lesson for researchers to try to anticipate ways in which their work might be misinterpreted and to attempt to address possible misinterpretations when they write research articles.

Even when research is accurately interpreted, researchers of color may face personal criticisms because of the controversial nature of ethnic research (S. Sue & Sue, 2003). Opponents of multicultural research may criticize it as racist because it focuses on differences between groups rather than similarities. Researchers of color may face criticism in their own ethnic communities for their research not being practical or for not being politically involved enough in community issues.

The publication of a research article in a scientific journal is not necessarily the end of a culturally competent research project. Most ethnic community members are unlikely to read the article. Therefore, the researcher bears some responsibility to communicate the results to the community. Most research involves some form of debriefing following the study in which participants can ask questions. Disseminating results also might involve a community education forum or discussing the results with community leaders. In some ethnic communities, community approval of a research article is required before the researcher submits it for publication. Another way to broadly disseminate research findings is to create a Web site describing the findings. In communicating information on a Web site, however, care must be taken to protect the confidentiality of participants. For example, it is not appropriate to provide information that might allow participants to be identified, unless identification is the participants' stated desire (C. B. Fisher et al., 2002). Researchers can also affect public policy by serving as expert consultants to political leaders.

In summary, cultural competence is necessary in communicating and disseminating research findings. Nevertheless, misinterpretation of research findings is possible, as is personal criticism of researchers who engage in multicultural research. A culturally competent research project will attempt to offer tangible benefits to the community being studied.

Conclusion

Cultural competence is important throughout the research process, from the development of theories to designing research to conducting research to communicating and disseminating findings. A well-developed theory will guide each phase of the research process. Identifying, recruiting, and assessing samples of color are each challenging tasks. Data analyses should be oriented toward identifying the bases or mechanisms of racial, ethnic, or cultural influences. Qualitative methods can capture rich contextual data that are often overlooked in quantitative approaches.

Unfortunately, much psychology research on race, culture, and ethnicity treats these topics in a superficial way, often as categorical variables, without attempting to address the complexity involved in multicultural research. In the following chapters, I have selected topics for which there exists culturally competent research. Having read this chapter, you may find flaws even in this culturally competent research, which may motivate you to correct these flaws by designing and conducting your own research.

Discussion Questions

1. It is both challenging and expensive to recruit ethnically diverse research samples. Should psychology resign itself to the fact that its theories and methods are of limited applicability and that it may not be feasible to evaluate these theories and methods with diverse populations?

2. Research that adheres to the cultural competence principles in this chapter is the exception, rather than the rule, in psychology. What might motivate psychology researchers to implement culturally competent research methods?

3. Is a multicultural research approach inherently political? In other words, when a researcher considers culture and the voices of communities at every stage of the research process, does this mean that the researcher is choosing a particular political perspective?

CHAPTER 3

Biological Psychology

Biological approaches to human behavior emphasize universals between and within species. At first glance, the emphasis on universality in biological approaches may appear to be at odds with the emphasis on variability in multicultural psychology. Nevertheless, these approaches inform multicultural psychology because they help elucidate the relative contributions of biology and the cultural environment to behavior. In this chapter, we will consider genetic, evolutionary, and health research that is relevant to multicultural psychology.

In comparative psychology, the metaphor for human behavior is animal behavior. Humans share psychological mechanisms with other species, and psychological mechanisms are assumed to be shared within species. In cognitive science, the metaphor for the human mind is the computer. Individual differences, let alone cultural differences, are seldom considered in this metaphor.

An alternative metaphor for the human mind that incorporates variability, including culture, is the toolbox (M. Cole, 1996; Piaget, 1952; Vygotsky, 1978). Tools in the box to solve problems are psychological processes, including cognitive structures, emotions, and motivations (Norenzayan & Heine, 2005). Although all humans may have the same or similar toolboxes, cultural groups may vary in how they use tools. In the context of the biological approaches in this chapter, humans of all racial and ethnic groups may be biologically similar, but different groups may use their biological resources in different ways to respond to situations.

As an example of cultural differences in the use of biological tools, all humans have cognitive and verbal skills. As discussed in Chapter 2, Western cultures emphasize verbal expression, and "thinking aloud" facilitates problem solving for European Americans (H. S. Kim, 2002). Conversely, Asian American cultures value self-restraint and "thinking aloud" interferes with problem solving for Asian Americans. Both ethnic groups possess cognitive and verbal skills, yet one group uses both and the other uses only cognitive skills to solve problems. It could be argued that European Americans effectively use all their available tools or, alternatively, that Asian Americans are more economical by using fewer tools. However, the point is not that one approach is better, but that the two groups use their biological tools in different manners.

GENETIC PSYCHOLOGY

The biological tools that humans have at their disposal are almost identical across individuals and groups. Humans are 99.9% the same genetically (Bonham, Warshaeuer-Baker, & Collins, 2005). *Genes* are pieces of DNA (deoxyribonucleic acid) and are the functional and physical unit of heredity passed from parent to offspring. *DNA* is the chemical inside the nucleus of a cell that carries the genetic instructions for making living organisms. *Genotypes* are the actual variations of genes present in an individual. *Phenotypes* are the observable characteristics of an individual that may or may not correspond to genotypes. For example, an individual may have a genotype that creates a risk for antisocial behavior but not engage in antisocial behavior because he lives in a tightly controlled environment (e.g., a monastery) in which prosocial norms and few opportunities for antisocial behavior exist. *Heritability* is the ratio of genetic influence in an attribute (Sternberg, Grigorenko, & Kidd, 2005). *Environmentality* is the ratio of environmental influence on a phenotype.

There has been enthusiasm about associating particular genes with psychological disorders, such as schizophrenia or antisocial behavior, which would create the possibility of gene therapies to prevent such disorders. However, behavior, including disordered behavior, involves complex interactions of multiple genes and of genes and the environment (Kendler, 2005). Moreover, some genes have desirable as well as undesirable effects. Thus, gene therapies at best might have a limited effect on behavior and at worst might have unwanted effects on behavior (Jaffee, Caspi, Moffitt, & Taylor, 2004).

Just as there is no particular gene exclusively associated with a particular behavior, there is no single gene or genetic variant that is sufficient to classify human populations into racial categories (Bonham et al., 2005; Cavalli-Sforza, Menozzi, & Piazza, 1994). Moreover, there is more variation within than between groups that have been identified as races. Among ancestral population groups whose geographic origins are in Africa, Asia, and Europe, 80–90% of genetic variation occurs within these groups and only 10–15% of genetic variation occurs between them (Jorde & Wooding, 2004). Additionally, genetic boundaries between purported racial groups are permeable. An increasing proportion of the world's population does not have recent ancestors from a single geographic region, which is the basis of racial grouping (Bonham et al., 2005; Jorde & Wooding, 2004). Thus, concepts of racial groups as distinct genetic entities are of limited utility, given the growing population of mixed-race individuals. Moreover, as discussed in Chapter 1, meanings of race are socially constructed and have relatively little to do with biology or genetics. Nevertheless, genes are an important influence on behavior, even if they do not correspond to racial groupings.

A common method of studying genetic influences is twin studies (Whitfield & McClearn, 2005). Identical (*monozygotic*, MZ) twins, which share 100% of their genes, are compared with fraternal (*dizygotic*, DZ) twins of the same sex, which share 50% of their genes as do other sibling pairs. Relative genetic and environmental influence on a characteristic can be determined with the correlations among MZ and among DZ twins on a characteristic, such as extraversion. Stronger correlations would be expected among MZ twins on characteristics that are genetically influenced.

Are genes an unalterable blueprint for human behavior? Such a deterministic view suggests that humans can do little to change their genetic programming. Thus, maladaptive behaviors (e.g., aggression, sexual infidelity) can be blamed on the genes inherited from our ancestors. However, there is an increasing body of evidence suggesting gene expression interacts with environmental contingencies (Lickliter & Honeycutt, 2003). Humans inherit not only genes but the ability to use genes as resources in response to the environment (Richardson, 1998). Thus, genes may be considered some of the tools in an individual's cognitive toolbox to be applied or not applied as a function of environmental demands (cf. Lickliter & Honeycutt, 2003; Norenzayan & Heine, 2005; Richardson, 1998).

As an example of environmental and genetic interactions, cultural norms may influence genetic risk for antisocial behavior. Antisocial behavior includes rule violations that may be aggressive (e.g., destroying property, fighting, attacking others, threatening others) or nonaggressive (e.g., truancy, shoplifting, drug use). The *social push hypothesis* suggests that for those exposed to adverse early environments (e.g., child maltreatment), social influences (e.g., antisocial cultural norms) on antisocial behavior may camouflage genetic influences (Raine, 2002). Indeed, in a Swedish twin study, environmental influences (69% of the variance) on antisocial behavior (i.e., self-reported property offenses, drug-related offenses, violent offenses) were stronger than genetic influences (1% of the variance) under conditions of neighborhood socioeconomic disadvantage, as determined by percentage of persons born outside Europe, North America, Australia, and New Zealand and educational level, unemployment level, net income, and crime rates (Tuvblad, Grann, & Lichtenstein, 2006). Under conditions of neighborhood socioeconomic advantage in this Swedish study, genetic influences were stronger (37% of the variance in antisocial behavior) than environmental influences (13% of the variance in antisocial behavior).

Additionally, cultural norms may confer protection against genetic risk. Social order may be maintained in cultural contexts through informal social control, which involves social norms and structural constraints that are placed on people to limit their behavior and choices. According to the *social control hypothesis*, in settings of high social control, a large percentage of the people will exhibit the same phenotype (e.g., prosocial behavior) regardless of their genotypes, whereas in settings marked by low social control, people's choices and behaviors are more likely to reflect their genotype (Shanahan & Hofer, 2005).

Studies on alcohol use in situations of high and low social control support Shanahan and Hofer's (2005) hypotheses. Dick, Rose, Viken, Kaprio, & Koskenvuo (2001) examined the effects of community stability on alcohol use among adolescent twins in Finland. As community migration in and out of an area increases, community monitoring and personal accountability decrease. In highest migration areas, the genetic effect was high and the environmental effect was low. In the area with the lowest migration, the environmental effect was much greater than the genetic effect. Similarly, in the same Finnish sample, environmental factors had a greater influence in adolescent alcohol use in rural settings in which social control is relatively high, whereas genetic factors had a greater influence among adolescents residing in urban areas, in which there is relatively low social control (Rose, Dick, Viken, & Kaprio, 2001). Religiosity is another form of informal social control. In a study of adolescent and young adult twins in Holland, Koopmans, Slutske, van Baal, and Boomsma (1999) found that genetic influences accounted for 40% of the variance in alcohol use initiation in nonreligious females, compared to 0% in religiously raised females.

Being a member of an interdependent group and a strong identification with the group can be a source of social control or social push. In a study by Wong (1999), adherence to Chinese culture was a protective factor against delinquency, and acculturation to North American values was a risk factor among Chinese Canadian youths aged 10–20. Conversely, ethnic identity was positively associated with delinquency among adolescent Cambodian American males (Go & Le, 2005). Cambodian ethnic identity was associated with trauma and war experience, which may have caused it to be a risk factor. Genetic influences were not examined in the Wong or Go and Le studies. Nevertheless, ethnic identity can serve as a protective or control factor, or as a risk or push factor that may moderate the relative influence of genes on behavior. In the following sections, we will use research examining ethnic differences in intelligence and alcohol use as examples of evaluating the role genes play in determining behavior in these areas.

Genes and Intelligence

One of the most controversial areas in psychology is the study of intelligence, race, and genetics (Sternberg et al., 2005). Studies in psychology of race differences in intelligence began in the early 20th century with the development of tests of verbal and nonverbal motor performance skills. One's verbal and nonverbal performance on intelligence tests relative to those of others of the same age results in an intelligence quotient (IQ). Psychological studies of intelligence use tests of intellectual functioning, which primarily assess past learning and capture only part of the broader construct of intelligence. In other words, test performance or the IQ derived from these tests are not equivalent to intelligence but comprise only a part of it. For example, creative and practical abilities are typically not assessed by most intelligence tests. It has been argued that racial differences in intelligence developed because those in northern climates were faced with greater survival challenges (e.g., cold weather) than those in southern climates (Rushton, 1995b). However, there are equal challenges to surviving in southern climates (e.g., harsh weather in the form of extreme heat; Sternberg et al., 2005). Moreover, no gene has been linked to intelligence. The difference between European American and African American IQ scores has decreased over the past five decades and is now about 10 points, or 0.6–0.7 standard deviation (Dickens & Flynn, 2006; Nisbett, 2005). Although there is not evidence that this difference is based on race, in part because race cannot be defined as a genetic or biological entity, there is evidence implicating socioeconomic factors. Children adopted into middle-class homes experience IQ gains relative to those in lower-class homes (Nisbett, 2005). The evidence that the test score gap has decreased and that children's IQs can gain suggest that intelligence is not a fixed, unchangeable entity but that it is susceptible to environmental influences.

James Watson, who shared the Nobel Prize in 1953 with Francis Crick for their discovery of the structure of DNA, claimed in October of 2007 that tests indicate that the intelligence of people in Africa is not the same as that of persons of European ancestry. These claims echo those of psychologists in the early 20th century who assumed that persons of color were inferior to European Americans (Holliday, in press). Watson also claimed that these test differences are evolutionarily based. He later apologized for these statements. These statements assume that tests measure intelligence, that differences measured by the tests are important, and that the differences are genetically based. None of these assumptions is accurate (Nisbett, 2005; Sternberg et al., 2005).

Genetics and Alcohol Use

One genetic difference that has some association with ethnicity is the presence of the aldehyde dehydrogenase gene *ALDH2* and the alcohol dehydrogenase gene *ADH1B*, which are associated with protection from alcohol dependence (Luczak, Glatt, & Wall, 2006). Physiological effects of these genes associated with alcohol use include skin flushing (reddening), headaches, subjective sensations of being drunk with relatively low alcohol dosages, and severe hangovers. Thus, *ALDH2* and *ADH1B* might be considered a form of genetic antabuse. The *ALDH 2*2* allele, an alternative form of the *ALDH2* gene, is relatively common in persons of Northeast Asian ancestry but relatively rare in others. Population samples indicate that approximately 31% of Chinese, 45% of Japanese, 29% of Koreans, 10% of Thais, and 0% of Western and Central European Whites possess at least one *ALDH2*2* allele (Goedde et al., 1992). Similarly, population samples indicate that approximately 92% of Chinese, 84% of Japanese, 96% of Koreans, 54% of Thais, and 1–8% of Western and Northern European Whites possess at least one *ADH1B*2* allele (Goedde et al., 1992). Although these genes are associated with Northeast Asian ancestry, they are not markers for race or ethnicity, as less than 100% of each ethnic group has these genes and there is some overlap with other ethnic groups.

Alcohol dependence is characterized by (a) tolerance, which involves either a need for markedly increased amounts of alcohol to achieve intoxication or a markedly diminished effect with continued use of the same amount of alcohol, or (b) withdrawal, involving autonomic hyperactivity (e.g., sweating or fast pulse rate), hand tremors, insomnia, nausea or vomiting, hallucinations, agitation, anxiety, or seizures (American Psychiatric Association, 2000). In a meta-analysis of 15 studies with 1,980 cases and 2,550 controls, Luczak and colleagues (2006) found that possessing one *ALDH2*2* allele reduced the risk for alcohol dependence to approximately one-fourth and that possessing two *ALDH2*2* alleles reduced the risk to approximately one-ninth. *ADH1B*2* has a protective effect against alcohol dependence above and beyond that of *ALDH2*2*. Possession of one *ADH1B*2* allele reduced the risk for alcohol dependence to approximately one-sixth, and possession of two *ADH1B*2* alleles reduced the risk to approximately one-eleventh. Cultural effects may influence alcohol dependence in addition to these genetic effects. Japanese participants in the studies reviewed were least likely to experience alcohol dependence. Japanese culture places importance on men drinking in social contexts without becoming addicted, which may result in fewer instances of alcohol dependence (Luczak et al., 2006).

This genetic research on alcohol has personal significance. I experience unpleasant physiological sensations, including skin flushing, every time I take a drink of alcohol. I have long suspected that I had the anti-alcohol genes described above, and I joked about this during a paper presentation at the 2004 Convention of the Association for the Advancement of Behavior Therapy. In the audience was Tamara Wall, a researcher on genetic and ethnic effects on alcohol and a coauthor of the meta-analytic study discussed above. Dr. Wall said that she could genotype me with a blood sample. She sent me a kit that required me to puncture my finger and stain blood on a slide. I mailed the blood sample to Dr. Wall and waited for the results. These results would be a day of reckoning for me, not only in terms of my difficulties in drinking alcohol but because a large percentage of persons of Northeast Asian ancestry have the *ALDH2*2* gene. My maternal grandparents were from Japan, and although my phenotype is ambiguous, I wanted my genotype to prove that I have something in common with other Japanese people! Sure enough, my genotype indicated that I have the *ALDH2*2* gene. Although there is no gene that distinguishes any ethnic group, I have a gene and experiences with alcohol that are the same as those of many other persons of Northeast Asian ancestry. I consider my *ALDH2*2* gene (and my flushing response to alcohol) as my Asian American membership card.

Summary

The promise of genetics research is not that racially or ethnically based differences will be identified. Rather, genetics research can help determine relative contributions of the cultural environment to behavior. Genes interact with the environment to produce behavior. Additional research on cultural factors that can promote or prevent the expression of genetic predispositions is needed.

EVOLUTIONARY PSYCHOLOGY

Evolutionary psychology is the study of human adaptations that enhance species survival. *Adaptation* refers to a creature changing and becoming better suited, or *fit*, to the demands of the environment (Schmitt & Pilcher, 2004). Adaptations are genetically transmitted from generation to generation. Ancestral humans during the Pleistocene period varied in adaptive characteristics. Natural selection favored those characteristics associated with survival, such as fertility and physical strength.

Those humans possessing adaptive characteristics were more likely to survive and pass these characteristics to the next generation. Modern humans have inherited these historical adaptations, even if they are not as adaptive as they once were. For example, among ancestral humans, aggressive behavior may have been necessary to procure resources or defend oneself in interactions with animals and other humans. Aggressive behavior is much less necessary for survival among modern humans, yet modern humans retain an inherited capacity for aggression.

Not all genes that are transmitted from generation to generation are necessarily adaptive. Although fitness may be associated with fertility, not all fit or fertile persons have children. Genetic transmission may also be the result of chance events (e.g., availability of mating partners, natural disasters), known as *random genetic drift* (Sternberg et al., 2005). *Mutations* are another source of random changes in genes passed from generation to generation that may have behavioral consequences (Sternberg et al., 2005). Thus the presence of a gene or behavior does not necessarily mean that it was selected for its adaptive qualities.

One evolutionary adaptation is *reproductive strategy*, which involves two approaches (Pianka, 1970). The first approach, known as r-selected, is to have many offspring and to put little energy into raising them. The alternative, known as K-selected, involves having few offspring and putting much energy into raising them. Humans are the most K-selected species (Peregrine, Ember, & Ember, 2003).

Rushton (1995a) has contended that there exists racial variation in reproductive strategies. According to Rushton, all humans initially had an r strategy until they left Africa. Those who remained in Africa retained the r strategy, while those who moved to the colder climates of Asia evolved the K strategy. Those in Europe evolved a reproductive strategy between those in Africa and Asia. Based on this model, Rushton predicted that persons of African ancestry would have frequent marital dissolutions, high sexual precocity, frequent infidelity, frequent child neglect or abuse, high criminality, low social organization, and low technological sophistication. Persons of Asian ancestry would be at the other extremes on these variables, and persons of European ancestry would be in between. Rushton's model is obviously controversial. In a study of 186 societies on these variables, there was no support for Rushton's predictions (Peregrine et al., 2003). Moreover, adaptations are assumed to be universal (Schmitt & Pilcher, 2004), so it is not clear why one racial group in a K-selected species would be r-selected. There also is no fossil evidence for these racially different mating strategies, and such speculations are essentially folk beliefs to justify societal inequities (Cooper, 2005; Sternberg et al., 2005).

Evolution and Ethnic Identity

Although there is no evidence for racially based mating strategy differences, could there be other evolutionary-based group differences? Is it possible that racial or ethnic identity, as discussed in Chapter 1, is adaptive? Our hunter–gatherer ancestors lived in bands and came into conflict with neighboring bands. Survival involved distinguishing friends from enemies. A primitive method of detecting coalitions and alliances was shared appearance (Cosmides, Tooby, & Kurzban, 2003). Thus, humans developed neurocognitive machinery that processes phenotypic characteristics as a means of *alliance detection.*

Neuroscience evidence supports the hypothesis that humans are more interested in their racial ingroup than in racial outgroups. The fusiform face area of the brain is activated during face processing. In a functional magnetic resonance imaging (fMRI) study, Golby, Gabrieli, Chiao, and Eberhardt (2001) had 9 African American and 10 European American men view 42 African American and 42 Europrean American men's faces, as well as control stimuli (42 antique radios, fixation cross). fMRI is a scan of brain activity during a task, which in this case was face processing. Fusiform face area activation was significantly greater for participants while they viewed same-race faces versus while they viewed different-race faces. A second set of African American and European American faces and control stimuli was presented, half of which the participants had not previously seen. Recognition of same-race faces was significantly greater than recognition of different race faces.

Of course, not all primitive alliances were based on phenotypic similarity. Enemies could develop within one's racial group and alliances could develop outside one's racial group (Cosmides et al., 2003). Thus, the neurocognitive machinery to detect phenotypic characteristics would need to respond to environmental contingencies. Are preference and recognition of racially similar faces "hardwired", or can these abilities respond to the cultural environment?

Two studies suggest that facial preference and recognition are influenced by the environment. Bar-Haim, Ziv, Lamy, and Hodes (2006) examined the amount of time that 3-month-old infants spent looking at pairs of photos of the faces of White and Black individuals. Looking time was determined by the direction of the infants' gaze and amount of time spent gazing in that direction. Twelve of the infants were White Israelis who had been raised in a White environment in Israel, 12 were Black Ethiopians raised in a primarily Black environment in Ethiopia, and 12 were Black Israelis raised in a primarily White environment that was an immigration center in Israel. There was not a group of White infants raised in a primarily Black environment. The White Israeli infants raised in a White environment spent significantly more time looking at the White faces than at the Black faces. The opposite was true of Black Ethiopians in Ethiopia. However, the Black Israelis raised in a White environment did not differ in the amount of time spent looking at White versus Black faces. This study involving infants provides evidence that facial preference is malleable at an early age.

In another study involving differential exposure to racial groups, Sangrigoli, Pallier, Argenti, Ventureyra, & de Schonen (2005) studied the face recognition abilities of 12 Korean adults who were adopted between ages 3 and 9 by White families in Europe, 12 native Korean adults, and 12 White French adults. Similar to the Bar-Haim et al. (2006) study of infants, there was not a group of White adults in this study that was raised in an Asian environment. The participants were presented pictures of White and Japanese faces and then asked to recognize these pictures among a second set of pictures that included pictures they had not previously viewed. Native Korean adults were better at recognizing the Japanese faces than the White faces, and the opposite was true for White French adults. The recognition accuracy pattern for the Korean adoptees was similar to that of the White French adults, with superior recognition of White versus Japanese faces. These data suggest plasticity (changeability) in facial recognition abilities as late as 9 years of age. The Bar-Haim et al. and Sangrigoli et al. studies have implications for interethnic relations. Experience with other ethnic groups may reduce one's ingroup preference or prejudice toward outgroups.

In addition to reproductive strategy and alliance detection, *altruism* is relevant to survival (Nowak & Sigmund, 2005). Altruism involves cooperation between persons who are genetically, and sometimes phenotypically, dissimilar. Although natural selection might be assumed to favor those who are strong and selfish, cooperation can lead to greater payoffs than an individualistic strategy, even for individuals. Such cooperation is essential in communities and societies in which survival depends on individuals' abilities to share resources. Of course, there are some individuals who maintain a selfish strategy despite the possibility of greater benefits from a cooperative strategy.

How does an individual decide with whom to cooperate? Cooperation with one's ingroup enhances survival but may not provide the level of benefits of added cooperation with outgroup members. Nowak and Sigmund (2005) have contended that cooperation and altruism involving persons who are not genetically similar are based on reputation. An individual is most likely to cooperate with someone whose reputation suggests that they are likely to reciprocally cooperate. Just as there are some who maintain a selfish strategy without regard to the payoffs of a cooperative strategy, there are some who will maintain a cooperative strategy even with those who do not reciprocate. Nevertheless, most will assess the reputation of another person or group before they decide to cooperate.

A person's reputation may be based on direct experiences with the person. Experience can change preference, as demonstrated by the Bar-Haim et al. (2006) and Sangrigoli et al. (2005) studies on facial preference and recognition. In the absence of direct experiences, reputation is based on indirect experiences, including the experiences of others (Nowak & Sigmund, 2005). Sometimes one's interpretation of these indirect experiences can be inaccurate and lead to stereotypes about another person's reputation. Such stereotypes may prevent cooperation or sometimes enhance it. The likelihood of developing stereotypic information about another person or group may be reduced by actual experiences with that person or group. Intergroup relations are part of social psychology, which will be discussed in Chapter 5.

Summary

Evolutionary approaches emphasize that the persistence of behaviors throughout history is based on adaptation. However, not all behaviors that persist are as adaptive as they once were, nor are all existent behaviors necessarily selected. Some behaviors appear because of chance events, such as mutations. Although the emphasis in evolutionary psychology is on species universals, this approach is relevant to multicultural psychology because it addresses the adaptive aspects of racial and ethnic identity.

HEALTH PSYCHOLOGY

Physical health is biologically based but also influenced by cultural and sociocultural factors. Ethnic differences in eating disorders, blood pressure, substance abuse, birth outcomes, and chronic health problems have been studied. Cultural norms that differ across ethnic groups and sociocultural factors, such as discrimination, may influence these ethnic differences.

Health-enhancing behaviors are adaptive. Signs of physical health, such as youthfulness, are desirable in mates. The sexual competition hypothesis suggests that females compete for male commitment and that appearing youthful makes females more desirable to males (Abed, 1998). Thinness may be a sign of youthfulness, which suggests that a drive for thinness, resulting in eating disorders in some cases, may have an evolutionary basis (Faer, Hendriks, Abed, & Figueredo, 2005). In the following sections, we will review the literature on the following health topics with regard to ethnic populations and cultural considerations: eating disorders, blood pressure, substance use, birth outcomes, and chronic health problems.

Eating Disorders

Major eating disorders are anorexia nervosa, bulimia nervosa, and binge eating disorder (American Psychiatric Association, 2000). *Anorexia nervosa* involves a refusal to maintain a minimally accepted standard of weight. Weight is lost either by restricting caloric intake or by binge eating and purging food (e.g., vomiting, laxative abuse). *Bulimia nervosa* involves recurrent episodes of binge eating followed by inappropriate compensatory behaviors used to prevent weight gain, including purging, fasting, or excessive exercise. This syndrome features recurrent episodes of binge eating without compensatory behaviors. Binge episodes in *binge eating disorder* are characterized by feelings of loss of control, extremely rapid eating, eating without hunger, eating alone, and feelings of disgust or depression regarding eating episodes.

In a cross-historical and cross-cultural literature review, Keel and Klump (2003) concluded that bulimia nervosa is specific to Western cultures but that anorexia nervosa is not. However, this review did not consider racial, ethnic, and cultural diversity within Western cultures. Although eating disorders were initially assumed to be culturally-specific to young, upper-middle-class European American women, these disorders also occur among women of color. Cultural standards of beauty are assumed to contribute to eating disorders (Gilbert, 2003). Thus, cultural values, attitudes, and beliefs, as well as acculturation, need to be considered in research as the possible basis of ethnic differences. Sociocultural issues associated with minority status, including barriers to educational and economic opportunities, and discrimination also need to be considered.

There is some evidence that eating disorders and body dissatisfaction are more common among European American than among African American women. In a large sample of 19–20-year-old women from California, Ohio, and Washington, DC, 1.5% of European American women and no African American women met the diagnostic criteria for anorexia nervosa (Striegel-Moore et al., 2003). In the same study, 2.3% of European American and 0.4% of African American women met the criteria for bulimia nervosa, and binge eating was present among 2.7% of European American and 1.4% of African American women. In a review of 42 studies of European Americans and African Americans, dieting behavior was significantly greater among African Americans in only 2 studies (Crago & Shisslak, 2003). These differences may be a result of different levels of body satisfaction. In a nationally representative sample of women 18–45 years of age, African Americans had lower concerns and dissatisfaction than European Americans or Latinas (Bay-Cheng, Zucker, Stewart, & Pomerlau, 2002).

Why might African American women be more satisfied with their bodies than European American women are? It is possible that African American and European American women have different reference groups with whom they are comparing themselves. European American women tend to compare themselves with media images of thin, European American women (Gilbert, 2003). Because of large and cohesive kinship networks, and because there are relatively few media images of African American women, African American women's body images may be influenced by family members. African American females may also receive more positive than negative feedback about their appearance from family members and friends (Franko & Striegel-Moore, 2002).

Other research suggests that rates of eating disorders are similar between European American and African American women. There were few differences between European American and ethnic minority women in a review of 28 studies of binge eating and 19 studies of purging (Crago & Shisslak, 2003). O'Neill (2003) came to the same conclusion regarding binge eating in a meta-analysis of 18 studies of European American and African American women.

Across studies, Asian Americans tend to have similar levels of body dissatisfaction to European Americans but lower rates of diagnosable eating disorders (Cummins, Simmons, & Zane, 2005). However, some of these studies have included small samples of Asian Americans, which do not provide the statistical power to detect differences. Moreover, the reason for the lower rates of diagnosable eating disorders among Asian Americans is unknown.

Most of the above studies of ethnic differences in eating disorders have used a one-item self-report measure of ethnicity, as discussed in Chapter 2. Given the variability within ethnic groups, it is surprising that between-groups differences are found. Sources of variability within ethnic groups include acculturation, ethnic identity, and discrimination (Crago & Shisslak, 2003).

Research on the association between acculturation and eating disorders has produced mixed results, in part because of varying definitions and measures of acculturation (e.g., generation in the United States). Acculturation and eating disorders were investigated in a Los Angeles community sample of Mexican American women (Cachelin, Phinney, Schug, & Striegel-Moore, 2006). Acculturation was assessed with the Acculturation Rating Scale for Mexican Americans-II (ARSMA-II; Cuellar, Arnold, & Maldonado, 1995), a validated and commonly used measure of acculturation. The ARSMA-II includes language usage and preference, ethnic identity and classification, cultural heritage and ethnic behaviors, and ethnic interaction. The scale measures orientation to Mexican culture and to Anglo culture. Examples of Mexican orientation scale items are "I enjoy speaking Spanish" and "My family cooks Mexican foods." Examples of Anglo orientation items are "I associate with Anglos" and "I enjoy listening to English language music." The Multigroup Ethnic Identity Measure (Phinney, 1992) was used to assess ethnic identity. Eating disorders were assessed with the Structured Clinical Interview for DSM-IV-TR (First, Spitzer, Gibbon, & Williams, 2001) and the Eating Disorders Examination (EDE; Fairburn & Cooper, 1993). The EDE assesses frequency of binge eating during the past 6 months, frequency of purging behaviors (vomiting, laxative, and diuretic abuse) during the past 6 months, degree of dietary restriction in the past 6 months, degree of distress regarding binge eating, and importance of weight or shape. Interviews and measures were administered in participants' preferred language (English or Spanish). Anglo orientation was significantly associated with eating disorders, but Mexican orientation and ethnic identity were not (Cachelin et al., 2006). Mexican culture does not emphasize body image as European American culture does, which may explain these results.

The previous studies have examined eating disorders among females. Do eating disorders exist among males? Although the rates of eating disorders are lower among males than among females, males are more likely to develop problems associated with the pursuit of muscularity (Ricciardelli & McCabe, 2004). In a review of 27 studies on African American and European American males, Ricciardelli, McCabe, Williams, and Thompson (2007) found African Americans to have a more positive body image and prefer a larger body size. These findings are similar to those for African American females. However, African American males were more likely than European American males to engage in extreme weight loss behaviors (e.g., chronic dieting, use of diet pills, laxatives and diuretics, and vomiting) and binge eating. Although having a positive body image and eating disorders may seem to be at odds, achieving a muscular physique may create a positive body image but may also involve an alternation between binge eating to gain muscle mass and weight loss behaviors to reduce weight gain (Ricciardelli et al., 2007).

Similar to the findings with females, Latino American and European American males' body images and body size preferences were not significantly different across 26 studies (Ricciardelli et al., 2007). Similar to African American males, Latino American males were more likely to engage in extreme weight loss and binge eating than European American males. Although the basis of eating disorders among Latino American males has not been investigated, it is possible that disordered eating among male Latino American immigrants is associated with loss of status in the United States relative to their countries of origin, which affects men more than women (Ricciardelli et al., 2007).

Evidence on body image and size and on eating disorders was inconsistent across 22 studies of Asian American males (Ricciardelli et al., 2007). Pacific Islander American males exhibited a more positive image than European American males in three of four studies, but eating disorders have not been studied among Pacific Islander American males. There have been only five studies comparing body image, disordered eating, or related behaviors between American Indians and European Americans. Nevertheless, the evidence from these studies suggests that American Indians have more body image concerns and engage in extreme weight loss and binge eating more than European Americans do. American Indians were found to have a greater body mass index than European Americans.

Discrimination and Blood Pressure

In addition to eating disorders, there has been much interest in ethnic differences in other health problems. African Americans disproportionately experience diabetes, heart disease, hypertension, and obesity relative to other U.S. ethnic groups (Mays, Cochran, & Barnes, 2007). The gap in health between African Americans and European Americans has not changed over the past two decades (Farmer & Ferraro, 2005). Because European Americans as the majority group in North American generally do not experience race based discrimination, discrimination may contribute to the health disparities between European Americans and persons of color in North America. Perceived race-based discrimination among African Americans is associated with poorer self-rated health, higher blood pressure, smoking, and alcohol use (Mays et al., 2007; Nazroo, 2003).

Poverty does not account for these health disparities. Discrimination may transcend socioeconomic status. In fact, in a 5-year study of 10–12-year-old African Americans, higher socioeconomic status children were more likely to experience racial discrimination than lower socioeconomic status children (Brody et al., 2006a). Higher socioeconomic status persons are more likely to come into contact with persons from other racial and ethnic groups and also likely to experience more opportunities for discrimination. During the 1960s, a newly minted African American Ph.D. was excited to tell Malcolm X of his academic accomplishment. Malcolm poignantly asked this young man what White racists call African American PhDs. Malcolm's answer was "n——".

D. R. Williams, Neighbors, and Jackson (2003) reviewed 11 community studies on discrimination and blood pressure among African Americans. Three studies revealed a positive association, five revealed a positive association under certain conditions, including coping style and gender, and three revealed no association. Studies conducted since the D. R. Williams et al. review have attempted to clarify the conditions under which perceived discrimination is associated with blood pressure among African Americans. These studies reviewed below suggest that the effects of discrimination on African Americans' blood pressure are not necessarily intuitive.

The effects of perceived discrimination on blood pressure may be indirect. Clark (2006a) examined the effects of perceived racism on blood pressure among African American high school students. Perceived racism was assessed with the Everyday Racism Scale (Forman, Williams, & Jackson, 1997). The scale asks participants, "In your day-to-day life, how often have any of the following things happened to you because of your race?" Examples of events from the scale are: treated with less respect, received poorer service, people act as if you are not as smart, people act as if they are afraid of you, called names, and threatened or harassed. Ninety-six percent of the sample reported experiencing racism.

The participants also completed a measure that assessed how frequently anger is experienced and had their diastolic and systolic blood pressure assessed (Clark, 2006a). Perceived racism was not associated with blood pressure among participants who were high in anger. It appears that

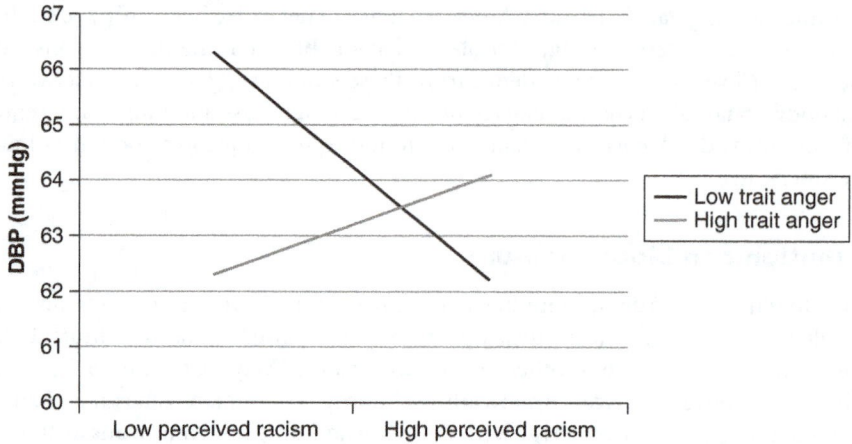

FIGURE 3.1 Perceived Racism and Diastolic Blood Pressure Among African Americans

the effects of high anger on blood pressure override the effects of racism. However, among those low in anger, high perceived racism was associated with lower blood pressure (Figure 3.1). It is possible that African American adolescents who are low in anger are less likely to experience anger following racist incidents and more likely to withdraw from potentially stressful situations, both of which may result in lower blood pressure (Clark, 2006a). Also, participants low in both perceived racism and trait anger had higher blood pressure than those high in trait anger. African American adolescents who report having few stressful experiences (racism, anger) may be defensive, which may result in higher blood pressure. The assumption is that racism against African Americans exists and that high blood pressure is a way of compensating for not perceiving racism.

In a second study with African American college women, Clark (2006b) again found the effects of perceived racism on blood pressure to be indirect. In this study, participants were asked about experiences of racism in nine domains (employment, law, finances, education, community, family–social relationships, emotional well-being, physical health, and public assistance). Seeking social support (e.g., I talk to someone about how I feel) when dealing with racism was also assessed. Blood pressure was assessed before and after a stressful task, which involved answering aloud five questions concerning animal rights. Among participants who were low in seeking social support, blood pressure increased following the stressful task for participants high in perceived racism more than for those low in perceived racism. Blood pressure was not reactive to the stressful task among participants who were high in seeking social support. Thus, social support may buffer the negative health effects of racism.

If an African American received unfair treatment while shopping, would their blood pressure rise more in response to blatant racist statements or to the same unfair treatment without racist statements? Merritt, Bennett, Williams, Edwards, and Sollers (2006) had African American men listen to a scenario of the unfair treatment of a shopping customer that included or did not include blatantly racist statements. After hearing the scenario, participants rated how much they thought racism played a role in the unfair treatment of the customer. They then discussed their thoughts and feelings about the scenario and how they would react to the situation. Blood pressure was continuously assessed throughout the experiment. Diastolic blood pressure was higher for those who heard the scenario that did not include the racist statements than for those who heard the racist scenario. Moreover, those who heard the nonracist scenario and perceived high levels of racism in the scenario showed larger increases in blood pressure than those who did not perceive racism in the scenario. Thus, an ambiguous situation led to cardiovascular reactivity more than a blatant racist situation. Blatant racism is becoming less common that subtle racism but is easy to detect and does not require intensive cognitive processing. The subtle condition may have required more cognitive processing, and accompanying cardiovascular reactivity, to determine if the event was discriminatory (Merritt et al., 2006).

What is the association between racial/ethnic identity and blood pressure? In the only study that has directly assessed ethnic identity and blood pressure, African American self-concept was found to be inversely associated with systolic blood pressure in males (Scribner, Hohn, & Dwyer, 1995). This finding suggests that African Americans who are highly racially identified are less reactive to stressors that might result in blood pressure increases. However, the models of racial and ethnic identity discussed in Chapter 1 suggest that a person who is more racially- or ethnically-identified might be more sensitive to discrimination and hence might be *more* susceptible to hypertension. Conversely, a person of color who is not racially- or ethnically-identified may be *less* sensitive to discrimination and could be less susceptible to hypertension. Nevertheless, Clark (2006a) found that African Americans who reported few experiences of discrimination had higher blood pressure than those who reported more experiences of discrimination. More research on the effects of racial and ethnic identity on blood pressure is needed, as is research on groups of color in addition to African Americans.

Discrimination and Substance Use

Another health consequence of discrimination is substance use. Gibbons, Gerrard, Cleveland, Wills, and Brody (2004) conducted a 20-month follow-up study of discrimination and substance use among community samples of African American 10- or 11-year-olds and their parents. This longitudinal design allowed the determination of how discrimination affected later substance use. Discrimination was assessed with the Schedule of Racist Events (Landrine & Klonoff, 1996b), which includes negative experiences attributable to being African American (e.g., "How often have you been treated unfairly because you are African American?" "How often has someone treated a member of your family unfairly because they were African American?"). Among both children and parents, 91% reported experiences with discrimination. Substance use included lifetime and past 12-month tobacco, alcohol, and drug use. Children were also asked about their friends' substance use. Eleven percent of children used at least one substance at the first assessment (Time 1) and 22% at the second assessment (Time 2). Friends' substance use was 31% at Time 1 and 39% at Time 2. Parental substance use was 54% at Time 1 and 56% at Time 2. Risk images of substance users were also assessed by rating peers who used tobacco, alcohol, or drugs on six adjectives: *popular, smart, cool, good-looking, childish,* and *dull.* Children's willingness to use tobacco, alcohol, and drugs was also assessed.

Level of perceived discrimination among parents at Time 1 was associated with parents' increased substance use or maintaining a high level of substance use at Time 2 (Gibbons et al., 2004). The association between discrimination and children's drug use was mediated by distress. Children who experienced distress as a result of discrimination were more likely to use substances at Time 2. Substance use may be a way of coping with this distress. Moreover, those children who experienced distress because of their parents' experiences with discrimination were more likely to use substances at Time 2. Children's perceived discrimination was also associated with affiliating with peers who used substances, which also was associated with children's substance use.

Children's perceived discrimination was also associated with more positive images of substance users, which in turn was associated with a greater willingness to use substances and actual substance use. Thus, discrimination may cause African American children to feel excluded from peer groups who do not use substances and may cause them to turn to peers who do use substances.

Discrimination and Birth Outcomes

Yet another area in which discrimination has negative health effects is in birth outcomes. Discrimination may produce prenatal stress in African American women, which may lead to infant mortality, low birth weight, and preterm delivery (Giscombé & Lobel, 2005). Infant mortality, defined as death within the first year after birth, was 5.7/100,000 for European Americans and 13.3/100,000 for African Americans in 2002 (Arias et al., 2003). Low birth weight (<2,500 g) affected 7% of European American infants versus 13% of African American infants, and 11% of European American infants versus 17% of African American infants were born preterm (<37 weeks; Arias et al., 2003). Low birth weight and preterm delivery are the leading causes of infant mortality in African Americans (Giscombé & Lobel, 2005). Low birth weight is also associated with later difficulties, such as cognitive deficits and cardiovascular disease.

The ethnic disparity in birth outcomes is not explained by socioeconomic status. After controlling for income, maternal age, education, substance use, prenatal care, and educational status, the disparity in adverse birth outcomes continued to be approximately two times or more (Giscombé & Lobel, 2005). However, African American women may be more susceptible than European American women to prenatal stress. A major component of stress for African American women is race-based discrimination. Race-based discrimination creates stress beyond other general stressors. Klonoff, Landrine, and Ullman (1999) found that race-based discrimination was associated with distress (anxiety, somatization, obsessive compulsive symptoms, interpersonal sensitivity, depression) among African American women even when socioeconomic status and general stressful events (e.g., getting married, going on welfare, getting arrested, changing jobs) were accounted for. In four studies, racism in school, medical care, service at a restaurant or store, housing, and work settings experienced by African American women has been found to be associated with low infant birth weight or preterm delivery (Giscombé & Lobel, 2005). Although there are no published studies on ethnic differences in cardiovascular response to stress and racism in pregnant women, it is possible that the stress created by race-based discrimination may result in hypertension, which is a risk factor for low birth weight (Giscombé & Lobel, 2005).

Discrimination and Chronic Health Problems

Most of the literature on health consequences of discrimination has involved African Americans. However, Gee, Spencer, Chen, and Takeuchi (2007) reported on the health effects of discrimination in a large household survey of Asian Pacific Americans. Because Asian Pacific Americans are often assumed to be a "model minority," they are also often assumed not to experience discrimination that might have deleterious consequences. Chronic health problems were assessed with the World Mental Health Composite International Diagnostic Interview, a self-report checklist of lifetime physical and psychophysiological disorders. These problems included arthritis or rheumatism, chronic back or neck problems, frequent or severe headaches, other chronic pain, hay fever and other seasonal allergies, stroke, heart attack, heart disease, high blood pressure, asthma, tuberculosis, other chronic lung disease, diabetes or high blood sugar, ulcer in stomach or intestine, HIV/AIDS, epilepsy or seizure, and cancer. Discrimination was assessed with the Everyday Racism Scale (Forman et al., 1997), as discussed above. Everyday discrimination was significantly correlated with composite chronic health problems. Similar to the above studies on African Americans, discrimination was associated with cardiovascular problems. Discrimination was also associated with respiratory problems and with pain conditions. These data suggest that the negative health effects of race-based discrimination apply to multiple groups of color, including those who are assumed not to experience discrimination or its effects.

The above discussion is on discrimination at a personal level. However, discrimination has deleterious health effects at the broader societal level (Nazroo, 2003; D. R. Williams et al., 2003). Residential segregation is an effect of discrimination and has negative effects on health. Segregated communities are typically poor, and poor communities have limited access to health care and social services (S. A. Roberts). Although poverty does not account for ethnic health disparities, as discussed above, once an ethnic minority person develops a health problem, their health may deteriorate because of a lack of resources and health hazards, such as air pollution, lead, dust, dirt, and smog, in the physical environment. Social connectedness is also likely to be low in environments of unemployment, substandard housing and schools, drugs, crime, gangs, and violence. Constant coping to maintain homeostasis and adapt to acutely stressful events, known as *allostasis*, with a concentration of poverty and violence creates biological risk for coronary heart disease, inflammatory disorders, and cognitive impairment (Mays et al., 2007). Although ethnically concentrated communities can be a source of social support (Cutrona, Russell, Hessling, Brown, & Murry, 2000), conditions of poverty can offset such social support. It should be kept in mind that most persons of color are not poor. Nevertheless, almost all African Americans, including children, in the studies discussed above experienced race-based discrimination. As Malcolm X observed, discrimination transcends social boundaries.

Summary

There is some evidence of ethnic differences in health problems. However, evidence of differences does not reveal the basis of these differences. There is much variability within ethnic groups. Two sources of variability that affect health outcomes are discrimination and acculturation. Most of the research in health psychology has been conducted with African Americans, with relatively limited attention to other groups of color. Research with diverse groups, adequate sample sizes, and consistent use of valid measures is needed in multicultural health psychology.

Conclusion

Biological approaches emphasize universals. Although humans are biologically similar, they may differ in their responses to the environment. Cultural norms may promote or prevent genetic expression. Racial and ethnic identity might have origins as an adaptive behavior, in terms of detecting alliances. Furthermore, environmental contingencies that affect physical health, such as discrimination-related stress, may differ by ethnic group. Thus, consideration of race, ethnicity, and culture is important in biological approaches because they create influential contexts in which behavior occurs.

Discussion Questions

1. There has been much more scientific and public enthusiasm about genetic influences on behavior, such as juvenile delinquency or eating disorders, than on cultural factors, such as ethnic community norms, that might offset or exacerbate genetic risk. Genetic factors are, for the most part, not modifiable, whereas cultural factors are. Why is there such a disproportionate interest in what we can't control versus what we can?

2. Humans detect and prefer faces of the race of familiar people from infancy. Thus, those who claim to be "color-blind" with respect to race and ethnicity probably are not. What implications do studies of racial/ethnic detection and preference have for intercultural relationships?

3. Discrimination disproportionately affects the health of people of color. Ambiguous situations in which people of color are mistreated that do not involve blatant race-based discrimination may be even more problematic than situations that do involve blatant race-based discrimination because the reason for discrimination is obvious in the latter situations. Given the history of race-based discrimination in North America, will it ever be feasible for people of color not to worry about their race or ethnicity as a factor in people's negative actions toward them?

CHAPTER 4

Developmental Psychology

Developmental psychology focuses on human development across the life span. Many of the studies in this field involving populations of color have been designed to replicate theories and research that have been developed with European Americans. In contrast, the focus in this chapter is on developmental research on experiences that are unique to persons of color. The framework for this chapter is on the development of racial and ethnic identity and how this identity influences behavior across the life span. There is also a consideration of the effects of acculturation of persons of color to European American culture. The chapter begins with a review of the literature on parents' racial and ethnic socialization practices, which form the basis for children's racial and ethnic identity. Next we will consider the effects of racial and ethnic discrimination, which is the context within which racial and ethnic identity develops. In Chapter 3 we reviewed the physical health effects of discrimination, and in this chapter we will review the psychological effects of discrimination across the life span. The subsequent sections of the chapter focus on how identification with one's own ethnic group or with European Americans affects behavior, as well as on how racial and ethnic discrimination affects behavior. These sections of the chapter are organized chronologically, beginning with early childhood and proceeding through childhood, adolescence, and early adulthood.

How early in life does racial and ethnic identity develop? Neurocognitive evidence presented in Chapter 3 suggests that infants as young as 1 month show a preference for faces of the race of persons in their environment (Bar-Haim et al., 2006). Such an ability to differentiate faces may be evolutionarily adaptive in terms of identifying allies (Cosmides et al., 2003). These neurocognitive abilities soon translate into attitudes about ingroups and outgroups.

Children as young as 3 years of age have been demonstrated to develop ingroup biased attitudes. Patterson and Bigler (2006) assigned 3-to-5-year-olds to social groups in which they wore a red or blue shirt for 3 weeks. The participants were randomly assigned to experimental or control conditions, with gender and ethnic composition in each condition roughly equivalent. In the experimental condition, teachers referred to the color labels and organized their classes according to group color. Teachers in the control condition did not mention the color groups. Ingroup preference (i.e., how much participants liked to play with children from each group, predictions of winners in a group competition, and preferences for toys presented as group favorites) was observed in both the experimental and control conditions. In addition, participants in the experimental group rated ingroup members as more likeable and preferred unfamiliar ingroup members more than did participants in the experimental group. Although this was not a direct test of ethnic or racial preferences, the study demonstrated that young children develop ingroup preferences and inferences based on external characteristics. Moreover, ingroup preference can develop merely by categorizing children into groups (cf. Tajfel & Turner, 1986).

RACIAL AND ETHNIC SOCIALIZATION

If ingroup preference can develop when children are arbitrarily assigned to categories, such as blue and red (Patterson & Bigler, 2006), it follows that racial and ethnic identity, which include ingroup preference as a component, will develop when children are aware of racial and ethnic groups. Moreover, if ingroup preference can develop without information about the meaning of arbitrary categories, it follows that racial and ethnic identity will strongly develop when information is provided about the meaning of race and ethnicity. Children's racial and ethnic identities are influenced by their parents' values and perspectives about race and ethnicity.

It could be argued that such a focus on racial and ethnic differences might foster ingroup favoritism or racism. Why emphasize differences, or why not allow a child to spontaneously learn about group differences without overemphasizing them? Unfortunately, the default mode for racial socialization in society is "color-blindness," which implicitly views the world through the eyes of the mainstream while ignoring or devaluing the experiences of diverse groups, as discussed in Chapter 1.

The transmission of parental values and perspectives about race and ethnicity to children is known as *racial socialization* and *ethnic socialization* (Hughes et al., 2006). Research on racial socialization usually has focused on African Americans' efforts to cope with societal racism. Ethnic socialization research has included multiple ethnic groups. During the 1980s, research on racial and ethnic socialization focused primarily on African Americans. The scope of this research during the 1990s broadened to include multiple groups of color. Four themes have emerged in the way parents socialize their children to their own perspectives on race and ethnicity: egalitarianism, cultural socialization, preparation for bias, and promotion of mistrust (Hughes et al., 2006).

Egalitarianism involves an emphasis on individual qualities (e.g., hard work, self-acceptance) over racial or ethnic group membership and may also involve a silence about race (Hughes et al., 2006). This approach may include a "color-blind" perspective on society. Twenty to 50% of parents of color do not discuss race and ethnicity with their children.

Cultural socialization includes (a) talking about important historical or cultural figures; (b) exposing children to culturally relevant books, artifacts, music, and stories; (c) celebrating cultural holidays; (d) eating ethnic foods; and (e) encouraging children to use their family's native language (Hughes et al., 2006). Estimates of the rates of cultural socialization range from 33 to 85% in Asian American, Latino American, and African American families. This wide range is probably influenced by parental education, economic factors, and parental cultural identification, as discussed below. Cultural socialization probably occurs in all ethnic groups, including European Americans. European American cultural socialization is likely in contexts in which ethnicity is salient, such as communities in which there are relatively large numbers of persons of color (Hughes et al., 2006).

Education and economic status are factors that have been found to influence the amount of cultural socialization parents engage in. Parents of color with higher education and income are more likely to culturally socialize their children and prepare them for bias than parents with a lower income and educational attainment (Caughy et al., 2002; McHale et al., 2006). These parents of higher socioeconomic status are more likely to have the resources (e.g., time, knowledge) to be able to culturally socialize their children (Caughy et al., 2002) and also may be more aware of prejudice and discrimination (D. Williams, 1999). Moreover, higher education and income are associated with more interactions with persons of different racial and ethnic backgrounds, which create more opportunities for interracial and interethnic prejudice (Brody et al., 2006a). However, upper-socioeconomic-class African American parents have been found to culturally socialize their children less than middle-socioeconomic-class African American parents (Caughy et al., 2002). It is possible that upper-class parents are able to shield themselves from discrimination or may be trying to assimilate and do not view culture, race, and ethnicity as important as middle-class parents do.

As might be expected, parental cultural identification is associated with cultural socialization of children. Immigrants are more likely to culturally socialize their children than later-generation parents (Waters, 1990). African American (A. Thomas & Speight, 1999), Dominican and Puerto Rican (Hughes, 2003), and Mexican/Mexican American (Knight et al., 1993; Romero, Cuellar, & Roberts, 2000) parents who are more attached to their ethnic groups are also more likely to culturally socialize their children than parents in these groups who are less attached to their ethnic groups.

Preparation for bias involves making children aware of discrimination and teaching them how to cope with it. Preparation for bias may occur less frequently than cultural socialization and may be more frequent among African Americans than among other groups because of long-standing racism against African Americans (Caughy, O'Campo, Randolph, & Nickerson 2002; Hughes et al., 2006). Parents who have experienced discrimination are more likely than parents who have not experienced discrimination to prepare their children to cope with discrimination (Hughes, 2003; Umaña-Taylor & Fine, 2004). Strong ethnic identity is associated with preparation for bias among Latino parents (Hughes, 2003; Knight, Bernal, Cota, Garza, & Ocampo 1993; Knight, Bernal, Garza, Cota, & Ocampo 2003). Overall, there may be ethnic variations in discussion of bias, as Asian American families have been found to discuss prejudice against Asian Americans relatively infrequently (Nagata & Cheng, 2003). This could be associated with cultural values that emphasize emotional restraint and maintaining harmony.

Although there have not been studies of racial and ethnic socialization using the Sellers et al. (1998) Multidimensional Model of Racial Identity (see Chapter 1), Hughes and colleagues (2006) hypothesized how racial identity in terms of the Sellers et al. model may affect racial and ethnic socialization. Parents high in racial centrality who believe that their group is held in low public regard may be likely to discuss discrimination with their children. Group pride is likely to be emphasized by those high in racial centrality and high in private regard. Research is needed to test these hypotheses.

Parents are more likely to discuss racial and ethnic issues, particularly discrimination, with adolescents than with younger children (McHale et al., 2006). Adolescents undergo an identity-seeking process and are more likely to experience discrimination than children. Nevertheless, younger children are capable of processing racial and ethnic socialization messages, and it is possible that early racial and ethnic socialization could prevent later negative effects of discrimination. Stevenson, Herrero-Taylor, Cameron, and Davis (2002) found that ethnic minority boys may be perceived as more threatening than ethnic minority girls, so differences in parental racial and ethnic socialization practices by child gender might be expected. In one study, African American fathers were found to racially socialize their sons more than their daughters. However, mothers' racial socialization practices did not differ by their children's gender (McHale et al., 2006), which is consistent with other research on mothers' racial socialization (Caughy et al., 2002; Frabutt, Walker, & MacKinnon-Lewis, 2002).

In addition to parent and child characteristics, neighborhood characteristics may influence the likelihood of racial and ethnic socialization. Preparation for bias has been found to be more common among African American parents in racially integrated neighborhoods than in all–African American neighborhoods (Stevenson et al., 2002; Stevenson, McNeil, Herrero-Taylor, & Davis, 2005). Thus, both individual and contextual factors affect which families are more likely to discuss discrimination and how to cope with it.

Promotion of mistrust involves the need for wariness and distrust in interethnic interactions. Parental messages that promote caution and wariness about other groups are different from preparation for bias messages because they contain no advice for coping with or managing discrimination (Hughes et al., 2006). Promotion of mistrust typically is targeted at European Americans but also may target other groups of color.

Racial socialization messages associated with promotion of mistrust are less common among African American parents living in primarily European American neighborhoods than among African American parents who have less contact with European Americans (Caughy, Nettles, O'Campo, & Lohrfink, 2006). In addition to neighborhood demographics, interracial conflicts in neighborhoods may influence parents' racial and ethnic socialization behavior (Hughes et al., 2006). In a study of urban African American first-graders, parental messages emphasizing racism and mistrust were positively associated with negative neighborhood social climate (perceived physical/social disorder, fear of retaliation, and fear of victimization; Caughy et al., 2006).

Thus far, the literature on the racial and ethnic socialization of children and adolescents suggests that there are four ways in which parents convey their perspectives on race and ethnicity: egalitarianism, cultural socialization, preparation for bias, and promotion of mistrust. Of course, racial and ethnic socialization does not occur in only one manner. As we have reviewed, various characteristics—parental, child, and contextual—affect who is more likely to be socialized and the topics more likely to be discussed (e.g., parents of a higher socioeconomic status are more likely to discuss bias, families of color are more likely to discuss cultural values and traditions, etc.). However, racial and ethnic socialization is only one aspect to the development of an individual's racial and ethnic identity. Contextual factors, such as discrimination, can also strongly influence one's identity development.

RACIAL AND ETHNIC DISCRIMINATION

Discrimination is not necessary for the development of racial identity, but it is the context in which racial identity develops (Yip et al., 2006). Children know about racial stereotypes by age 4 or 5 (Aboud, 1988). By age 10, 99% of ethnic minority children judge ethnic name-calling as discriminatory (Verkuyten, Kinket, & van der Weilen, 1997).

Which groups experience the most racial and ethnic discrimination? In a study of African American 10- to 12-year-olds 67% had been insulted because they were African American, 46% had experienced racial slurs, and 43% had been suspected of doing something wrong because they were African American (Simons et al., 2002). Similarly high percentages of discrimination occur for African American college students. Eighty percent of a college sample of African Americans reported being treated as if they were stupid or being talked down to because of their race, and more than 80% reported being ignored, overlooked, not given service, treated rudely or disrespectfully, or being reacted to by others as if they were afraid or intimidated because of their race (Sellers & Shelton, 2003). In a study of 9th- and 10th-graders in a New York City high school in which there were few European Americans, Asian Americans (primarily Chinese Americans) and non–Puerto Rican Latinos (primarily Dominican Americans) reported experiencing more discrimination from adults and from peers than did Puerto Rican Americans or African Americans (Greene, Way, & Pahl, 2006). The Asian American and non–Puerto Rican Latino American groups were primarily immigrants, which may have resulted in greater discrimination than that experienced by the non-immigrant groups. In a study of college students, African Americans and Latino Americans perceived more ethnic discrimination than did European Americans (Levin, Sinclair, Veniegas, & Taylor, 2002). Thus, most persons of color experience discrimination, and the relative amount of discrimination is a function of social context.

A DEVELOPMENTAL MODEL OF CHILDREN'S PERCEPTIONS OF DISCRIMINATION

C. S. Brown and Bigler (2005) proposed that children perceive discrimination based on (a) cultural and social cognitions, (b) situational factors, and (c) individual differences. *Cultural cognition* is the awareness that individuals, including the self, can be sorted into racial and gender categories and that cultural stereotypes are associated with racial and gender categories. Young children are exposed to these stereotypes via family, peers, and the media. *Social cognition* has four components: (1) understanding that others have cognitions that differ from one's own, (2) understanding of classification into hierarchical categories, (3) moral reasoning (understanding that others, including adults, and institutions, such as schools, may act unfairly), and (4) use of social comparisons. Preschoolers are capable of social cognition, based on their development of a theory of mind—the awareness that different individuals have different minds (Carlson & Moses, 2001).

A key situational factor involved in the perception of discrimination is whether the target of the discrimination is the self or someone else. Individuals are more likely to perceive discrimination if the target is someone else than if the target is oneself. For example, a Latina American student might perceive her teacher ignoring the only other Latina American student in class when the other student has her hand raised as discrimination, but she may not attribute the teacher's same behavior as discrimination when it involves her. This discrepancy is referred to as the *personal/group discrimination discrepancy* (PGDD; Crosby, 1984). One explanation of PGDD is the complexity of knowledge about the self versus others (Quinn, Roese, Pennington, & Olson, 1999). An individual may have a self-view that includes multiple identities (e.g., female, Latina American, student, high achiever), whereas such knowledge is not as available about others. Thus, in the case of another Latina American student being ignored by a teacher, the most salient characteristic about the other student is that she is Latina American and the inference is that her ethnicity is the basis of discrimination. Another reason for the PGDD involves the psychological costs of perceiving oneself as a victim of discrimination (Crosby, 1984). Self-perception as a victim may lead to a feeling of powerlessness in a situation. Thus, it would be preferable to attribute an event (e.g., being ignored by the teacher) to some cause other than discrimination (e.g., the teacher didn't see my raised hand, the teacher tends not to call on smarter students because the other students need more attention) to avoid such a feeling of powerlessness.

Another important situational factor that influences perceptions of discrimination is knowledge of the possible perpetrator. If a child knows that a teacher has a history of discriminating against ethnic minority children, then the child may be likely to perceive the teacher's negative behavior (e.g., ignoring them) as discrimination. Perceptions of discrimination also are influenced by the availability of a comparison other. If there is not another person similar to oneself (e.g., a Latina American) in the same context, it would be unclear if a potentially discriminatory behavior was directed toward a particular group of individuals. Relevance of the discrimination to a stereotype is another situational factor that influences perceptions of discrimination. For example, if the Latina American student is aware of a stereotype that Latina American students do not work hard, she may interpret her teacher ignoring her as discrimination because she thinks her teacher does not believe that she works hard. Perceived social support also is associated with the perception of a negative event as discriminatory. If the other Latina American student or family members agreed that the teacher's behavior is discriminatory, the student would be more likely to perceive the behavior as discriminatory than if the other student or family members disagreed that the behavior is discriminatory.

Several years ago, my daughter was one of two Asian Americans in the third grade in her school. Each year, the music teacher, who taught all the students, held a public recital in which many individual students sang or played a musical instrument. Each year, she confused the names of my daughter, who is Japanese American, and the other Asian American girl, who is Chinese/Korean American, and the girls corrected her. Was this a form of bias or even discrimination? Granted, there were many children's names that the teacher had to keep track of. However, the teacher seemingly had no difficulty differentiating among the many blue-eyed, blond boys and girls in the group. The presence of a comparison other (i.e., another Asian American) demonstrated that the teacher's identification error was specific to Asian Americans. My wife (who is a teacher) interpreted the teacher's behavior benignly, as a memory difficulty. However, if she or I presented the possibility of discrimination to our daughter, our daughter may have interpreted the teacher's behavior accordingly.

Additionally, there are individual differences that may facilitate perceptions of discrimination. Members of minority groups are more likely to perceive group-based discrimination than members of majority groups because discrimination based on majority group status is relatively unlikely. Knowledge about discrimination will also facilitate perceptions of discrimination. For example, awareness of racism may make persons of color acutely aware of the possibility of discrimination (A. N. Alvarez et al., 2006).

Attitudes toward social groups are another individual difference that influences perceptions of discrimination. Those who believe in egalitarianism are more likely to perceive discrimination when a group is treated differently than those who believe in stereotypes (C. S. Brown & Bigler, 2005). Another individual difference influencing perceptions of discrimination is strength of group identity. Persons with strong group identities are more likely to perceive discrimination than those with weak group identities. Racial centrality (Sellers et al., 1998) is an example of a strong group identity. Parental socialization practices also influence perceptions of discrimination. For example, a person of color whose parents practiced racial socialization may be more likely to perceive negative behavior as discriminatory than a person of color who has not received such socialization because the former person may be more aware of racial and cultural differences.

Thus far, we have discussed discrimination in individual or small-group situations. Children may also perceive discrimination perpetrated by institutions. The U.S. government's slow response to the victims of Hurricane Katrina was viewed by many to be a result of racism: In 2005, approximately 150,000 people were stranded by the hurricane for a week without aid.

What did African American children attribute as the reason for the delayed relief efforts in Hurricane Katrina? Second-graders were equally likely to attribute the delayed efforts to logistics (e.g., there were too many people to rescue, people lived in difficult areas for rescuers to reach), individual culpability (e.g., people didn't follow directions or listen to police), class discrimination (e.g., people weren't rescued because they were poor), or race discrimination (e.g., people weren't rescued because they were African American; Brown, Mistry, & Bigler, 2007). Fourth- and sixth-graders perceived the reason for the delayed relief as logistics more than individual culpability or race or class discrimination. Eighth-graders strongly disagreed that individual culpability was the reason for delayed relief and were more likely than the younger children to attribute race and class bias as reasons. Older children also rated President Bush's response to Hurricane Katrina more negatively than did younger children.

In summary, persons of color are highly likely to experience discrimination based on race or ethnicity. Perpetrators of discrimination against people of color are European Americans and other people of color. Perceptions of discrimination are influenced by characteristics of the target, perpetrator, and context, as well as individual differences and attitudes. As children become older, they become aware that perpetration of discrimination is not restricted to individuals but may involve institutions.

We will now shift to a focus on the effects of racial and ethnic socialization on behavior from early childhood to adulthood. Racial and ethnic identities are achieved, in part, because of racial and ethnic socialization. The focus will also be on the behavioral effects of acculturation and of racial and ethnic discrimination across the life span.

EARLY CHILDHOOD

Racial socialization has been found to have academic benefits among preschoolers. An Africentric home environment (i.e., African or African American toys, photos, clothing, household items) was associated with greater general factual knowledge and problem-solving skills as assessed by the Kauffman Assessment Battery with African American 3 and 4-year-olds (Caughy et al., 2002) and for first-graders (Caughy et al., 2006). Among fourth-grade African American children, perceived racial barriers ("Even with education my color affects me"; "No matter how hard I try, my color affects me") were negatively associated with scores on tests of math and reading achievement, whereas cultural pride ("People should be proud of their color"; "I feel good about my culture and heritage") was positively associated with these achievement measures (Smith, Atkins, & Connell, 2003). Thus, promoting a secure sense of racial or ethnic identity may be important for parents in helping their young children succeed in school.

Mental health effects of racial and ethnic socialization occur in the areas of internalizing and externalizing behavior. *Internalizing behavior* includes psychological problems within an individual, such as depression and anxiety. *Externalizing behavior* involves conflicts with others, such as rule violations and fighting. In Caughy et al. (2002), cultural socialization was significantly associated with fewer internalizing and externalizing problems among African American 3 and 4-year-old boys and was marginally associated with fewer of these problems among girls. These effects of cultural socialization went beyond the effects of parent involvement. However, Caughy and colleagues (2006) subsequently found that parents' promotion of mistrust was associated with higher externalizing problems for African American first-grade boys and internalizing problems for African American first-grade girls. Such a parental emphasis on barriers may be the basis of these problems for young African American children.

MIDDLE/LATE CHILDHOOD

Racial and ethnic socialization have also been found to have mental health benefits during middle to late childhood. In a study of African American fourth-graders, ethnic identity was positively associated with self-esteem and behavioral control and negatively associated with child problems (D. E. Thomas, Townsend, & Belgrave, 2003). Ethnic identity involved the Swahili *Nguzo Saba* (seven principles), including unity, self-determination, collective work and responsibility, collective economics, creativity, and faith, as well as attitudes toward African American physical appearance, competency, and behaviors.

Among middle-schoolers in a predominantly African American parochial middle school, cultural socialization was associated with greater self-esteem in family and peer contexts (Constantine & Blackmon, 2002). However, mainstream socialization was associated with lower self-esteem in the school context. These findings suggest that African American identity is adaptive in an African American context, whereas a mainstream identity may be less adaptive in this context. Preparation for bias has also been associated among middle-schoolers with greater self-esteem in family contexts (Constantine & Blackmon, 2002) and with seeking support and problem-solving strategies in hypothetical situations of discrimination (Scott, 2003).

Racial socialization has also been found to reduce the likelihood of using tobacco and alcohol during late childhood. In a study of rural African American children, whose mean age was 11 years, racial socialization was positively correlated with ethnic pride (e.g., "I am happy that I am Black"; "I believe that because I am Black I have many strengths"), which in turn was positively correlated with substance-resistance efficacy (e.g., "I would take the cigarette and smoke it"—disagree; "I would tell my friend no and not smoke it"), which was negatively correlated with willingness to use substances (e.g., "Suppose you were with a group of kids and there was some alcohol you could have if you wanted. How willing would you be to drink one drink, have more than one drink, get drunk?"; Wills et al., 2007). Thus, racial socialization creates ethnic esteem, which is a protective factor against substance use.

Among immigrant children, identification with their culture of origin appears to be more important to adjustment than identification with the host culture. Costigan and Dokis (2006) assessed acculturation among Chinese parents and their children (mean age = 11.87 years) who immigrated to Canada. Chinese values assessed included collectivism, following social norms, and humility. Canadian values were assessed as beliefs regarding the amount of independence adolescents should be allowed (e.g., "It is all right for girls over the age of 18 to decide when to marry and whom to marry"). Adjustment included conflicts with parents (e.g., "who your friends should be," "watching TV," "going places without parents"), depressive feelings, and achievement motivation (e.g., "Be one of the best students in your class"). Costigan and Dokis found that acculturation and Canadian values were not associated with adjustment among Chinese immigrant children to Canada. Children's Chinese language and media use and Chinese values were associated with lower parental conflict, lower depressive feelings, and higher achievement motivation, particularly when their parents used Chinese language and media and retained Chinese values. Thus, acculturation is not necessarily adaptive in immigrant families. This study was cross-sectional, so the direction of the cultural identification-adjustment association is unknown.

Just as racial and ethnic identification with one's culture of origin tend to have positive effects during middle and late childhood, racial and ethnic discrimination have negative effects. In a study of African American and European American fifth-through eighth-graders, discrimination (e.g., being called names because of your race or ethnicity, being excluded by other kids because of your race/ethnicity, expected to be good or not good at a sport because of your race or ethnicity) was directly associated with emotional problems among African Americans but not among European Americans (DuBois et al., 2002). Discrimination and prejudice-related events during the previous 6 months in the domains of school, family, peer relations, physical appearance, and sports/athletics were assessed. Emotional problems involved internalizing behavior and behavior problems. Ethnic identity was positively associated with global self-esteem (e.g., "I am happy with myself as a person"), which was negatively associated with emotional and behavioral problems for both African Americans and European Americans. Thus, ethnic identity has positive effects not only for persons of color but also for European Americans.

Consistent with the DuBois et al. (2002) findings, perceived discrimination among African American 10–12-year-olds was associated with self-reported depression and conduct problems (e.g., shoplifting, physical assault, lying, fire setting, cruelty to animals, vandalism, burglary, robbery) 2 and 5 years later (Brody et al., 2006a). However, the impact of perceived discrimination was diminished when children (a) received nurturant-involved parenting (use of warmth, involvement, inductive reasoning (i.e., deriving a general rule from a specific case), communication skills, and monitoring), (b) had friends who encouraged involvement in prosocial activities (e.g., working hard for good grades, taking part in school activities, helping with chores at home, taking care of younger siblings, taking part in community activities), and (c) performed well in school. Therefore, the impact of discrimination can be offset by parents, peers, and the school environment.

To summarize the findings on early and middle childhood, racial socialization has positive effects on academic achievement and mental health. Racial and ethnic socialization may be most adaptive when one is in a social context in which such socialization is valued, such as family settings or school settings with predominantly same-race or same-ethnicity peers. Race-based discrimination adversely affects the mental health of African Americans, but such effects apparently do not occur for European Americans. Conversely, ethnic identity has mental health benefits for African Americans and European Americans. Parents, peers, and schools can offset the negative effects of discrimination.

ADOLESCENCE

Racial and ethnic socialization would be expected to facilitate adolescents' racial and ethnic identity development. Indeed, cultural socialization has been associated with identity exploration and development, positive group attitudes, and group-oriented ethnic behaviors among African American and Mexican American adolescents and adults (O'Connor et al., 2000; Supple, Ghazarian, Frabutt, Plunkett, & Sands, 2006; Umaña-Taylor & Fine, 2004) and among cross-racially adopted Korean youths in the United States (D. C. Lee & Quintana, 2005; Yoon, 2001, 2004). Although most of the literature on racial and ethnic socialization has focused on African Americans, these studies suggest that racial and ethnic socialization have positive effects across groups of color in the United States.

Developmental Changes in Ethnic Identity During Adolescence

Exploration of racial and ethnic identity may increase during adolescence and decrease as adolescents become older and more secure in their identities (Phinney, 1989). French, Seidman, Allen, and Aber (2006) found that ethnic identity exploration increased for African American and Latino American fifth- and sixth-graders, and eighth- and ninth-graders over a 3-year period. Group esteem ("I feel good about being in my racial/ethnic group"; "I want to raise my children to be aware of their own cultural or racial/ethnic background"; "I feel comfortable among people of my own group and at least one other group") also increased over time in both ethnic groups.

In a 2-year study of African American and Latino American eighth-graders, racial and ethnic identity increased slightly (Altschul, Oyserman, & Bybee, 2006). Racial and ethnic identity was assessed with measures of (a) *connectedness*, involving a positive sense of ingroup belonging (e.g., "I feel part of the Black community"); (b) *awareness of racism* (e.g., "Because I am Black, others may have negative expectations of me"); and (c) *embedded achievement*, involving the belief that achievement is valued by the ingroup (e.g., "It is important for my family and the Black community that I succeed in school"). The slight increase in racial and ethnic identity from eighth to ninth grade may reflect the deceleration in identity exploration as adolescents become older (Phinney, 1989).

The pervasiveness of racism directed at particular groups (e.g., African Americans), may result in a more extended period of exploration that does not decrease during adolescence as much as it does for other groups (Pahl & Way, 2006). Consistent with this hypothesis, Pahl and Way (2006) found that exploration decreased more among Latino/a American urban high school students over 5 years than it did among African American urban high school students. Moreover, African Americans perceived more discrimination from adults (e.g., "How often are you treated unfairly by adults because of your race or ethnicity?"; "How often are you insulted by adults because of your race or ethnicity?") than did Latino/a Americans. Perceived discrimination by peers (e.g., being treated unfairly, insulted, threatened, or harassed) was positively associated with exploration for both ethnic groups, and this association was particularly strong for African Americans.

Yip, Seaton, and Sellers (2006) used the Marcia (1980)/Phinney (1989) model of identity development (see Chapter 1) in studying African American adolescents, college students, and adults. Only 6% of the total sample had a *diffused* status, in which the individuals had neither explored nor committed to the meaning of their ethnicity. Twenty percent of the total sample had a *foreclosed* status, in which they were committed to a definition of ethnicity without further exploration. A *moratorium* status, which involves active exploration without a commitment to a specific definition of ethnicity, was characteristic of 31% of the total sample. The largest group in the sample (43%) had an *achieved* status, which involves both active exploration and a commitment to a specific definition of ethnicity. Persons from all age groups were in each of the status categories (Figure 4.1). However, adolescents were more likely than the other groups to have a moratorium status and less likely to have an achieved status. Nevertheless, this was not a longitudinal study, and it is unclear how individuals' racial and ethnic identities change across the life span.

Identity development does not always involve a neat, linear progression through the stages of various theories. Seaton, Scottham, and Sellers (2006) subsequently conducted a 2-year longitudinal study of ethnic identity with African Americans whose mean age was 14 at the beginning of the study. At the end of the study, 39% of the participants remained in the same identity status (diffuse, foreclosed, moratorium, achieved), 33% progressed to a more mature identity status,

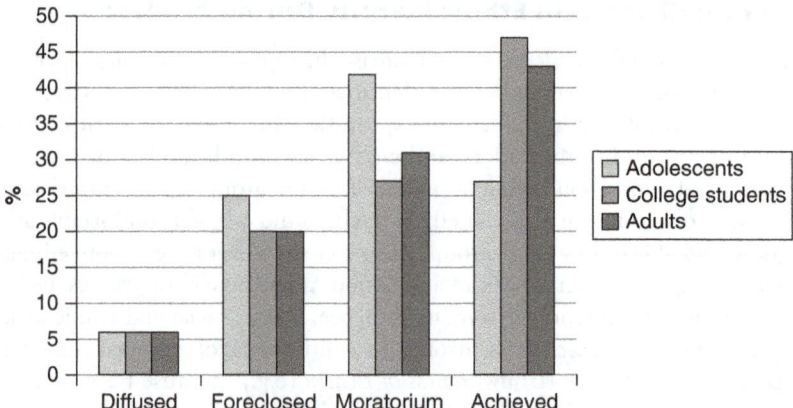

FIGURE 4.1 Ethnic Identity Status by Age Group Among African Americans

and 28% regressed to a less mature identity status. Such regression has been termed *recycling*, in which a person experiences an event that is incompatible with his or her existing identity and then attempts to reconstruct his or her identity (Cross & Fhagen-Smith, 2001; Parham, 1989).

Effects of Racial and Ethnic Identity During Adolescence

Racial and ethnic identity tends to be associated with positive emotions and perceptions among adolescents of color. Kiang, Yip, Gonzales-Backen, Itkow, & Fuligni (2006) conducted a daily diary study over 14 days on the stressful demands that Mexican American and Chinese American ninth-graders experienced each day and how happy and anxious they felt. Adolescents with higher ethnic regard were happier and less anxious over the 14-day period.

In another study with African American twelfth-graders, who had a grade point average of 3.0 or lower during eighth grade, private regard was negatively correlated with perceived stress (e.g., "You have been upset because of something that happened that you did not expect"; "You found that you could not deal with all the things that you had to do"; "You felt that you had so many problems that you could not deal with them"; Caldwell, Zimmerman, Bernat, Sellers, & Notaro 2002). Thus, positive feelings about one's racial group in a race-conscious society may be a protective factor against stress. However, racial centrality was positively associated with stress. This positive association may result from the interpretation of ambiguous events (e.g., being ignored by a teacher when raising one's hand to answer a question in class) as being race related (Shelton & Sellers, 2000). Nevertheless, this was a cross-sectional study, so it is unknown if perceived stress was an antecedent or effect of racial identity. For example, it is possible that perceived stress in one's life causes one to feel more negatively about one's racial group.

Ethnic identity as conceptualized in models other than the Sellers et al. (1998) model has also been associated with positive effects. In a sample of European American, Asian American, Latino American, African American, and mixed-ethnicity ninth-graders (Giang & Wittig, 2006), ethnic identity was positively associated with personal self-esteem (e.g., "I feel that I am a person of worth, at least on an equal basis with others"), and collective self-esteem (e.g., "The ethnic group I belong to is an important reflection of who I am"). Using the same measures of ethnic identity and self-esteem, Yip and Cross (2004) found the same positive associations in a sample of Chinese American high school students. Similarly, among Mexican American middle and high school students, Edwards and Lopez (2006) found that Mexican orientation was associated with life satisfaction. However, Anglo orientation was not significantly associated with life satisfaction (Edwards & Lopez, 2006).

The effects of racial and ethnic identity on academic performance have also been examined among adolescents. L. Y. Flores, Carrubba, and Good (2006b) failed to find an association between Mexican orientation and educational goals among rural Mexican American high school students, 81% of whom were born in the United States. Anglo orientation was significantly associated with educational goals, as indicated by participants' reports of highest level of education they expected and hoped to complete. It appears that these rural Mexican American adolescents associated education with European American culture (L. Y. Flores et al., 2006b).

Consistent with the L. Y. Flores et al. (2006b) results, Guzman, Santiago-Rivera, and Haase (2005) found that ethnic identity was not significantly associated with attitudes toward school and education or grade point average among Mexican American high school students, 78% of whom were born in the United States. However, willingness to interact with other ethnic groups was positively correlated with both attitudes toward school and education and with grade point average. The L. Y. Flores et al. and Guzman et al. results suggest that willingness to interact with other ethnic groups may be a component of academic success for Mexican Americans.

In studies using the Sellers et al. (1997) model of racial and ethnic identity, in which there are multiple identity dimensions, racial and ethnic identity have been demonstrated to have positive academic effects. In the Altschul et al. (2006) study described above, racial-ethnic identity, as assessed by connectedness, awareness of racism, and embedded achievement, was positively associated with grade point average in eighth and ninth grade among African Americans and Latino Americans. In another study of second-generation (U.S. born) Latino American adolescents (mean age = 14 years), ethnic identity affirmation was positively associated with teachers' reports of student grades, work habits, and cooperation behaviors (Supple et al., 2006). Similarly, ethnic identity was positively, albeit modestly, associated with grades among Latino American sixth-, seventh-, and eighth-graders, 86% of whom were born in the United States (Schwartz, Zamboanga, & Jarvis, 2007). The ethnic identity–grades association was mediated (see Chapter 2 for definition of *mediation*) by self-esteem. Strong ethnic identity was associated with self-esteem, which in turn was associated with higher grades.

Fuligni, Witkow, and Garcia (2005) also found positive associations between ethnic identity and academic attitudes among Mexican American, Chinese American, and European American ninth-graders. Scores on the centrality and private regard scales of the MIBI (Sellers et al., 1997) were positively associated with (a) the belief that education is integral for their future success (e.g., "Going to college is necessary for what I want to do in the future"; "Doing well in school is the best way for me to succeed as an adult"), (b) the intrinsic value of school (i.e., attitudes toward schoolwork), (c) the belief that school is useful for one's present and future life (e.g., "Right now, how useful do you find things you learn in school to be in your everyday life?"; "In the future, how useful do you think the things you have learned in school will be in your everyday life?"), (d) academic value (e.g., doing well in school, getting good grades, going to college), (e) the belief that one is valued and respected by the teachers and other adults at their school (e.g., "The teachers at my school treat students fairly"; "I feel that the adults at school respect the work I do"), and (f) students' identification with their school (e.g., "I feel close to people at my school"; "I feel like I am a part of my school"; "I am happy to be at my school"). Thus, a strong ethnic identity was not associated with being disconnected from school but was associated with positive academic attitudes for all groups in the study, including European Americans. Unlike the Altschul et al. (2006), Schwartz et al. (2007), and Supple et al. (2006) studies, ethnic identity was not significantly associated with students' grades in the Fuligni et al. study, possibly because different measures of ethnic identity were used across studies. Chavous et al. (2003) also did not find that the MIBI was associated with grades among African American twelfth-graders.

In a 2-year study of African American twelfth-graders using the Sellers et al. (1998) racial identity model, those who had high racial centrality, high private regard, and perceptions of low public regard for African Americans were more likely than others to go to college (51% did so; Chavous et al., 2003). This identity was referred to as *buffering*. In contrast, those who had (a) low racial centrality, high private regard, and perceptions of low public regard (*low connectedness*); (b) high racial centrality, high private regard, and perceptions of high public regard (*idealized*); or (c) low racial centrality, low private regard, and perceptions of low public regard (*alienated*) were less likely to go to college. Youth having a buffering identity persisted in school because they had strong connections to their racial group and had realistic perceptions of how society regards African Americans. In contrast, youth with low connected identities lacked social support for persisting in school. Idealized youth were likely to face disappointment when they faced the reality of low public regard for African Americans. Alienated youth had negative regard for African Americans and perceived the public's regard similarly, which may have interfered with persistence in school. Figure 4.2 presents the identity types and college outcomes.

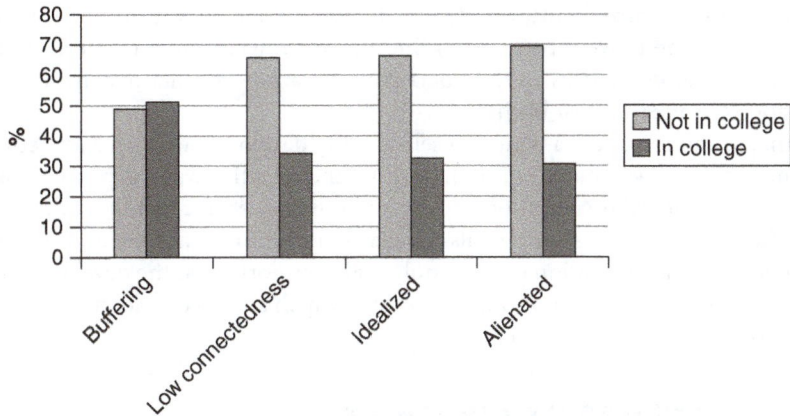

FIGURE 4.2   Racial Identity and College Outcomes 2 Years After High School

Similar to the protective effects of racial identity against substance use found in children (Wills et al., 2007), Caldwell, Sellers, Bernat, & Zimmerman (2004b) found racial identity to be a protective factor against alcohol use among African American twelfth-graders from the Caldwell et al. (2002) study described above. Adolescents for whom race was a central part of their identity and who had high private regard for their group were less likely to use alcohol than other adolescents. However, the association among these racial identity variables and alcohol use was modest and the study was cross-sectional.

Thus far, we have discussed the effects of racial/ethnic socialization and identity on individual adolescents. However, most adolescents are involved in and influenced by their families, and the development of racial and ethnic identity occurs in this context. Farver, Narang, and Badha (2002) classified Asian Indian American immigrant parents and their U.S.-born high school children as integrated (bicultural), assimilated (identified with European American culture), marginalized (disconnected from cultures), or separated (overly identified with one's culture of origin), based on Berry's (1974) model of acculturation (see Chapter 1). The dependent variable was family conflict, which involved parents' and adolescents' self-reports of frequency and intensity of discussions associated with specific issues that might arise in the home (e.g., telephone calls, doing homework, table manners). Based on both parent and adolescent reports, family conflict was greater in separated and marginalized families than in integrated or assimilated families. Moreover, family conflict was greater between parents and adolescents who had different styles of acculturation (e.g., integrated vs. marginalized) than among parents and adolescents who shared the same acculturation style.

In a subsequent study of parent/child acculturation match, Lau et al. (2005) found that parent/youth acculturation discrepancies were not associated with family conflict or youth conduct problems (conduct disorder, oppositional defiant disorder) in 260 Mexican American families with a youth from 12 to 17 years of age. All the youth in the study were receiving public services (i.e., alcohol or drugs, child welfare, juvenile justice, mental health, and public school services for youth with serious emotional disturbance), and 86% of the youth were born in the United States. Acculturation was assessed with language use, values and beliefs, social environment, ethnic identity, and cultural traditions and practices. Youth conduct problems were associated with a marginalized cultural identity for the parent or youth. The differences be-tween this study and the Farver et al. (2002) findings with Asian Indian American families in which acculturation discrepancies were associated with family conflict may be a result of dif-ferent populations or measures or both.

In summary, adolescence is a period of self-identity development. Racial and ethnic social-ization can impact this development in both positive and negative ways, depending on an indi-vidual's experience. Cultural socialization and racism influence ethnic identity, which in turn can affect critical areas, such as educational goals and academic performance, for adolescents. Finally, the ethnic identity and acculturation of the family is also important to the developing identity of an adolescent, as it is one of the main contexts through which adolescents learn family values and perspectives about racial and ethnic identity.

LATE ADOLESCENCE/EARLY ADULTHOOD

Similar to the findings with children (Constantine & Blackmon, 2002) and adolescents (Giang & Wittig, 2006), ethnic identity is associated with self-esteem in college students. In one study, eth-nic identity, as measured by exploration (e.g., "I have attended events that have helped me learn more about my ethnicity"), affirmation (e.g., "I wish I were of a different ethnicity"—disagree), and resolution (e.g., "I have a clear sense of what my ethnicity means to me"), was associated with self-esteem among European American, Latino American, Asian American, and African Ameri-can college students in the Midwest and in California (Umaña-Taylor & Shin, 2007). The strength of the association between ethnic identity and self-esteem varied somewhat across ethnic groups and geographic region, but all associations were positive.

Pride in Chinese culture and proficiency in Chinese and English languages were associ-ated with self-esteem among Asian American college students (Tsai, Ying, & Lee, 2001). The General Ethnicity Questionnaire (Tsai et al., 2000) was used to assess Chinese and American pride, social affiliation, and language use. American pride and social affiliation were not as-sociated with self-esteem. It was predicted that Chinese social affiliation would be negatively associated with self-esteem because of the Chinese norm of self-effacement, and this predic-tion was supported (Tsai et al., 2001).

In a subsequent study of Asian American college students (B. S. K. Kim & Omizo, 2006), *enculturation,* which involves the process of socialization to one's indigenous culture, was associated with collective self-esteem. In another study, European American values, which involve child-rearing practices (e.g., "I think it is fine for an unmarried woman to have a child"), marital behavior (e.g., "The idea that one spouse does all the housework is outdated"), autonomy (e.g., "I'm confident in my ability to handle most situations"), and sexual freedom (e.g., "It is okay to allow others to restrict one's sexual freedom"; reverse-scored), were also associated with collective self-esteem among Asian American college students (B. S. K. Kim & Omizo, 2005). Thus, a bicultural identity with engagement in two cultures is adaptive (B. S. K. Kim & Omizo, 2005, 2006; LaFromboise, Coleman, & Gerton, 1993). The differences between the results of the Tsai et al. (2001) and B. S. K. Kim and Omizo stud-ies are likely a function of different measures. The measure in the Tsai et al. study involved cultural pride, social affiliation, and language use, whereas the measures in the B. S. K. Kim and Omizo stud-ies involved acculturation and cultural values.

Racial socialization has also been found to be associated with adjustment to college. In Anglin and Wade (2007), African American students at a primarily European American university and at an ethnically diverse college whose parents or caregivers communicated messages regarding cultural or racial pride, racial struggle, cultural survival, and spiritual and religious coping rated themselves as having better academic, social, emotional, and institutional adjustment to college than did those who did not receive these messages.

Preparation for bias does not have uniformly positive effects. In one study, among African American teenagers, preparation for bias in combination with cultural socialization was associated with less fighting and initiation of fighting (Stevenson et al., 2002). However, A. Alvarez, Juang, and Liang (2006) found that Asian American college students who had discussions of race and racism as children with family members and other important adults were more likely to perceive experiences of racism than those who did not have such discussions. A young person sensitized to the possibility of discrimination could become hypersensitive and prone to feeling stigmatized (Brega & Coleman, 1999). Nevertheless, societal discrimination against persons of color is a reality, and sensitivity to the possibility of discrimination may be adaptive (Ridley, 1984).

In two studies by Castillo and colleagues of Latino American college students in predominantly European American environments, comfort in such environments appears to be more influential on behavior than ethnic or cultural identity. Comfort with European American cultural values was associated with lower distress among Mexican American female undergraduates and graduate students, 77% of whom attended predominantly European American universities (Castillo, Conoley, & Brossart, 2004). However, behavioral acculturation (e.g., "I associate with Anglos"; "I enjoy listening to English language music") was not associated with distress. The lack of association between acculturation and distress may have been a function of 47% of the sample being acculturated second-generation Mexican Americans, whereas the studies in which the association has been found have primarily included immigrant groups. The findings of this study suggest that it is not necessarily one's own cultural identity, but comfort with European American cultural values that decreases distress in predominantly European American settings. As with other cross-sectional studies, the direction of the effects in this study cannot be determined.

Castillo and colleagues (2006) found that ethnic identity was negatively associated with persistence attitudes in college (e.g., "It is important for me to graduate from college") in a subsequent study with Latino American students in a predominantly European American university. However, perceptions of the university environment (e.g., "I do not feel valued as a student on campus"; "The university seems like a cold, uncaring place to me") mediated the relationship between ethnic identity and persistence attitudes. Students who had negative perceptions of the university environment were less likely to have persistence attitudes, independent of their ethnic identity. Although acculturation was not assessed, it is likely that most of the participants were acculturated because they were college students. The results of the Castillo et al. (2004, 2006) studies are consistent with studies of high school Mexican Americans, in which willingness to interact with other ethnic groups was a component of academic success for Mexican Americans. (L. Y. Flores et al., 2006b; Guzman et al., 2005).

Consistent with the research on children (Wills et al., 2007) and adolescents (Caldwell et al., 2004b), in Hugh and Bry (2007), ethnic identity was negatively associated with beer or hard liquor use, wine use, and marijuana use among African American college students. This negative association between African American identity and substance use counters stereotypes of African American young adults as substance abusers. Ethnic identity was a stronger influence on beer or hard liquor use and wine use than was friends' use of these substances, but friends' use of marijuana was more influential on marijuana use than was ethnic identity. Marijuana availability may be more a function of social networks than is alcohol availability.

Similar to the effects of racial discrimination on internalizing disorders in children (DuBois et al., 2002), racial discrimination is associated with internalizing disorders in young adults. Discrimination has been found to be associated with stress among Asian Americans (Liang, Alvarez, Juang, & Liang, 2007) and psychological distress among Latino Americans (Moradi & Risco, 2006) and African Americans (Sellers & Shelton, 2003).

Discrimination is also associated with externalizing problems. Racial discrimination (e.g., "others reacting to you as if they were afraid or intimidated"; "being insulted, called a name, or harassed"; "not being hired for a job") was associated with violent behavior among African American young adults (mean age = 20; Caldwell et al., 2004a) in a follow-up of the Caldwell et al. (2002) cohort. Violent behavior included being in a fight, being in a group fight, carrying a gun, using a knife or gun, and intentionally hurting someone enough to need bandages or a doctor. Although discrimination predicted violent behavior regardless of gender, racial centrality, as measured by the MIBI (Sellers et al., 1997), decreased the risk of discrimination for violent behavior for males only. For both genders, the association between discrimination and violent behavior was moderated (see Chapter 2 for definition of *moderation*) by perceptions of positive public regard for African Americans, such that African Americans who experienced discrimination and had positive regard for African Americans were more violent than those with low positive regard for African Americans. Perceptions of positive public regard for African Americans may be unrealistic, and this inconsistency between these perceptions and discrimination may lead to violent behavior (Caldwell et al., 2004a). The participants in this study had a grade point average of 3.0 or less when they were in the eighth grade, so these results do not necessarily apply to all African American youth.

It might be expected that ethnic identity protects against the effects of discrimination. However, in a series of studies with Asian American college students, R. M. Lee (2003, 2005; Yoo & Lee, 2005) demonstrated that ethnic identity generally is not a buffer against the effects of racism. Consistent with Lee's findings, perceptions of discrimination were not significantly associated with commitment to one's ethnic group in the 5-year study of African American and Latino/a American high school students discussed above (Pahl & Way, 2006). Thus, it appears that something in addition to a strong ethnic identity is necessary to protect against the effects of discrimination for people of color.

A strong ethnic identity does not necessarily mean that a person is prepared for discrimination. Using the MIBI, Sellers and Shelton (2003) found that racial centrality and a nationalist ideology were positively associated with perceived discrimination among African American college students. If race is an important part of one's identity, he or she is likely to be aware of discrimination. Also indicated in Sellers & Shelton, discrimination was associated with psychological distress in this study. However, discrimination was less distressing for those who perceived low public regard for African Americans than for those who perceived higher public regard for African Americans. This finding is similar to the association between discrimination and violence being moderated by public regard for African Americans among African American youth (Caldwell et al., 2004a). A strong ethnic identity without a realistic view of public perceptions of one's ethnic group may lead to distress when discrimination is experienced. Thus, preparation for discrimination may be a more direct and effective method of buffering discrimination than a strong ethnic identity alone.

In summary, racial and ethnic identity continue to have positive effects on mental health and academic performance during late adolescence and early adulthood. In some instances a strong ethnic identity and preparation for bias were associated with negative outcomes, including not being persistent in college and hypersensitivity to discrimination. There is also evidence that a mainstream identity can be adaptive for people of color, particularly in mainstream settings in which they are in the minority. As with younger persons, discrimination has negative mental health and behavioral effects. Ethnic identity alone does not protect against the negative effects of discrimination, but a realistic view of how people of color are regarded in society has been found to offset these negative effects.

Conclusion

Many parents of color socialize their children with respect to culture and preparation for bias. Likelihood of racial and ethnic socialization occurring is a function of parental characteristics, such as socioeconomic status and experiences with discrimination; child characteristics, such as age; and neighborhood characteristics, such as demographics and intergroup conflicts. Outcomes of racial and ethnic socialization include children's greater ethnic identity, as well as positive academic and mental health consequences.

Exploration of racial and ethnic identity generally increases during adolescence and decreases during early adulthood when identity becomes established. Parents and children who have the same levels of ethnic identity experience less conflict than those whose ethnic identities are mismatched. Engagement with persons outside one's ethnic group may be important for success in settings in which one is the ethnic minority, such as in school. A bicultural identity is adaptive in negotiating the demands of one's ethnic group and the demands of the ethnic majority.

Perceptions of racial and ethnic discrimination vary as a function of individual and situational differences. Unlike racial and ethnic socialization, discrimination has negative effects. Although racial or ethnic identity alone is not a protective factor against discrimination, parental preparation for discrimination may diminish the negative effects of discrimination.

Much of the work on development has been conducted with African Americans. More work on other groups of color is needed. Future research should also be longitudinal, as most studies in this area are cross-sectional and cannot definitively identify the directionality of effects. There is also a need for racial and ethnic identity research on older adults.

Discussion Questions

1. Intergroup attitudes form early in a child's development. Is it easier for a child than an adult to learn healthy intergroup attitudes, similar to how it is easier for a child to become fluent in a second language than it is for an adult to do so? Is there a critical period for developing cultural competence with multiple groups?

2. Most people of color experience discrimination. When parents of children of color do not prepare their children for such discrimination, could this be considered a form of parental neglect? Does preparing children for discrimination make them overly sensitive to the possibility of discrimination?

3. Racial and ethnic socialization are generally associated with positive mental health and academic outcomes from early childhood through early adulthood. Are these positive outcomes sufficiently important that schools should share with parents and families the responsibility for racial and ethnic socialization of children?

CHAPTER 5

Social Psychology

In Chapter 4, we focused on development in individuals, families, and neighborhoods. Social psychology focuses on intergroup relations. Most social psychology research on prejudice, racism, and discrimination is on the perspectives of perpetrators, and most of this research has been on European Americans. *Prejudice* is a positive or negative attitude or belief about a person that is generalized from attitudes or beliefs held about the group to which the person belongs (J. M. Jones, 1997). *Racism* assumes that group differences are biologically based, that one's own race is superior, and that practices that formalize the domination of one racial group over another are justifiable (J. M. Jones, 1997). *Discrimination* involves harmful actions toward others because of their membership in a particular group (Fishbein, 1996).

In the late 1990s, studies began to focus on the perspectives of persons being targeted by prejudice, racism, and discrimination (Mays et al., 2007). Although much research in social psychology focuses on the attitudes and behavior of European Americans in relation to persons of color, the focus of this chapter will be on the attitudes and behavior of persons of color in relation to other groups. Racial and ethnic identity influence intergroup relations, similar to their influence on the behaviors reviewed in previous chapters.

Although persons of color have lived in North America and have been involved in North American society for centuries, and constitute over one-third of the U.S. population, they are perceived as less American than European Americans. Devos and Banaji (2005) found that European American, African American, Latino/a American, and Asian American college students rated African Americans and Asian Americans as less American than European Americans, and Asian Americans as less American than African Americans. Ratings for all ethnic groups were for persons born in the United States. "American" for many Americans means White or European American. To the extent that persons of color are viewed as less American than are European Americans and because of other social inequities that result in discrimination (see Chapters 1 and 4), persons of color are devalued in American society.

CURRENT FORMS OF DISCRIMINATION

It could be argued that discrimination in North America does not continue to exist in the 21st century. Racist laws that restrict privileges for persons of color have been abolished. "Political correctness" dictates sensitivity in intergroup race and ethnic relations. Blatant forms of racism, such as denying privileges based on race, seem not to be common and create attention when they occur.

Racism and discrimination may not be obvious because they now occur in a more subtle fashion (J. M. Jones, 1997). Subtle forms of racism have been referred to as *modern racism* (McConahay, 1986), *symbolic racism* (Sears, 1988), and *aversive racism* (Dovidio, et al., 2002). Ostensibly non-racial reasons are used as a rationale for attitudes that are anti–African American or against other racial or ethnic groups (Gaertner & Dovidio, 2000). Modern racists disclaim personal bigotry by strong and rigid adherence to traditional American values (e.g., individualism, self-reliance, hard work) and view responsibility for success or failure as residing within the individual (D. W. Sue et al., 2007). An example of symbolic racism would be opposition to affirmative action not ostensibly because of overt prejudice toward ethnic minority groups but based on a belief that ethnic minority groups already have the benefits that affirmative action is intended to provide. Thus racism is not overt or direct but symbolic in that it opposes a policy that provides benefits to multiple racial and ethnic groups. Aversive racists are strongly motivated by egalitarian values, which operate at a conscious level, as well as antiminority feelings, which are less conscious and usually covert (D. W. Sue et al., 2007). Thus, an aversive racist might philosophically oppose affirmative action because it discriminates among groups and is not egalitarian, conveniently ignoring the fact that in many cases diversity and opportunities for minority groups will not exist without affirmative action.

Although some might assume that persons who are politically liberal might be considered less racist than those who are politically conservative, modern and symbolic racism are associated with political conservatism whereas aversive racism is associated with political liberalism (Dovidio & Gaertner, 1996, 2000). The assumption of each of these forms of subtle racism is that treating all persons equally without regard to race or ethnicity will result in equal outcomes for all persons. However, as discussed below in the section on affirmative action, this seemingly egalitarian approach results in bias in favor of the majority group.

How is subtle racism expressed? Everyday occurrences of subtle racism involve *microaggressions*, which involve "brief, everyday exchanges that send denigrating messages to people of color because they belong to a racial minority group" (p. 273, D. W. Sue et al., 2007). The forms of microaggressions are (a) microassaults, (b) microinsults, and (c) microinvalidation. *Microassaults* involve "verbal or nonverbal attacks intended to hurt another person via name-calling, avoidant behavior, or purposeful discriminatory actions" (p. 274, D. W. Sue et al., 2007). Although some microassaults are not subtle, subtle examples of microassaults include calling someone "colored" or "Oriental" (terms considered derogatory by persons of color) and serving a European American patron before a patron of color. Microassaults tend to be intentional.

Less intentional and less conscious are microinsults and microinvalidation. A *microinsult* involves "communications that convey rudeness and insensitivity and demean a person's racial heritage or identity" (p. 274 D. W. Sue et al., 2007). Microinsults communicate that a person is less valued because of his or her membership in a racial category, which may be associated with different levels of intelligence, abnormality, and criminality. For example, an apparent compliment that "you are so articulate" might carry the implication that you are so articulate for being Black, Asian, Latino, etc. *Microinvalidation* involves communications that exclude, negate, or nullify the psychological thoughts, feelings, or experiential reality of a person of color (D. W. Sue et al., 2007). For example, a person whose ancestors immigrated to the United States from Asia might be complimented on how well they speak English, despite the fact that the person and their ancestors were born in the United States. Included in microinvalidation is the belief that racial or ethnic minority citizens are foreigners, color-blindness (see Chapter 1), the belief in the myth of meritocracy that race or ethnicity plays no role in life success, and the denial that one has personal responsibility for racism.

Although perpetrators or even bystanders may minimize the intention or impact of microaggressions (e.g., "You are being too sensitive"; "He really didn't mean to insult you"), they are a form of discrimination. Microaggression research is a new area, but it is probable that the effects of microaggression are similar to those of other forms of discrimination, including negative physical and psychological health effects on persons of color (see Chapters 3 and 4). The harm of microaggressions is that they communicate that persons of color are less valued than others in society.

INTERGROUP STEREOTYPES AND SOCIAL DOMINANCE

Intergroup relations are strained when some groups in a society are valued less than others. Ingroups and outgroups may develop stereotypes of each other. A stereotype is a generalization about members of a group that assumes a high degree of similarity of all group members (J. M. Jones, 1997). Image theorists, whose work is based on international relations in political science, have identified five generic outgroup images perceived by ingroups based on relative status, power, and goal compatibility: ally, enemy, barbarian, dependent, and imperialist (Herrmann & Fischerkeller, 1995). Goal compatibility involves the perception that benefits for the outgroup (e.g., African Americans) also benefit the ingroup (e.g., European Americans). For example, the ingroup may perceive affirmative action to recruit members of the outgroup to a university as beneficial in preparing the ingroup to live in a multicultural world.

Outgroups whose status and power are equal to the ingroup and whose goals are compatible with those of the ingroup have an *ally image* (Herrmann & Fischerkeller, 1995). An *enemy image* of the outgroup involves equal status and power but incompatible goals. Lower status, higher power, and incompatible goals characterize the *barbarian image*. Outgroups with lower status and power and incompatible goals have a *dependent image*. Higher status and power of an outgroup combined with incompatible goals constitute an *imperialist image*.

Data from African American, American Indian, and European American high school students suggest that each group holds stereotypes of the other group (Alexander, Brewer, & Livingston, 2005). The strongest image that African Americans and American Indians held of European Americans was the imperialist image. Thus, persons of color may perceive European Americans as having higher status and power than their own, as well as incompatible goals. Conversely, the strongest image that European Americans held of African Americans was barbarian/enemy and of American Indians was dependent. Similar to the perceptions of persons of color of European Americans, European Americans may perceive African Americans' goals as incompatible with their own insofar as gains for the outgroup are viewed as coming at the expense of the ingroup.

Such zero-sum gain perceptions may be explained by social dominance theory. Social dominance theory suggests that societies are organized into group-based hierarchies with inequitable distribution of resources favoring dominant groups at the expense of subordinates (Sidanius & Pratto, 1999). Gains by subordinate groups come at the expense of dominant groups. Thus, the dominant group in North American societies, European Americans, may view progress toward racial equality as relatively great because they perceive such progress as coming at the expense of their own privileges. Perceptions of progress toward racial equality are particularly great among European Americans having a social dominance orientation (e.g., "This country would be better off if we cared less about how equal all people were"; Eibach & Keegan, 2006). Conversely, many persons of color do not perceive much racial progress because, despite any gains, their racial group continues to be devalued in North American societies.

I have personally witnessed these divergent views of progress in my work at different universities on diversity initiatives. Many members of the dominant European American group perceived such goals as recruiting faculty and students of color and including students' perceptions of faculty sensitivity to diversity in faculty teaching evaluations as too far-reaching. In contrast, many persons of color viewed these goals as small steps and insufficient to change the campus diversity climate. Of course there were many European Americans who agreed that these goals were too modest, and a few persons of color who agreed that these goals were too far-reaching. However, even when I worked with a group whose members had diverse opinions on how to achieve diversity and offered guidelines to a university based on the consensus of this group, there was still resistance, primarily from European Americans.

It is this context of inequality and ethnic group-based divergent perceptions of inequality that persons of color must contend with. Even when persons of color attempt to assimilate into the mainstream, they still may be perceived by others as members of a devalued group. Moreover, the attitudes and behaviors of persons of color may be influenced by negative perceptions of their group (e.g., intellectual or social deficits), even if they personally do not believe that these negative perceptions are accurate. Nevertheless, being in diverse social situations generally benefits persons of all ethnic backgrounds. We will review the benefits of diversity in this chapter.

In summary, ingroups tend to hold negative stereotypes of outgroups. Gains by the outgroup are often viewed as losses by the ingroup. Dominant groups tend to view the progress of subordinate groups as relatively great because dominant groups perceive such progress as coming at their expense. The same amount of progress may be viewed as minimal by subordinate groups who may believe that progress is incomplete until their subordinate status has changed.

INTERGROUP RELATIONS IN SCHOOL SETTINGS

Recall from Chapter 3 that persons tend to prefer others from their own racial or ethnic group. This preference may have been advantageous in identifying allies at one time in human history. How do racial and ethnic friendship preferences currently develop in social settings in which there is diversity? School situations often create contact between multiple racial and ethnic groups. The first contact that some children have with racial and ethnic groups other than their own may be when they begin school.

Elementary students tend to select few cross-race friends and even fewer as they grow older (Aboud, Mendelson, & Purdy, 2003). Cross-race friendships are relatively unlikely among adolescents in settings in which the number of students of color is relatively small (Quillian & Campbell, 2003). In such school settings, students of color may seek friendships with others of their own group to protect their identity from being subsumed by the majority. However, cross-race friendships tend to increase as a function of school diversity; there are more cross-race friendships among adolescents in diverse schools (Quillian & Campbell, 2003). In diverse settings, power across groups may be relatively proportional, and students of color may feel less of a need to protect their identities.

Children of color may have different experiences than other children as soon as they enter school. In one study, in kindergarten and first-grade classrooms in which European Americans were typically the majority, African Americans experienced more peer rejection and teacher–child conflict and less teacher–child closeness and mutual friendships with peers (i.e., consistency with peers in nominations of best friends) than did European Americans (Ladd & Burgess, 2001). The ethnicity of the teachers and nominated best friends was not specified, but presumably most of the teachers were European Americans and at least some best friends nominated by African Americans were European Americans. These findings suggest that African American children in primarily European American schools may experience stressors and find it difficult to find support from teachers and peers.

Discrepant experiences between African Americans and European Americans also occur in high school when African Americans are in the minority. Mattison and Aber (2007) found that African American students experienced more racism, detentions, and suspensions and had more negative perceptions of the school's racial climate than did European American students in a public school in a Midwest university town. However, positive perceptions of the school's racial climate were associated with higher grades and fewer detentions for all students. Racial identity was not assessed in this study, and it is unknown if those African American students who had positive perceptions of the school's racial climate were less racially identified than those who had negative perceptions of the school's racial climate.

What are the experiences of students of color when they are in the majority? Pfeifer et al. (2007) studied first- or second-generation Chinese, Dominican, and Russian immigrants, as well as African Americans and third-generation or later European Americans (i.e., grandparents were born abroad), in New York City neighborhoods. Ethnic minority children lived in neighborhoods where their ethnic group constituted the majority, but Russian and European American children lived in more heterogeneous neighborhoods. Second- and fourth-graders were more positive (endorsed items like rich, friendly, smart, good at sports, and honest) and less negative (endorsed items like bad, ugly, selfish, lazy, and shy) toward Americans in general (of any ethnicity, including their own) and Spanish/Dominican Americans than toward African Americans (Pfeifer et al., 2007). The children were least positive toward Chinese Americans and most negative toward African Americans. Immigrant children were more positive and less negative toward their own groups than toward African Americans, which may suggest that they have adopted U.S. norms of bias against African Americans, although children who were not recent immigrants displayed significantly less bias than those who were. Because some groups were rated more negatively than were Americans in general, these results imply that some groups were perceived as less American than others (cf. Devos & Banaji, 2005). African Americans in the Pfeifer et al. (2007) study did not exhibit differences in positivity or negativity toward any group, which may reflect lack of bias or may be a result of the relatively small sample of African Americans in the study ($N = 43$).

A strong ethnic identity among the children of color was associated with a positivity bias favoring their own group over others in both second and fourth grades, as well as (for older children only) a negativity bias against other groups relative to their own (Pfeifer et al., 2007). Children in groups of color who reported feeling more American than ethnic reported less favoritism toward their own group over others than did children in groups of color who reported feeling more ethnic than American. Importantly, they felt more positive and less negative toward ethnic outgroups, not less positive and more negative toward their own ethnic group. Although it might be tempting to conclude that an American identity is the solution to intergroup bias, assimilation may not be possible for all groups and may create a particular risk for psychological distress when discrimination is encountered (Major, Kaiser, O'Brien, & McCoy, 2007; Sellers & Shelton, 2003). As discussed in Chapter 4, a bicultural identity may be most adaptive. Keep in mind also that the Pfeifer et al. (2007) study took place in contexts in which immigrant children had relatively limited contact with ethnic groups other than their own.

The findings of negative perceptions toward African American children in the Ladd and Burgess (2001) and Pfeifer et al. (2007) studies were replicated in a study of fifth graders in classrooms in a southeastern state in which African Americans were the minority or the majority and in which there were African American or European American teachers (M. F. Jackson,

Barth, Powell, & Lochman, 2006). European American children were liked and perceived as leaders by African American and European American children more than African American children in classrooms in which the percentage of African American children was up to 66%. In classrooms in which the percentage of African American children was two-thirds or greater, African Americans were liked and perceived as leaders by African American and European American children more than European American children. However, even in classrooms in which the percentage of African American children was two-thirds or greater, European American children were rated relatively high on likeability and leadership.

M. F. Jackson et al. (2006) also found that children's likeability ratings covaried with teacher ethnicity. African American children were rated as more likeable than European Americans in classrooms in which the teacher was African American and the opposite was true in classrooms in which the teacher was European American. Classrooms with African American teachers usually had a majority of African Americans. However, teacher ethnicity was not associated with the ethnicities of students perceived as leaders. African American children were also rated as fighting more than European American children regardless of the percentage of African Americans in the classroom. Teacher ethnicity was not associated with fighting ratings. A limitation of the M. F. Jackson et al. study is that the ethnicity of the children making the ratings was not identified, and the actual rates of fighting were unknown. Nevertheless, African American children were rated negatively unless they were in the majority, and even when they were in the majority, they were rated as fighting more than European American children.

Being in the majority has also been shown to have benefits for African American adults (Postmes & Branscombe, 2002). African American women college students from environments in which an average of 83% were African American perceived less ingroup rejection, greater identification with African Americans, and greater self-esteem than did those from environments in which an average of 39% were African American. However, African American women from environments in which they were the majority were also more likely to perceive outgroup rejection than African American women from environments in which they were the minority. Such perceptions of outgroup rejection may be associated with limited interactions with the outgroup.

The results of the Postmes and Brancombe (2002) study suggest that ingroup majority environments for persons of color, such as Historically Black Colleges and Universities, may have some psychological benefits for persons of color. Most African American and Latino American children attend segregated schools (Pettigrew, 2004). Nevertheless, segregated schools limit intergroup contact, which prepares students for life and opportunities in a multicultural world.

Ethnically diverse classrooms have also been found to have psychological benefits for students of color. Juvonen, Nishina, and Graham (2006) hypothesized that greater diversity promotes perceptions of safety and lessens feelings of vulnerability because students in diverse settings belong to one of many ethnic groups that share a balance of power. African American and Latino/a American sixth graders in classrooms in Los Angeles felt safer in school, were less harassed by peers, felt less lonely, and had higher self-worth in classrooms in which there were relatively high representations of multiple ethnic groups (Latino, African American, Asian American, European American, and multiracial) than in classrooms in which there was less diversity (i.e., fewer different groups or relatively low representations of different groups or both).

Ethnic diversity also has positive effects in higher education settings. Hurtado (2005) surveyed more than 4,400 students in their first year and again in their second year at 10 public colleges and universities, which ranged from 5% to 95% students of color. Positive interactions with diverse peers were predictive of analytical problem-solving skills and complex thinking skills in all ethnic groups. As might be expected, positive interactions with diverse peers were also predictive of cultural awareness, interest in social issues, pluralistic orientation, interest in poverty issues, and concern for the public good. In contrast, negative interactions with diverse peers were predictive of the belief of fundamental value differences with students from other racial/ethnic groups and greater identification with others in the same racial category.

In another context, simulated juries that consisted of African Americans and European Americans deliberated longer, considered a wider range of information, and made fewer factual errors than did simulated juries that consisted only of European Americans (Sommers, 2006). Although critics might suggest that diversity in working groups may create conflict, the level of conflict was not significantly different between the diverse and nondiverse simulated juries. Unfortunately, the study design did not include a simulated jury of only African Americans, so it is unclear if the diverse simulated jury would have outperformed a simulated jury of only African Americans.

Although the effects of intergroup relations on European Americans are not the focus of this chapter, ethnic diversity also benefits European American students in that it contributes to their listening, critical thinking, and writing skills by helping them learn to incorporate multiple perspectives (Antonio et al., 2004; Gurin et al., 2004; Hurtado, 2005). This psychology research on the benefits of diversity for students of all ethnic backgrounds influenced Supreme Court Justice Sandra Day O'Connor in writing an opinion in favor of affirmative action in the 2003 *Grutter v. Bollinger* case, discussed below.

What is the effect of ethnic identity in ethnically diverse contexts? Sidanius, Van Laar, Levin, and Sinclair (2004) examined the effects of involvement in ethnic student organizations for Asian American, African American, and Latino American students and in Greek organizations (fraternities, sororities) for European American students at UCLA. Involvement in ethnic student organizations predicted ethnic identity, ethnic activism (e.g., voting in terms of what is good for your particular group, participating in demonstrations, signing petitions), and a sense of being part of the university community. However, involvement in ethnic student organizations was also predictive of the perception that ethnic groups are in a zero-sum competition with one another (e.g., "More good jobs for other groups come at the expense of fewer good jobs for members of my group") and with a sense of victimization as a result of one's ethnicity. Similar effects of Greek membership were found for European American students.

Ethnic and Greek organizations emphasize the ingroup. What may be missing in these organizations is the cultivation of a bicultural or multicultural identity that involves identification with one's ingroup as well as with one or more other groups. A bicultural or multicultural identity may be more adaptive than identification solely with the ingroup or the outgroup (B. S. K. Kim & Omizo, 2005, 2006; LaFromboise et al., 1993).

Other research with a community sample of Latino Americans, African Americans, and European Americans suggests that ethnic identity and superordinate American identity are not incompatible (Huo, 2003). In each of these groups, ethnic identity and American identity were positively correlated. Thus, the members of these groups had a bicultural identity, in that they were identified with American and ethnic cultures, and one identity did not come at the expense of the other.

In summary, persons of color tend to choose other persons of color as friends. Nevertheless, diverse social settings generally benefit persons of all ethnic backgrounds, particularly when one ethnic group is not disproportionately large. An important moderator of the effects of diversity is whether intergroup relations are positive or negative (Hurtado, 2005). However, diversity alone does not eliminate intergroup stereotypes that may influence persons of color.

STEREOTYPE THREAT

The discomfort persons feel when they are at risk of fulfilling a negative stereotype about their group has been termed *stereotype threat* (Aronson, Quinn, & Spencer, 1998; Steele, 1997). Anxiety about poor performance may interfere with performance. For example, an African American student in an elite university in which there are few students of color may believe that African Americans are less capable than other students and less qualified because they are in the university only because of affirmative action. Anxiety about this belief may interfere with this student's academic test performance.

Persons do not need to believe a stereotype to be threatened by it. Awareness may be sufficient to interfere with performance. An African American who does not believe in negative stereotypes about African American academic performance may nevertheless experience excess pressure to disprove such stereotypes, which may interfere with his or her performance. The more one is invested in a domain (e.g., school), the more vulnerable he or she may be to stereotypes.

For members of stigmatized groups, simply observing an ingroup member confirming a stereotype may affect performance. African American college students at an Ivy League university performed more poorly on the Graduate Record Examination (GRE) verbal test than when they were exposed to an African American who was struggling on an IQ test than when they were exposed to an African American who was struggling on an art test or a European American who was struggling on an IQ test (Cohen & Garcia, 2005). An African American struggling on an IQ test confirms a stereotype and is threatening, whereas a European American struggling on the same test or an African American struggling on an art test does not confirm a stereotype.

Repeated experiences of rejection for stigmatized groups lead to expectations of rejection, which is known as *rejection sensitivity* (Mendoza-Denton, Downey, Purdie, Davis, & Pietrzak, 2002). Rejection sensitivity may be particularly acute in contexts in which stereotyping has occurred, such as in academic contexts for ethnic minority groups. In a study of African American students at a predominantly European American university, those who were sensitive about race-based rejection experienced a steady decline in their GPAs over their first five semesters, whereas the GPAs of those who were less sensitive about race-based rejection remained consistent (Figure 5.1). Thus, decreasing expectations of rejection and increasing a sense of belonging might be beneficial in reducing stereotype threat.

Relatively simple interventions to increase a sense of belonging have been demonstrated to reduce the effects of stereotype threat (Walton & Cohen, 2007). Most college students experience self-doubt about their abilities when they observe the abilities of others. If a person belongs to a stigmatized group, such self-doubt may lead them to question whether they belong in college. In the study by Walton and Cohen, experimenters told African American and European American college students in an experimental condition that most students, regardless of race, worry during their first year of college about whether they belong in college but that these worries decrease with time. Students in a control condition were told that their political views would become increasingly sophisticated over time. All students' grade point averages (GPA) were assessed in the fall semester of their freshman year in college before the experiment and again in the fall semester of their sophomore year. The GPA increase of African American students in the experimental condition was significantly greater than that of students in the other conditions. Thus, reducing stigmatization by creating a sense of belonging (i.e., self-doubt is characteristic of all college students) improved the performance of a stigmatized group but did not affect the performance of a nonstigmatized group.

Many years ago I was accepted into a training program that included another trainee who was the child of a faculty member in the program. The other trainee experienced self-doubt

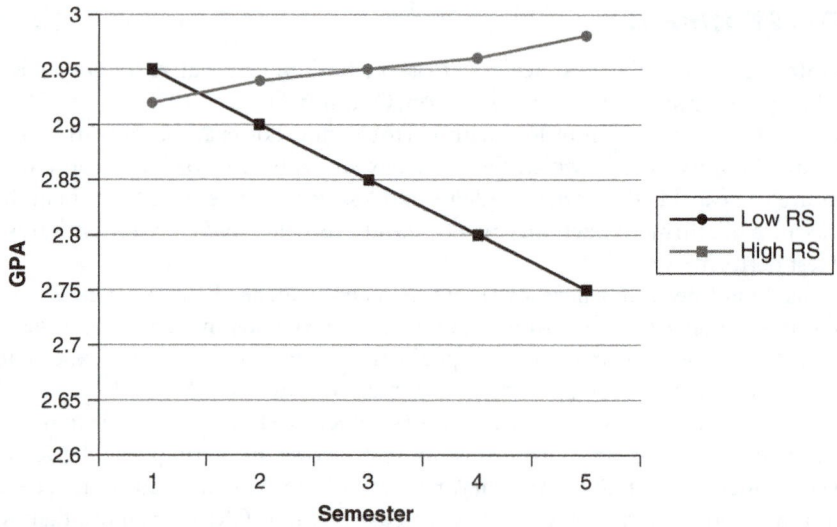

FIGURE 5.1   GPA and Rejection Sensitivity Based on Race Among African Americans

about whether he had been admitted to the program because of his qualifications or because of his parent. Because I am a person of color, this trainee asked me, "How does it feel to be here because of affirmative action?" I snidely could have replied, "I don't know, how does it feel?" However, I told the trainee that I was in the program because I was qualified to be. Nevertheless, I did pause to think about whether others might view me as a product of affirmative action. My own self-doubt was laid to rest when I later received an award from the training program, which made me feel that I was as deserving to be in the program as any of the other trainees. The award gave me a sense of belonging in the training program.

As my personal example illustrates, the effects of stereotype threat are not specific to African Americans. Schmader and Johns (2003) told one group of Latino American college students that a memory test was highly predictive of performance on intelligence tests and that their performance would be used to help establish norms for different groups. This group was also asked to indicate their ethnicity. A second group of Latino American college students was told that the memory test was a test of working memory capacity and were also asked their ethnicity. Groups of European Americans were given the same instructions as either the first or second Latino American group and were also asked their ethnicity. The first Latino American group in the intelligence condition performed more poorly on the memory test than any of the other groups (Schmader & Johns, 2003). Thus, Latino Americans may be susceptible to academic performance stereotypes similar to those of African Americans. European Americans, who are not targeted by negative academic stereotypes, were not affected by stereotype threat.

Are there ethnic group stereotypes that might enhance academic performance? A stereotype about Asians is that they have superior quantitative skills compared to other groups. As discussed in Chapter 2, Asian American college women who were asked about being an Asian American (e.g., non–English language knowledge, generation in the United States) performed significantly better on a quantitative task than when they were not asked about being an Asian

American or when they were asked about being a woman (e.g., questions about coed/single-sex dorms; Shih, et al., 1999). Thus, the stereotype about Asians having superior quantitative skills appears beneficial.

Could there be situations in which a seemingly positive stereotype could create undue pressure? The Asian identity cues in the Shih et al. (1999) study were relatively subtle, involving language spoken and generation in the United States Cues that are more blatant, such as "Overall, my race is considered good by others," "I am a worthy member of the racial group I belong to," and "Asian Americans are good at mathematics," have been demonstrated to create pressure that interferes with math performance (Cheryan & Bodenhausen, 2000; Shih, Ambady, Richeson, Fujita, & Gray, 2002). Even a seemingly positive stereotype is still a stereotype. People of Asian ancestry do not excel at math in all circumstances, nor are all Asians inherently good at math, and such stereotypes can interfere with identifying students who are indeed in need of help.

How does one deal with membership in a devalued group? Tajfel and Turner (1986) described three strategies: (a) individual mobility, (b) social creativity, and (c) social competition. *Individual mobility* involves disidentifying with a devalued group. For example, a person of color may emphasize their other group memberships (e.g., student, professional) that are valued by others and deemphasize their racial or ethnic group membership. This is similar to the Cross (1971) Pre-Encounter stage of racial identity or low racial centrality in the Sellers et al. (1998) model of racial identity. Moreover, a person focusing on individual mobility may be attempting to assimilate into mainstream American society (Sellers et al., 1998).

African Americans and Latino/a Americans who believe that individuals from all ethnic backgrounds are able to advance in American society have been found to perceive less discrimination than those from the same groups who do not believe in individual mobility (Major et al., 2002). Those who believe that they can move away from a devalued group may also believe that they can escape discrimination. Moreover, they may view members of their group as personally responsible for their devalued status (Major et al., 2007). However, when persons from devalued groups who believe in individual mobility do perceive discrimination, it may be more harmful to their self-esteem than it is for persons from devalued groups who do not believe in individual mobility and realize that others devalue their group (Major et al., 2007; Sellers & Shelton, 2003).

Social creativity involves redefining the meaning of racial or ethnic group membership by comparing one's ingroup with the outgroup on a dimension on which the ingroup is superior or by changing the values assigned to the ingroup from negative to positive (Tajfel & Turner, 1986). For example, persons of color who are interdependent on their family and community might be viewed by others as overly dependent on these groups. Alternatively, interdependent behavior could be defined by persons of color as a type of social skill and that they have a greater degree of social skills than those who are independent of others. Social creativity is consistent with aspects of Cross's (1971) Immersion-Emersion stage. In the Sellers et al. (1998) model, race or ethnicity may be central to the identity of a socially creative person of color, they may have high private regard for their racial or ethnic group, and they may have a nationalist ideology in that they may desire limited input from others concerning their group. Social creativity may be a risky strategy unless the ingroup is large and powerful enough to define valued behavior and reward it.

Social competition involves fighting the current system to change the societal hierarchy of group membership. For example, as depicted in the 2006 movie *Glory Road*, Texas Western College (now the University of Texas at El Paso) men's basketball team, with an all–African American starting lineup, defeated the powerhouse and all–European American University of Kentucky men's basketball team for the 1966 National Collegiate Athletic Association championship. Although it may seem incredible, given the dominance of African Americans in basketball today, many Americans in the South in the 1960s considered African Americans to be inferior basketball players to European Americans. The Texas Western victory was a first step in desegregating college basketball teams in the South, eventually including the University of Kentucky. Social competition is also consistent with the Cross (1971) Internalization stage and with the oppressed minority ideology in the Sellers et al. (1998) model in which one identifies with the oppression of others. As with social creativity, the size and power of the ingroup may determine the effectiveness of a social competition strategy.

In summary, persons of color are susceptible to stereotype threat because of influential stereotypes. Interventions to create a sense of belonging may reduce stereotype threat (Walton & Cohen, 2007). Persons of color may adopt various strategies to cope with being members of stereotyped groups, including individual mobility, social creativity, and social competition (Tajfel & Turner, 1986). In addition to these individual coping strategies, methods of reducing prejudice have been evaluated and are reviewed next.

REDUCING INTERGROUP PREJUDICE

Cameron, Rutland, Brown, and Douch (2006) examined the prejudice-reduction benefits of emphasizing a bicultural identity among White British 5- to 11-year-olds. A bicultural identity condition focused on unique ingroup (White British) characteristics as well as commonalities with outgroups (refugees). A decategorization condition focused on a deemphasis on group membership in which persons are perceived as individuals. A third condition emphasized a common superordinate identity between the ingroup and outgroup. The children in experimental conditions in the study were read stories weekly for six consecutive weeks about contact between White British children and refugee children. The stories emphasized (a) dual identity with a focus on unique ingroup characteristics (British vs. refugee) and on commonalities (same school), (b) decategorization with a focus on individual characteristics with only a single reference to group membership, or (c) commonalities (same school). A control group did not hear the stories.

Following the stories, dual-identity participants' ratings of refugees were more positive than the ratings of refugees by participants in the other conditions (Cameron et al., 2006). Children in the dual identity group were also more likely to want to play with a refugee than were children in the other conditions. Although the participants in this study were not children of color, the results suggest that neither an emphasis on individual uniqueness nor on commonalities across individuals, which are the goals of assimilation (LaFromboise et al., 1993; see Chapter 1), is effective in reducing prejudice. Rather, a bicultural approach, in which commonalities between the outgroup and the ingroup in combination with an emphasis on the ingroup, was most effective in reducing prejudice. The Cameron et al. (2006) findings are consistent with other experimental work with adults of color on prejudice reduction in which an emphasis on both ingroup and common identities have been most effective (Carpenter, Zárate, & Garza, 2007; Zárate & Garza, 2002).

A classic finding in the social psychology literature is that contact between ingroups and outgroups reduces prejudice (Allport, 1954; Pettigrew, 1998). Actual experiences with individuals from outgroups may demonstrate that stereotypes are not true, which may reduce prejudice. However, the results of a meta-analytic study suggest that the effects of intergroup contact in reducing prejudice are weaker for ethnic minority groups that they are for the ethnic majority (Tropp & Pettigrew, 2005). Whereas intergroup contact may cause members of the majority to become aware of their prejudiced attitudes, intergroup contact for ethnic minority persons may become a reminder of their devalued status in society. Moreover, in their everyday lives, ethnic minority persons may have more intergroup experiences with majority persons because the majority tends to be well represented in most settings, such as school, business, and government. Conversely, majority persons may not have as many opportunities for interactions with ethnic minority persons. Intergroup contact interventions to reduce prejudice usually attempt to create optimal conditions, such as equal status, common goals, cooperation, and institutional support (Tropp & Pettigrew, 2005). However, members of ethnic minority groups may be skeptical about how successfully such conditions can be implemented.

Although reducing prejudice in all ethnic groups is important, perpetrators of prejudice tend to be part of the majority and members of minority groups tend to be targets (Tropp & Pettigrew, 2005). In addition, majority group prejudice that targets minorities tends to be more harmful than prejudice in the opposite direction in that the majority group generally has more societal power than minority groups. Perpetrators of abusive behavior are responsible for it and are also responsible for stopping it, the targets are not (G. C. N. Hall, 1996). Thus, it is incumbent on perpetrators of prejudice of all ethnicities to stop it. To the extent that intergroup contact reduces prejudice particularly among the majority, majority group members should actively seek opportunities for contact with persons of color. Reduction of prejudice among the majority would reduce discrimination that creates the deleterious physical and psychological health effects for persons of color discussed in Chapters 3 and 4.

Despite the potential benefits of intergroup contact, both ethnic majority and minority groups tend to avoid such contact (Shelton & Richeson, 2005). African American college students reported that they would like to have more European American friends than they believed European American students would like to have African American friends (Shelton & Richeson, 2005). Similarly, European American students reported that they would like to have more African American friends than they believed African American students would like to have European American friends. European Americans may fear that they will be perceived as prejudiced and be rejected in such intergroup interactions. Members of minority groups may also fear that they will be rejected, but because of being perceived in a stereotypic manner.

Although majority and minority groups fear rejection from the other, they may infer that the other group does not interact with them because the other group is not interested. Such behavior may reflect *pluralistic ignorance*, in which people observe others behaving similarly to themselves but believe that the behavior reflects different motives than their own (Prentice & Miller, 1996). Consistent with a pluralistic ignorance explanation, both African American and European American college students reported that they would not interact with the outgroup because of fear of being rejected by the outgroup because of their race but that that the outgroup would not interact with them because of lack of interest (Shelton & Richeson, 2005).

Although expectations may be similar between African Americans and European Americans, interpretations of rejection once it occurs may not. Mendes, Major, McCoy, and Blascovich (2008) had African American and European American college students give brief speeches on "Why I Make a Good Friend" and gave the students ratings that indicated a same-race or different-race confederate had socially accepted or rejected them. African Americans rejected by a different- race confederate were more likely to attribute this rejection to discrimination than when the rejection was by a same-race confederate. European Americans were not more likely to attribute rejection to discrimination when the confederate was the same versus a different race. Thus, personal experiences and historical racism against African Americans may have primed African Americans to perceive rejection by a European American as discrimination toward African Americans.

Even interracial social acceptance may be interpreted differently by African Americans and European Americans. Rejection for both European Americans and African Americans in the

Mendes et al. (2008) study resulted in cardiovascular responses consistent with threat (e.g., increased blood pressure) and less positive emotion. These responses were more pronounced when the rejecting confederate was of a different race. However, when African Americans were accepted by a European American confederate, they also exhibited cardiovascular responses consistent with threat and showed less positive emotion than when they were accepted by an African American confederate. These responses did not differ among European Americans when they were accepted by a same- or different-race confederate. It is possible that the African American participants perceived the European American confederate's responses as disingenuous because of social pressure for European Americans to appear "politically correct" in their interactions with African Americans (Mendes et al., 2008). Thus, even interracial interactions that are apparently positive do not necessarily have positive consequences for persons of color.

Prejudice reduction may require much more than positive intergroup contact. Optimal conditions, such as equal status, common goals, cooperation, and institutional support, may be necessary for prejudice reduction to occur (Tropp & Pettigrew, 2005). Such optimal conditions are not easily achieved at the individual or group level and may require systemic change. One method of creating optimal conditions and leveling the playing field for groups of all ethnic backgrounds is affirmative action.

AFFIRMATIVE ACTION

Affirmative action involves organizations, such as schools or businesses, making efforts to ensure that people are not discriminated against based on the group they belong to (Crosby, Iyer, & Sincharoen, 2006). By making groups more diverse, affirmative action rearranges the social structures that inform us about who is in our ingroup and who is in the outgroup (Tajfel & Turner, 1986). Affirmative action helps prepare individuals to live in a society that is becoming increasingly diverse.

In the United States, affirmative action policies began in 1965 with Executive Order (EO) 11246, which required the government and organizations funded by the government to exercise fairness in selection decisions. The focus of EO 11246 was on women, African Americans, Asian Americans, Latino/a Americans, and American Indians. When an organization has an affirmative action policy, the availability of persons from these groups in a field (e.g., psychology PhDs) relative to the representation of persons in the organization (e.g., psychology faculty) is evaluated. If there is a discrepancy between the availability of women and persons of color in a field versus their representation in the organization, the organization must make efforts to eliminate the discrepancy. When candidates are qualified for a position or an opportunity (e.g., scholarship), group membership such as gender or ethnicity that may help diversify an organization is considered to be a "plus factor" along with other factors, such as special talents, region of residence, or legacy status (Crosby et al., 2003). It is important to note that group membership is considered among qualified candidates, and group membership does not qualify someone who is otherwise unqualified.

Affirmative action is predicated upon a supply of diverse persons in a particular field. Therefore, an organization could contend that it does not need to enact affirmative action policies because the supply of diverse persons in a field, such as psychology, is limited. Although an organization that draws from a field that is not diverse might be technically justified in not enacting affirmative action, such a lack of diversity would be a strong rationale for efforts to make the field more diverse! If the pool of diverse applicants is limited in a field, the field needs to make efforts to attract diverse applicants to create a diverse pipeline for the future. As discussed above, diversity contributes to listening, critical thinking, and writing skills (Antonio et al., 2004; Gurin et al., 2004; Hurtado, 2005), which are beneficial to all fields or organizations.

In psychology, training programs to create an ethnically diverse pipeline to the field have been developed. In a program that I developed for undergraduates of color who were majoring in psychology and had strong grades and faculty recommendations, more than half of the students who participated in a summer research training program applied to graduate school in psychology, whereas only 31% of undergraduates of color who did not participate in the program applied (G. C. N. Hall & Allard, in press). Although all the students had academic credentials that would have made them competitive to apply to graduate school, without the training program, nearly 70% of these excellent students did not apply. Thus, affirmative action programs that target diverse groups may be necessary to diversify a field.

The effects of past discrimination may be redressed by affirmative action (Crosby et al., 2003). For example, even if there are not current ostensible barriers to equality, affirmative action may require efforts to change the effects of historical barriers. If persons of color were historically excluded from an organization, affirmative action may involve active recruitment efforts. Ironically, to the extent that European American men have created selection criteria for organizations that favor others similar to them, European American men have benefitted from their own form of affirmative action. For example, standardized testing, such as the SAT I, has produced gaps between European Americans and persons of color, yet the ethnic gap in these tests has often been larger than the ethnic gap in actual job or school performance (Crosby et al., 2003). Thus, the historically established standardized tests may select European Americans, who are expected to perform well, and exclude persons of color whose performance is underpredicted by the tests. Rather than selecting based on a narrow range of abilities that may favor a particular group, a more comprehensive approach that includes analytical abilities, creative abilities, and practical abilities might not only have better predictive validity but also be more fair to all groups (Sternberg & Williams, 1997).

Affirmative action differs from equal opportunity. *Equal opportunity* assumes that when there is no overt discrimination, equal opportunity exists for all persons (Crosby et al., 2003). This is a passive policy in that action is taken only when there is evidence of explicit discrimination. In contrast, affirmative action involves a proactive policy to determine whether equal opportunity actually exists and a plan to eliminate barriers and establish equality if it does not (Crosby et al., 2003).

Proactive affirmative action plans work, in that public organizations that are required to implement affirmative action policies (e.g., government organizations, public universities) are more ethnically diverse and have more opportunities for advancement for people of color than private organizations (Crosby et al., 2003). The primary beneficiaries of affirmative action have been European American women, who are better represented in all levels of public organizations than they were before EO 11246. European American women are also better represented in public organizations than persons of color are.

As might be expected, affirmative action has faced legal challenges. In separate legal cases in 1997, European American women who were denied admission to the University of Michigan undergraduate program and to its Law School sued the University for admitting African American students who had lower grades and test scores than they did. These were the *Gratz et al. v. Bollinger* and *Grutter v. Bollinger* cases. In 2003, the Supreme Court ruled that race-sensitive admissions policies were constitutionally permissible because the state has a compelling interest in assuring diversity among the student bodies of state-sponsored schools (Crosby et al., 2006). However, the Court ruled that such race-based considerations need to be applied on a case-by-case basis, which occurred in the University of Michigan Law School, and that broad applications of race-based considerations, which occurred in the University of Michigan undergraduate program, were not permissible. Nevertheless, the Court ruled that race is a legitimate consideration in college admissions to achieve diversity.

Is affirmative action fair? Critics contend that it is not, because it violates the rights of individuals. Proponents of affirmative action contend that racial and ethnic justice is a more fundamental moral concern than individual rights and that societal-level injustices exist that are not easily solved at the individual level (Vasquez & Jones, 2006). In educational settings, proponents of affirmative action wonder why it is singled out for criticism whereas other forms of preferential admissions to universities, such as being the child of a graduate or being an athlete, are not (Crosby et al., 2006; Vasquez & Jones, 2006). Race- and ethnicity-based discrimination continues to exist in society with the harmful physical and psychological effects discussed in Chapters 3 and 4. Discrimination also creates disparities in educational opportunities, rates of pay, receipt of adequate medical care, and treatment in the judicial system. Proponents of affirmative action contend that there is not a viable alternative method of achieving fairness in organizations. Affirmative action programs may prevent discrimination from occurring or may be able to correct it before it becomes pervasive (Crosby et al., 2006).

Critics of affirmative action may argue that a consideration of characteristics other than race or ethnicity, such as social class, will achieve diversity. Nevertheless, affirmative action based on social class usually does not achieve ethnic diversity (Kane, 2003). Moreover, although class-based discrimination is deleterious, it is possible to change one's social class. Race, on the other hand, is not changeable, and race-based discrimination has had serious and long-lasting damaging consequences in North America (Crosby et al., 2006).

A question critics of affirmative action might ask is why victims of discrimination themselves cannot individually seek to right wrongs rather rely on the government to do so. Victims of discrimination may be reluctant to come forward because of fear of additional victimization in the form of retaliation or ordeals in the justice system (Crosby et al., 2006). Persons of color who claim that they are discriminated against are viewed more unfavorably by European Americans than persons of color who attribute negative treatment to personal characteristics or causes other than discrimination (Kaiser, Dyrenforth, & Hagiwara, 2006). Because of the personal/group discrimination discrepancy (Crosby, 1984), discussed in Chapter 4, victims of discrimination may be able to perceive discrimination directed toward others but may have difficulty defining prejudicial behavior toward themselves as discrimination. It also may be difficult to identify a particular person as the source of a problem when discrimination is endemic to an organization (Vasquez & Jones, 2006). Moreover, perpetrators of discrimination may have difficulty acknowledging discrimination, but perpetrators, not victims, are responsible for victimization (G. C. N. Hall, 1996). The government has power and resources to change organizational discrimination that may not be readily available to individual victims of discrimination.

Another criticism of affirmative action is that it drives a wedge between members of communities of color; those who benefit from affirmative action leave their communities behind. However, there is not evidence that well-educated people of color disengage themselves from their racial or ethnic communities. Alumni of color have been found to make disproportionately high contributions to their communities relative to their peers (Crosby et al., 2006).

Critics of affirmative action also argue that group-based policies may hurt their intended beneficiaries by creating stereotypes about their ability to succeed without the policies (Crosby et al., 2006). Affirmative action may be viewed by these critics as setting up its beneficiaries for failure. Nevertheless, in a study of 80,000 students who had completed degrees at 28 elite colleges and universities in 1951, 1976, and 1989, students of color who were admitted to college on the basis of affirmative action graduated from college and attended and graduated from professional and graduate schools at the same rate as European American students and also held professional jobs at the same rate (Bowen & Bok, 1998).

So how do persons of color feel about affirmative action? Persons who are the targets of affirmative action, including women and persons of color, are more favorable toward it than are those that it does not target (Harrison, Kravitz, Mayer, Leslie, & Lev-Arey, 2006). As might be expected, those stronger in racial or ethnic identity are also more supportive of affirmative action than those whose racial or ethnic identity is less strong (Elizondo & Crosby, 2004; Schmerund, Sellers, Mueller, & Crosby, 2001). Support for affirmative action is inversely associated with racism and sexism (Harrison et al., 2006). Those who oppose affirmative action may believe that discrimination is not the cause of societal inequities or may be trying to preserve the privileges they believe they have legitimately earned (Crosby et al., 2006).

An institution that voluntarily establishes an affirmative action program may create a very different environment for those who benefit from affirmative action than an institution in which affirmative action is imposed. Voluntary affirmative action was associated with a positive work climate (e.g., persons of color are not stereotyped) for faculty of color in a national sample, and positive climate was also associated with job satisfaction (Niemann & Dovidio, 2005). In addition, a positive work climate was negatively associated with self-doubt, which in turn was negatively associated with job satisfaction.

In summary, race- and ethnicity-based affirmative action is an effective means of achieving diversity that has positive outcomes for its beneficiaries and for society. Passive equal opportunity approaches do not achieve ethnic diversity. Affirmative action programs tend to be more satisfying when they are voluntary than when they are involuntary. Nevertheless, continuing affirmative action efforts may be necessary to ensure that persons from all backgrounds reap the benefits of diversity.

Conclusion

Persons of color and European Americans often live in different worlds, despite occupying the same geographic space. Social acceptance or rejection and academic success or failure are usually not interpreted through the lenses of race or ethnicity among European Americans. However, historical and personal experiences of racism among groups of color may cause social and academic experiences to be interpreted through the lenses of race and ethnicity for persons of color.

Positive intergroup contact in diverse settings in which no single group is in the majority is beneficial for persons of all ethnicities. Nevertheless, diversity alone does not eliminate stereotypes. Creating a sense of belonging for all persons in an organization may reduce the influence of stereotypes. Racial and ethnic segregation is the default mode in many social settings, and systemic approaches, such as affirmative action, may be necessary to diversify organizations.

Most of the social psychology literature on prejudice, racism, and discrimination has focused on the perspectives of European Americans. Although some research on the perspectives of persons of color, who are usually the targets of prejudice, racism, and discrimination, has been conducted over the past decade, much more research on persons of color is needed in social psychology. More research is also needed on interventions to reduce the effects of prejudice, racism, and discrimination. The effects of existing interventions reviewed in this chapter are promising.

Discussion Questions

1. Political liberals may consider themselves less racist relative to political conservatives. Yet, being politically liberal is associated with aversive racism, involving egalitarian beliefs and often involving opposition to affirmative action, which benefits people of color. How can political liberals come to grips with their own possibly racist tendencies? Is there a persuasive argument to get political liberals to support affirmative action?

2. The Mendes et al. (2008) study on interracial interactions suggests that even positive social contact with European Americans may be perceived by African Americans as threatening. Given the history of racism in North America, is it feasible to try to reduce the perceived threat involved in interracial interactions? If so, how, and whose responsibility is it?

3. Affirmative action is similar to taxes. Most people value the benefits, but they won't participate unless mandated to do so. Affirmative action creates ethnic and cultural diversity that benefits everyone. Is there a viable alternative to affirmative action to achieve ethnic and cultural diversity in organizations?

Psychology in the Context of Multicultural Issues

CHAPTER 6

African Americans

"I am because we are; we are, therefore I am"

—AFRICAN WORLDVIEW (NOBLES, 1973)

African Americans are 13.4% of the U.S. population at 40.2 million persons, which makes them the second largest ethnic minority group in the U.S. following Latino/a Americans (U.S. Bureau of the Census, 2007). Ninety-three percent of African Americans' ancestors were brought here from Africa as slaves (Spickard, 2007). A minority of African Americans are recent immigrants, most of whom are persons of African ancestry who have immigrated to the United States from Latin America.

Among African Americans 25 years old and above, 81% have at least completed high school and 18% have completed college (U.S. Bureau of the Census, January 2006). There are 2.3 million African American college students. Advanced degrees (masters, doctorate, medical, law) are held by 1.3 million African Americans. More than one in four African Americans work in management or professional positions. However, about one in four African Americans meets national poverty standards, which are $20,614 in income for a family of four and $10,294 for an individual.

This chapter begins with an overview of African American history from early immigration in the 1600s to the present. Next, African American cultural values are reviewed followed by reviews of the psychological literature on family issues, mental health, academic achievement, and career development. African American cultural values and identity influence all these areas.

HISTORY

Since 1976, February has been African American History Month. Although it is important for all Americans to give special recognition to African American history, it is also important to understand that African American history is part and parcel of American history. African Americans have been influenced by and have influenced American history. A synopsis of African American history follows to provide a context for current theory and research in psychology.

1600s–1800s: Slavery and the Civil War

The earliest African immigrants to the United States probably were not slaves. Twenty Africans came to America in 1619 as servants (Takaki, 1993). Similar to many other European immigrants, these Africans were probably indentured servants who were bound by contract for 4 to 7 years to pay for their transportation expenses. Unlike slaves, these servants could eventually earn their freedom.

Black and White servants began to be treated differently during the 1640s (Takaki, 1993). Unlike Black servants, when White servants escaped they could blend into European American communities (Spickard, 2007). American Indians were enslaved by European Americans for a brief period, but they also could easily escape into non-slave Indian communities. European Americans also felt less guilty enslaving Blacks because they regarded Indians as human savages but regarded Blacks as subhuman beasts (Spickard, 2007).

Although the slave trade was controlled by Europeans, slaves were kidnapped in Africa by Africans from outside their communities who worked for the Europeans. The slaves were chained together and transported across the ocean to the United States in tightly packed ships. Many Africans died in transit, and dead bodies were simply thrown overboard. When they arrived in North America, the slaves were kept in forts or cages to be auctioned as merchandise for the purpose of performing unpaid labor on European American tobacco and cotton plantations. Tobacco and cotton were extremely labor-intensive to produce.

Despite originating from culturally diverse ethnic groups in West Africa, Blacks who came to North America became generically regarded as Negroes (Spickard, 2007). However, many African Americans retained their African cultures in terms of language when communicating with other African Americans. The struggle to survive slavery became a common bond for these Americans from diverse African backgrounds. These cultural and sociocultural aspects of unity were the beginnings of Black identity in the United States.

Black servants began to be treated as slaves for life in 1642 in Virginia. In 1648, the children of slaves began to be regarded as slaves. To keep the part-White children of European American slave owners and African American slave women as slaves, the one-drop rule established that any person with any known African ancestry was regarded as Black (Spickard, 2007). Laws also explicitly indicated that conversion to the European Americans' Christianity did not change slave status.

Between 1720 and 1760, 159,000 Africans came to the United States as slaves, whereas only 105,000 Europeans immigrated to the United States during this period (Spickard, 2007). This increase in African slaves in the South decreased the need for White servants, and African labor was less expensive than White labor. The Virginia legislature formally began to define a slave as property in 1669. Later, in 1691, the Virginia legislature denied slaves the right to vote, to hold office, and to testify in court. Although they could not vote, each slave was counted as 3/5 of a person for states to be represented in Congress and in the Electoral College. Despite not having rights as citizens, approximately 25% of George Washington's Continental Army in the Revolutionary War was African American (Spickard, 2007).

Slavery did not develop on a large scale in New England because of the absence of a staple crop that required slaves (Takaki, 1993). In 1777 when Vermont became a state, its constitution outlawed slavery, and Massachusetts outlawed it in 1781 (Spickard, 2007). However, ship captains in New England continued to profit from transporting slaves. New York and Philadelphia also depended on slave labor for their docks and industries (Spickard, 2007). Nevertheless, children born to slaves after 1780 were declared free (although their parents and other existing slaves were not) by the Pennsylvania legislature, and New York gradually began freeing slaves in 1799. Unlike the South, the abolition of slavery in Northern states had limited economic impact.

The slave trade was abolished by Congress in 1807. However, ending the slave trade did not free those who were already slaves. Slavery continued to flourish from 1820 to 1850 in Alabama, Mississippi, and Louisiana because of cotton production. Slaveowners depended on slave women to bear children. African American men were used as breeders, and frequent changes of partner were common for African American men and women (Hines & Boyd-Franklin, 1996). Slaves had been prohibited from marrying to prevent family bonds from being established that would interfere with the trade of individual slaves. Such destruction of family unity is at odds with African communal traditions. Some European American owners would rape slave women to produce children (Takaki, 1993).

By the Civil War, 4 million African Americans were enslaved (Takaki, 1993). The Civil War freed African Americans by law from slavery with the 13th Amendment of the Constitution in 1865. African Americans played a critical role in the Civil War. Approximately 86,000 African Americans served, one-third of whom were subsequently missing or dead. In 1865, near the end of the Civil War, Union Army general William Tecumseh Sherman issued Special Field Order 15, which awarded 40 acres of farmland and a mule to each of the former slaves. President Andrew Johnson quickly rescinded this order, returning the land to the former slave owners. This would have been a token form of reparations for slavery and other forms of oppression but would have represented a recognition of the debt owed to African Americans. No other form of reparations or even an apology has been issued by the U.S. government since then.

Following the Civil War, the vestiges of slavery were prominent despite laws to create civil rights for African Americans. The 14th Amendment in 1868 stated that all persons born or naturalized in the U.S. are citizens and are entitled to the privileges and protections of citizens. The Civil Rights Act of 1875 gave African Americans the right to equal treatment in public settings, inns, theaters, and public amusement places, but the act was ruled unconstitutional in 1883. The 1896 Supreme Court's "separate but equal" decision in *Plessy v. Ferguson* legalized racial segregation of schools. Nevertheless, the separate schools were anything but equal, with European American schools and other facilities having far superior resources (Spickard, 2007).

1900s–1930s: Racism and Separatism

Racism consists of beliefs, attitudes, institutional arrangements, and acts that tend to denigrate individuals or groups because of phenotypic characteristics or ethnic group affiliation (Clark, Anderson, Clark, & Williams, 1999). Racism can be attitudinal or behavioral. Some individuals may suffer the negative effects of racism without attributing their problems to racism. For example, institutional racism may reduce access to resources (Clark et al., 1999), but individuals may attribute their lack of resources to their own inabilities. Although slavery was abolished in the 19th century, racism continued in the United States as a legacy of slavery during the 20th century.

Conflicts between European Americans and African Americans continued during the early 1900s. From 1900 to 1910, anti-Black race riots occurred in the North, and lynching and burning in the South (J. M. Jones, 1997). Lynch mobs were as likely to consist of European American employers and their henchmen trying to terrorize African Americans into accepting lower wages as they were to consist of Ku Klux Klan members (Spickard, 2007). In response, the National

Association for the Advancement of Colored People was established in New York City in 1909. Between 1910 and 1920, there was a large migration of African Americans north for jobs. However, many European Americans did not want African Americans in their neighborhoods.

The Social Darwinism and eugenics movements contended that there was an evolutionary basis for the inferiority of African Americans. Natural selection, or "survival of the fittest," favored European Americans. African Americans were viewed as a burden to the progress of European Americans. The field of social psychology, which emphasized the interdependence of individual personality and societal influences, developed in response to the biological emphasis of Social Darwinism (J. M. Jones, 1997). Race relations problems were redefined as a problem of European American prejudice rather than African American inferiority. Unfortunately, Social Darwinian thought did not cease in the early 1900s but continues to have proponents among those who posit biologically based race differences (e.g., Rushton, 1995a, 1995b).

Separatist movements also developed during the early 1900s. Marcus Garvey made plans for African Americans to return to Africa but was later deported by the U.S. government. W. E. B. Dubois, the leader of the NAACP, had initially supported integration but began to support the establishment of a separate African nation. Dubois immigrated to Ghana shortly before his death.

1940s–1970s: Civil Rights

Several landmark civil rights events occurred during the late 1940s and 1950s. President Truman desegregated the military in 1948. One year later, Jackie Robinson became the first African American Major League Baseball player. In 1954 in the *Brown v. the Board of Education of Topeka* decision, the Supreme Court declared the "separate but equal" doctrine invalid. On December 1, 1955, Rosa Parks sat at the front of the colored section of a bus in Montgomery, Alabama, and refused to move farther back for a White patron when the White section became full. This incident sparked the Montgomery bus boycott, led by Dr. Martin Luther King, Jr.

Civil rights activism and legislation continued to blossom during the 1960s. The decade began with four students from North Carolina A & T State University staging a sit-in at a Greensboro lunch counter in February of 1960. These students had been refused service because they were African Americans. The Student Nonviolent Coordinating Committee (SNCC) organized in 1960 and coordinated sit-ins. In 1961, an integrated busload of freedom riders traveled south from Washington, DC. In Montgomery, Alabama, the riders were beaten and the bus burned. Attorney General Robert Kennedy sent 600 federal marshals to restore order. The March on Washington for jobs and freedom occurred in 1963, culminating in the "I Have a Dream" speech by Rev. Dr. Martin Luther King, Jr.

The Civil Rights Act of 1964 mandated constitutional rights without discrimination or segregation on the grounds of race, color, religion, or national origin. Affirmative action legislation was signed by President Lyndon Johnson in 1965. Whereas the Civil Rights Act of 1964 created equal opportunity, the purpose of affirmative action was to take proactive steps to include underrepresented groups such that equal outcomes could be achieved. In the equal opportunity approach, employers are able to adopt a passive stance by claiming that they do not actively discriminate against persons or groups. However, affirmative action goes beyond creating opportunities by assessing whether outcomes reflect the goals of diversity (Crosby & Cordova, 1996).

Parallel to these efforts toward integration, the separatist movement that began in the early part of the century continued. Elijah Muhammad and Malcolm X led the Black Muslim movement. Goals of Black Muslims were to replace the negative effects of slavery with positive values and behavior and to develop independence from the dominant culture. Malcolm X broke away from Elijah Muhammad to practice orthodox Islam. In 1965, SNCC moved from the goal of integration to Black power under the leadership of Stokely Carmichael. European American members were informed that their role would be secondary. The Black Panther Party was formed as a protective vigilante group in Oakland, California, in 1966.

The progress of the 1960s spilled over into the early 1970s. The Kwanzaa celebration was established as an integration of African, European American, and Jewish influences (J. M. Jones, 1997). Afro-American studies were established at universities, followed by the initiation of women's studies, Asian American studies, Latino studies, and American Indian studies.

The progress of the 1960s and 1970s began to be halted near the end of the 1970s. The Supreme Court ruled in the *Bakke* case in 1978 that a separate admissions process for minority groups was illegal. Allan Bakke was initially denied admission to medical school at the University of California, Davis, because 16 of 100 slots were allotted to African American, Latino American, and American Indian students who had lower test scores than his. As a result of the Supreme Court decision, Bakke was later admitted to the medical school. Nevertheless, the Bakke decision allowed that race could be taken into account in the admissions process. Justice Blackmun wrote, "In order to get beyond racism we must first take account of race. . . . In order to treat persons equally, we must treat them differently" (*Regents of the University of California v. Bakke,* 1978).

Psychology in the 1960s and 1970s shifted from individual to cultural and societal explanations of prejudice (J. M. Jones, 1997). Childhood socialization and conformity were viewed as causal mechanisms of prejudice. Desegregation, which allowed social contact between African Americans and European Americans, was viewed as the solution to prejudice. However, optimism about solutions to prejudice decreased when the civil rights movement began to focus on institutional racism, including voting rights, jobs and income disparities, that affected both the North and South (J. M. Jones, 1997).

By the 1960s, there was a critical mass of African American psychologists that allowed the development of African American psychology (Holliday, in press). In 1968, the Association of Black Psychologists (ABPsi) was established in San Francisco at the American Psychological Association (APA) convention in protest of APA's lack of responsiveness to African American psychologists and communities. ABPsi presented APA with a Petition of Concerns that included (a) the low numbers of Black psychologists and psychology graduate students; (b) APA's failure to direct its efforts to social concerns, including poverty and racism, and to address social problems in communities of color; and (3) the inadequate representation of Blacks in the APA governance structure (Holliday, in press). The Black Students Psychological Association (BSPA) was established at the Western Psychological Association meeting in Vancouver, BC, in 1969. Later that year at the APA convention, the group interrupted the APA presidential address and voiced their concerns, which they were allowed to present the next day to the APA Council of Representatives, the governing body of APA. BSPA demanded greater recruitment and retention of Black faculty and students. APA's council supported the students' concerns. In 1969, ABPsi called for a moratorium on educational testing that was biased against African American children and in 1970 developed a 10-point plan for recruitment and retention of African American students. In 1974, ABPsi launched the *Journal of Black Psychology,* which focuses on psychological theory and research involving African Americans.

1980s–2000s: Dismantling of Affirmative Action, but Hope for the Future

Many Americans in the 1980s, led by President Reagan proclaiming that it was "morning in America", contended that racism was no longer existent. Although blatant forms of racism may have decreased somewhat, subtle racism continued (Dovidio & Gaertner, 1996; J. Jones, 1997). Subtle forms of racism include the belief that discrimination no longer exists and valuing a single way of life. African Americans may be sensitive to subtle racism because of negative personal experiences with racism (Franklin, 1999). What may have been morning for some Americans was dusk for many others. Whereas many Americans would not express overt antagonism toward African Americans, they did believe that many gains of African Americans were undeserved. Many of the civil rights gains of the previous four decades began to be dismantled. Because many Americans believed that discrimination was a thing of the past, they believed that fairness involved not providing special treatment to African Americans or any other historically disadvantaged group. These critics were not without data to support their arguments. African Americans with college and graduate degrees earned more than their White counterparts from the mid-1970s until 1980. Nevertheless, the reverse occurred from 1981 to 1993, which may reflect changing attitudes concerning affir-mative action (J. M. Jones, 1997). Adversarial relationships between European Americans and people of color continued, resulting in the Hate Crimes Act of 1989. However, those who opposed acts of intolerance were viewed by some as hypersensitive and driven by political correctness.

Despite the belief or wish of some Americans that racism is a thing of the past, nearly all African Americans experience some form of racism during their lifetime (Klonoff & Landrine, 1999). There is also evidence that European Americans have more negative and crystallized attitudes toward African Americans than toward other ethnic minority groups (Sears, Citrin, Cheleden, & van Laar, 1999). Subtle racism may be more prominent for higher socioeconomic status African Americans while overt racism may be more prominent for lower SES African Americans (Clark et al., 1999). Nevertheless, there is evidence that overt racism is a problem even for higher SES African Americans (Brody et al., 2006a).

Discrimination also has negative mental health consequences. Racist discrimination is associated with anxiety, anger, frustration, resentment, somatization, obsessive-compulsive symptoms, interpersonal hypersensitivity, fear, paranoia, helplessness-hopelessness, and depression among African Americans (Clark et al., 1999; Klonoff, Landrine, & Ullman, 1999). These problems occur across social classes, but working-class African Americans may be the targets of discrimination more than middle-class African Americans (Clark et al., 1999; Hughes & Dodge, 1997).

A positive development in psychology in 1986 was the founding of the Society for the Psychological Study of Ethnic Minority Issues, which is a division (Division 45) of APA. Division 45 adopted a multicultural model with leadership that has included African Americans, Asian American/Pacific Islanders, Latino/a Americans, and American Indians. This group has attracted many psychologists and students of color to become active in APA.

Racism and its negative consequences were overlooked as the dismantling of affirmative action continued in the 1990s. The Civil Rights Act of 1991 forbade adjustment of test scores or the use of cutoffs based on race, color religion, sex, or national origin, which modified the Civil Rights Act of 1964 (Wittig, 1996). However, the 1991 Act pronounced it unlawful for employers to engage in practices that have a disparate impact on racial/ethnic, sex, religious, national origin, or disability groups when not required by business necessity. Thus, qualified applicants from any of these groups should not be discriminated against. Although such legislation may seem fair, the broader issue of how to get qualified ethnic minority applicants into the employment pipeline was not addressed, nor were actions or resources for training potential ethnic minority applicants provided.

Subsequent legislative decisions in education even more directly outlawed affirmative action. The 1996 *Hopwood* decision in Texas pronounced the preferential admission of Black and Latino students to the University of Texas Law School unconstitutional. This decision overturned the clause from the *Bakke* decision that race could be taken into account during the admissions process. During the same year, affirmative action was effectively dismantled by the Board of Regents of the University of California, when Proposition 209 was approved. Similar anti–affirmative action legislation followed in Washington state.

By 2000, the 1954 *Brown v. Board of Education* ruling invalidating segregation seemed to have been reversed (Pettigrew, 2004). During 2000, 70% of African American children went to predominantly African American schools, and 30% went to schools that had 90% or greater African American students. Such segregation was the result of the rulings of five conservative justices (Rehnquist, Kennedy, O'Connor, Scalia, Thomas) appointed to the Supreme Court by Republican presidents (Nixon, Reagan, Bush). These justices emphasized local over federal authority and providing resources for segregated schools, rather than affirming *Brown* and integrating schools (Pettigrew, 2004).

Despite these political and legal setbacks, psychological theory and research in the 1980s and 1990s offered hope for understanding African American identity and multicultural relations. Against the backdrop of conservativism and the much broader context of centuries of African American oppression, the construct of Afrocentrism was being developed. Afrocentrism espouses African ideals at the center of one's approach to problem solving (Asante, 1987). Another important development in psychology over the past two decades is the multicultural movement (D. W. Sue, Bingham, Porche-Burke, & Vasquez, 1999). This movement emphasizes that different cultural groups have differing worldviews. Recognizing and understanding these worldviews allows intercultural communication. Psychology has developed within a Western worldview. However, many persons of color have non-Western worldviews. Multicultural psychology attempts to understand persons within their own cultural context and in their own terms.

CULTURAL VALUES AND IDENTITY

Based on African cultural worldviews, J. M. Jones (1986) proposed five important attributes: *t*ime, *r*hythm, *i*mprovisation, *o*ral expression, and *s*pirituality, or TRIOS. Traditional West African cultures valued the slow movement of time, patience, and waiting, whereas capitalistic societies view time as an externally imposed organizer of behavior that evaluates productivity, morality, and worth. Rhythm involves the patterning of behavior in response to externally imposed time. Synchrony occurs when the person and environment are in good fit, whereas asynchrony occurs when rhythm is blocked, such as in cases where discrimination occurs. Improvisation is the combination of expressiveness and creativity under time pressure, particularly unanticipated events. In the context of discrimination, improvisation involves a creative, adaptive response. Oral expression confers meaning on events, reveals truths (e.g., stories, proverbs), and creates common bonds among people. Spirituality is a belief in nonmaterial causation by a life force that does not reside solely in individuals but is shared by humans and resides in the universe.

Boykin (1994) identified nine salient cultural dimensions for African Americans that are consistent with traditional African belief systems: communalism, affect, expressive individualism, spirituality, harmony, orality, movement expressiveness, verve, and social time perspective. Communalism involves the priority of duty and commitment to one's social group over individual privileges. Affect involves the centrality of emotional cues and expressiveness. Expressive individualism involves the cultivation and expression of uniqueness. Spirituality involves the nonmaterial forces that permeate one's life. Harmony involves a commitment to oneness with nature in contrast to an effort to control nature. Orality is the special importance of knowledge gained through words or speech. Movement expressiveness refers to the importance of movement, music, syncopation, and dance. Verve involves receptiveness to high levels of sensory stimulation. Social time perspective implies a commitment to time as social phenomenon, such that people control time (e.g., an event begins when everyone arrives) rather than time controlling people.

African American cultural values are also expressed in the Nguzo Saba, the principles of the celebration of Kwanzaa (Grills & Longshore, 1996):

1. *Umoja* (Unity)—to strive for and maintain family, community, and racial unity
2. *Kujichagulia* (Self-Determination)—to define ourselves, name ourselves, create for ourselves, and speak for ourselves instead of being defined, named, created for, and spoken for by others
3. *Ujima* (Collective Work and Responsibility)—to build and maintain our community together and make others' problems our problems to solve them together
4. *Ujamaa* (Cooperative Economics)—to build and maintain our own businesses and to profit from them together
5. *Nia* (Purpose)—to make our collective vocation the building and developing of our community to restore our people to their traditional greatness
6. *Kuumba* (Creativity)—to do always as much as we can, in the way we can, to leave our community more beautiful and beneficial than we inherited it
7. *Imani* (Faith)—to believe in our people, our parents, our teachers, and the righteousness and victory of our struggle

Common to all the above conceptualizations of African American cultural values are individuals in the context of families and communities. Although communalism is important in the lives of African Americans, so is individualism. Consistent with the cultural dimension of African American expressive individualism (Boykin, 1994), across studies, African Americans have been found to be more individualistic than European Americans, as discussed in Chapter 2 (Oyserman, Coon, & Kemmelmeier, 2002). However, African American individualism may serve the collective (J. M. Jones, 1997), in that individual efforts benefit other African Americans. Thus, African American individualism may promote communalism.

FAMILY ISSUES

African American families are diverse in terms of their functioning. Using family environment and parenting style data, Mandara and Murray (2002) identified the following types of African American families: cohesive-authoritative, conflicted-authoritarian, and defensive-neglectful. Cohesive-authoritative families were characterized by high family cohesion and being supportive, nurturing, and involved with their children. Racial socialization, regular church attendance, and high educational expectations were also present in cohesive-authoritative families. Married parents were the heads of 58% of these families with other family constellations constituting the remaining 42%.

Conflictive-authoritarian families experienced conflict, and parents were controlling, critical, and expressed unhappiness with their children's performance and abilities (Mandara & Murray, 2002). Although these families emphasize achievement, there is limited intellectual stimulation. Religious socialization and church attendance is emphasized, and racial socialization is moderate. Married parents headed 63% of conflictive-authoritarian families.

Defensive-neglectful families emphasized a dislike for other racial groups but did not teach their children to be proud of being African Americans (Mandara & Murray, 2002). Parents exhibited limited concern and emotion about their children. Similar to conflictive-authoritarian parents, defensive-neglectful parents were controlling, critical, and expressed unhappiness with their children's performance and abilities. Defensive-neglectful families also did not emphasize achievement or religious/moral development. Single mothers headed 73% of these families. However, the difficulties in defensive-neglectful families should not be attributed to single mothers, as there were single mothers in each family type (Mandara & Murray, 2002), and single mothering has been demonstrated not to affect children's cognitive and emotional functioning (Foster & Kalil, 2007).

Census data suggest that the number of African Americans raised by single mothers continues to grow (U.S. Bureau of the Census, January, 2006). A priority of federal government under the George W. Bush administration was promotion of marriage and fatherhood with the assumption that two-parent families are more beneficial to children than single-parent families are (U.S. Department of Health and Human Services, 2006). Yet, data indicate that living with both parents does not appear to have specific benefits for African American children, in terms of cognitive achievement and emotional adjustment, beyond other family constellations (Dunifon & Kowaleski-Jones, 2002; Foster & Kalil, 2007).

The cognitive and emotional effects of living with mother only, father and mother, mother and male partner who was not the child's biological father, and mother and grandmother were examined in a national sample of low-income African Americans, Latino Americans, and European Americans during their first 6 years of life (Foster & Kalil, 2007). Cognitive and emotional outcomes were assessed with interviews and psychological tests. There were no differences in cognitive and emotional outcomes by family living arrangement or by ethnic group. Thus, two-parent families do not appear to be more beneficial than other family constellations, at least among low-income families.

An extended-family model of parenting is consistent with African American cultural values. Many single African American mothers reside in the homes of relatives or have relatives reside with them. This may be a matter of economic necessity, as nearly half of single African American mothers live below the poverty threshold (D. J. Jones, Zalot, Foster, Sterrett, & Chester 2007).

A key to the effectiveness of extended family parenting is the mother's relationship with the extended family members. When the mother's relationship with her mother (i.e., the child's grandmother) is positive, the grandmother is viewed as helpful and the single mother's and child's adjustment is better than when the relationship is strained (C. B. Gee & Rhodes, 2003; D. J. Jones et al., 2007; Oberlander, Black, & Starr, 2007). Similarly, biological fathers are viewed as helpful to single mothers, and the single mother's and child's adjustment is better when the father's relationship to the mother is positive (D. J. Jones et al., 2007). Relationship quality with the mother also influences the effectiveness of co-parenting with adults other than grandmothers and biological fathers.

Respect for authority is an important component of the African American cultural dimensions of communalism and harmony. Among middle-class third-grade girls, African Americans were observed during a 5–7-minute discussion of conflicts to respect their parents more than did European Americans (Dixon, Graber, & Brooks-Gunn, 2008). Children's respect involved attending to, showing interest in, and validation of what their mothers were saying and also involved not ignoring or disobeying their mothers. Moreover, children's low respect was perceived more as a source of the frequency and intensity of conflicts for African American mothers than for European American mothers.

Communalism is important for effective functioning of African American families. Communal values, including cooperating with others, thinking about family, and learning about African American values and history, were negatively associated with violent behavior and positively associated with empathy among fifth-grade African American children (Jagers, Sydnor, Mouttapa, & Flay, 2007). Violence avoidance efficacy, which is the ability to stay away from a fight, was also positively associated with communal values.

African American parents may have greater involvement in decision making with their adolescent children than European American parents do with their adolescent children. African American parental involvement in decision making with their adolescents may protect against racism and discrimination across class and may protect against danger in poor families (Gutman & Eccles, 2007; Smetana, Campione-Barr, & Daddis, 2004). Among African American early adolescents, parental involvement in decision making regarding conventional issues (whether to do assigned chores, how to talk to parents, whether to use manners, what type of language to use) and prudential issues (whether to smoke cigarettes, drink alcohol, take drugs, have sex) was positively associated with adjustment (Smetana et al., 2004).

Low family cohesion has been found to be associated with depression among African American adolescents but not among European American adolescents (K. C. Herman, Ostrander, & Tucker, 2007). In the same study, family conflict was associated with depression among European American adolescents but not among African American adolescents. Consistent with African American values of family unity, family connections and positive family relations may protect against depression for African American adolescents, whereas reducing family conflict may not (K. C. Herman et al., 2007).

A prevention program was designed to strengthen African American families via involved-vigilant parenting, clearly articulated parental expectations for alcohol use, communication about sex, and racial socialization (Brody et al., 2004). This program, known as Strong African American Families, has increased parent-child relationship quality, which in turn increases youth self-control (Brody et al., 2005). The Strong African American Families program also has been found to reduce preadolescent risky sexual behaviors (Murry, Berkel, Brody, Gibbons, & Gibbons 2007), preadolescent alcohol use (Brody et al., 2006b; Gerrard et al., 2006), and parental depression (Beach et al., 2008) among African American families.

Even seemingly negative family interactions among African Americans are not necessarily harmful. Approximately 90% of African American children have experienced spanking (Dodge, McLoyd, & Lansford, 2005). Physical punishment of children has been found to be associated with psychological problems, such as depression and aggressive behavior, among European American children. However, in a family context of warmth and acceptance, mild physical punishment in the form of spanking does not have the deleterious effects on African American children that it does on European American children and in some instances is beneficial (Dodge et al., 2005). In African American family contexts of warmth and acceptance, spanking is a predictable response to misbehavior, rather than an unpredictable angry reaction of parents.

Other work on the effects of seemingly negative interactions in African American families involves schizophrenics. Critical and intrusive behavior of relatives of African American schizophrenics observed in interactions between the relatives and the schizophrenics was associated with a lower likelihood of relapse of schizophrenic symptoms (Rosenfarb, Bellack, & Aziz, 2006a). Critical behavior involved dissatisfaction or disapproval of past schizophrenic patient behaviors without indicating how the patient might change in the future (e.g., "You don't contribute anything to the family"). Intrusive behavior involved special knowledge of the schizophrenic patient's attitudes, knowledge, or feelings (e.g., "You don't really care about me"). Unlike African Americans, critical and intrusive behavior of relatives of European American schizophrenics was associated with a higher likelihood of relapse of schizophrenic symptoms. Although critical and intrusive behaviors are confrontive, it is possible that these behaviors by relatives are interpreted in African American families as expressions of caring and concern (Rosenfarb et al., 2006b). Consistent with results among adolescents (K. C. Herman et al., 2007), family conflict is not necessarily associated with psychopathology. Moreover, African American families of schizophrenics are less burdened by and less rejecting of schizophrenic family members than are European American families (Rosenfarb et al., 2006a).

In summary, cohesive African American families, regardless of their configuration, tend to have positive psychological effects on their members. Families may be more involved in the lives of African Americans than of European Americans. Seemingly negative family interactions among African Americans are not necessarily associated with psychopathology, including depression and schizophrenia relapse. As discussed below, African American identity may serve as a protective factor against psychopathology.

MENTAL HEALTH

Among children and adolescents, African Americans tend to be more depressed than European Americans (Costello, Swendsen, Rose, & Dierker, 2008; Kistner, David-Ferdon, Lopez, & Dunkel, 2007). As discussed in Chapter 2, ethnic or racial differences alone do not inform us about the basis of the differences. Although discrimination was not assessed in theses studies, persons of color experience discrimination more than European Americans do (Levin, Sinclair, Veniegas, & Taylor, 2002).

Discrimination has negative effects on the mental health of African Americans. In a study of New Hampshire adults, discrimination was strongly associated with lower scores on a generic measure of mental health among African Americans after age, gender, education, employment, income, insurance, and nativity (born in U.S. vs. born outside U.S.) were controlled (G. C. Gee, Ryan, Laflamme, & Holt, 2006). Discrimination may have greater effects on African Americans' mental health than does general stress. Among college students, experiences of racism were more strongly associated with scores on a measure of somatization, anxiety, and depression than were other stressful life events (Utsey, Giesbrecht, Hook, & Stanard, 2008).

Discrimination was more strongly associated with depression among African American college students with Assimilationist and Humanist ideologies (see Chapter 1) on the Multidimensional Inventory of Black Identity than among those who were less identified with these ideologies (Banks & Kohn-Wood, 2007). Persons having Assimilation and Humanist ideologies may attempt to reach out to other groups, and discrimination from these groups may have more of an impact than on persons who are not attempting to reach out to other groups.

Conversely, African American identity appears to buffer the association between discrimination and depression. Church attendance among African Americans decreased the effects of discrimination on depression (Bierman, 2006). Although the type of church attended was not specified in the study, most of the African Americans attended conservative Protestant churches that presumably were African American churches. African American churches are an important component of African American identity and communal values.

Depression is a risk factor for suicidal ideation and suicide attempts. Among depressed African American college students, those with a strong African American ethnic identity were less likely to have suicidal ideation (Walker, Wingate, Obasi, & Joiner, 2008). Ethnic identity did not moderate the association between depression and suicidal ideation among European American college students. Similarly, among African American patients at a public hospital, suicide attempters had a lower ethnic identity than those who had not attempted suicide (Kaslow et al., 2004).

In summary, discrimination may have deleterious effects on African Americans' mental health and may have greater effects than general stress. An African American identity may buffer the effects of discrimination on depression and may also reduce the risk of suicidal ideation and suicide attempts. As discussed below, an African American identity also has positive effects on academic achievement.

ACADEMIC ACHIEVEMENT AND CAREER DEVELOPMENT

African American parents' facilitation of their children's academic success may be culturally based. In a study of 8–12-year-olds, well-educated European American parents translated their expectations of academic success for their children via the instrumental task of reading to their children (Davis-Kean, 2005). Conversely, well-educated African American parents translated their expectations of academic success for their children not only via reading to their children but also via warmth in their relationships with their children. Parental warmth included conveying positive feelings toward the child and praising the child. Thus, African American children's academic success was achieved via both instrumental and relational means. The emphasis on relationships among African Americans is consistent with African American communal values.

Is academic achievement a source of status among African American children? For some young African American males, aggressive behavior may be a means of establishing social competence, protection, and pride (Lazur & Majors, 1995). However, in a lower-socioeconomic-status-inner-city group of African American first-, fourth-, and seventh-graders, where aggressive behavior might be expected to be valued, aggressive behavior was negatively associated with popularity in the first grade and not associated with popularity in the later grades (Xie, Boucher, Hutchins, & Cairns, 2006). The basis for popularity at all three grade levels was being a good student. These findings are encouraging, given societal stereotypes about African American violence and academic achievement.

Pride about being an African American has been found to be associated with academic achievement, as measured by standardized test scores and grades, among African American fourth-graders (Smith, Atkins, & Connell, 2003). Children who were proud about being African American were more likely to have parents who had college education. Moreover, children who perceived being African American as a barrier to their success had poorer academic achievement. Children who perceived this barrier tended to have parents who were less educated and teachers who also perceived that being an African American was a barrier to success.

Some have contended that African American children reject academic achievement as being White because it requires conformity to a school system that is inconsistent with African American values (Ogbu, 1986). Boykin and colleagues (2005) presented low-income African American and European American fifth-graders descriptions of high-achieving students that were individualistic, competitive, communal, or vervistic. The individualistic student was described as performing better on school tasks when working independently and enjoying solving problems all on her or his own efforts. The competitive student was described as liking the challenge of seeing who is the best and disliking having the second highest test score in the class. The communal student was described as feeling that it is a good idea for students to help each other learn and that students can learn a lot of important things from each other. The vervistic student was described as enjoying working on several different subjects within a class period and not bothered should music be

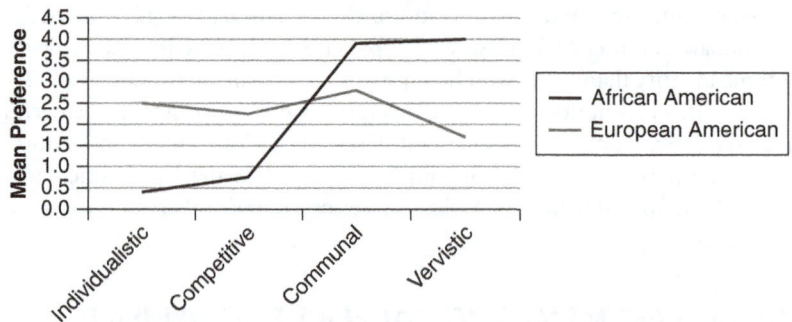

FIGURE 6.1   Preference of Student Learning Style by Ethnic Group

played in the background while she or he was working. Whereas European American students preferred individualistic and competitive students as friends, African American students preferred communal and vervistic students as friends (Figure 6.1). Thus, African Americans do not summarily reject high academic achievers but prefer culturally congruent academic achievers.

Success in high school has also been found to be associated with African American identity. Among African American high school students, maternal racial socialization is positively associated with grades and negatively associated with delinquent behavior (T. L. Brown & Krishnakumar, 2007). Paternal racial socialization was also negatively associated with delinquent behavior and with depression. High school students reported that their mothers engaged in greater levels of racial socialization than their fathers did.

Higher education is valued by African Americans for the same reasons persons from other ethnic groups value higher education, including intellectual development, status, and income (Phinney, Dennis, & Osorio, 2006). However, relative to European Americans, African American freshman were more likely to endorse helping their family financially as a reason to attend college. This desire to help one's family financially was not a result of lower socioeconomic status among African Americans, as socioeconomic status was controlled in the analyses. Such a desire to help one's family financially after achieving personal success is consistent with African American communal values.

Although African Americans may value academic achievement, many African Americans are educated in settings in which they are the minority and European Americans are the majority. Thus, feeling comfortable with European Americans may be important for African Americans to thrive in White majority educational institutions. Indeed, comfort with European Americans has been found to reduce anxiety and increase intergroup contact among African American college students (E. R. Cole & Yip, 2008). In addition, comfort with European Americans was found to reduce concerns about academic abilities and performance among African American male students and to increase well-being among African American female students.

Similar to the E. R. Cole and Yip (2007) findings, Anglin and Wade (2007) found that an internalized multicultural identity was positively associated with social and academic adjustment to college for African Americans in a predominately European American university and in an ethnically diverse college. However, an internalized Afrocentric identity was negatively associated with college adjustment. Thus, a multicultural identity was more adaptive than identity exclusively involving one's own group. As might be expected, Pre-Encounter and Immersion-Emersion identities were both negatively associated with college adjustment.

In summary, a strong African American identity facilitates academic achievement. Academic achievement is valued by African American children, particularly that which is culturally congruent. A bicultural identity is adaptive in educational settings in which African Americans are in the minority. Issues of identity and minority status also influence African Americans after they complete their education and embark on careers.

CAREER DEVELOPMENT

Although the evidence reviewed above suggests that African American identity is generally positively associated with academic achievement, African Americans may still hold race-based stereotypes about various careers (Bigler, Averhart, & Liben, 2003). African American first- and sixth-graders reported that African Americans were more likely to perform low-status (e.g., fast food worker, maid, cashier) and medium-status (e.g., police officer, hair dresser, school teacher) jobs than high-status jobs (e.g., airline pilot, doctor, college professor). However, the children indicated that both European Americans and African Americans should perform all occupations. Moreover, the children preferred the high-status jobs over the low-status jobs. When descriptions and pictures of novel jobs (e.g., *tenic,* "a person in charge of creating handicapped parking spaces for city buildings and stores") were presented in which the race of the workers in the pictures was varied (only European Americans, only African Americans, European Americans and African Americans), jobs depicted with only European Americans were rated higher in status (e.g., more difficult to learn and perform, receiving higher pay, being more important) than jobs depicted with only African Americans. Children preferred the jobs depicted with only European Americans over those depicted with only African Americans or with both European Americans and African Americans (Figure 6.2). Thus, African American children are aware of race-based occupational stereotypes, but this awareness does not interfere with the belief that all jobs should be performed by persons of any racial background or with the desirability of jobs that are seen as the purview of European Americans.

Similar to occupations that are race based, there are occupations that are gender based. Ethnic identity has been demonstrated to have a bearing on young African Americans' choices of gender-traditional careers (Gushue & Whitson, 2006). African American ninth-graders with a strong ethnic identity also had confidence in their ability to effectively engage in career decision-making tasks. Such confidence was negatively associated with the selection of gender-traditional careers. Thus, ethnic identity may expand career choices for African Americans.

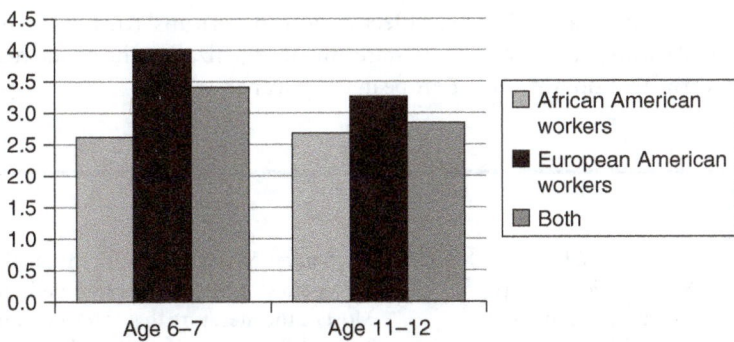

FIGURE 6.2 African American Children's Interest in Jobs by Race of Workers

It is one thing to prefer or to select an occupation and quite another to try to cope with the actual demands of an occupation in the organizations in which the occupation exists. African Americans' perceptions of a business organization may be influenced by organizational diversity and the organization's diversity policies. African American professionals were found to trust an organization if it was depicted in a photo as having a high representation of ethnic minorities, regardless of the organization's diversity policies (Purdie-Vaughns et al., 2008). When an organization was depicted in a photo that did not include ethnic minorities, these professionals trusted an organization that valued diversity (e.g., other firms try to shape their staffs into a single mold; we believe that embracing our diversity enriches our culture) more than one that had a color-blind policy (e.g., other firms mistakenly focus on their staff's diversity; we train our diverse workforce to embrace their similarities). Also, when a European American was promoted and an African American fired, African American professionals did not view the personnel actions as race based when there was high ethnic minority representation in the organization. However, when there was low ethnic minority representation, African American professionals were more likely to perceive the personnel actions as race-based in organizations that had color-blind policies than in organizations that valued diversity. African American professionals trusted a nondiverse organization with color-blind policies only when they had evidence of an independent audit that the organization's procedures were fair.

In solo status situations in which they are the only member of their group in an organization, African Americans may fear that poor performance may not only reflect poorly on themselves but on their whole race. European Americans, who tend to be individualistic and not connected to a group, may not experience such concerns in solo status situations. Indeed, Sekaquaptewa, Waldman, and Thompson (2007) found African Americans' racial centrality increased when they believed they were the only African American in a group that was to perform a learning task versus when they were in a group with another African American, whereas racial centrality did not increase for European Americans in solo versus nonsolo status. Solo status African Americans also believed that their performance would reflect on their race and that they were representing their race more in solo than in nonsolo conditions. Such race-based performance apprehension and representativeness did not differ for European Americans by solo versus nonsolo condition. Thus, race-based concerns about solo status may be a burden that interferes with African Americans' performance, whereas European Americans may not have such race-based concerns when they have solo status.

In summary, African American children may hold stereotypes about careers, but having a strong ethnic identity enables African Americans to effectively make career choices. The relative amount of diversity in an organization may affect African Americans' trust in the organization. Moreover, when an African American has solo status in an organization, he or she may be subject to race-based concerns that do not affect European Americans.

Conclusion

African American culture and identity have thrived, despite centuries of oppression in the United States. African American families are functional in various configurations, and strong African American families have positive effects on mental health and academic achievement. Families nurture an African American identity that is associated with adaptive career functioning. Nevertheless, African Americans face race-related career stressors that European Americans do not face.

Most of the literature that is reviewed in this chapter is socioculturally informed. Cultural constructs, such as racial or ethnic identity, and sociocultural constructs, such as discrimination, are conceptualized and measured. On the other hand, most of the psychology literature on African Americans that is not reviewed in this chapter is not socioculturally informed and does not consider the unique characteristics of African Americans. When African Americans are considered, it is usually as a homogeneous group in a single racial category. There is a pressing need for additional research on all the topics covered in this chapter that goes well beyond the ethnic-group-differences approach to examine the cultural and sociocultural bases of African American behavior.

Discussion Questions

1. What are the enduring psychological effects of the legacy of oppression that African Americans have experienced in United States? How much does the election of an African American president undo these psychological effects?

2. Single-parent households are viewed by many as problematic for children and particularly so for African American children. Yet, there is not evidence that single-parent households are associated with significantly different cognitive or emotional outcomes than are dual-parent households in any ethnic group. In the face of this lack of evidence, why do many continue to view single-parent African American households as deviant?

3. To be successful in academic and occupational settings, competence in European American culture is often required of African Americans. Can you envision a time and setting where competence in African American culture will be a criterion for success?

CHAPTER 7

Asian Pacific Americans

To forget one's ancestors is to be a brook without a source,
a tree without a root.

—CHINESE PROVERB

Asian Pacific Americans are immigrants and descendants of immigrants from East and South Asia and the Pacific Islands. They constitute at least 29 different groups whose cultural customs are distinct from most other groups in the United States. The term "Asian Pacific American" will be used as a term in this chapter to include Americans of East Asian (e.g., China, Japan, Korea), Southeast Asian (e.g., Vietnam, Thailand, Cambodia), South Asian (e.g., India), and Pacific Island (e.g., Philippines, Hawaii, Samoa) ancestry, whereas the term "Asian American" will be used to refer to persons of East Asian ancestry and not to the other groups. Most research in psychology has been on Americans of East Asian ancestry, with a developing literature on Southeast Asian and South Asian Americans. The literature on Pacific Island Americans is quite limited.

Chinese, Japanese, and Korean Americans are influenced by Confucian traditions, although each culture has developed these traditions in somewhat unique ways. Hong Kong has been influenced by Chinese culture as well as its former status as a British colony. Vietnamese Americans have been influenced by Chinese culture as well as by French colonization. Vietnamese, Cambodian, and Thai Americans all are likely to have been influenced by the Buddhist religion. Indian Americans may have multiple religious influences, including Hinduism, Islam, Sikhism, and Jainism (Min, 1995). British colonization resulted in the adoption of English as the official language in India. Spanish colonization exposed Filipino Americans to Roman Catholic influences. Colonization by the United States introduced American influences in the Philippines, including the English language. Over 70% of Korean Americans are Protestant Christians as a result of American missionary influences in Korea beginning in the late 1800s (Kitano & Daniels, 1995; E. Lee, 1997).

Of the total U.S. population, 4.2% (11.9 million people) have Asian ancestry (U.S. Bureau of the Census, December 2004a). Asian Indian, Chinese, Filipino, Korean, and Vietnamese Americans accounted for 80% of the Asian American population, and Japanese, Cambodian, Hmong, Laotian,

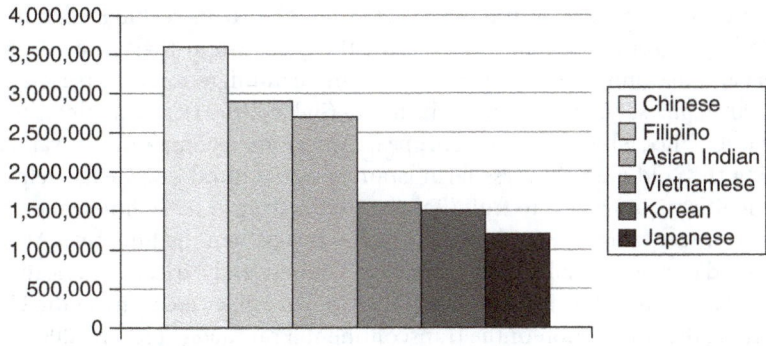

FIGURE 7.1 Americans of Asian Ancestry

Pakistani, and Thai Americans accounted for 15 percent. Chinese Americans are the largest Asian American group (Figure 7.1). About 64% of Asians in the United States were born in Asia, which means that most Asian Americans are immigrants (U.S. Bureau of the Census, August 2005).

Forty-four percent of Asian Americans have earned at least a bachelor's degree, compared to 24% in the total population (U.S. Bureau of the Census, August 2005). However, according to the 2005 census, 60% of Hmong and about half of Cambodians and Laotians had less than a high school education. Seventy-eight percent of all Native Hawaiians and Pacific Islanders had completed high school, which was similar to that of the national population (80%). However, only 14% had a bachelor's degree or more, compared to 24% for the national population.

The median annual income of Asian American families is $59,000. The median income for all U.S. families is $50,000. This discrepancy is partially due to more wage earners in Asian American families. Asian Americans were more likely to be in married-couple families than the national population, with over 60% of Asian American households reporting being in a married-couple family. Moreover, Asian Americans tend to be concentrated in parts of the country in which there is a high cost of living (e.g., California, Hawaii, New York). There is much diversity between ethnic groups in income among Asian Americans. Asian Indian and Japanese families' median income is the highest of all Asian Americans (over $60,000) and Cambodian and Hmong families' median income is the lowest ($30,000–35,000).

Although poverty rates for Asian Americans (12.6%) are similar to that of the total population (12.4%), Hmongs and Cambodians had the highest individual poverty rates (37.8 and 29.3%, respectively). About one of every six Native Hawaiians and Pacific Islanders (17.7%) and nearly one in five Asian immigrants lived below the poverty threshold, which is higher than the national population (U.S. Bureau of the Census, August 2005).

HISTORY

Early Immigration

The late 1700s was the first period of Asian Pacific immigration to America, although the total number of immigrants was small. Chinese and Filipino sailors who arrived on Spanish ships founded settlements in Louisiana during this time, and South Asians and Malaysians arrived on English ships on the East Coast as slaves (Agbayani-Siewert & Revilla, 1995). During the 19th century, approximately 250,000 Chinese persons immigrated to the United States (Spickard, 2007).

A cohort of Chinese men came to the United States in the 1820s seeking work in railroads or mines, as did a larger group to California following the gold rush in 1849. The Burlingame Treaty between China and the United States encouraged Chinese immigration for a period. By the 1860s, there were 24,000 Chinese men working in the mines (Takaki, 1993). Asian miners were subjected to a Foreign Miners' Tax, which provided European Americans a competitive advantage.

Following the gold rush, Chinese farm laborers' agricultural knowledge helped transform California agriculture from wheat to fruit (Takaki, 1993). Over 12,000 Chinese men were hired to build the transcontinental railroad. They received lower pay than the European American workers, and 1,000 died during the railroad construction. Chinese and African American workers were conspicuously absent from drawings depicting the Golden Spike ceremony in the Utah Territory in 1869, signifying the completion of the transcontinental railroad (Spickard, 2007).

The American economy was depressed at the end of the 1800s, and Chinese immigrants were often scapegoats. Additional Chinese immigration to the United States ended in 1882 with the Chinese Exclusion Act, motivated in part by perceived competition between Chinese and European American laborers. This was the first law that excluded immigrants on the basis of nationality, and it was not repealed until 1942. In 1885 and 1886, Chinese residents of Tacoma, Seattle, and Rock Springs, Wyoming, were attacked, killed, and driven out of these communities by European Americans (Spickard, 2007).

Most Chinese immigrants had families in China and intended to eventually return there. However, these men could not have become United States citizens even if they had wanted to. A 1790 federal law reserved naturalized citizenship for Whites, and Asians were not allowed to become naturalized citizens until 1952 (Takaki, 1993).

Because there were very few Chinese women in California, only 4% of Chinese in the United States in 1900 were American-born (Takaki, 1993). Roles for Chinese women were extremely limited in the United States. In 1870, 61 percent of the 3,536 women in California listed their occupation as prostitute (L. Lee, 1998). This statistic must have come to federal attention, as the 1875 Page Law prohibited immigration of women who were being brought into the United States for "lewd and immoral purposes" (Spickard, 2007). Selective enforcement of this law further reduced the immigration of Chinese women to the United States. Chinese men were unable to marry European American women in California as a result of a 1880 California law that prohibited marriage between a White person and a "negro, mulatto, or Mongolian" (Takaki, 1993).

Chinatowns were developed at the end of the 1800s for economic and social support. Many Chinese Americans were forced into self-employment, including stores, restaurants, and laundries, as a result of discrimination and language barriers. Thus, the existence of Chinese restaurants and laundries in the United States is not necessarily a result of a Chinese affinity for these businesses. However, many European Americans began to view Asian American men as feminized, as cooking and washing were traditionally female tasks for European Americans (Spickard, 2007).

Over 6,000 Asian Indian men immigrated to California between 1904 and 1911 (Jensen, 1988). Most of these men worked as farmers. About half were married, but most were unable to bring their wives to the United States until legislation allowed this in 1946. Similar to the Chinese immigration experience, the relative absence of women prevented a lasting Asian Indian presence. Indeed, many of the 1,000 Indian students who came to the United States in the 1920s intended to learn science and technology and to return to India and apply this knowledge (Sheth, 1995). Financial hardships caused by British colonial rule motivated many Indians to emigrate to the United States (Sheth, 1995). However, improved social, political, and economic conditions following India's independence from Great Britain in 1947 curtailed Indian immigration to the United States until 1965.

A wave of immigrants to the United States from Japan followed the Chinese Exclusion Act in 1882. The 1908 Gentleman's Agreement between the United States and Japan allowed Japanese family members to immigrate to the United States. This law allowed many Japanese immigrants to remain with their families in the United States, unlike the Chinese immigrants whose families remained in China. Japanese immigrants came to California to seek employment and economic opportunities, finding independent employment in shop keeping and in farming. However, the immigrants' opportunities were restricted by the Alien Land Law of 1913, which prohibited non-citizens from owning land. Nevertheless, their American-born children were able to own land as citizens. By 1940, Japanese Americans grew 95% of beans, 67% of tomatoes, 95% of celery, 44% of onions, and 40% of green peas in California (Takaki, 1993).

Asian Pacific Americans in Hawaii

The Asian Pacific American diversity in Hawaii is a result of labor force issues. During the early 1900s, many Asian Pacific groups were brought by European Americans to Hawaii to prevent any particular Asian group from becoming the majority (Takaki, 1993). However, the Asian workers in Hawaii united across ethnic groups, eventually became the majority, and unionized (Takaki, 1993). Over 60% of the current population of Hawaii has Asian Pacific American ancestry.

The recruitment in Hawaii of Asian laborers resulted in over 7,200 Koreans emigrating from 1903 to 1905 (Min, 1995). Between 1906 and 1923, the primary groups of Korean immigrants to the United States were the wives of the workers, students, and political refugees (Min, 1995). Asian immigration to the United States, other than that of Filipinos, was completely halted in 1924 with the Asian Exclusion Act.

The United States gained possession of the Philippines in 1898 after the Spanish-American War. Between 1906 and 1940, Filipinos were imported to Hawaii and the West Coast of the United States as a cheap source of farm labor (Agabayani-Siewert & Revilla, 1995; Edman & Johnson, 1999). Similar to Chinese immigration, Filipino immigration primarily involved men (Agabayani-Siewert & Revilla, 1995). During the Depression in the 1930s, 2,000 Filipino Americans left the United States under pressure from the federal government to "repatriate" to the Philippines (Spickard, 2007). Such repatriation occurred on a much larger scale during the 1930s with Mexican Americans, who were also perceived as a threat to the employment opportunities of European Americans (see Chapter 8). Many Filipinos served in the United States armed forces during World War II, and those who served were allowed to become U.S. citizens in 1943. The Philippines gained independence from the United States in 1946.

Before and after World War II, European Americans controlled the social and political systems of Hawaii (Spickard, 2007). Their goal with Japanese Americans was to Americanize them in the public schools by teaching standard English and other U.S. customs, such as table manners. However, Japanese Americans used these tools to take political control of Hawaii.

Japanese American Incarceration During World War II

The largest act of discrimination by the United States government against any Asian American group occurred against Japanese Americans during World War II. Japanese American agricultural productivity was perceived as an economic threat to European American farmers in California and provided much of the impetus for the incarceration of 120,000 Japanese Americans in United States internment camps during World War II.

Two-thirds of the Japanese Americans who were incarcerated were United States citizens. The official reason for Japanese American wartime internment was that they were a threat to national security. However, no acts of sabotage against the United States by Japanese Americans were committed before or during World War II (Nakanishi, 1988). Even military leaders debated over the actual threat that Japanese Americans posed to national security (Commission on Wartime Relocation and Internment of Civilians, 1982). All Japanese American on the West Coast of the United States were incarcerated, whereas very few Japanese Americans in Hawaii were similarly incarcerated, nor were Japanese Americans who lived in other parts of the United States. Moreover, the United States was also at war with Germany and Italy, but there were not mass incarcerations of German and Italian Americans. Another irony is that Japanese American men were recruited from the internment camps to serve in the United States military in Europe and the Pacific. Somehow these men's parents and younger siblings constituted a threat to the national security, but they did not.

It took 35 years for the United States government to apologize to the incarcerated Japanese Americans (Spickard, 2007). In 1988, the U.S. government enacted redress legislation to provide $20,000 to each camp survivor or the children of those who died. Twenty thousand dollars is a token sum, considering the traumas that Japanese Americans endured in the areas of education, employment, and health. In 2008, colleges and universities in Oregon and Washington state made symbolic efforts to recognize how the internment interrupted the education of internees by awarding honorary degrees to their former students who were removed from college because of the internment. However, many of the former internees had died before these degrees were awarded.

Repeal of Immigration Restrictions

In 1943, Congress repealed the Chinese Exclusion Act because China had become a U.S. ally (Takaki, 1993). This allowed 105 Chinese persons to immigrate annually to the United States. Many of these Chinese immigrants were women, which resulted in a population of American-born Chinese. Chinese wives of Chinese American soldiers were allowed to come to the United States via war brides acts, which were intended to allow American soldiers to bring home women they had married abroad during World War II (Spickard, 2007). Chinese students and professionals who were in the United States after the 1949 Communist Revolution in China and did not wish to return were also permitted to remain in the United States because of refugee status.

Immigration opportunities were opened for Filipinos and Asian Indians in 1946 in separate congressional acts that allowed the annual immigration of 100 persons from each group (Fong, 1998). The legislation also allowed Filipinos and Asian Indians to apply for United States citizenship. However, it was not until the Immigration and Naturalization Act of 1965 that Asians were again allowed to immigrate in large numbers to the United States.

During and following the Korean War in the early 1950s and through 1964, Korean and Japanese women immigrated to the United States as wives of American soldiers. Orphaned Korean children were also part of this wave of immigration. Asian immigrants for the first time became eligible for U.S. citizenship in 1952 with the passage of the McCarran-Walter Act (Nishi, 1995). Exposure to Americans during the Korean War caused over 27,000 Koreans to come to the United States between 1950 and 1964 as nonimmigrant students (Min, 1995). During the 1970s and 1980s, over 3,000 Korean orphans were adopted by U.S. citizens per year (Min, 1995). This wave of adoptions ended, in part, because of negative world publicity during the 1988 Seoul Olympics about Koreans not caring for their own orphans.

The Immigration Act of 1965 repealed the restrictions of the 1924 Asian Exclusion Act. Immigrants from all countries were allowed into the United States if they had valuable occupational skills, were being reunified with family members, or were vulnerable to political or religious persecution. A quota of 20,000 immigrants per country was established.

Southeast Asian Immigration

Following the Vietnam War in 1975, refugees began emigrating from Southeast Asia. These Southeast Asians had become refugees because of the political conflicts that had resulted from United States political and military involvement in Southeast Asia. Many of the first-wave immigrants were Vietnamese, educated, and spoke English (Nishio & Bilmes, 1987). This group included Vietnam government and military personnel (Fong, 1998). The 1975 Indochinese Resettlement Assistance Act was passed by Congress to assist these refugees. The immigration of this initial wave of Southeast Asians was relatively smooth and complete by the time the Resettlement Assistance Act expired in 1977.

After the Immigration Act of 1965, many Asian professionals immigrated to the United States. However, the flow of Asian professional immigrants was severely restricted by the Eilberg Act and the Health Professions Assistance Act in 1976 (Min, 1995). These acts eliminated valuable occupational status as an eligibility criterion for immigration. Thus, a large portion of the Asian immigrants since 1976 has been family members of persons already in the United States and refugees.

From 1979 to 1984, Vietnamese, Cambodian, Laotian, and Hmong refugees settled across the United States. Many were involuntary immigrants because they had become refugees in their own countries for assisting the United States, war effort. These groups had been evacuated from their homes, placed in "reeducation camps," forced to labor in rural regions, attacked with bombs and chemical weapons, had family members executed, and forced to flee to refugee camps in Thailand. At least half of these refugees experienced post-traumatic stress (Sack & Clarke, 1996). Hundreds of thousands of refugees attempted to escape in boats on the South China Sea, with at least 100,000 drowning in these escape attempts (Rumbaut, 1995). Immigrants in this second wave were primarily rural, of lower socioeconomic status, and unable to speak English (Nishio & Bilmes, 1987). The 1980 Refugee Act allowed 50,000 refugees to enter the United States annually and initially provided 36 months of assistance, after which time the refugees could become eligible for welfare benefits. The length of assistance was reduced to only 18 months in 1981.

Recent Immigration

Over a half million Koreans came to the United States between 1970 and 1990 (Min, 1995). The Korean American community has been highly cohesive because of language barriers and because many immigrants are immersed in the Korean American community, including Korean Christian churches and businesses. Most Korean Americans are either self-employed or work for Korean companies (Min, 1995). Korean businessmen have been described as a middleman minority, which distributes products produced by the group in power to the masses (Min, 1995). Following the not guilty verdict in 1992 involving the White police officers who assaulted Rodney King in Los Angeles, the media focused on African Americans vandalizing and destroying Korean businesses. However, the media coverage of these riots has been perceived by Korean Americans as an attempt by the media to shift public attention from African American–European American conflicts, which were likely the primary source of dissatisfaction in the African American community. Less than half of the property damage during these incidents involved Korean American businesses (Spickard, 2007). Moreover, there were more Latino Americans among the 12,000 arrested than African Americans (Gonzalez, 2000).

Korean Americans have described those who were born in Korea but came to the United States with their families as young children as the 1.5 generation (Spickard, 2007). They are more likely to speak the Korean language better and are usually more identified with Korean culture than Korean Americans born in the United States However, 1.5 generation Korean Americans are able to speak English and are acculturated to Western traditions as well, which makes them similar to Korean Americans born in the United States. All immigrant groups have similar individuals who immigrated as children, but Korean Americans have coined the 1.5 generation term for themselves (Spickard, 2007).

The Asian Pacific American population has continued to change during the past two decades. Since 1971, Filipinos have been the largest group of Asian Pacific immigrants to the United States and will be the largest group of Asian Pacific Americans within 30 years. The United States has been particularly attractive to Filipinos because of cultural influences during American colonization and because of intermarriage of Filipinos and U.S. military personnel (Agabayani-Siewert & Revilla, 1995). Many nurses were trained in the Philippines during the Vietnam War to serve the U.S. troops who were hosted there. The United States experienced a shortage of nurses, and in 1989 Congress passed the Immigration Nursing Relief Act, which attracted many nurses to the United States from the Philippines, where there was a surplus of nurses after the Vietnam War (Spickard, 2007).

Since 1965, approximately 1 million South Asians, from India, Pakistan, Bangladesh, Sri Lanka, Nepal, Bhutan, and Sikkim, have immigrated to the United States Many of these immigrants have been well educated and have had the occupational skills that were desirable in the 1965 Immigration Act (Spickard, 2007). Their economic resources allowed them to travel to South Asia and maintain contact with their families, unlike other Asian immigrants who seldom were able to return to their ancestral homelands. Other South Asian immigrants who were less educated became motel operators, convenience store managers, and cab drivers, among other occupations.

Asian American Identity and Civil Rights

Asian American identity began to galvanize in the late 1960s, particularly on the West Coast, in the context of the civil rights movement. The Asian American movement demanded civil and political rights for Asian Americans, created pressure for universities to begin Asian American studies programs, and helped established community services for disadvantaged and poor Asian Pacific Americans (Fong, 1998). The movement was pan-Asian, including Asian Pacific Americans of all ethnic groups. Asian American activists recognized the similarities of their own concerns to those of other ethnic minority groups and the power in uniting with these groups in common struggles. One of the major events of the movement was the Third World Strike in 1968–1969, which shut down San Francisco State College for 5 months. This strike resulted in the establishment of the first School of ethnic studies, which included Asian American studies. Permanent Asian American studies programs were also established at major universities in California, including UCLA and the University of California at Berkeley, and at the University of Washington. Asian American student groups were also formed at universities in other parts of the country, and Asian American studies programs were established in response to student initiatives.

Coinciding with the civil rights movement in the late 1960s was the perpetration of the myth of Asian Americans as a "model minority." Critics of affirmative action argued that Asian Americans had become successful in society without the benefit of affirmative action, so why couldn't other minority groups succeed as well without affirmative action? This argument ignored the centuries of oppression in the United States faced by non-Asian groups that has placed them at a competitive disadvantage in society, as well as discrimination against Asian Americans. Although Asian Americans may be regarded as competent, they are also regarded as unsociable and threatening to the opportunities of other groups, which may exclude them from full acceptance and participation in mainstream U.S. culture (Lin, Kwan, Cheung, & Fiske, 2005; Maddux, Galinsky, Cuddy, & Polifroni, 2008).

The Asian American Psychological Association (AAPA) was founded in 1972 by a group of Asian American psychologists in the San Francisco Bay area (Leong & Okazaki, in press). AAPA was formed to exchange ideas and to provide social support, and the emphasis has been on education and training of psychologists and improving mental health services for Asian Americans. Derald Wing Sue served as the AAPA's first president, and the association has grown from 185 members in 1979 to over 500 currently. AAPA has an annual professional convention and has recently relaunched a professional journal.

Asian Americans from many ethnic backgrounds became united following the murder of a Chinese American man, Vincent Chin, in 1982. Chin was murdered by two White autoworkers because they were angry at the competition of the Japanese auto industry and mistook him for being Japanese. The two men were convicted of relatively minor offense, and neither served jail time (Spickard, 2007). This is yet another example of a failure to distinguish Asian Americans from Asians, let alone a failure to distinguish within Asian American ethnic groups.

Such a failure to distinguish Asian Americans from Asians appears to be the basis of the U.S. government's handling of Wen Ho Lee. Lee was a scientist who came to the United States in the 1960s, earned a PhD at Texas A&M University, and became a naturalized citizen (Spickard, 2007). In the 1990s, the Los Alamos National Laboratory, where Lee worked as a physicist, came under criticism for lax security because other countries, including China, were making advances in weapons technology that were presumed to be based on stolen information. Lee became a suspect in 1996 because he had met some Chinese scientists and also probably was a suspect because of his Chinese ancestry. Based on a 1999 *New York Times* story that indicated that Lee was probably a spy, although the story did not name him, the Los Alamos Laboratory fired Lee (Spickard, 2007). The Justice Department subsequently indicted Lee on 59 counts of sharing bomb secrets with a foreign country. Lee was placed in solitary confinement for 278 days, during which time it was unknown how long he would spend in prison. Asian Americans and scientists criticized the government's mistreatment of Lee. The government ultimately dismissed all but one count of mishandling classified information, to which Lee pled guilty, and he was released from prison. Lee had downloaded to his home computer information that was not classified at the time, to work on it at home, something his colleagues commonly did (Spickard, 2007). Thus, it appears that Lee became the scapegoat for the Los Alamos Laboratory, in part because of his Chinese ancestry.

CULTURAL VALUES AND IDENTITY

Do most Asian Americans even think of themselves as Asian Americans, or do they not think of themselves in terms of culture and ethnicity? It could be argued that Asian Americans' relative amount of success in North American society means that they have assimilated and do not have a distinctive culture or identity that sets them apart from other Americans. Nevertheless, Asian Americans perceive themselves in terms of their ethnicity in social situations whether they are in the majority or the minority (Kim-Ju & Liem, 2003). Conversely, European Americans perceive themselves in terms of their ethnicity only in situations in which they are the minority, which is unusual. Thus, Asian Americans do perceive themselves in terms of their ethnicity.

B. S. K. Kim, Atkinson, & Yang (1999) identified six Asian cultural value dimensions: collectivism, conformity to norms, emotional self-control, family recognition through achievement, filial piety, and humility. These values are derived from East Asian cultures but also apply to varying degrees to other Asian cultures. Collectivism involves thinking of one's group and its needs before oneself and viewing individual achievement as the family's achievement. Conformity to norms involves conforming to family and gender social role expectations, concern about bringing disgrace to one's family reputation, and reciprocating others' gifts. Emotional self-control involves controlling and not expressing emotions. Family recognition through achievement is achieving academically and not bringing shame to one's family via failure. Filial piety involves respect for elders and an obligation to care for one's parents when they are unable to care for themselves. Humility involves modesty and not being boastful.

Because social roles are important in Asian American cultures, gender role stereotyping might be expected. Certain emotions and behaviors might be perceived as appropriate for one gender but not for the other. Indeed, Asian American men and women have been found to stereotype women as experiencing more disgust, distress, embarrassment, fear, guilt, love, sadness, shame, surprise, and sympathy than men, and men as experiencing more anger than women (Durik et al., 2006). Nevertheless, gender stereotypes of women and men on these emotions and behaviors were even more pronounced among European American men and women than among Asian Americans. Thus, gender role stereotyping does not appear to be greater among Asian Americans than among European Americans. It is possible that Asian Americans' value of collectivism influences them to perceive men and women as more similar than European Americans do, whereas European Americans' more individualist views may influence them to perceive men and women as more disconnected (Durik et al., 2006). However, collectivism and individualism were not assessed in the study, so it is unknown how collectivism and individualism influence gender role stereotyping.

There is much cultural variation among Asian American groups. Although Japanese Americans have been in the United States for multiple generations, their values tend to be more traditionally Asian than other Asian American groups (B. S. K. Kim, Yang, Atkinson, Wolfe, & Hong 2001). This may be because the Japanese culture that Japanese Americans are maintaining is the culture of Japan a century ago when their ancestors immigrated to the United States, which was more traditional than the contemporary Asian cultures that current Asian immigrants are from. In contrast, Filipino Americans tend to be less traditionally Asian than Asian Americans whose ancestors are from East Asia. This difference may be a result of Spanish influences on Filipino culture. Nevertheless, the cultural values of East Asian Americans and Filipino Americans are more traditionally Asian than are the values of European Americans.

Generation is the United States (i.e., immigrants are first generation, their children are second generation, their children are third generation) is sometimes used as a proxy for *acculturation,* with the assumption that those born outside the United States are more culturally traditional than those born in the United States. However, in a study of California college students, there were few differences between Asian-born and U.S.-born Asians on measures of interdependence and independence, and the differences that were found were small and sometimes counterintuitive (Abe-Kim, Okazaki, & Goto, 2001). For example, Asian-born Asians were more self-reliant (vs. interdependent) than were U.S.-born Asians. Thus, it cannot be assumed that Asian Americans born in the United States are less culturally traditional than those born outside the United States.

Acculturation is not necessarily a linear process, where a person acculturates to the United States and leaves his or her culture of origin behind. A bilinear or multilinear process can occur in which a person adheres to more than one culture (Miller, 2007). Adherence to one's culture of origin (e.g., Japanese culture) is known as *enculturation.* As discussed in Chapter 1, a bicultural orientation is considered optimally adaptive (LaFromboise, Coleman, & Gerton, 1993).

Moreover, even though overt traditional behaviors may diminish, such as using an Asian language, eating Asian foods, and associating with other Asian Americans, adherence to traditional values (e.g., emotional self-control, filial piety) may not.

Some Asian values may be more susceptible to acculturation than others. Second-generation Chinese Americans were less extroverted and more serious than European Americans at age 12 and also 5 years later (Huntsinger & Jose, 2006). Low extroversion and seriousness are consistent with Asian values of emotional restraint. However, Chinese Americans increased in dominance and excitability such that they did not differ from European Americans on these characteristics by age 17. Dominance, which involves asserting personal goals over those of others, and excitability, which involves emotional expression, are individualistic characteristics. Thus, Chinese Americans acculturated on these dimensions to European American norms during adolescence.

Although Asian Americans may adhere to some Asian traditions, they are Americans by virtue of birth or citizenship, or adherence to American values if they are not citizens. However, despite being in the United States for multiple generations and, in some cases, two centuries, Asian Americans are still viewed by some as foreigners. "Where are you from?" is a question that Asian Americans are commonly asked. In a study of college students in California, where most Asian Americans in the study were born in the United States, more than one-third of Asian Americans were mistaken as being from another country or being a non-English native speaker, versus 21% of Latino/a Americans, 10% of African Americans, and only 7% of European Americans (Cheryan & Monin, 2005). Asian American faces were also rated by European Americans as less American than European American faces. Such situations in which a person is not recognized as a member of the ingroup in known as *identity denial*.

A reaction to identity denial may be *identity assertion,* in which an individual or group attempts to prove that he or she it belongs (Cheryan & Monin, 2005). For example, an Asian American might assert his or her American identity via involvement in American sports or music or having non–Asian American friends. When I was living in the Midwest, I was occasionally asked about current events in Japan by non-Asians, as if I had some special knowledge of the country where my grandparents came from during the early part of the 20th century. I prided myself on not knowing about Japan and asked my friends why they didn't know about their ancestors' countries of origin, such as England or Germany. My lack of knowledge about Japan was an attempt to prove that I knew as little about my ancestral origins as other Americans did. Since that time, however, I have traveled to Japan, adopted two children from Japan, and taken introductory Japanese language courses. I have come to terms with my Japanese roots, but I have done this in the context of Japanese American culture, which is an integration of early 20th-century Japanese culture and early 21st-century American culture. My Japanese American culture offers little in terms of inherent expertise in 21st-century Japanese culture.

In summary, Asian Americans think of themselves in terms of their ethnicities and share cultural characteristics that distinguish them from other ethnic groups. Nevertheless, there is much diversity among Asian groups in terms of cultural characteristics. Generation in the United States is not necessarily associated with acculturation. Acculturation also is not necessarily a linear process, in which a person moves from one culture to another. A person may acculturate to one culture while maintaining ties to one or more others. Some cultural values may be more susceptible to acculturation (e.g., dominance) than others (e.g., emotional restraint). Asian Americans often experience identity denial, in which they are assumed not to be Americans. One response to identity denial is identity assertion, in which Asian Americans attempt to prove that they are Americans.

FAMILY ISSUES

Cultural value differences between Asian Americans and European Americans may influence perceptions of parenting. Individualistic self-enhancement motives may dispose European Americans to perceive themselves as successful parents, to attribute their children's successes to their own parenting abilities, and to not attribute their children's failures to their own parenting abilities (Bornstein & Cote, 2004). Conversely, collectivist motives to fulfill one's role may dispose persons of Asian ancestry to perceive successful parenting as a result of effort rather than of abilities. Values of modesty would prevent Asian American parents from taking credit for their children's successes, and concerns about loss of face would dispose them to take responsibility for their children's failure, as children's failure might be perceived as a lack of parenting effort. Consistent with individualist and collectivist motives, European American parents engaged in greater levels of self-enhancing cognitions regarding their parenting abilities and their children's successes and failures than did Japanese or Japanese immigrant parents (Bornstein & Cote, 2004; Figure 7.2). Japanese immigrant parents were in between Japanese and European American parents on self-enhancement, which suggest that Japanese immigrant parents had acculturated somewhat toward European American norms.

Intergenerational Cultural Gaps

Asian immigrant parents may begin to acculturate to European American values, but they still tend to adhere to traditional Asian values more than their children do. Such a gap in cultural values often results in parent-child conflicts. In one study, a perceived cultural gap among Chinese American immigrant parents of preadolescent children was associated with poor parent-child communication, uncertainty about how to parent, and dissatisfaction with children (Buki, Ma, Strom, & Strom, 2003). Among Chinese Canadian children, those who adhered to Chinese culture less than their parents were more likely to experience intense conflicts with their parents, greater depressive symptoms, and less achievement motivation than those whose adherence to Chinese culture was similar to that of their parents (Costigan & Dokis, 2006).

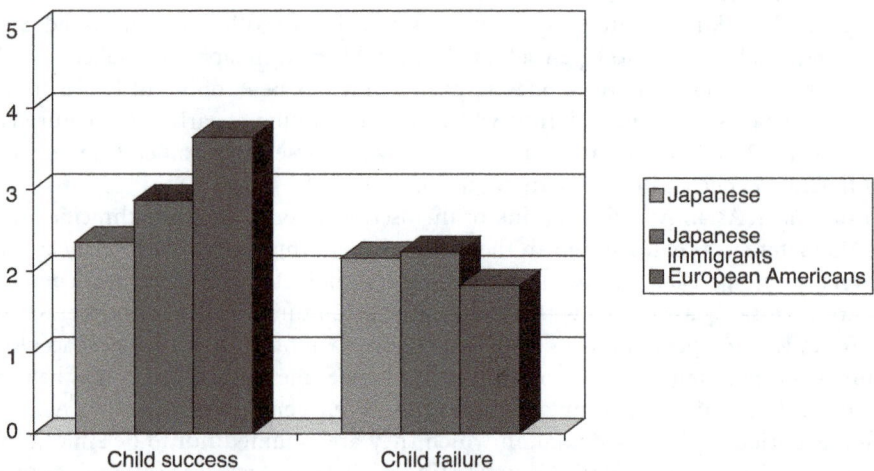

FIGURE 7.2   Children's Performance and Mother's Ability Attributions

Culturally based conflicts often arise over children placing their individual needs above those of the family (Hwang, 2006). Immigrant parents also may have difficulties communicating with their children in English, a language that their children may come to prefer, and children may gradually lose their ability to communicate in their parents' language. Children's acculturation to European American styles of nonverbal communication (e.g., physical display of affection) may cause children to view their parents as emotionally nonexpressive and parents to view their children as lacking emotional control (Hwang, 2006).

Gaps in cultural values between parents and children are not necessarily directly responsible for children's problem behavior. Choi, He, and Harachi (2008) proposed that intergenerational cultural value gaps are problematic particularly when they result in parent-child conflicts. Parent-child conflicts, rather than such cultural values gaps per se, lead to problem behaviors. However, such conflicts may be offset by parent-child bonding even when cultural values gaps exist. Consistent with this model, Vietnamese American and Cambodian American youths' perceptions of intergenerational cultural gaps (e.g., your parents tell you that a social life is not important at this age, but you think it is; your parents don't want to bring shame on the family, but you think they are too concerned with saving face) were associated with their perceptions of conflict with their parents (e.g., my parents never listen to my side of the story, my parents nag me a lot). However, even in the presence of intergenerational cultural gaps and parent-child conflict, children who felt bonded with their parents (e.g., I feel close to my mother or father) were less likely to engage in problem behaviors (e.g., teasing, lying, shoplifting, staying out late) than those who did not feel bonded to their parents (Choi et al., 2008). Thus, an Asian American child's relationship with his or her parents may be a more important predictor of behavior than intergenerational cultural gaps.

Intergenerational conflict may be most likely to occur when parents and children are born in different countries. In a study of Asian American young adults, those whose parents were born in the United States experienced less parental conflict around family expectations (e.g., spending time with family, learning one's own Asian language), education and career issues (e.g., time spent on studying, which school to attend), and dating and marriage (e.g., when to begin dating, whom to marry) than those whose parents were born in Asia (Chung, 2001). Japanese Americans who have been in the United States for multiple generations also experienced less parental conflict around family expectations and dating and marriage than Chinese Americans, Korean Americans, Filipino Americans, and Southeast Asian Americans. Similarly, immigrant Chinese Americans in high school felt closer to parents who were also born in China than did U.S.-born Chinese Americans whose parents were born in China (Chao, 2001).

Because children of immigrants in North America usually are more acculturated than their parents, they often communicate on behalf of the family with the English-speaking world and become culture brokers. This role could be construed as negative in that it creates parental dependence on children (Portes & Rumbaut, 2001). Alternatively, the role could be construed as positive in that the child makes an important contribution to the family (Orellana, Dorner, & Pulido, 2003). Culture brokering may have both negative and positive effects on immigrant families. Among Vietnamese American adolescents, culture brokering was associated with family conflict but also with adolescent input into family decision making (Trickett & Jones, 2007).

Family Obligations

Parental expectations of their children's involvement with their family may influence their children's actual family involvement. In one study, Chinese American high school students from immigrant families had greater respect for the authority of their families and felt more obligated to help their families now and in the future than did European Americans (Hardway & Fuligni, 2006). Similar results were found for Mexican American high school students from immigrant families, which suggests that immigrants may have a stronger sense of family obligation than nonimmigrants.

Might such family obligations limit the amount of time students can study? Fuligni, Yip, and Tseng (2002) found that Chinese American high school students from immigrant families spent approximately the same amount of time on family obligations as they did studying. In that academic achievement is an Asian cultural value, studying might be regarded as part of one's family obligation. However, family obligations did limit the amount of time that students were able to spend with peers.

Are the demands of balancing family obligations, academic responsibilities, and a social life stressful for Asian American youths? The answer apparently is no. Neither family obligations nor efforts to balance family obligations with other activities was associated with distress for Chinese American high school students from immigrant families (Fuligni et al., 2002). It is possible that the sense of identity that Asian American youths derive from family obligations offsets any negative effects of these obligations.

In summary, Asian American parents tend not to be as self-enhancing as European American parents. Parent-child acculturation gaps in Asian American families tend to be problematic only when they result in parent-child conflict, which is likely when parent and child are born in different countries. Conflicts based on acculturation differences may be offset by parent-child bonding. Asian Americans and other immigrants tend to feel obligated toward their families, but such obligations are not associated with distress, possibly because family obligations may create a sense of identity.

MENTAL HEALTH

Normative cultural patterns among Asian Americans may be misinterpreted by others as psychological problems. As discussed in Chapter 2, some Asian Americans may solve problems better silently than by thinking aloud (H. S Kim, 2002). Thus, if the expectation in a classroom is that students must solve problems by discussing them, thinking about problems without discussing them could be perceived as passivity, a lack of confidence, or social withdrawal.

Interdependent behavior, such as concern about not wanting to be the center of attention and trying to blend into a group, could be perceived as social anxiety. In a study of Korean Canadian and European Canadian college students, Korean Canadians were found to express more social anxiety symptoms that European Canadians did (J. J. Hong & Woody, 2007). However, the association between ethnicity and social anxiety symptoms was mediated by independence. Korean Canadians were less independent than European Canadians, but those who were more independent in both ethnic groups were less likely to express social anxiety symptoms. However, a culturally based concern about one's impact in a social situation is not necessarily pathological.

When Asian Americans do experience psychological problems, cultural values may influence the manner in which these problems are expressed. There is a tendency for Asian Americans to express distress more via physical symptoms (e.g., pain, sleep disturbance, headaches) than via emotional expression (Hwang, Myers, Abe-Kim, & Ting, 2008). Such physical expression of distress is consistent with the Asian value of emotional restraint. Even when emotion is expressed among less acculturated Asian Americans, it tends to be in physical terms, such as feeling dizzy (Tsai, Simeonova, & Watanabe, 2004).

Expressing such emotional distress may be perceived as creating burdens for the social support system. Indeed, S. E. Taylor and colleagues (2004) found that Asian Americans were less likely than European Americans to seek social support for distress because Asian Americans tended to be more concerned about the impact of seeking social support on their relationships with others. Thus, an internalized, intrapersonal expression of distress in the form of physical symptoms may be considered an illness that is the responsibility of the individual to cure rather than an interpersonal problem that is the responsibility of the group. Physical symptoms among Asian Americans are not necessarily subsumed within other disorders, such as depression or anxiety. In a community study of Chinese Americans, 78% of those who experienced physical symptoms did not meet the criteria for depression or anxiety (Zheng et al., 1997).

Asian Americans may face psychosocial stress associated with acculturation that results in psychological problems. For immigrants, relocation, adaptation to a new environment (e.g., learning a new language), and loss of social support networks are stressful. Acculturative stress, such as language difficulties, perceptions of a closed society, and a parent-child cultural gap, creates psychological distress above and beyond the effects of general stress (e.g., how uncontrollable, unpredictable, and overloaded one feels; Hwang & Ting, 2008). How acculturated one is to North American society is less critical in predicting psychological distress among Asian Americans than the amount of stress experienced in the acculturation process (Hwang & Ting, 2008).

Risk for psychological distress does not necessarily subside once immigrants are settled in North America. Hwang, Chun, Takeuchi, Myers, & Siddarth (2005) found that length of residence in the United States was positively associated with depression among Chinese Americans. Although it is unclear why more time in the United States was associated with depression, it is possible that the effects of discrimination become increasingly apparent over time as barriers to full participation in American society.

Perceptions of cultural inferiority are also associated with psychological problems. Among Filipino/a Americans, *colonial mentality* involves perceptions of cultural inferiority as a consequence of centuries of colonization of the Philippines by Spain and the United States (David & Okazaki, 2006). Components of colonial mentality include discrimination within Filipino/as (e.g., Americanized vs. less Americanized), denigration of the Filipino/a culture (e.g., embarrassment about Filipino/a traditions) or physical body (e.g., facial features or skin color), and tolerating historical or current discrimination against Filipino/as (e.g., belief that Spanish and U.S. colonization did not damage Filipino/a culture). Colonial mentality has been found to be strongly associated with depression among Filipino/as (David, 2008).

Although there are seemingly positive stereotypes associated with Asian Americans (e.g., intelligent, hardworking, mathematical, self-disciplined), they may experience discrimination because such positive stereotypes can be perceived as a threat to other groups' educational, economic, and political opportunities (Maddux, Galinsky, Cuddy, & Polifroni, 2008). In a national sample of Asian Americans, perceived discrimination was associated with psychological disorders including depression and anxiety (G. C. Gee, Spencer, Chen, Yip, & Takeuchi, 2007). Discrimination, involving unfair treatment based on ethnicity, was found to be a stronger predictor of psychological disorders than either acculturative stress or time spent in the United States. Subtle discrimination, such as being treated unfairly, being refused services, and being ignored because of one's ethnicity, has been found to be more strongly associated with depression than overt discrimination, such as being hit, insulted, or threatened because of one's ethnicity, among Korean immigrants in Canada (Noh, Kaspar, & Wickrama, 2007).

Does ethnic identity offset the effects of discrimination for Asian Americans? The protective effects of ethnic identity appear to depend on Asian Americans' age group (Yip, Gee, & Takeuchi, 2007). Whereas ethnic identity buffered the association between discrimination and mental health among U.S.-born Asian Americans aged 41 to 50 years, it actually exacerbated the negative effects of discrimination on mental health among U.S.-born Asian Americans aged 31 to 40 and 51 to 75 years of age. It is possible that persons in middle age cope better with discrimination than those that are younger or older, but the reasons for the age-related effects of ethnic identity on the relationship between discrimination and mental health are unclear.

In summary, normative Asian American behavior, such as emotional restraint and concern about blending into social groups, could be construed by non-Asians as pathological. When Asian Americans experience psychological distress, they tend to express it in physical symptoms and tend not to seek help out of concerns about burdening others. Stress associated with acculturation or discrimination influences psychological problems beyond the effects of general stress. Perceptions of cultural inferiority are strongly associated with depression. Ethnic identity appears to buffer the effects of discrimination for middle-aged Asian Americans but not for Asian Americans of other ages.

ACADEMIC ACHIEVEMENT AND CAREER DEVELOPMENT

School achievement and other desired behaviors are accomplished in Asian American families via training, in which hard work, self-discipline, and obedience are emphasized (Chao, 1994). This training model is similar to what European American models characterize as *authoritarian* parenting (Baumrind, 1991). Conversely, the most desirable style of parenting in European American models is *authoritative*, in which parents emphasize both control and warmth (Baumrind, 1991). Authoritative parents reason with their children, explain why they do what they do, and are firm but understanding.

In a study of high school students, authoritative parenting was positively associated with parent-youth closeness, youth effort in school, and youth grades, whereas authoritarian parenting was negatively associated with these characteristics among European Americans (Chao, 2001). Closeness and effort were also associated with grades among European Americans. In contrast, among immigrant Chinese Americans, neither authoritative nor authoritarian parenting was associated with effort or grades, although authoritative parenting was associated with parent-youth closeness. Only effort in school was associated with grades among immigrant Chinese Americans. Second-generation Chinese Americans were between immigrant Chinese Americans and European Americans. Thus, a particular style of parenting is not necessarily most desirable or effective among Chinese Americans, particularly those who are immigrants.

However, grades certainly are not the only criterion for parenting success or even academic success. There are both cultural and practical reasons for Asian Americans to excel academically. As discussed above, academic achievement is valued among many Asian Americans as a means of family recognition. For many immigrants, education in North America also is the route to economic and social mobility. Opportunities for education are often more available to the children of adult immigrants than to the adult immigrants themselves because of language barriers and available time to devote to education. Thus, many adult immigrants may value and emphasize education for their children (Tseng, 2006). Immigrant Chinese Americans had higher grades than U.S.-born Chinese Americans, who had higher grades than European Americans, in the Chao (2001) study.

Stereotypes of Asian Americans are that they have special aptitudes for math and science. First- and second-generation Asian American high school and college students are indeed more likely than European American students to choose math and science courses (Tseng, 2006). However, math and science are less dependent on English language skills than other areas of study. First- and second-generation Asian American students have been found to have lower English skills than European Americans on standardized tests and also perceive themselves to have lower English skills than European Americans (Tseng, 2006). Moreover, Asian American students may choose math and science careers not because of a particular aptitude in these areas but because careers in these areas have been more available to Asian Americans than careers in other areas (S. Sue & Okazaki, 1990).

As in academic contexts, there are seemingly positive stereotypes of Asian Americans in career contexts. Fictitious job applicants with Asian names are rated as highly qualified for high-status jobs, regardless of their qualifications (King, Madera, Hebl, Knight, & Mendoza, 2006). Nevertheless, not all Asian Americans benefit from such positive stereotypes. Asian Americans who are most acculturated to U.S. norms are most satisfied in their occupations, receive the most positive supervisor ratings, and experience the least occupational stress (Leong, 2001). In that about two-thirds of Asian Americans are immigrants and many are relatively unacculturated, it is probable that the majority of Asian Americans are not wholly accepted or valued in work settings and may experience job-related dissatisfaction and stress.

In summary, a parenting style in which hard work, self-discipline, and obedience are emphasized is emphasized is characteristic of many Asian Americans. Immigrants are particularly likely to view academic excellence as a route to success. Language issues and career opportunities may influence Asian Americans' decisions to pursue math and science in school. Although Asian Americans may be perceived as qualified for high-status jobs, acculturated Asian Americans fare better than unacculturated Asian Americans in the workplace.

Conclusion

Many Asian Americans have a strong ethnic identity and cultural value system. Acculturation to Western norms does not necessarily mean losing or rejecting Asian cultural traditions. Most Asian Americans are immigrants, but those who have been in the United States for several generations may not be fully accepted as Americans. Acculturative gaps between parents and children sometimes create conflicts. Acculturative stress, perceptions of cultural inferiority, and discrimination are associated with psychological problems among Asian Americans. Academic excellence among Asian Americans may be associated with cultural values and limited opportunities in non-academic areas.

Most of what is known in psychology about Asian Pacific Americans is based on persons of East Asian ancestry. Although there is an emerging literature on Southeast Asian and South Asian Americans, there is limited work on Pacific Islander Americans. More research is needed on the cultural diversity among various Asian American groups, as well as within particular Asian American groups on the influence on behavior of dimensions such as cultural values, acculturation, and discrimination.

Discussion Questions

1. Of all immigrant groups to the United States, Asian Americans are most likely to be mistaken as being from another country. Although nearly two-thirds of Asian Americans are from other countries, many are from families who have been in the United States for a century or more. Despite the ability to speak English without

an accent, Asian Americans whose families have been in this country for several generations are still often asked, "where are you from?" Is there something inherent about Asian Americans that makes other Americans perceive them as foreigners? What would need to take place for Asian Americans to be perceived as American as other Americans?

2. Asian values, such as humility and family obligation, seem to be at odds with mainstream American values, which are relatively competitive and individualistic. Yet, Asian American students having these values tend to have academic achievements that exceed those of other groups. Might Asian values enhance the academic performance of non-Asian groups?

3. Although there are positive stereotypes of Asian Americans, such as being intelligent, hardworking, mathematical, and self-disciplined, these characteristics could be perceived as threatening by other groups. Of course, these are stereotypes and not characteristic of all Asian Americans. Nevertheless, if a group about which there are positive stereotypes has difficulty gaining acceptance into mainstream American society, can any group of color ever be fully accepted into American society?

CHAPTER 8

Latino/a Americans

"Things don't change, you change the way of looking, that's all."

—Carlos Castañeda

What is the appropriate term to refer to the largest group of color in the United States? The search for a term for ethnic self-designation empowers ethnic groups and involves a rejection of colonization (Comas-Diaz, 2001). The terms *Hispanic* and *Latino* are political terms used within a U.S. context (Bernal & Enchautegui-de-Jesus, 1994). *Hispanic* is an English term and refers to persons having Spanish ancestry, including those from Puerto Rico, Cuba, Central and South America, and Spain. The federal government began to use the term *Hispanic* in the 1970s for census and federal program purposes (Bernal & Enchautegui-de-Jesus, 1994).

Latino/a refers to Latin American origins. The term *Latino* is masculine while *Latina* is feminine. Those who prefer the term *Latino/a* may disidentify with Spain and the term *Hispanic* because of the associations of the latter with colonization (Comas-Diaz, 2001). Some Mexican Americans prefer the term *Chicano/a*. Chicano/as view themselves as outsiders to both mainstream U.S. and Mexican cultures (Falicov, 1998). Those Latino/a Americans who have a pan-ethnic Latino/a American identity tend to be female, more educated, born in the United States, involved in politics, and to perceive discrimination (Masuoka, 2006). Because of Spanish influences, most Latino/as speak Spanish. About 70% of Latino/as are Roman Catholics (Perl, Greely, & Gray, 2006), although the number of practicing Latino/a Catholics may be decreasing.

Latino/a Americans can be from any racial group. There are large groups of Latino/as having African ancestry, as well as large groups having European ancestry. Many Latino/as are racially mixed. Those having Spanish and Indian ancestry are known as *mestizos*. Those with Spanish and African ancestry as known as *mulattos*, although this term is derogatory. However, race may be a problematic concept for many Latino/a Americans, as two-thirds of a national sample of Latino/a American adolescents chose No Race or Other rather than White, Black, Asian, or Native American to describe themselves (Kao & Vaquera, 2006). Ethnicity may be a more useful basis of identity, as Cuban Americans, Mexican Americans, and Puerto Rican Americans identify more with their particular Latino/a American ethnic group than Latino/a Americans as a whole (Huddy & Virtanen, 1995). Moreover, Latino/a American adolescents tend to form close

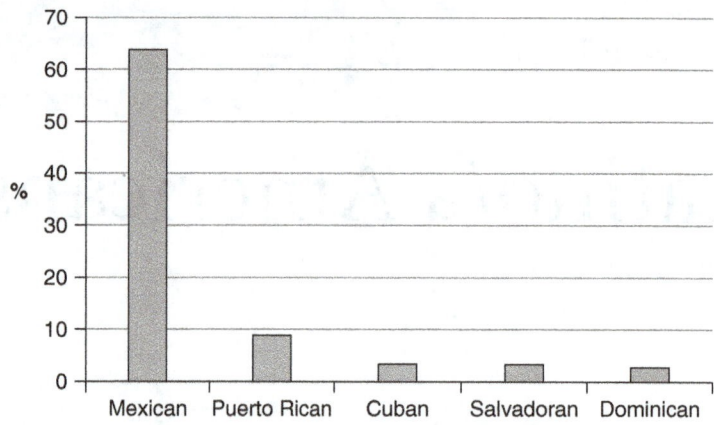

FIGURE 8.1 Percentage of Americans of Latin American Ancestry

friendships on the basis of ethnicity (i.e., Mexican, Chicano, Puerto Rican, Cuban, Central or South American, other Hispanic; Kao & Vaquera, 2006).

Latino/a Americans are over 13% of the U.S. population at over 40 million persons (U.S. Bureau of the Census, June 2004). Forty percent were born in Latin America. Since 2000, Latino Americans have been the fastest growing ethnic minority in the United States. People of Mexican origin are the largest group of the Latino/a Americans, representing 59 percent of the nation's total Latino/a American population (S. Chun, 2007). Percentages of all Latino/a groups are presented in Figure 8.1.

The population of Latino Americans is relatively young. In 2004, the median age was 26.7 years, the lowest of all ethnic groups (U.S. Bureau of the Census, June 2004) and about 9 years younger than the total population (U.S. Bureau of the Census, December 2004b). Over half of Mexican, Cuban, Central American, South American, and other Latino households were married-couple families, while less than half (42%) of Puerto Rican households reported the same.

In 2000, Latino Americans reported less educational attainment than the national population (U.S. Bureau of the Census, December 2004b). Fifty-two percent of Latino Americans had at least a high school diploma, and 10% had at least a bachelor's degree or higher, compared to 80% and 52%, respectively, for the total population. Of Latino Americans, South Americans reported the highest proportions of those with at least a high school diploma (77% and 76%, respectively), while Mexicans and Central Americans reported the lowest (about 46% each).

The median family income for Latino Americans was $34,400, which was lower than the median family income for all families ($50,000). In general, 23% of Latino Americans were in poverty, compared to 12% for the national population.

HISTORY

Highly developed cultures, with achievements in agriculture, textiles, and medical practices, existed in the regions that are now Central and South America long before the Spanish arrived there (Comas-Diaz, Lykes, & Alarcon, 1998). The Mayan, Incan, and Aztec empires were part of these cultures. Much of Central and South America was conquered by the Spanish in the late 15th and early 16th centuries. The Spanish also conquered the indigenous peoples of what are now New Mexico, Texas, and California in the 1500s.

Mexican Americans

Spanish missions were established throughout what is now California beginning in 1769. Mexican settlers, most of whom were poor, came to live and work at these missions. By 1821 there were 3,000 Mexicans in California (Takaki, 1993). European American settlers were initially welcomed by the Mexicans, although tensions developed between the groups. The Mexicans were viewed by the European Americans as idle and thriftless, while the Mexicans viewed the European Americans as having a sense of entitlement to the land (Takaki, 1993).

Mexico became independent from Spain in 1821 and began to encourage immigrants (Spickard, 2007). By 1836, the majority of the region of Mexico that is now Texas was European American. European Americans in Texas battled the Mexican army and proclaimed independence after capturing Mexican president Santa Ana. The Texas Republic applied for admission to the United States as a state but was initially denied because of the practice of slavery (Spickard, 2007).

The Mexican-American War, led by European American Texans, began in 1846 to gain the Southwest for the United States. Robbery, murder, and rape of Mexicans were common during the war (Takaki, 1993). In 1848, the Treaty of Guadalupe Hidalgo ceded Texas, California, New Mexico, Nevada, parts of Colorado, Arizona, and Utah to the United States. Mexico lost 45% of its national territory and over 100,000 of its people (Bernal & Enchautegui-de-Jesus, 1994). The treaty promised citizenship, freedom of religion and language, and maintenance of lands (Garcia-Preto, 1996a). However, similar to the many treaties between the U.S. government and American Indians, Mexicans in the United States were oppressed by these supposed agreements. The English language, U.S. laws and courts, and U.S. food and dress were imposed on these Mexicans, and lynching of Mexicans occurred (Spickard, 2007). Mexican landowners lost their land when it was determined by the U.S. government in 1851 that land grants under former Spanish and Mexican rule were no longer valid (Takaki, 1993). Those who did not lose their land by legal rulings often lost it because of an inability to pay high taxes.

The gold rush in 1849 resulted in a huge influx of European Americans to California. Before 1849, Mexicans outnumbered European Americans by 10 to 1 in California (Takaki, 1993). This situation was reversed in 1849, by which time there were 100,000 European Americans and 13,000 Mexicans in California. Although European Americans learned gold mining methods from Mexicans, foreign miners' taxes were imposed on Mexican miners, including U.S. citizens of Mexican ancestry. The tax was intended for anyone who was not White, as it was not levied against Europeans who were not U.S. citizens (Spickard, 2007).

Many Mexicans migrated to the United States during the early 1900s for better opportunities. The available work planting cotton, on railroads, and in mining was menial and often dangerous. Mexicans were a cheap source of labor, as they were paid less than European Americans for the same work (Takaki, 1993). Many Mexicans were migrant laborers, performing strenuous work alongside their families, including small children, and living in shacks or tents with no plumbing or running water (Spickard, 2007).

Mexican laborers organized strikes in California in the early 1900s. In 1903, Japanese and Mexicans formed the Japanese-Mexican Labor Association, which successfully orchestrated a strike in Oxnard, California, that forced a pay raise. This labor association attempted to join the American Federation of Labor (AFL) but decided not to when the AFL would not accept Japanese members (Takaki, 1993). Anti-Asian immigration laws later caused European American farmers to rely on Mexican labor.

Mexicans in California faced segregated public buildings, and their children were educated in segregated schools (Takaki, 1993). American teachers taught Mexican children to be obedient so that they could eventually replace their parents as workers. Mexican children were taught domestic skills and manual labor skills in school.

Mexicans began to be perceived as a source of competition for jobs during the Depression in the 1930s. Approximately 300,000 Mexicans were "repatriated" or deported on trains and dropped off at the Mexican border during the early 1930s (Bernal & Enchautegui-de-Jesus, 1994). Many were children who were born in the United States, which made them American citizens. However, the rights of American citizenship have been suspended for ethnic minority groups during other times of perceived national emergency, such as when over 120,000 Japanese Americans were later incarcerated during World War II.

During World War II, a farm labor shortage in the United States occurred because of involvement in the war effort (Bernal & Enchautegui-de-Jesus, 1994). The United States and Mexico issued Mexicans temporary permits to work in the United States. These temporary workers were known as *braceros*, who worked 10-hour days with few breaks, lived in tents or shacks, and had no medical care (Spickard, 2007). Over 5 million *braceros* came to the United States between 1942 and 1964. Mexican immigrants during and following World War II were primarily from rural areas (Bernal & Enchautegui-de-Jesus, 1994).

In 1962, Cesar Chavez, Dolores Huerta, and other Mexican American farmworkers organized the National Farm Workers Association in the San Joaquin Valley of California (Spickard, 2007). They began a strike against grape growers in 1965, which became a national boycott of table grapes. The strike ended in 1970 when better pay and working conditions were negotiated for the farm workers. In 1966, the National Farm Workers merged with a Filipino union and the combined groups eventually became the United Farm Workers of America in 1973. Strikes and boycotts were organized against lettuce and other crops. Chavez adhered to a strict ethic of nonviolence in these strikes (Spickard, 2007).

"Chicano Power" was proclaimed in 1968 by 10,000 students who walked out of classrooms in East Los Angeles in protest over poor educational conditions (Spickard, 2007). This movement was modeled after the antiwar, civil rights, and Black Power movements. These students were also angry about the Vietnam War, in which a disproportionately high number of Mexican Americans served and died.

Latino American psychologists began to unite in the late 1960s, as well. Edward Casavantes founded the Association of Psychologists por la Raza in 1969 (Padilla, in press). Later, in 1980, the National Hispanic Psychological Association was established, which is now known as the National Latino Psychological Association.

The Immigration Reform and Control Act of 1986 punished employers for hiring nondocumented immigrants (Spickard, 2007). However, employers of seasonal agricultural workers were not punished under this act. Moreover, this act provided amnesty for 3 million undocumented immigrants in the United States and allowed a path to citizenship.

In 1994, the United States began to invest in the U.S./Mexico border region following the North American Free Trade Agreement (NAFTA). This agreement caused many Mexicans to leave farming and seek jobs in the northern border region of Mexico and the United States because the reduced agricultural tariffs on U.S. crops, such as corn and wheat, drove the Mexican farmers out of business (Gonzalez, 2000). Mayan peasants in the Chiapas region of Mexico protested NAFTA in the Zapatista revolt. Mexican workers often took construction, crop picking, restaurant, and domestic work in the United States that paid too little for other workers or was too unhealthy, monotonous, or dangerous. Also in 1994, the Clinton administration began Operation Gatekeeper, which involved building steel walls topped by barbed wire at the San Diego–Tijuana, El Paso–Ciudad Juarez, and Brownsville-Matamoros borders, to keep Mexicans out of the United States (Spickard, 2007).

Mexicans who wished to find temporary work in the United States began to rely on *coyotes*, guides who smuggled them into the United States via desert routes (Hernandez, 1996; Spickard, 2007). The trips lasted weeks or months, and the refugees were often taken advantage of by these guides. Many refugees were ultimately captured by immigration officers and deported.

Puerto Rican Americans

Puerto Rico was colonized by Spain in 1493. Its native Taino Indian inhabitants were enslaved and killed (Comas-Diaz et al., 1998). Taino emphases on tranquility, kinship, and group dependence continue to persist in current Puerto Rican culture (Garcia-Preto, 1996b). Spanish influences included language, the Roman Catholic religion, and patriarchy (Garcia-Preto, 1996b). The Spanish brought African slaves, who also contributed language, religion, and medicine, as well as the fatalism of slavery (Garcia-Preto, 1996b). During the Spanish American War in 1898, Puerto Rico, Cuba, Guam, and the Philippines were invaded by the United States (Bernal & Enchautegui-de-Jesus, 1994). Puerto Rico has remained a colony of the United States since then. English was mandated as the official language of instruction in Puerto Rican public schools, although few Puerto Ricans, including teachers, spoke English (Garcia-Preto, 1996b). Congress allowed Puerto Ricans to become U.S. citizens in 1917. Nevertheless, many Americans do not regard Puerto Ricans as citizens (Garcia-Preto, 1996a).

Large numbers of Puerto Ricans emigrated to the northeastern United States in the 1940s and 1950s for economic reasons. Puerto Ricans often took menial, low-paying jobs that no one else wanted (Inclán & Herron, 1998). Available employment often involved domestic labor (e.g., housecleaning) that women were more willing to accept. Thus, women immigrants became more employable than men immigrants, which resulted in a power shift and gender conflicts in many families (Hernandez, 1996). Puerto Rico became a commonwealth in 1952, and Spanish was reinstituted as the language of instruction in public schools (Garcia-Preto, 1996b). Nevertheless, Puerto Rico still often functions as a colony of the United States (Comas-Diaz et al., 1998).

Cuban Americans

Cuba gained its independence from the United States in 1902 but continued to trade with the United States until the revolution in 1959. The revolutionary government created social, economic, and political changes in Cuba, prompting an economic embargo by the United States (Bernal & Enchautegui-de-Jesus, 1994). Political reasons were the motivation for initial waves of Cuban immigrants to the United States between 1959 and 1965. These initial immigrants were predominantly White and upper and middle class (Bernal & Enchautegui-de-Jesus, 1994). They also received over $1 billion in financial assistance from the U. S. government (Spickard, 2007).

The second wave, from 1965 to 1973, included middle-class, lower middle-class, and working-class persons, who were allowed to leave to be united with relatives in the United States. The third wave began in 1980, when Fidel Castro allowed anyone who wanted to leave Cuba to do so via boatlifts at the port of Mariel. This third migration wave included a broader spectrum of persons in terms of race, education, gender, and socioeconomic status (Bernal & Enchautegui-de-Jesus, 1994). This third wave also included a greater percentage (30%) of Afro-Cubans than the earlier waves (Bernal & Shapiro, 1996).

The higher socioeconomic status of the first two waves of Cuban immigrants in combination with federal resources that have not been available for other Latino/a groups has placed Cuban Americans in relatively better standing than other Latino/a groups. Indeed, most Cuban Americans, Mexican Americans, and Puerto Rican Americans perceive Cuban Americans as having the highest status among these Latino/a American groups (Huddy & Virtanen, 1995). Cuban Americans also have the strongest ethnic identity of Latino/a American groups, although most Latino/a Americans are strongly ethnically identified (Guarnaccia et al., 2007). Cuban Americans have been considered by some to be a "model minority," but the same stereotypes and disadvantages of being a model minority for Asian Americans that were discussed in Chapter 7 apply to Cuban Americans.

A fourth wave of Cuban immigration to the United States occurred in the 1990s (Bernal & Shapiro, 1996). Economic hardships became severe with the end of the Soviet Union, which had been sending aid to Cuba, and the United States economic blockade was still in effect. In 1994, thousands of *balseros* attempted to elude coastal police and come to Florida on makeshift rafts. The Cuban government again allowed persons to leave Cuba. The United States and Cuba entered an agreement to allow 20,000 Cubans to legally emigrate each year.

Other Latin Americans

Several waves of immigration to the United States from Latin America have occurred for economic and political reasons. Argentineans and Chileans left their countries for the United States in the 1960s and 1970s because of repressive regimes. Poor economic conditions caused Mexicans from urban areas to come to the United States during the 1970s and 1980s. Political conflicts in Nicaragua, El Salvador, Peru, and Guatemala in the 1980s caused many persons in these countries to leave for the United States. Conflicts have resulted from historic tensions between indigenous peoples and those with Spanish ancestry who have controlled the government. Maoist and Marxist groups have also engaged in guerilla warfare. Many women joined these guerilla efforts and participated in changing national politics, which constituted a shift in gender roles (Hernandez, 1996).

In an effort to oppose communist influence, the United States backed the governments of some Central American countries (Hernandez, 1996). Hundreds of thousands of civilians, including children and youth, have been murdered and indigenous cultures have been destroyed in conflicts involving the United States (Comas-Diaz et al., 1998). Nicaraguans were welcomed in the United States as political refugees of the Sandinistas, who the United States government opposed, whereas Salvadorans and Guatemalans were viewed as emigrating for economic reasons and were often deported (Bernal & Enchautegui-de-Jesus, 1994). Beginning in 1982, the Sanctuary movement, led by more than 200 U.S. churches, provided refuge for Central American refugees (Gonzalez, 2000).

In addition to these political and economic motivations for emigration, Latin American countries have been susceptible to the effects of natural disasters, including floods and earthquakes, which has been an additional motivation for immigration to the United States (Hough, Canino, Abueg, & Gusman, 1996). However, the United States has often not been hospitable to these refugees. In 1994, Proposition 187 in California denied public services to nondocumented immigrants and compelled employers to report undocumented immigrants to immigration officials (Falicov, 1996; Spickard, 2007). Latino/a Americans living in ethnic enclaves are particularly susceptible to investigations and deportation by immigration officials. The 1996 Personal Responsibility and Work Opportunity Act went further than Proposition 187 in that even legal immigrants were not eligible for Supplemental Security Income or food stamps until they became citizens (Spickard, 2007).

Some African Americans may perceive immigration as threatening their job security (Sears, Citrin, Cheleden, & van Laar, 1999). Because many Asian Americans and Latino/a Americans are themselves immigrants, these groups tend to be less likely to perceive immigration as having a negative effect on the economy. Latino/a Americans are more likely than other ethnic groups to support rights for illegal immigrants (e.g., work permits, citizenship for children of illegal immigrants who are born in the United States). Economic threat does not appear to be the reason that European Americans express less support for immigration than Asian Americans and Latino/a Americans do. Prejudice, rather than economic threat, may be the basis of European American opposition to immigration and societal diversity (Bobo, 1999; Sears et al., 1999). The primary economic beneficiaries of immigrant labor are businesses, which can hire workers at substandard wages (Spickard, 2007).

CULTURAL VALUES AND IDENTITY

Similar to African American and Asian American values discussed in previous chapters, Latino/a American values tend to emphasize interdependence. However, there are culture-specific Latino/a American values that differ somewhat from those of African Americans and Asian Americans. Latino/a cultural values that influence behavior include *familismo* (family orientation and commitment), *personalismo* (preference for relationships with individuals rather than with institutions), *respeto* (respecting the role of each member of the family), *confianza* (trust and intimacy in a relationship), *fatalismo* (fatalism), *controlarse* (self-containment or conscious control), *aguantarse* (the ability to withstand stressful situations during difficult times), *educacion* (academic, moral, and interpersonal education), *marianismo* (adherence to feminine gender roles, including being a strong care provider), and *machismo* (adherence to male gender roles, including protecting and providing for one's family); L. Alvarez, 2007; Halgunseth, Ispa, & Rudy, 2006; Santiago-Rivera, Arredondo, & Gallardo-Cooper, 2002).

Consistent with interdependent cultural values, in one study, 6- to 10-year-old children of Mexican immigrants to the United States were more likely than European American children to engage all three members of a group of three in a problem-solving task involving origami (Mejia-Arauz, Rogoff, Dexter, & Najafi, 2007). European American children tended to attempt the task individually or in a dyad, excluding one of the group members. Mexican American children whose mothers had 12 or more years of schooling in the United States also tended to work individually or in a dyad, which suggests that education in the United States may discourage group-based problem solving.

How do parents socialize their children to learn cultural values, and what effects might such socialization have on children's ethnic identity? Parents' ethnic socialization of their children, involving participation in cultural activities and contact with ethnic traditions, has been found to be associated with exploration of ethnic identity and clarity about the meaning of ethnicity among Latino American adolescents whose parents were from Mexico, Guatemala, and El Salvador (Supple et al., 2006). However, ethnic socialization was associated with adolescents' ethnic pride only in low-risk neighborhoods when parents were highly involved and not harsh with their children. Conversely, in high-risk neighborhoods when parents were not involved and were harsh with their children, ethnic socialization was found to decrease adolescents' ethnic pride. It is possible that in high-risk neighborhoods, culture and ethnicity may be seen by adolescents as negative because of the deviant behavior of community members, and efforts to promote culture and ethnicity may be resisted. Moreover, cultural messages of harsh parents may also be resisted as a reaction against their harsh parenting style.

As discussed in Chapter 7 in relation to Asian American cultural values, Latino/a American cultural values may appear to be gender role stereotyped. Latino/a Americans have been found to stereotype women as experiencing embarrassment, fear, love, sadness, and surprise more than men (Durik et al., 2006). However, similar to the findings for Asian Americans, perceived gender differences for these emotions and behaviors were more pronounced among European Americans than among Latino/a Americans. Thus, Latino/a Americans do not appear to be more gender role stereotyped than European Americans. Moreover, young Mexican American women were found to more strongly endorse feminist attitudes than young European American women (L. Y. Flores, Carrubba, & Good, 2006b).

Similar to the findings on acculturation among Asian Americans discussed in Chapter 7 (Abe-Kim et al. 2001), acculturation among Latino/a Americans is not necessarily a linear process that increases as a function of generation in the United States. Among Mexican American adults, Mexican cultural identity was strong for both Mexican- and U.S.-born persons and did not decrease as a function of time spent in the United States (Rodriguez, Mira, Paez, & Myers, 2007). Mexican American youth have been found to adhere less to familismo than their parents, but also been found not to differ from their parents on machismo (L. Alvarez, 2007). Thus, traditional family roles may change more quickly than traditional gender roles.

Adherence to familism may also vary within Latino American adults. Importance of family, which is a component of familism, was greater among U.S.-born than among Mexican-born Mexican American adults (Rodriguez et al., 2007). It is possible that Mexican-born immigrants may be more likely to live near family members and may not need to deliberately emphasize the importance of family, whereas those born in the United States may be less likely to live in close proximity to family members and may feel a need to emphasize family importance as a way of maintaining familial and cultural ties. Although acculturation might seem to lead to family conflict because of cultural clashes, acculturation was not associated with family conflict in this study.

In one study, four patterns of acculturation were identified among Latino/a American (Central American, Cuban, South American, Caribbean) immigrant youth: (a) bicultural (45% of the sample); (b) assimilation (23%); (c) maintenance of Latino/a culture while avoiding involvement in U.S. culture (4%); and (d) moderate involvement in Latino/a and U.S. culture (27%; Coatsworth, Maldonado-Molina, Pantin, & Szapocznik, 2005). Bicultural youth had greater academic achievement and more peer social support than the other groups. Youth in the assimilation group had lower parental monitoring than the other groups and more classroom difficulties. The maintenance group had relatively low levels of academic achievement and peer social support. The moderate involvement group was characterized as transitioning to another form of acculturation (bicultural or assimilated). This group had spent less time in the United States, had lower academic achievement and English language skills, and less peer social support than the assimilation or bicultural groups. Consistent with the LaFromboise et al. (1993) models of acculturation discussed in Chapter 1, a bicultural orientation appears to have been the most adaptive and also was the most common acculturation pattern (Coatsworth et al, 2005).

Much research on acculturation uses simple proxy measures, such as generation in the United States, length of residence in the United States, and language use. As discussed in Chapter 7, such proxy measures are not necessarily associated with identification with one's culture of origin or with identification with mainstream U.S. culture. Most models assume that acculturation of immigrants is toward European American culture. However, persons of color (e.g., Latino/a Americans) may also acculturate to the cultures of other persons of color (e.g., African Americans). Acculturation of people of color or of European Americans toward the cultures of other people of color has not been considered in psychological research (Abraído-Lanza, Armbrister, Flórez, & Aguirre, 2006).

In summary, Latino/a American cultures tend to be interdependent but have specific interdependent cultural values that differ from those of other interdependent groups. The likelihood of Latino/a Americans adopting a Latino/a American identity may be a function of their perception of the value of such an identity in family and community contexts. Although Latino/a American cultural values may appear to be gender role stereotyped, the data suggest that European Americans are no more gender role stereotyped than European Americans. Latino/a American acculturation is not a linear process but may occur at different rates for different cultural values and may have different patterns as a function of relative involvement in Latino/a American and European American cultures.

FAMILY ISSUES

Latino American parents often have goals of teaching their children cultural values, which may affect their parenting style (Halgunseth et al., 2006). Whereas European American parents may attempt to foster independence in their preschool children, Latino American parents may indulge their preschool children because they do not believe that their children are yet capable of independent behavior. This may include more physical control of preschool children among Latino Americans, which has been found to result in secure attachment in Latino American children but not in European American children. Children at about age 6 are perceived by Latino American parents as capable of adjusting their behavior to others, and Latino American parents may react by exerting greater control (e.g., unilateral decision making, more rules, corporal punishment, parental monitoring) than European American parents when their children fail to meet parental expectations. Greater parental control among Latino Americans versus European Americans may also be a reaction to acculturative stress and a desire to see children adhere to cultural traditions.

Consistent with the above findings on parental control and similar to Asian American parents as discussed in Chapter 7, many Latino American parents may be more authoritarian than European American parents. Mexican American parents have been found to be more authoritarian not only than European American parents but also than Mexican parents in Mexico (Varela et al., 2004; Figures 8.2 and 8.3). Why would Mexican American parents be more

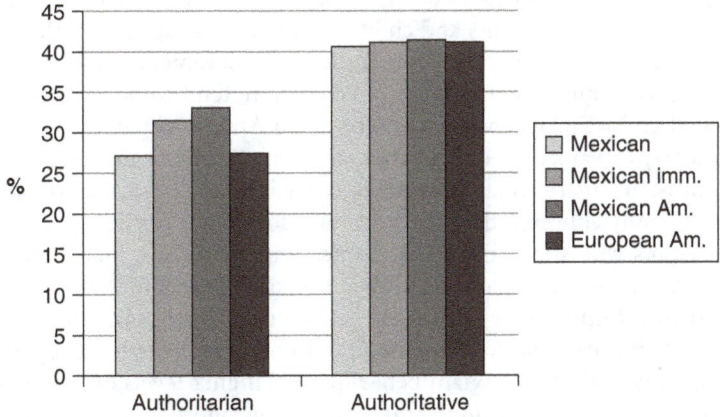

FIGURE 8.2 Mothers' Parenting Styles

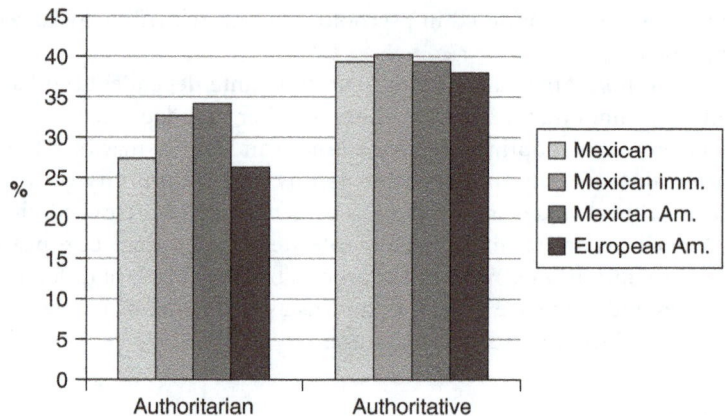

FIGURE 8.3 Fathers' Parenting Styles

authoritarian than the other parents? Mexican American parents were the only parents having minority status in their country and may use authoritarian methods in reaction to accultura-tive stress and in an effort to control their children and to preserve cultural traditions. Never-theless, all groups of parents in the Varela et al. (2004) study were more authoritative than authoritarian, which suggests that parents may use a variety of parenting strategies and may not always be characterized by a single strategy.

Similar to findings with European American children, physical punishment is associated with psychological problems, including anxiety and depression, in Latino American children (Halgunseth et al., 2006). Lower socioeconomic status Latino American parents are more likely to use physical punishment than are higher socioeconomic status Latino American parents. Among lower socioeconomic status parents, economic pressures may lead to depression, which in turn leads to hostile, physically punitive parenting (Parke et al., 2004).

Parental goals for children may also differ between Latino Americans and European Amer-icans (Halgunseth et al., 2006). Respeto is important in Latino American families as a means of maintaining harmonious relationships. Latino/a American children and adolescents have been found to respect their parents more than European American children of similar ages do (Dixon et al., 2008; Fuligni & Pedersen, 2002; Hardway & Fuligni, 2006). However, the degree of empha-sis on respeto may decrease for parents and children with acculturation. Another Latino Ameri-can parental goal is educacion, which involves academic achievement, good manners, and high morals. Children's social skills, a component of educacion, tend to be valued more by Latino American parents than by European American or Asian American parents (Halgunseth et al., 2006). Social skills may be valued even more than children's cognitive abilities.

In many European American families, adolescence is a time of increased independence. In one study, whereas family cohesion decreased during adolescence for European Americans and for Mexican Americans who spoke English at home, family cohesion increased during adoles-cence for Mexican Americans who spoke Spanish at home (Baer & Schmitz, 2007). Latino Amer-ican parents tend to monitor their adolescents more than European American parents do (Halgunseth et al., 2006). Parental monitoring of Latino adolescents has been associated with lower levels of smoking and other deviant behaviors and higher levels of academic motivation and educational goals. Latino American parents tend to have more family rules for their adoles-cents and exercise more control (e.g., stricter curfews) over activities outside the family than do

European American parents. Restrictions on extrafamilial activities may reduce acculturative influences and allow greater cultural socialization from the family.

Even time spent outside the family does not necessarily acculturate Latino Americans to the mainstream. When Latino American children spend time outside their families, it is often with Latino American peers. One study revealed that Mexican American seventh-graders spent more than twice as much free time with Mexican American than with non–Mexican American peers in a multiethnic community (Updegraff et al., 2006). Parents' Mexican identity was associated with the likelihood of spending time with Mexican American peers.

Similar to the findings with Asian Americans discussed in Chapter 7, Latino American parent-child acculturation gaps are not necessarily directly associated with children's problems. Among at-risk Mexican American early adolescents (e.g., involved in services for drug or alcohol problems, mental health, juvenile justice), parent-child acculturation gaps were not associated with parent-child conflict or with youth conduct problems (Lau et al., 2005). However, youth conduct problems were associated with parents or youths who were marginalized from Mexican American and American cultures and with parents being more aligned than their children with American culture. It is possible that parents who were more aligned with American culture provided more autonomy and less monitoring than their children needed, which resulted in conduct problems. Parents' acculturation has also been found to be associated with antisocial behavior among Puerto Rican and Puerto Rican American children (Duarte et al., 2008). Unfortunately, there is limited research on the effects of generation gaps in Latino American families. Nevertheless, in research with Southeast Asian American immigrant families, discussed in Chapter 7, acculturation gaps between parents and children were not directly associated with children's problem behavior unless these gaps were associated with parent-child conflicts (Choi, He, & Harachi, 2008).

Similar to the role of children as culture brokers in Asian American families discussed in Chapter 7, Latino/a American children often serve as language brokers for their parents by communicating with the English-speaking world. Language-brokering begins at about age 8 or 9 and it is more common for girls (Morales & Hanson, 2005). Those Latino/a American children who have multiple language-brokering responsibilities tend to be more depressed than those who have fewer language-brokering responsibilities (Love & Buriel, 2007). Strong bonds with their parents and a bicultural identity offset the depressive effects of language-brokering responsibilities for boys. Being in charge of household responsibilities, which may be a form of status, offset the depressive effects of language-brokering for girls.

Among adults, acculturation has been found to result in more direct expressions of feelings and conflicts in Mexican American couples (E. Flores, Tschann, Marin, & Pantoja, 2004). Such direct expressions may be desirable in mainstream U.S. culture and among mainstream therapists relative to the control of emotions that are part of the Latino/a value of controlarse. Nevertheless direct expressions of feelings and conflicts do not have uniformly positive consequences. Such directness was associated with verbal aggression by men and women and physical aggression by women (E. Flores et al., 2004).

In summary, Latino/a American parents often exert more control of their children than European American parents do. Latino/a American parental control is associated with beliefs concerning child development and with minority status, and it tends to be a protective factor against problem behavior. Psychological problems may occur among Latino/a American youth who are culturally marginalized or who do not receive adequate parental monitoring. Other family sources of psychological problems include excessive culture brokering responsibilities and overly direct expressions of feelings and conflicts among Latino/a American couples.

MENTAL HEALTH

Traditional cultural influences may be positively associated with mental health among Latino/a Americans. Consistent with the traditional Latino/a value of familismo, family support is associated with lower levels of psychological problems. Familism has been found to be a protective factor against aggression among primarily U.S.-born youth whose parents were from Mexico or Central or South America (Smokowski & Bacallao, 2006). Perceived support of parents offset the effects of acculturative stress on anxiety and depression among Mexican American college students (Crockett et al., 2007). Similarly, a parent training intervention that considered the influences of acculturation and discrimination was found to prevent aggression and substance use among mostly Mexican American middle school students (Martinez & Eddy, 2005).

Family variables may also have a protective role against schizophrenic symptoms among Latino/a Americans. Family warmth, which involved a positive tone of voice, expression of positive regard, and expressions of concern, understanding, and interest, was associated with fewer posthospitalization psychotic symptoms among Mexican American schizophrenics (S. López et al., 2004). In contrast, family warmth was not associated with psychotic symptoms among European American schizophrenics. In contexts in which family ties are valued, family support in the form of warmth may be critical to health. Family support may be less critical in contexts in which autonomy is valued (S. López et al., 2004).

Involvement in a religious community may have a greater impact on Latino Americans' behavior than personal religious beliefs. In a sample of Latino Americans seen in the emergency room of a large hospital, religious beliefs, including perceived religiosity and spirituality, were not associated with abstinence from alcohol (Bazargan, Sherkat, & Bazargan, 2004). However, both being Roman Catholic and attending church were associated with abstinence. Thus, it appears that community norms concerning alcohol use influence Latino Americans' drinking behavior.

In addition to traditional values, competence in mainstream U.S. culture may be associated with mental health. In a study of primarily Mexican American adults, perceived social, academic, and career competence in mainstream U.S. culture was found to protect against psychological problems brought about by acculturation (Torres & Rollock, 2007). Thus, actual behaviors, such as language and social skills, may be more important protective factors than nonbehavioral factors, such as mainstream U.S. knowledge, values, and identity.

Acculturation

Acculturation to mainstream U.S. culture might be expected to reduce psychological problems among Latino/a Americans because of competence in mainstream U.S. culture. Conversely, acculturation could be expected to increase psychological problems because of a loss of Latino/a culture. The evidence of the association between acculturation and mental health among Latino/a American is mixed (Torres & Rollock, 2007).

Similar to Asian Americans (Hwang & Ting, 2008), acculturation alone may not have direct effects on the mental health of Latino/a Americans. Stress experienced during acculturation was found to be significantly associated with anxiety and depression among Mexican American college students, whereas acculturation was not (Crockett et al., 2007). Acculturative stress as a result of a deterioration of family values has been found to be associated with alcohol use among Latino/a American youth (Gil, Wagner, & Vega, 2000). In a sample of primarily U.S.-born youth whose parents were from Mexico or Central or South America, acculturation was not significantly associated with aggressive behavior (Smokowski & Bacallao, 2006). However, acculturation conflicts (e.g., problems with family because of a preference for American customs), parent-child conflicts, and discrimination were.

Sources of acculturative stress may vary as a function of acculturation level. Among Mexican Americans, immigrant youth were found to experience stress about needing better English at school and generally experienced more stressors than U.S.-born youth (Romero & Roberts, 2003). Conversely, U.S.-born Mexican American youth experienced stress over needing to speak better Spanish and over being different from other youth because of their parents' culture. For both immigrant and U.S.-born youth, acculturative stress was associated with depression (Romero & Roberts, 2003).

Is it more stressful to be less acculturated or to be more acculturated to mainstream U.S. culture? In a national sample of Latino/a American adults, those who were less acculturated experienced more acculturative stress than those who were more acculturated (Caetano, Ramisetty-Mikler, Vaeth, & Harris, 2007). Acculturative stress included conflicts with family and friends because of changes in values, problems with communication in English, and adjustment problems associated with Latino cultures. Thus, acculturation to U.S. norms may be particularly stressful for those who are relatively unacculturated.

Acculturative stress was predictive of domestic violence in a longitudinal study of Latino American adult couples (Caetano et al., 2007). Differences in acculturation levels between members of a couple can result in acculturative stress, which leads to domestic violence. Even when members of a couple are matched in acculturation levels, domestic violence may occur if either member of the couple experiences acculturative stress. Whereas acculturative stress was predictive of domestic violence, alcohol use was not. This lack of an association between drinking and domestic violence may mean that Latino/a Americans have different expectancies for the effects of alcohol than other ethnic groups do or that drinking patterns in the community sample studied by Caetano and colleagues (2007) are lighter than those in clinical populations in which drinking has been associated with domestic violence.

Discrimination

As with other groups of color, perceived discrimination among Latino/a Americans is associated with psychological distress (Moradi & Risco, 2006). In a national sample of Latino/a Americans, 30% reported experiencing discrimination (Perez, Fortuna, & Alegria, 2008). Darker skinned Latino/a Americans may experience more discrimination than lighter skinned Latino Americans (Ramos, Jaccard, & Guilamo-Ramos, 2003). Latino/a Americans having Spanish accents may also experience greater discrimination than those without (National Survey of Latinos, 2002).

The association between discrimination and mental health problems is stronger for Latino/a American immigrants who have spent more time in the United States (G.C. Gee et al. 2006). Latino/a Americans who have spent more time in the United States may expect discrimination to decrease and may be more impacted by discrimination when it occurs than recent immigrants, who may perceive discrimination as a fact of life. Moreover, Latino/a Americans who are not fluent in English may be linguistically isolated from perceptions of discrimination (Perez et al., 2008).

Ethnic identity may protect against the negative effects of discrimination. In a study of Latino/a American adolescents, most of whom were Mexican American, discrimination was associated with depressive symptoms (Umaña-Taylor & Updegraff, 2007). However, adolescents with high self-esteem were less likely to become depressed when they experienced discrimination. Ethnic identity was associated with self-esteem, which means that ethnic identity indirectly buffered the effects of discrimination by creating higher self-esteem.

Another protective factor against the psychological effects of discrimination is education. Although persons with more education may be exposed to a greater number of situations in which discrimination might occur (Perez et al., 2008), they also may have the intellectual resources to cope with discrimination. Indeed, the relationship between perceived racism and negative emotions was weaker among Latino/a American adults with more education than among those with less education (Brondolo et al., 2008).

In addition to the direct effects of discrimination by others on mental health, membership in an ethnic minority group may have indirect effects on mental health. Concern about fulfilling group stereotypes (e.g., low intelligence) was associated with anxiety, depression, and loss of behavioral and emotional control among primarily Mexican American college students (Chavez & French, 2007). Thus, the perceptions of others may have negative effects on a group even in the absence of overt acts of discrimination. Fortunately, the effects of stereotype threat can be overcome when information about the inaccuracy of stereotypes is presented (Good, Aronson, & Inzlicht, 2003).

In summary, traditional Latino/a cultural values as well as competence in European American culture tend to be protective factors against psychological problems among Latino/a Americans. Acculturative stress, rather than acculturation per se, is associated with psychological problems. Discrimination is another source of psychological problems, particularly for Latino/a Americans who have spent more time in the United States and who expect discrimination to subside. Ethnic identity, education, and the knowledge of the inaccuracy of stereotypes can offset the negative effects of discrimination.

ACADEMIC ACHIEVEMENT AND CAREER DEVELOPMENT

Although there exist negative stereotypes of Latino/a American academic performance, actual academic performance varies within ethnic groups. In a national sample of Mexican American, Puerto Rican, and Cuban American adolescents, nearly half had approximately a B grade point average (Crosnoe, 2005). Cuban Americans were most likely to have a B average or better. Among Mexican Americans, immigrants had higher grades than those born in the United States, but this was not true for the other ethnic groups.

Latino American parents' expectations of their children's long-term educational attainment are consistent with the cultural value of educacion. In a national sample of 5-year-old children, parents of Latino American and Asian American children expected their children to go to school beyond college, whereas parents of European American and African American children expected their children to complete college (Suizzo & Stapleton, 2007). Because many of the Latino American and Asian American parents were immigrants, it is possible that their high expectations are unencumbered by experiences or perceptions of discrimination, which they may have yet to encounter as barriers to their children's educational attainment. Nevertheless, young adult children of immigrants to the United States also tend to have higher social and economic aspirations than their peers whose parents were born in the United States (Tseng, 2006). Education may be culturally valued by immigrants, and it also can be an avenue to upward social and economic mobility, as discussed in Chapter 7.

Children of immigrants may enter school at an academic disadvantage because their parents do not speak English. In a longitudinal study of Latino/a American children whose parents were born in Mexico or Central America, mathematics achievement scores from first through eighth grades were relatively low and stable, ranging from the 37th to 44th percentile (E. M. Lopez, Gallimore, Garnier, & Reese, 2007). Mathematics achievement was associated with preschool home literacy activities (e.g., parents reading to children) and with the children's English literacy. Thus, interventions to support immigrant Latino/a American parents' and their children's literacy may not only improve their literacy skills but also the children's mathematics skills (E. M. Lopez et al., 2007).

Limited English proficiency, however, is not equivalent to limited intelligence. There are important nonverbal aspects of intelligence, including planning abilities, attention, simultaneous processing (integrating stimuli into interrelated groups), and successive processing (ability to process and recall sequences of information) (Naglieri, Rojahn, & Matto, 2007). On a measure of these nonverbal dimensions, Latino/a American children were not significantly different than non-Latino children (Naglieri et al., 2007). Thus, on these measures of nonverbal abilities that are not dependent on specific verbal or mathematics content that English-proficient children might be exposed to, Latino/a American children were found to have abilities equal to those of other children. Moreover, tests administered in the English language do not assess language proficiency in Spanish.

Institutional barriers may interfere with Latino/a American academic achievement. Latino/a American middle and high school students were found to be less satisfied with school resources and to experience more discrimination than non-Latino students (Martinez, DeGarmo, & Eddy, 2004). Dissatisfaction with school resources and discrimination were associated with lower grades and school dropout.

Cultural factors may facilitate academic achievement among Latino/a Americans. As discussed in Chapter 4, ethnic identity is generally associated with academic achievement among Latino/a Americans (Altschul et al., 2006; Ong, Phinney, & Dennis, 2006; Schwartz et al., 2007; Supple et al., 2006). However, competence in mainstream U.S. culture is also critical to Latino Americans' success in predominantly European American academic settings (Castillo et al., 2004, 2006; L. Y. Flores et al., 2006b; Guzman et al., 2005). Thus, combined competence in Latino and in mainstream U.S. cultures may be optimal for Latino/a American academic success. Indeed, a bicultural identity, involving identification with Latino/a Americans and the larger society, was associated with higher grades among middle school Latino/a Americans (Oyserman et al., 2003).

In cultures that value the family, family support may be as important as individual variables in academic achievement. Parental academic encouragement (e.g., rewarding good grades, giving consequences for school failure) was associated with a greater amount of homework, which in turn was associated with better grades among Latino/a American middle and high school students and was a protective factor against dropout (Martinez et al., 2004). Among Latino American college students, family interdependence and family support for education were associated with college grade point average (Ong et al., 2006), as was time spent with family (Sy, 2006).

The U.S. workforce does not accurately reflect the number of Latino/a Americans in the population. Latino/a Americans tend to be concentrated in service and administrative support employment sectors and underrepresented in managerial and sales sectors (R. Roberts, Swanson, & Murphy, 2004). Whereas Latino/a Americans are 13% of the U.S. population, they constitute only 3% of faculty in degree-granting institutions of higher education (U.S. Department of Education, 2004).

Workplace diversity influences the psychological functioning of Latino/a Americans. In one study, either being a token (i.e., the only Latino/a American or one of a few) or being segregated (i.e., all other coworkers are Latino/a Americans) was associated with psychosomatic symptoms and with lower well-being, life satisfaction, and job satisfaction among Dominican Americans, Mexican Americans, and Puerto Rican Americans (Enchautegui-de-Jesús, Hughes, Johnston, & Oh, 2006). The optimal workplace environment involved actual diversity in which there were many Latino/a Americans as well as many persons from other ethnic groups. These findings also applied to African Americans.

In summary, education is a Latino/a American cultural value and it also is a means of social and economic mobility. A lack of English language proficiency is a barrier to academic and career achievement for many Latino/a Americans. Family support and bicultural competence are associated with academic success. Workplace ethnic diversity is associated with both personal and occupational well-being for Latino/a Americans.

Conclusion

Latino/a Americans are the largest ethnic group of color in the United States Although Latino/a American groups are diverse with divergent historical experiences, there are specific Latino/a American cultural characteristics that are generally common across groups. Latino/a Americans acculturate to European American culture at different rates and have different patterns of adherence to Latino/a American and European American cultures. Latino/a cultural values tend to have a protective effect against psychological problems, as does bicultural competence. Bicultural competence also is associated with academic and career success.

The amount and quality of psychological research on Latino/a Americans does not reflect their status as the largest group of color in the United States. Much of the research reviewed in this chapter indicates that models of behavior developed for European Americans do not necessarily apply to this large American ethnic group. More basic research on the influences of Latino/a American cultures and language on behavior is needed. Much more research is also needed on how Latino/a American cultures influence other ethnic and cultural groups in multiethnic contexts.

Discussion Questions

1. Latino/a Americans are the largest ethnic group of color in the United States. Many speak Spanish, as 40% were born in Latin America. Yet, there have been efforts throughout the United States to restrict or eliminate bilingual education. From a different perspective, it would be useful for all Americans to learn Spanish as a first step toward cultural competence in the Americas. What is the likelihood of the U.S. education system promoting bilingual education?

2. Acculturation among Latino/a Americans does not appear to be directly associated with mental health problems, but acculturative stress does. What can be done to reduce acculturative stress among Latino/a American families?

3. Latino/a American immigrants have higher academic aspirations for their children than do U.S.-born Latino/a Americans. Are lower academic aspirations more realistic? Is it possible to maintain high academic aspirations and the value of education among Latino/a Americans?

CHAPTER 9

American Indians and Alaska Natives

When you were born, you cried and the world rejoiced.
Live your life so that when you die, the world cries
and you rejoice.

—WHITE ELK

The current existence of American Indians, Alaska Natives, and their cultures is a tribute to their resilience. These groups have survived attempts of outsiders toward extermination, relocation, and destruction of their language, culture, and religion. American Indians and Alaska Natives could not escape this oppression because it was occurring in their own homeland (Duran, Duran, Brave Heart, & Yellow Horse-Davis, 1998). The oppression that native groups have experienced in this country has been conceptualized as hate crimes, although American Indians and Alaska Natives receive limited attention as hate crime victims (Herring, 1999). Yet American Indians and Alaska Natives remain vibrant and growing groups in the United States.

There are 4.5 million American Indians and Alaska Natives in the United States, which is 1.5% of the country's population (U.S. Bureau of the Census, November 2007). Alaska Natives constitute about 19% of Alaska's population. Although psychological research often focuses on reservation Indians, only one-third of American Indians live on reservations, and most live in urban areas (U.S. Bureau of the Census, February 2006). However, the majority of Alaska Natives live in rural areas (Haycox, 2002). Poverty on reservations has caused many Indians to leave reservations to seek employment. Similarly, unemployment and poverty in Alaska Native villages has also caused an exodus to urban areas. The poverty rate among American Indians and Alaska Natives is 27%, which is higher than any of the other groups discussed in this book.

Despite being one of the numerically smallest ethnic groups discussed in this book, American Indians and Alaska Natives are among the most diverse. There are 562 federally recognized Indian tribes and Alaska Native villages (Bureau of Indian Affairs, 2002). A *tribe* is a social organization based on ancestry (Spickard, 2007). Most American Indian tribes have their own languages. Twenty-eight percent speak a language other than English at home. The largest Indian tribes are the Cherokee and the Navajo, each with more than 250,000 members (U.S. Bureau of the Census, February 2006). The largest Alaska Native tribe is the Eskimo, at over 47,000 members (U.S. Bureau of the Census, February 2006).

The Bureau of Indian Affairs defines an Indian as an enrolled or registered member of a federally recognized Indian tribe or as at least one-fourth Indian or more in blood quantum who can legally demonstrate that to BIA officials (Trimble & Thurman, 2002). However, being an American Indian not only involves ancestry but also cultural identity (Herring, 1999). Because many Indian tribes are sovereign nations, many Indians have dual citizenship in their tribal nation and in the United States (Castro, Proescholdbell, Abeita, & Rodriguez, 1999). Moreover, at least 100 tribes are not federally recognized but have members with a strong Indian identity (Trimble & Thurman, 2002).

The designation "American Indian" is accepted by many Indians themselves (LaFromboise & Graff Low, 1998; Trimble et al., 1996) and will be the term used in this chapter. However, "Indian" in this usage is a misnomer, coined by Europeans who, when they reached this continent, believed that they had reached India. All the indigenous people living on this continent were referred to by Spanish explorers as "*indios*", despite the diversity among these indigenous groups (Sutton & Broken Nose, 2005). Although the many diverse groups that were on this continent before Europeans arrived did not consider themselves to be part of a single group, the European perception of Indians as a single group persists (Spickard, 2007). The term "Native American" is confusing, insofar as many who are not American Indians who were born in the United States consider themselves native Americans. Canada's indigenous peoples refer to themselves as First Nations Peoples.

There are nine major geographic areas in which American Indian nations have shared an ecological environment (Hodge & Fredericks, 1999): the Northeast, Southeast, Southwest, Northern Plains, Northwest Coast, Plateau/Great Basin/Rocky Mountains, Oklahoma, California, and Alaska. Although different tribes have shared the same geographic environment, their cultures and languages have not necessarily been shared. The cities having the largest populations of American Indians are Los Angeles and New York (Sutton & Broken Nose, 2005).

HISTORY

American Indian and Alaska Native history did not begin with European contact (Hays, 2006; Page, 2003). Indian cultures were highly developed by the time European explorers first reached this continent (Hodge & Frederick, 1999; Spickard, 2007). Many tribes had sophisticated systems of agriculture, government, and commerce with other tribes. Knowledge in medicine, astronomy, and the arts was also developing. There was more cultural and linguistic diversity on this continent when Columbus arrived than there was in Europe (Duran & Duran, 1999).

Indian tribes treated the environment with respect. Agriculture, hunting, and fishing were primarily for subsistence purposes. The land was not misused or polluted, nor were animals killed that were not for food. Indian attempts to maintain a balance between the land's resources and their own survival needs were consistent with the spiritual value of harmony within nature (Hodge & Frederick, 1999). Non-Indians have desecrated the land by polluting the air, water, and soil, creating health hazards for many Indians (Hodge & Fredericks, 1999). Pollution and industrialization have also limited farming, hunting, and fishing opportunities. For example, Indians could not hunt buffalo, which were exterminated by settlers.

Displacement by Europeans

Despite the existence of advanced Indian cultures, European explorers viewed Indians as savages, dominated by passions, especially sexuality (Takaki, 1993). American Indians were treated as part of the natural landscape, similar to antelopes and cougars (Spickard, 2007). When the natural landscape becomes threatening, it can be removed and exterminated. Indians may have viewed the unfamiliar White explorers as gods or at least may have feared them because of their metal weapons (Spickard, 2007). They soon learned that Europeans were out to exploit them, their land, and their possessions.

Within 50 years of Columbus's arrival to this continent, European settlers began to displace Indians in the southeastern area of this country (Hodge & Fredericks, 1999). According to Spickard (2007), these early European settlers can be considered our country's first illegal immigrants. English settlers in Virginia during the early 1600s believed that the Indians, who grew corn, were not using the land properly. Thus, confiscating Indian land was not considered robbery (Takaki, 1993). Although the Indians had initially assisted the English settlers, the English attacked Indians in 1608 and destroyed their villages to get food supplies. The European settlers' need for land increased in 1613 when they began exporting tobacco to England. In 1622 the Indians attempted to forcibly drive the settlers out. Migration from the East to the Plains began in 1650 when European settlements drove Indians west (Hodge & Fredericks, 1999).

The Indian population decreased dramatically between 1610 and1675 because of the introduction of European diseases (e.g., smallpox), to which they were not immune (Spickard, 2007; Takaki, 1993). The Indian population in what is now the United States is estimated to have dropped from 5 million in 1600 to only 600,000 in 1800 (Spickard, 2007). Many colonists interpreted Indian deaths as divine intervention and confirmation that they should have taken the land (Takaki, 1993).

Wars were another cause of Indian deaths. In 1637, 700 Pequots were killed by colonists, and 6,000 Indians died from combat and disease during 1675–1676 in King Philip's War (Takaki, 1993). Violence against Indians was justified by Europeans as driving out the devil. Sadly, the ethnic group that was once the largest on this continent is now the smallest (McDonald & Gonzalez, 2006).

Another source of health problems that was introduced to Indians by Europeans was alcohol use. Most Indians did not have experience with alcohol prior to European contact (Beauvais, 1998). European colonists produced large amounts of potent, distilled alcoholic beverages and modeled heavy drinking. Drinking alcohol for European colonists was a means of avoiding contaminated drinking water and fighting illness (Spillane & Smith, 2007). Fur traders and political officials also used alcohol as a currency of trade for Indian resources.

Early American History

American statesman and founding father Thomas Jefferson's view of Indian culture mirrored that of the early European settlers. In 1776, Jefferson believed that Indians should either be civilized, which meant adopting European methods of farming, or exterminated (Takaki, 1993). "Civilizing" the Indians would limit their needs for hunting lands. Jefferson contended that lands had been fairly and legally purchased from Indians. He blamed Indian cultural practices for the decline in numbers of Indians. Ironically, he publicly stated that both Indians and colonists were Americans, born in the same land, and hoped the two could be friends. Such duplicity was not unknown to Jefferson, who publicly opposed slavery but personally owned hundreds of slaves who were never freed.

The U.S. government, not long after it was established, began a repeated pattern of removing Indians from their lands and marginalizing them from American society. Even the leftover lands that Indians were given were often taken from them. The Northwest Ordinance of 1783 and the 1790 Trade and Intercourse Acts gave Indian tribes sovereignty and protection in exchange for their lands (Carson & Hand, 1999). Although sovereignty and protection might appear to be at least somewhat beneficial, the Naturalization Act of 1790 excluded non-White immigrants and Indians from U.S. citizenship (Takaki, 1993). Indian land in the South became valuable for cotton production, and the government forced Indians to sell their land in Alabama, Mississippi, and Louisiana between 1814 and 1824. The Bureau of Indian Affairs was created within the U.S. War Department in 1824 to oversee relationships with tribes.

Andrew Jackson was elected president of the United States in 1828 in part because he had been a hero in wars against the Indians (Takaki, 1993). Jackson believed that efforts to civilize Indians had failed and that Indians should be removed. In 1830, the Indian Removal Act moved 70,000 Indians west of the Mississippi (Carson & Hand, 1999). Most of the Indians in Oklahoma settled there because they were removed from other areas, primarily the South (Hodge & Fredericks, 1999). From 1829, over 10,000 Cherokee, Choctaw, Chickasaw, Creek, and Seminole Indians were forced to leave their sacred homelands and burial grounds in the South without their belongings, often during winter. Between 4,000 and 8,000 Indians died in transit (Takaki, 1993). This forced exodus is known as the Trail of Tears.

Throughout American history, over 600 treaties were made with Indian tribes, often by force or with subgroups of Indians who did not represent tribal wishes (Duran et al., 1998; Takaki, 1993). Ancestral tribal lands are considered sacred by Indians (Trujillo, 2000); thus, the government's removal of Indians from their ancestral tribal lands is analogous to a church being seized by the government and the prohibition of its members from worshipping there. By the mid-19th century, European Americans had developed an ideology, *manifest destiny*, in which seizing the lands of non-Whites on the North American continent was viewed as their God-given right (Spickard, 2007).

Indians in California were also exploited during Spanish colonization during the 19th century. Spanish settlers sought to turn these Indians into laborers and to convert them to Christianity. Diseases introduced by Europeans and violence from non-Indian settlers and the U.S. military completely exterminated some tribes.

Government Interventions

Banishing Indians to previously uninhabited regions of the nation was not the end of government interference. In order to connect the country for commerce, railroads through Indian territories were needed (Takaki, 1993). The Indian Appropriation Act of 1871 stated that "no Indian nation or tribe within the territory of the United States shall be acknowledged or recognized as an independent nation, tribe or power with whom the United States may contract by treaty." This Act allowed railroads to be built through the Plains and also allowed buffalo, which were the Plains Indians' sustenance, to be killed by non-Indians.

A major provision of the Indian Appropriation Act was the establishment of Indian reservations. The purpose of these reservations was a temporary support to help Indians make the adjustment to assimilate into U.S. society (Takaki, 1993). U.S. policies regarding reservations were arbitrary, sometimes forcing enemy tribes onto the same reservation, such as the Modoc, Klamath, and Paiutes in southern Oregon (Spickard, 2007). Conditions on the reservations varied but often involved inadequate food, nonpure water, fuel shortages, disease, abuse by military personnel, and even raids by other tribes. Because Indians were federally mandated to live on reservations, those who refused to be displaced to reservations could be attacked with impunity. For example, the Nez Perce, led by Chief Joseph, attempted to flee to Canada after European Americans discovered gold on their reservation in northeast Oregon and ordered the Nez Perce to a far smaller reservation in Idaho in 1877 (Spickard, 2007). Following many battles that killed tribal leaders, Chief Joseph capitulated to the U.S. government, which imprisoned the Nez Perce in Kansas. By 1911, 98% of Nez Perce territory was leased by the U.S. government to non-Indians (Wilkinson, 2005).

Indian children were taken from their families and forced to live in boarding schools, often hundreds of miles from their families, beginning in 1879 in Pennsylvania at the Carlisle Indian Industrial School (Brucker & Perry, 1998). Church attendance was mandatory at boarding schools, and Indian traditions and religions were regarded as pagan and uncivilized (LaFromboise, Berman, & Sohi, 1994). Teachers at these boarding schools often physically punished children for any displays of traditional culture (Thompson, Hare, Sempier, & Grace, 2008). The motto of the founder of the Carlisle School, Captain Richard Henry Pratt, was "Kill the Indian and save the man" (Spickard, 2007; Wilkinson, 2005). Boarding schools were later established in Alaska for Alaska Native children (Hays, 2006).

Federal policy in the late 1800s outlawed traditional Indian religion and spirituality (Trujillo, 2000). It is possible that the removal of these coping mechanisms may have contributed to Indians seeking maladaptive coping mechanisms, such as alcohol abuse (Spillane & Smith, 2007). Christian churches collaborated with the U.S. government to "civilize" Indians by attempting to convert them to Christianity (Garrett & Pichette, 2000). In 1882, Presbyterian missionary Sheldon Jackson and other Protestant Christian leaders divided Alaska into religious territories in which specific Protestant denominations could work without interference from other groups (Hays, 2006). Catholics already had influence in Alaska. However, neither the Protestants nor the Catholics consulted with Alaska Natives about their plans to spread Christianity in Alaska.

Sixteen years after reservations were established, Congress passed the 1887 Dawes Act, which sought to discontinue reservations and help Indians become property owners and U.S. citizens (Takaki, 1993). Part of the rationale for making Indians property owners was to convert them to farmers, rather than hunters and gatherers (McDonald & Gonzalez, 2006). Farming was considered to be more "civilized" than hunting and gathering and did involve limited access to the lands that were formerly inhabited by Indians. Those considered by the U.S. governments to be the "Five Civilized Tribes" (Cherokee, Chickasaw, Choctaw, Creek, Seminole) adopted European American agricultural systems, government, churches, and schools (McDonald & Gonzalez, 2006). However, these tribes learned that European Americans were more interested in their land than in their assimilation into U.S. society.

The Dawes Act encouraged individual landownership, and each Indian family was given 160 acres for 25 years. Ironically, 19 years after the Dawes Act, the Burke Act nullified the 25-year trust provision of the Dawes Act. Large areas of land from the reservations were taken from the Indians and sold to non-Indians. "Last arrow" pageants that marked the transition to American citizenship were established (Takaki, 1993). In these pageants, Indians wore a traditional costume and shot an arrow. They then entered a teepee and changed into "civilized" clothing, emerged from the teepee, and were given a plow and an American flag.

Despite the oppression that Indians suffered as non-Indians began to occupy their lands, many were undaunted and maintained their ancestral traditions. In 1890, Wovoka of the Paiutes claimed to be the messiah and believed that Indian customs, lands, and buffalo would be restored. The time when the White man would leave Indian lands was celebrated with the tradition of ghost dancing (Takaki, 1993). Ghost dancers wore muslin shirts decorated with sacred symbols that they believed would protect them from their enemies. To quell this growing Indian nationalism, Sitting Bull, a Ghost dance leader, was arrested and then killed by Indian policemen who worked for the U.S. government. Sioux Indians were also arrested and taken to the Wounded Knee camp, where hundreds were massacred when they attempted to escape.

The presence of Europeans in the Indians' homelands forced them into a peripheral existence in the United States. Whereas there were estimated to be 6 million Indians in what is now North America before the arrival of Europeans, this number was reduced to 1.3 million by 1800 and to only 250,000 by 1900 (Spickard, 2007). Disease, killing, and poor conditions on reservations were the primary reasons for this population decline.

Civil Rights

American Indians and Alaska Natives gained some civil rights during the early 20th century. They became official U.S. citizens in 1924, although this act alternatively could be viewed as an effort by the U.S. government to abolish an Indian identity separate from other Americans (Spickard, 2007). The 1934 Indian Reorganization Act allowed tribal land acquisition and self-government. Nevertheless, these rights were in many ways empty to people whose presence on this continent predated those who were offering these rights. Also, as with many other government treaties and laws involving Indians, the apparent freedom that these acts provided proved to be temporary. From 1933 through 1945, the federal government reorganized Indian groups into councils that adopted Western structures (Hodge & Fredericks, 1999). Following World War II, Indians returning from military service or from work in factories in the war effort were offered a bus ticket, low-cost housing, and new clothing as incentives to move to urban areas, as part of the Voluntary Relocation Program (Garrett & Pichette, 2000). Beginning in 1946, the government sought to terminate tribes by taking their land, Indian status, and services and by relocating them from reservations to urban areas (Hodge & Fredericks, 1999; Norton & Manson, 1996).

During the 1960s, a supra-tribal identification as Indians began to develop (Nagel, 1995). In 1968, the American Indian Movement (AIM) was founded in Minneapolis by a group of urban Indians (Spickard, 2007). During the same year, the Indian Civil Rights Act, which allowed Indian self-governance, was passed and self-determination became the government's policy toward Indians (Hodge & Fredericks, 1999). In 1969, students from San Francisco State University with involvement in AIM took over Alcatraz Island, a former penitentiary in the San Francisco Bay (Nagel, 1995). According to the 1868 Fort Laramie Treaty between the United States and the Sioux, abandoned federal facilities could be claimed by Indians (Spickard, 2007). The island was reclaimed in the name of all Indians. The purpose of the occupation was to establish cultural and training centers on the island. The protesters were removed from Alcatraz in 1971 by local and federal authorities. Although the cultural and training centers were not established, Alcatraz spawned other Indian protests and became a rallying point for "Red Power" activism during the 1970s.

The 1970s saw the passage of the Alaska Native Claims Settlement Act (1971), the Indian Self-Determination Act (1975), the Indian Child Welfare Act (1978), and the Religious Freedom Act (1978). These acts all provided increased authority and autonomy to Indian tribes. The Indian Child Welfare Act limited the removal of Indian children from their tribe for purposes of adoption or foster care, whereas such removal was common before this act. In 1976, a lawsuit by an Alaska Native student forced Alaska to support the rights of students to be educated in their home villages rather than in boarding schools (Hays, 2006). Oil revenues in the 1970s allowed the state to build schools in villages that had 15 or more high school–age children (Haycox, 2002).

Federal funding for Indian tribes declined in the 1980s, but Indians continue to work for control over reservation government and industry.

Indian fishing rights created conflict with non-Indian fisherman in the Pacific Northwest. During the 1940s and 1950s, dams built on the Columbia and Snake rivers in the Pacific Northwest flooded Indian fishing areas, such as Celilo Falls in Oregon, and made Indian net fishing impossible (Wilkinson, 2005). Although Indians took just 6% of the overall fishing harvest in the Puget Sound area of Washington state, state officials in the 1960s began to restrict Indian fishing because of complaints from non-Indian commercial and sport fishermen. This resulted in the court case *United States v. Washington*, in which conservative judge George H. Boldt ruled in favor of Indian fishing rights in 1974.

Conflicts between AIM and the FBI developed in 1973 at the Pine Ridge reservation in South Dakota. Tribal chairman Richard Wilson asked the FBI for help in removing AIM from the reservation (Spickard, 2007). The FBI, armed with machine guns, helicopters, and armored vehicles, surrounded the AIM group and engaged in gun battles in which two Indians were killed. AIM was removed from the reservation after two and a half months. There was continued violent conflict between the FBI and AIM in which several Indians were killed. In 1975, two armed FBI agents entered an AIM encampment and engaged in a battle that killed the agents and one Indian. The AIM leader, Leonard Peltier, was incarcerated, and still remains so, for the officers' deaths, although there is inconclusive evidence that he was responsible for the deaths. Human rights organizations consider Peltier to be a political prisoner (Spickard, 2007).

CULTURAL VALUES AND IDENTITY

Each American Indian and Alaska Native community has unique cultural characteristics. Because American Indians and Alaska Natives are small groups with whom most outsiders have had limited contact, many people believe in Pan-Indianism or the idea that all Indians are the same (McDonald & Gonzalez, 2006). This is a stereotype. Nevertheless, a common ethnic identity has helped create social and political power for American Indians and Alaska Natives (Trimble & Thurman, 2002).

Although there is much diversity among Indian and Native groups, there are some cultural characteristics that are common across these groups. Navajo cultural identity includes the elements of family, spirituality, and the environment (Rieckmann, Wadsworth, & Deyhle, 2004). The family element involves an identity as a family member as well as a responsibility to care for one's family. Spirituality includes traditions and ceremonies and connection with spirits and Indian deities. Most Indian beliefs are animistic in which all things animate and inanimate possess a spirit, and communication with a spirit world is accepted (McDonald & Gonzalez, 2006). Each person is viewed as having the facets of mind, body, and spirit, and harmony among the three is the definition of health. The environment element involves respect for the environment and appreciation of the natural processes of the universe. Traditionally, Indian and Native groups have had a subsistence approach to the environment, which involves use of the land and its resources (e.g., trees, animals) for no more than what is necessary for survival.

Do American Indian groups currently have a cultural identity, or have they been assimilated into mainstream U.S. culture? The Lumbee tribe, which resides in North Carolina, is not federally recognized nor has it ever been placed on a reservation (Bryant & LaFromboise, 2005). Moreover, the tribe does not know its native language as well as many other tribes do, nor has its history been documented. Nevertheless, a survey of Lumbee high school students indicated a bicultural identity, with strong American Indian and European American identities (Bryant &

LaFromboise, 2005). Thus, even with less access to Native culture than other American Indian groups, Lumbee youth retained a strong Indian identity. As with the other groups in this book, cultural identification has positive effects for American Indians. Among Lumbee adolescents, interest in Indian culture was associated with lower levels of social problems and aggression and with higher levels of social support (Newman, 2005).

What is the cultural identity of American Indians on reservations? Northern Plains, Pueblo, and Southwest Indian adolescents on reservations have been found to have a strong Indian identity, in terms of speaking Indian languages, Indian traditions and way of life, spiritual and religious practices, and plans to participate in the community as an adult (Whitesell, Mitchell, Kaufman, & Spicer, 2006). Indian identity was stronger than European American identity, as measured by engagement in White or Anglo ways of life and traditions, but European American identity was also relatively strong among these adolescents. Both Indian and European American identification increased among the participants over 3 years. Indian identity was positively correlated with community-mindedness, in terms of fulfilling community obligations (e.g., helping elders) and community expectations (e.g., pleasing elders or friends), whereas European American identity was not. This finding is consistent with the interdependence of Indian cultures. Moreover, those who were most community-minded at the beginning of the study identified less with a European American identity over 3 years. Despite the disadvantages of reservation life, Indian adolescents also reported high self-esteem, possibly because most adolescents report high self-esteem or because these adolescents resided with ethnically similar peers.

Despite their own identification as Indians, many American Indians may be misperceived by others as belonging to non-Indian groups. Indians display a range of phenotypic characteristics in terms of body size, skin and hair color, and facial features (Pewewardy, 1999). At least half of Indian youth have non-Native ancestry (Herring, 1999). American Indians are commonly misclassified as European Americans or Asian Americans (Campbell & Troyer, 2007). Such misclassifications can be considered microaggressions (see Chapter 5) in that they often involve a denial of cultural identity. The psychological effects of such misclassification are not trivial, as misclassified American Indians who identify as Indians are more likely to have considered and attempted suicide than those who identify as Indians and are correctly classified.

Five levels of Indian acculturation and cultural identification have been discussed (Garrett & Pichette, 2000). *Traditional* Indians adhere to Indian culture and speak in their Native language and may or may not speak English. *Marginal* Indians maintain aspects of their Native culture and have acquired aspects of European American culture but do not strongly identify with either culture. *Bicultural* Indians are competent in and identify with both European American and American Indian cultures. *Assimilated* Indians have attempted or have been forced to adopt European American culture and do not practice Indian cultures or speak Indian languages. Assimilation may represent an attempt to protect oneself and one's family from the negative connotations and stereotypes of being an Indian (Trimble & Thurman, 2002). *Pantraditional* Indians have been assimilated but have made a conscious choice to return to Indian cultures and speak both English and Indian languages (Garrett & Pichette, 2000).

Some persons with Indian ancestry may be opportunistic and may not claim an Indian identity until it becomes advantageous (Trimble & Thurman, 2002). For example, one might want to benefit from the profits of the Indian gambling industry. Others who are not otherwise identified with Indian culture might claim an Indian identity if it allows career benefits, such as admission to college or being hired for a job.

Alaska Native cultures include two major language groups: (a) the Eska-Aleutian language spoken by Inupiat and Yupiit (also known as "Eskimos," which is considered pejorative by some), and Aleut, and (b) the Na-Dene languages spoken by the Athabascans, Eyak, Tlingit, Haida, and Tsimshian (Hays, 2006). The Inupiat from the far north and the Yupiit from southwestern Alaska constitute over half the Alaska Native population. They are known for flexibility, knowledge of the environment, and survival skills (Hays, 2006). Aleuts are known for cooperation and sharing and respect that helps ensure the balance among human, natural, and spiritual realms. Na-Dene speakers are more acculturated to European American cultures because of more contact and intermarriage than the Eska-Aleutian groups (Hays, 2006). Tlingit, Haida, and Tsimshian groups reside in southeast Alaska and have been traditionally matrilineal, in which family relationships are determined by one's mother, analogous to determination by one's father in patrilineal societies. However, traditional roles and activities in Alaska Native cultures are gender specific, with men hunting and trapping and women sewing clothing (Hays, 2006).

In summary, American Indians and Alaska Natives maintain cultural traditions despite centuries of attempts to eliminate these traditions. Such traditions are maintained even when Indians or Natives do not reside on reservations or Native villages. There is much diversity across groups, although family, spirituality, and the environment are common cultural emphases. Many Indians and Natives have become bicultural, which has social benefits. Nevertheless, Indians and Natives have varying degrees of contact and identification with their traditional cultures.

FAMILY ISSUES

Who one's relatives are and where one is from are central components of Indian identity. In many American Indian families, the primary relationship is with one's grandparents (Sutton & Broken Nose, 2005). About 1 in 10 American Indian adults lives with a grandchild (Mutchler, Baker, & Lee, 2007). This is similar to the percentage of adults living with a grandchild among African Americans and Latino/a Americans, but higher than the percentage for European Americans. Indian elders are respected and often viewed as sacred (Bucko, 2007). In addition to cultural reasons for these interconnections, economic hardships have caused tribes to share their child-rearing resources and have created alternative family constellations to children living with biological parents (Fitzgerald, 2007).

In many American Indian families, cousins and in-laws are referred to as sisters or brothers (Sutton & Broken Nose, 2005). Some Indian languages do not have terms for "cousin" (Fitzgerald, 2007). Similar to other American families of color, persons can be considered family members even if they are not blood relatives.

There is much tribal variability in family customs, partly because each tribe historically lived in relative isolation from other tribes. Hopi and Dine'h (Navaho) men often move in with their wife's family when they marry, whereas Havasupai women move in with their husband's family when they marry (Sutton & Broken Nose, 2005). Similar to the Hopi and Dine'h traditions, Iroquois tribal membership is inherited through one's mother. Thus, if an Iroquois woman marries outside the tribe, the children are still considered Iroquois. Some tribes may sanction cohabitation as a valid marriage (Bucko, 2007).

A common cultural tradition across tribes is that families care for their members' emotional, spiritual, and economic needs (Fitzgerald, 2007). For example, some tribes do not have a word in their language for "I" (McDonald & Gonzalez, 2006). Although such interdependence could be construed by outsiders as enmeshment or overdependence, Indians might perceive those who do not offer such support as not taking care of their families (Bucko, 2007).

Another Indian family value that might be misunderstood is noninterference (Bucko, 2007). Not intervening in the affairs of family members may be perceived as respect for the natural order of the universe and a way of maintaining harmony. Children may not want to burden their elders with their own problems because they may perceive their problems as trivial relative to the traumas that their elders have experienced (Evans-Campbell, 2008).

Some general requirements to be accepted as an adult member of a tribe have included knowledge of (a) cultural heritage, (b) spiritual/religious practices, and (c) survival skills (Tafoya & Del Vecchio, 2005). Caregivers of children are expected to transmit this knowledge to Indian children. This knowledge has been communicated via storytelling and hands-on instruction. Unfortunately, many Europeans who immigrated to this continent did not understand Indian culture and engaged in acts discussed above that compromised the ability of Indian families to share their cultural knowledge with their children. For example, boarding schools destroyed both physical and cultural bonds among Indian families (Tafoya & Del Vecchio, 2005). The assumption of these attempts to "civilize" Indians was that their cultures and family bonds, which had existed long before Europeans came to this continent, would dissolve and that Indians would be transformed into "Americans" (Bucko, 2007). It was also assumed that Indians were not competent to raise their own children.

Indian families have formal and informal methods of maintaining their cultures. Pow-wows are cultural events that involve ceremony, food, and interaction among Indian families (Fitzgerald, 2007). These events are opportunities for cultural transmission and for maintaining extended family connections. Although the primary purpose of pow-wows is to strengthen extended family ties, they are often open to the public, and many college and university campus Indian organizations organize annual pow-wows. However, some tribes are more protective of their cultural traditions and attempt to insulate themselves from outsiders and outside influences. A less formal method of maintaining culture for urban Indians is contact with reservations or even returning to live there (Bucko, 2007).

In summary, many American Indians and Alaska Natives have strong ties with extended family members. Although there is much variability across tribes and villages, a responsibility to care for the emotional, spiritual, and economic needs of family members is common across groups. Another responsibility of Indians and Natives is to transmit cultural values and traditions to their children.

MENTAL HEALTH

Mental health exists in American Indian and Alaska Native cultures when mind, body, and spirit are in harmony or balance. If one follows a path of maintaining this harmony and keeping tribal and sacred laws, one's spirit will be strong enough to withstand negative events (Trimble & Thurman, 2002). Psychological problems are the result of imbalance among mind, body, and spirit (McDonald & Gonzalez, 2006). For example, if the body is ill, the spirit and mind must compensate for the imbalance. Addressing psychological problems among Indian and Native persons requires attention to mental, physical, and spiritual issues.

Alcohol and substance abuse rates vary widely across Indian and Native communities (Hawkins, Cummins, & Marlatt, 2004), but it is considered a major mental health concern among American Indians and Native Alaskans. Inhalant use often precedes substance use among American Indian youth (Wallace et al., 2002). American Indian teens tend to drink alcohol more frequently and consume larger quantities than other teens (Hawkins et al., 2004). However, much American Indian and Native Alaskan substance abuse involves experimentation, and there are few heavy users of any substance (Hawkins et al., 2004).

There may not be significantly greater percentages of drinkers among American Indians than among European Americans, but the consequences of drinking to American Indians are more severe (Spillane & Smith, 2007). These consequences include legal problems (e.g., arrests for driving while intoxicated), hangovers, blackouts, liver disease, fetal alcohol syndrome, and death, which are more common among Indian drinkers than among European American drinkers. These different health consequences may be associated with Indians' greater likelihood of binge drinking, as American Indians may consume greater amounts of alcohol per drinking occasion than European Americans do.

A risk factor for American Indian and Alaska Native substance abuse is historical trauma, involving repeated colonization and cultural destruction as discussed above (Hawkins et al., 2004). The numbing effects of trauma combined with indirect forms of communication may make it difficult for American Indians and Alaska Natives to deal with historical trauma by talking about it (Evans-Campbell, 2008). Moreover, many traditional Indian and Native cultural methods of coping with trauma have been lost or destroyed during centuries of domination (Trimble & Thurman, 2002). A method of coping with historical trauma, albeit maladaptive in many situations, is substance use. Discrimination and poverty, which are ongoing effects of historical trauma, are also risk factors for substance abuse (Hawkins et al., 2004).

Indian youth with low self-esteem are particularly susceptible to the influences of peers (Radin et al., 2006). If peers drink, then Indian youth are likely to drink as well. The influence of peers on youth with low self-worth is stronger for younger than for older Indian adolescents, who may be less susceptible to peer influences and may rely less on peers to obtain access to alcohol.

Parental substance abuse has been shown to be even more influential than peer influences on the substance abuse frequency of younger Indian youth (Kulis, Okamoto, Rayle, & Sen, 2006). This greater parental influence may be a result of parents having more access than peers to various substances, which they can share with their children. Thus, intervention and prevention programs need to consider the context of Indian substance abuse, and such programs may require attention to youth, their peers, and their parents, as well as historical traumas in American Indian and Alaska Native communities.

People's expectancies of the effects of alcohol use also influence whether they will use it. Those who have positive alcohol expectancies (e.g., alcohol makes people more caring, friendly, puts them in a better mood, allows them to have fun, helps teenagers to do their homework) are more likely to consume alcohol (B. T. Jones, Corbin, & Fromme, 2001). In a large study of adolescents in Iowa, American Indians had more positive alcohol expectancies than African Americans, Asian American, European Americans, or Latino/a Americans (Meier, Slutske, Arndt, & Cadoret, 2007). American Indians were also more likely than the other ethnic groups to have initiated alcohol use and to have engaged in binge drinking in the past month. Across ethnic groups, those having positive alcohol expectancies were also more likely to engage in delinquent behavior. Although the reasons why American Indians' alcohol expectancies were more positive than those of other groups were not investigated, an emphasis on the negative effects of alcohol might be important in preventing both drinking and delinquent behavior among adolescents. However, in contexts, such as reservations, in which there may not be negative consequences for heavy drinking (Spillane & Smith, 2007), it may be difficult to convincingly emphasize the negative effects of alcohol.

Reservation Indians may be at particular risk for alcohol abuse because of this lack of negative consequences and also because of few other sources of reward, such as education and employment (Spillane & Smith, 2007). Although the quality of housing and health services for reservation Indians is variable, both are provided by the U.S. government. Thus, alcohol abuse does not necessarily compromise access to housing or health care. Educational opportunities may not be attractive to some reservation Indians because they would involve leaving the Indian context both physically and culturally. Available employment tends to offer low wages. Thus, the immediate effects of alcohol consumption may be perceived as more rewarding than the unappealing aspects of education or employment. It should be kept in mind, however, that reservation Indians constitute only about one-third of all American Indians. Moreover, American Indians are heterogeneous, and conditions vary across reservations (Beals et al., 2009).

Similar to the findings with other groups in this book, bicultural competence is associated with less risk for substance abuse among American Indian youth (Hawkins et al., 2004). Bicultural competence allows youth to negotiate risky situations by increasing positive coping skills, self-efficacy, and social support. In contrast, disengagement with Indian or mainstream culture or both may be a risk factor for substance abuse. Bicultural competence may be more important in urban settings than in reservation settings, where there are few European Americans (Spillane & Smith, 2007).

Similar to Asian Americans, as discussed in Chapter 3, some American Indians may have genetic protection against alcohol abuse. In one study, Indians who possessed an *ALDH1A1*2* gene were less likely than Indians who did not have this gene to be dependent on alcohol (Ehlers, Spence, Wall, Gilder, & Carr, 2004). This gene was also associated with a lower likelihood of tobacco use. As discussed in Chapter 3, the presence of the *ALDH* gene is associated with physiological discomfort when substances are used.

Another effect of alcohol abuse and dependence among American Indians is suicide risk (Beals et al., 2005). Suicide rates are higher among American Indian youth than among other ethnic groups (Goldston et al., 2008). The conflicting demands of Indian and European American cultures (LaFromboise & Bigfoot, 1988), loss of ethnic identity (Olson & Wahab, 2006), and discrimination (Walls, Chapple, & Johnson, 2007; Whitbeck, Adams, Hoyt, & Chen, 2004) create stress that is associated with suicide risk. However, there is some evidence that an Indian cultural spiritual orientation is associated with a reduced history of suicide attempts (Garroutte et al., 2003).

In summary, American Indian and Alaska Native mental health involves a balance among mind, body, and spirit. Psychological problems result when there is an imbalance of these three elements. Historical trauma may be a risk factor for the abuse of alcohol and other substances in Indian and Native communities. Life on reservations is replete with many risk factors for substance abuse. Alcohol abuse also creates a risk for suicide. Fortunately, there exist both cultural and spiritual protective factors against mental health problems in Indian and Native communities.

ACADEMIC ACHIEVEMENT AND CAREER DEVELOPMENT

Optimal education for American Indian and Alaska Native children would incorporate Native cultures and languages, which would be a stark contrast to historical efforts to destroy these cultures and languages (Thompson et al., 2008). The development of such an educational curriculum would require the input of tribal leaders. Such educational efforts might be most feasible on reservations where there are relatively large groups of Indians in proximity. Nevertheless, reservations may include more than one tribe, which presents challenges in teaching multiple cultures and languages. Moreover, educators having skills in Native cultures and languages are scarce.

In a large, longitudinal study of a nationally representative sample of children, American Indians and Alaska Natives entering kindergarten had comparable reading and math skills to Latino/a Americans and African Americans (Marks & Coll, 2007; Figures 9.1 and 9.2). Although American Indians' and Alaska Natives' reading and math skills were lower than those of European American kindergartners, the gap between American Indians/Alaska Natives and European Americans was even greater by third grade. Unfortunately, there is also evidence that Indian middle

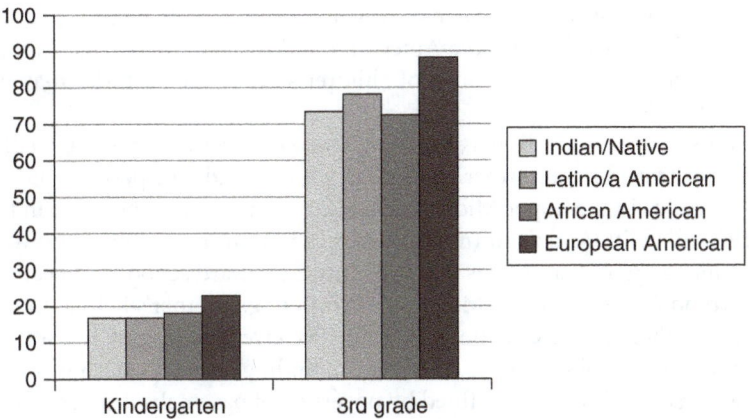

FIGURE 9.1 Mathematical Thinking by Ethnic Group

school children also become less academically engaged as they grow older (LaFromboise, Hoyt, Oliver, & Whitbeck, 2006).

Marks and Coll (2006) also found for all ethnic groups that teacher-perceived positive attitudes toward learning (e.g., accepts new ideas well, willingness to try, adherence to classroom rules) were associated with higher baseline reading and math skills and greater growth in these skills through third grade. Thus, it is critical for educators and parents to promote positive attitudes in children toward learning. Promoting positive attitudes toward learning may be particularly critical for American Indians and Alaska Natives so that they do not lose ground once they enter school. Positive attitudes toward school may also have benefits outside school. For example, positive attitudes toward school lowered the risk of cigarette smoking among American Indian youth (LeMaster, Connell, Mitchell, & Manson, 2002).

Insofar as teachers' perceptions of positive attitudes toward learning were associated with academic success (Marks & Coll, 2007), it is critical for teachers not to stereotype American Indians and Alaska Natives and other children of color as having negative attitudes toward learning. Teachers' lower expectations of Latino/a American and African American elementary students relative to

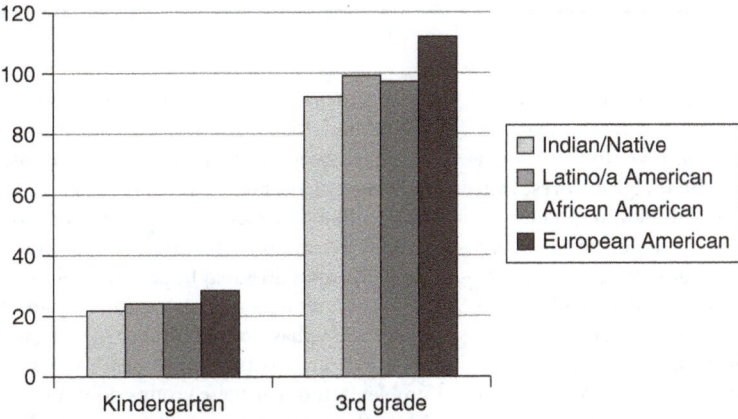

FIGURE 9.2 Reading Skills by Ethnic Group

their expectations of European American and Asian American elementary students result in lower academic performance for Latino/a Americans and African Americans (McKown & Weinstein, 2008). Thus, teacher misperceptions of children's academic attitudes may interfere with progress in school.

Similar to its positive educational effects discussed elsewhere in this book, cultural identity appears to have positive effects on American Indian youths' academic performance. In a study of Indian 10–15-year-olds in the upper Midwest, enculturation (i.e., participation in traditional activities), identification with American Indian culture, and traditional spiritual involvement were associated with higher grades, as well as positive attitudes toward school and academic plans for the future (LaFromboise et al., 2006). Maternal warmth (e.g., mother's help with problems) was also associated with these positive school outcomes. Perceived discrimination was negatively associated with positive school outcomes. Despite the finding that over 60% of the youth in the study lived in adverse conditions, as defined by poverty and parental substance abuse, 60% were also considered prosocial, as indicated by positive school outcomes and limited problem behaviors (e.g., substance abuse, externalizing behavior). Thus, many Indian youths are academically resilient even under adverse conditions.

Rates of high school graduation among American Indians and Alaska Natives are comparable to those of the total U.S. population (U.S. Bureau of the Census, February 2006). This is a remarkable achievement, given the stressors and barriers to success discussed above that many American Indians and Alaska Natives face. However, only 11% have bachelor's degrees or higher, which is approximately one-fifth that of the total U.S. population (U.S. Bureau of the Census, February 2006). Consistent with interdependent cultural values, American Indian college students reported that they were more emotionally attached to their families than to their work and also spent more time with their families than on work (C. Brown & Lavish, 2006). Thus, higher education may need to accommodate the family and cultural contexts of Indian and Native students in order for these students to remain in college and complete their education.

In summary, there may be an academic gap between American Indian and Native Alaskan students and European American students that widens over time. However, positive teacher expectations and cultural identity may facilitate Indian and Native students' academic performance. Rates of high school graduation among Indians and Natives are similar to those of other groups, but rates of college graduation are lower.

Conclusion

Although there is a dearth of psychological research on American Indians and Alaska Natives, it is critical that this void is not filled with culturally insensitive studies. Indian community participation should be integral to research projects in their conceptualization, design, implementation, data collection and interpretation, report writing, and dissemination (Cochran et al., 2008). Research efforts should also have tangible benefits to Indian and Native communities. However, gaining the collaboration of Indian communities in research projects may be challenging. Many Native communities may distrust researchers, who may be perceived as an arm of the government that has oppressed them.

An area of research that warrants greater emphasis is the cultural strengths of American Indians and Alaska Natives. There has been much emphasis on problems, particularly alcohol abuse and suicide. These problems certainly are worthy of attention; however, proposed solutions to these problems that are generated from outside American Indian and Alaska Native communities may be perceived within these communities as a continuation of oppression (Whitbeck, 2006). Moreover, the emphasis on problems makes it easy to assume that all American Indians and Alaska Natives experience these problems and that these groups do not have cultural assets. Thus, the protective aspects of American Indian and Alaska Native cultures should be further investigated.

Discussion Questions

1. Can American Indians and Alaska Natives be adequately understood apart from a context of historical trauma? Does historical trauma affect the way American Indians and Alaska Natives currently live?

2. American Indian and Alaska Native people, languages, and cultures have survived, despite centuries of efforts in North America to eliminate them. Although American Indians and Alaska Natives are often portrayed as having problems, such as alcohol abuse, they are remarkably resilient. Why are these people, languages, and cultures so resilient?

3. For the first time, the 2000 census allowed respondents to designate more than one ethnic category. An Indian or Native identity seems to have become popular, as the most common additional ethnic category was American Indian or Native Alaskan. What does it mean for someone who has a small amount of Indian or Native ancestry and little or no contact with Indian or Native culture to identify themselves this way?

CHAPTER 10

Multiracial Americans

But I have asserted a firm conviction—a conviction rooted in my faith in God and my faith in the American people—that working together we can move beyond some of our old racial wounds, and that in fact we have no choice if we are to continue on the path of a more perfect union.

—BARACK OBAMA

Barack Obama is the first multiracial president of the United States. Because he is multiracial, millions in the United States and around the world see in him someone who can unite people of diverse backgrounds. Yet, he is commonly referred to as the first Black or African American president. However, Obama's mother is European American, so why is he not referred to as White? Obama in his "More Perfect Union" speech on March 18, 2008, in Philadelphia observed that "At various stages in the campaign, some commentators have deemed me either 'too black' or 'not black enough.'" Similarly, abolitionist Frederick Douglass, National Association for the Advancement of Colored People (NAACP) founder W. E. B. Dubois, poet Langston Hughes, and civil rights leader Martin Luther King, Jr., all had mixed-race ancestry but were referred to as Black. Perhaps these monoracial categorizations are part of a tradition of multiracial persons being classified as members of monoracial minority groups. We will consider such issues of racial/ethnic identity of multiracial Americans in this chapter.

Multiracial persons defy traditional definitions of race. As discussed in Chapter 1, these definitions involve ancestry from a single geographic region and phenotypic similarities. Multiracial persons often meet neither of these definitional criteria and do not fit neatly into existing racial categories. A multiracial category for race would be as heterogeneous as other monoracial categories (e.g., American Indian), as multiracial persons can have any combination of two or more racial ancestries. To combine all multiracial individuals is to create a group that is as heterogeneous as any previously discussed in this book. Multiracial persons are both racially and ethnically diverse. For example, a person whose parents are European American and African is racially and ethnically different from a person whose parents are Latino American and Asian American. Moreover, even when two multiracial individuals have the same racial or ethnic heritage, they may differ on levels of identification with the racial or ethnic groups that they belong to, just as monoracial individuals from the same group differ in racial or ethnic identity.

Phenotypic appearance even among multiracial persons with the same racial background (e.g., Asian American/European American) may vary widely and is not necessarily a good clue to racial ancestry. Multiracial individuals may phenotypically appear to belong to one or more of the racial and ethnic groups discussed in this book, including European Americans. Several years ago, I was a new member of a review group that met to evaluate research grant proposals. No one in the review group knew my own racial background. In one grant proposal, the researchers intended to study race differences and planned to identify the races of their participants based on appearance. When it was time to discuss this proposal, I asked the members of the review group to look at me and identify my race. Because I had posed a question about race, most of the group probably assumed that I was not European American. Those who replied guessed Latino or Jewish. No one correctly guessed Asian American/European American. This exercise demonstrated to the group the folly of determining one's race by appearance, especially if the person is multiracial.

A working assumption in U.S. history has been that people belong to one racial group. Until 2000, multiracial individuals were forced to choose one racial group on the U.S. Census. Whereas there were approximately 500,000 persons in the United States who identified as biracial in 1970, 6.8 million people, or 1 in 40, identified themselves as multiracial in the 2000 census (Shih & Sanchez, 2005; Spickard, 2007). It is likely that 6.8 million is an underestimate of the actual number of multiracial Americans, as many multiracial Americans were accustomed to choosing a single racial group. Moreover, many racial and ethnic minority organizations encouraged multiracial persons not to designate more than one race out of fear of losing resources for minority groups (e.g., persons having European American ancestry counted as European Americans and not as minorities) or of policies that might adversely affect minority groups (Daniel & Castaneda-Liles, 2006; Suyemoto, 2004). Of those who indicated more than one race on the census, 93% indicated two races, 6% three races, and 1% four or more races. The ethnic groups having the largest percentages of persons who indicated that they were multiracial were Native Hawaiians/Pacific Islanders (45%) and American Indians/Alaska natives (36%). Twelve percent of Asian Americans indicated that they were multiracial, whereas only 2% of European Americans indicated that they were multiracial (J. Lee & Bean, 2004). However, because European Americans are a large proportion of the U.S. population, there were over 5 million multiracial persons with European American ancestry.

Although the Census Bureau has estimated that at least 75% of African Americans have multiracial ancestry, only 4% of African Americans indicated multiracial ancestry. It is possible that racism against African Americans prevents their acknowledgment of multiracial ancestry (J. Lee & Bean, 2004). Moreover, many of the sexual unions between European American men and African American women during slavery were not consensual, which is another reason to deny European American ancestry.

The U.S. census is a metaphor for the historic status of multiracial individuals in society. Because there were relatively few individuals who identified as multiracial until the past 40 years, multiracial persons have often been forced to identify with one part of their identity but not the others. Other multiracial persons choose not to identify with one particular racial or ethnic group and consider themselves to be biracial or multiracial (Shih & Sanchez, 2005). Still others identify with the specific components of their heritage, such as Eurasian or Black/White. Golfer Tiger Woods describes himself as "Cablinasian"—a combination of Caucasian, Black, (American) Indian, and Asian. Some do not identify themselves in terms of race or ethnicity, although others might attempt to force them to do so with the question commonly posed to multiracial persons: "What are you?"

This "what are you?" question may be rooted in perceptual tendencies. The immediate perceptual reaction (200 ms from the onset of the stimulus) of European Americans is to classify a racially ambiguous face (graphically morphed Asian-White or African-White faces) as White rather than Asian or Black (Willadsen-Jensen & Ito, 2006). Later in the perceptual process (500 ms), European Americans differentiate racially ambiguous faces from White faces. This initial tendency to perceive a racially ambiguous face as White and later determine that it may not be White could be an impetus for European Americans to attempt to classify multiracial persons by asking them what racial category they fit into.

Similar to the other groups of color previously discussed, multiracial persons are the targets of discrimination. However, unlike these groups of color for which the perpetrators of such discrimination are primarily from groups other than their own, multiracial persons often face discrimination from their own ethnic groups and even from their own families (Shih & Sanchez, 2005). Although some monoracial people of color may perceive that multiracial persons can "pass" for a racial group against which there is less discrimination (e.g., European Americans), there is evidence that multiracial persons report experiencing more discrimination than do monoracial persons of color (Brackett et al., 2006; M. Herman, 2004). Perhaps this greater level of discrimination results from the fact that multiracial persons are minorities in most settings, which means that there are more opportunities to be targets of discrimination than there are for monoracial persons of color.

Another explanation for the greater amount of discrimination experienced by multiracial persons is that persons lower in a social hierarchy (i.e., multiracial persons) are more sensitive to social feedback than those who are higher (i.e., monoracial persons), which would make multiracial persons more sensitive to incidents of discrimination. This idea that persons in higher social positions have less accurate knowledge of events than those in lower social positions is known as *standpoint theory* (Wood, 1997). For example, you are probably able to think of people in higher social positions than you (e.g., parents, professors) who are less aware than you of social interactions (e.g., gossip, fights) among your peers. Consistent with standpoint theory, biracial persons having African American ancestry perceive greater discrimination than biracial persons who do not have African American ancestry (e.g., Asian/Latino/a American, Asian/European American, Latino/a/European American), presumably because African Americans have a lower social position in society than the other groups (M. Herman, 2004).

Monoracial persons may find it difficult to accept multiracial persons as part of their group. In a study of immediate perceptions of Asian-White racially ambiguous faces in a study with a similar methodology to the Willadsen-Jensen and Ito (2006) study discussed above, Asian Americans perceived these faces as White (Willadsen-Jensen & Ito, 2008). This perception of racially ambiguous faces as White rather than as Asian may be a result of the Asian Americans in the study being in primarily European American social contexts in which the default mode for race was White. Thus, the initial tendency of Asian Americans may be to classify multiracial Asian Americans as part of the outgroup.

Other monoracial groups may perceive multiracial persons as members of the outgroup. African American and European American college students were asked to assess the peer acceptance of a biracial (African American/European American) child (Chesley & Wagner, 2003). African American students perceived the biracial child to have greater peer acceptance when the child's friends were European Americans than when the biracial child's friends were African Americans.

The opposite was true of European American students. They perceived the biracial child as having greater peer acceptance when the biracial child's friends were African Americans than when they were European Americans. Thus, the students perceived the biracial child to fit better in the racial outgroup.

Exclusion of multiracial persons from monoracial groups, including monoracial groups of color, may benefit monoracial groups (Suyemoto & Dimas, 2003). When there are limited resources for a group (e.g., Bureau of Indian Affairs benefits), monoracial groups may resist expanding their boundaries to include multiracial persons. Some monoracial persons may believe that inclusion of multiracial persons in their group will dilute their identity and hence their hard-earned political power. For some groups, racial "purity" is valued, and anyone whose appearance is dissimilar to the others in the group is excluded. All too often, multiracial individuals who associate with a monoracial group but do not phenotypically resemble it are asked, "What are *you* doing here?" Multiracial persons with European American ancestry may symbolize White oppression and dominance of minorities to some monoracial persons of color. Even when a person's ancestry involves two groups of color (e.g., Korean/Japanese), the person may be despised by monoracial groups because of a history of conflicts between the person's ancestral groups (C. C. I. Hall, 2003).

Monoracial persons typically do not face disagreement about their choice of racial identity, whereas a multiracial person may face discrimination if they identify with a monoracial group because the group does not accept them. Acceptance may be greater among other multiracial persons, but identified multiracial groups are often small or unavailable. Thus, many multiracial persons find themselves without a racial or ethnic reference group.

In summary, multiracial Americans defy traditional racial and ethnic categories and boundaries. Although 6.8 million Americans identified themselves as multiracial in the 2000 U.S. census, this may be an underestimate, as many multiracial persons may have indicated only one race, which was the only census option until 2000. Most multiracial Americans are biracial and are likely to have European American, Native Hawaiian/Pacific Islander, or American Indian/Alaska Native ancestry. Multiracial persons may experience a greater amount of discrimination than monoracial persons of color and may also experience difficulties in being accepted by monoracial groups.

HISTORY

Multiracial persons have been in North America since different racial groups first had contact. The focus in the United States has primarily been on African Americans and European Americans because of centuries of European American dominance over African Americans and larger numbers of African Americans relative to other groups of color. Clear racial boundaries were necessary to maintain White privilege (Suyemoto & Dimas, 2003). Efforts to prevent interracial unions began in the United States in the 1600s. In 1661, Maryland created a law that forced European American women (mostly servants) who married a slave to serve the slave's master (Teo, 2004). In 1662, Virginia imposed fines for sexual contact between European American women and African American men. To keep the part-White children of European American slave owners and African American slave women as slaves, the one-drop rule, also known as *hypodescent*, established that any person with any known African ancestry was regarded as Black (Spickard, 2007). Thus, biracial children could be regarded as property rather than as family members by European American slave owners.

Beginning in the 1600s in Louisiana and South Carolina, persons of African American/ European America ancestry who were not slaves were accorded a different status than mixed-race slaves (Davis, 2006). Free mixed-race persons were considered White rather than Black and could marry into White families. However, such acceptance of mixed-race persons into White society ended in 1808 in Louisiana and the 1840s in South Carolina when antimiscegenation laws, which made interracial marriage illegal, were enacted.

The term *mulatto* first appeared in the 1850 census to refer to persons having European and African ancestry (Suyemoto & Dimas, 2003). *Mulatto* is a pejorative term, derived from the word *mule*, which is a sterile animal produced by a donkey and a horse (C. C. I. Hall, 2003). An implication of this category was that multiracial persons were less fertile than monoracial persons. Psychologists in the 1800s also had negative views of multiracial individuals. Paul Broca, the brain researcher for whom the Broca's speech area is named, suggested in 1864 that mixture of closely related races (e.g., groups with northern European ancestry) is beneficial, whereas mixture of distant races (e.g., groups with European ancestry and groups with African ancestry) would result in offspring who would be inferior in fertility (Teo, 2004). State supreme courts in Missouri in 1883 and in Georgia in 1869 upheld miscegenation laws based on this untested assumption that interracial progeny would be inferior to monoracial progeny (Tucker, 2004). Sir Francis Galton, a pioneer in psychometrics, contended that racial mixing could be advantageous to intellectual ability, but only by mixing among "pure" races (Teo, 2004). G. Stanley Hall, the first president of the American Psychological Association, agreed with Broca about the negative consequences of mixing of distant races.

In the early 20th century, studies of the intellectual performance of African American/ European American individuals relative to monoracial individuals were conducted by Strong and Ferguson (Teo, 2004). In 1913, Strong reported that the performance of darker children was closest to "normal" (i.e., the performance of European Americans) and that the performance of lighter children was variable, both above and below normal. Ferguson in 1916 concluded that intellectual performance was negatively associated with African ancestry. Similarly, Hunter and Sommermier in 1922, Garth in 1923, and Jamieson and Sandiford in 1928 concluded that American Indian blood in multiracial children was negatively associated with intellectual performance (Teo, 2004).

The term *mulatto* was removed from the 1930 census, and multiracial African Americans were categorized as "Negroes", marking a return to the rule of hypodescent (Suyemoto & Dimas, 2003). However, there was continuing interest among academics in multiracial persons. The idea of multiracial persons being culturally marginal in society was proposed in 1928 by Robert E. Park, a professor of sociology at the University of Chicago (Teo, 2004). Also included in Park's "marginal man" idea were monoracial persons living in transition and crisis. Park wrote the introduction to Stonequist's 1937 book *The Marginal Man*, which popularized this concept. Cultural marginalization has persisted into contemporary models of acculturation (e.g., Berry, 1974).

Multiracial Americans on the West Coast of the United States having Japanese ancestry were placed in internment camps during World War II along with other Japanese Americans, as described in Chapter 7. Any person having 1/16 or more Japanese ancestry was placed in an internment camp (Nakashima, 2005). Because Japanese people first came to the United States in 1885, the 1/16 rule covered everyone in the United States with Japanese ancestry. It is unclear how being 1/16 Japanese would create a security risk, which underscores that the internment camps were created more for racial and political reasons than to reduce actual risk to the national security.

Biracial children of American servicemen and women in Asia during the Korean and Vietnam wars faced rejection both in Asia and in the United States (Davis, 2006). Because citizenship in Korea and Vietnam is paternal, these children could not become citizens in these countries and were further rejected because of prejudice against mixed-race persons. Children of American males born out of wedlock outside the United States were also ineligible for U.S. citizenship (Davis, 2006). The United States began to allow these children to emigrate in 1982, but, similar to their status in Asia, these biracial persons have often been regarded as outcasts in the United States.

Thirty-eight states in the United States have had antimiscegenation laws. My father, who was European American, and my mother, who was Japanese American, were married in 1949 in the state of Washington, which did not have antimiscegenation laws, but they could not have been legally married in any of the neighboring West Coast or Mountain West states. One of the major objections to the integrated schools that resulted from the 1954 Supreme Court *Brown v. Board of Education* ruling was that integrated schools would lead to interracial relationships and offspring (Tucker, 2004). The 1967 Supreme Court decision *Loving v. Virginia* invalidated the last antimiscegenation laws in 16 states in the South. Mildred Jeter, who was African American, and Richard Loving, who was European American, were unable to be legally married in Virginia and had to go to Washington, DC, to get married in 1958. A subsequent lawsuit on their behalf was taken before the U.S. Supreme Court.

Although antimiscegenation laws had been repealed, multiracial persons continued to be regarded as monoracial in many communities. In 1972, the National Association of Black Social Workers rejected the terms *biracial* and *racially mixed* and passed a resolution that African American children, including multiracial African American children, should not be adopted by European American parents (Davis, 2006). This was an effort to help children with African American ancestry affirm their African American identity. This resolution drastically reduced the numbers of adoptions of multiracial children with African American ancestry by European American parents. Although cross-racial adoptions have subsequently increased, many adoption court proceedings require adoptive parents to propose a plan for how they intend to preserve their adopted child's culture(s).

During the 1970s, after antimiscegenation laws had been repealed, multiracial persons began to be viewed by researchers as equivalent to monoracial persons (Shih & Sanchez, 2005). However, Scarr and Weinberg revived the research of the 1920s in comparing the intellectual functioning of biracial (African American/European American) children with that of monoracial African American children, as did Rushton in the 1990s (Teo, 2004). Moreover, personality psychologist Raymond B. Cattell, developer of the 16 Personality Factor Test, persisted in the 1970s through the 1990s with his beliefs first expressed in the 1930s that racial mixing was dangerous and that racial segregation should be maintained (Tucker, 2004). Against this anti-multiracial research backdrop, the multiracial movement began to develop. Interracial/Intercultural Pride (I-Pride) was a multiracial group formed in the late 1970s in Berkeley, California, that was successful in petitioning the local school board to add "interracial" as a designation to school demographic forms (Daniel & Castaneda-Liles, 2006).

Researchers in the 1970s assumed that models of racial identity development for monoracial persons were applicable to multiracial persons. However, monoracial models did not account for the possibility of identification with multiple racial groups (Poston, 1990). In response, alternative models of racial/ethnic identity were developed for multiracial persons, such as Poston's (1990) biracial identity development model reviewed in Chapter 1. The stages in the Poston model were personal identity, choice of group categorization, enmeshment/denial, appreciation, and integration. The growing influence of multiracial Americans was reflected in the founding of the Association of Multiethnic Americans in 1988 as a legal lobbying organization that emphasized the freedom to acknowledge all of one's ancestries.

During the 1990s, a shift from viewing multiracial persons as deviant to consideration of the positive aspects of multiracial identity was initiated by Maria Root in two influential books, *Racially Mixed People in America* (1992) and *The Multiracial Experience* (1996). She and other multiracial colleagues addressed conceptual, psychological, and methodological issues involving multiracial persons and identity, and empirical studies were included. This was one of the first instances of a group of multiracial psychologists addressing multiracial issues, rather than these issues being addressed by psychologists who were not multiracial. Root served as a consultant to the U.S. Census Bureau and helped persuade the Bureau to allow the option of indicating more than one racial designation in the 2000 census.

In 2003, conservative politicians in California attempted to capitalize on the multiracial movement to promote Proposition 54, otherwise known as the racial privacy initiative (K. M. Williams, 2006). Proposition 54 would have prevented the state from collecting racial and ethnic data because these data were considered private, race and ethnicity were considered artificial constructs, and to collect such data would amount to discrimination. This initiative was proposed on the heels of Proposition 209, which portrayed affirmative action as a form of discrimination and had been approved by California voters. The purported appeal of Proposition 54 to multiracial persons was that they would no longer have to categorize themselves by race. Opponents argued that race and ethnicity data were important for healthcare, in that some racial and ethnic groups are disproportionately affected by disease and that some groups may not have adequate access to healthcare. Proposition 54 was defeated 64% to 36%, which suggests that the majority of Californians perceived race and ethnicity as having some utility.

CULTURAL VALUES AND IDENTITY

Multiracial persons were considered marginalized in early work on racial identity. Similar to monoracial persons who identify neither with their culture of origin nor with their host culture (Berry, 1974; Chapter 1), multiracial persons who are marginalized are not identified with any of the races or ethnicities in their heritage. Such persons are dual minorities in that they are minorities within mainstream society as well as minorities within the minority community (Shih & Sanchez, 2005).

Are most multiracial individuals marginalized, or do they self-identify with one or more groups? When asked to choose a single monoracial group that best described them, the most common response among biracial high school students having ethnic minority ancestry was to choose an ethnic minority group, particularly among those having African American ancestry (M. Herman, 2004). Choosing a multiracial identity was not generally available until relatively recently.

Rockquemore (1999) suggested that African American/European American biracial persons have four racial identity options. The first is a *singular* identity in which one is exclusively African American or European American. The second *border* identity is exclusively biracial. A third *protean* identity involves sometimes being African American, sometimes being European American, and sometimes being biracial. A fourth option is *transcendent*, in which a person has no racial identity.

In a study of adults with African and European ancestry in which biracial identification was an option, the majority of the sample (62%) identified themselves as biracial (Rockquemore

& Brunsma, 2001). Only 15% identified as African American and less than 3% identified as European American. Approximately 5% had a flexible identity as a function of the racial composition of their social networks. Twelve percent did not define themselves based on existing racial categories.

Consistent with the Rockquemore and Brunsma (2001) results, 46% of African American/ European American adults and 64% of Asian American/European American adults identified themselves as biracial, whereas 33% of African American/European Americans identified themselves as African American and 19% of Asian American/European Americans identified themselves as Asian Americans (Suzuki-Crumly & Hyers, 2004). The percentages of biracial persons who did not define themselves in terms of racial categories were relatively high, at 21% of African American/European American adults and 14% of Asian American/European American adults. Thus, a biracial identity is modal for biracial persons, and a minority identity is the second most common identity.

Adolescents of color have been found to have stronger ethnic identities than European American adolescents. Biracial adolescents are in between with stronger ethnic identities than European American adolescents but weaker ethnic identities than monoracial adolescents of color (Bracey, Bámaca, & Umaña-Taylor, 2004; M. Herman, 2004). It is possible that biracial persons may have limited access to biracial groups or that the customs of biracial groups are not well defined or well known, which may limit the ability to have a biracial identity. Nevertheless, most biracial persons identify themselves in terms of ethnicity.

Cultural variables also influence the racial/ethnic identification of multiracial persons. The use of a language other than English at home increases the likelihood that a multiracial person will identify with the cultural group associated with the non-English language (Khanna, 2004; J. Lee & Bean, 2004). Participation in a U.S. ethnic community of color and visits to one's ancestral country also increase the likelihood of a multiracial person identifying with the culture associated with that community or country.

Identification among multiracial persons as monoracial or multiracial may be influenced by perceptions of acceptance and rejection in monoracial and multiracial communities. Among adults with Japanese and European American ancestry, a sense of belonging to Japanese American, European American, or multiracial communities was associated with identification with these communities (AhnAllen, Suyemoto, & Carter, 2006). Conversely, perceived exclusion from these communities was inversely associated with identification with these communities. In addition, perceived exclusion from the multiracial community was associated with less identification with Japanese American communities but was not significantly associated with European American identification. It appears that exclusion from one minority group (multiracial community) is associated with not identifying with another minority group (Japanese Americans).

Perceived belonging or exclusion from monoracial communities was also influenced by multiracial persons' physical appearance (AhnAllen et al., 2006). Those who had a Japanese physical appearance were more identified with the Japanese American community, whereas those who had a European physical appearance were more identified with the European American community. This finding is consistent with the findings of another study of Asian American/European American adults in which physical appearance was stronger than other influences (gender, socioeconomic status) in determining a person's identification as Asian American or European American (Khanna, 2004).

Given that multiracial persons belong to more than one group, does their racial identity change over time? In a study in which the racial identification of adolescents was assessed and assessed again 6 years later, 41% of African American/European Americans, 45% of Asian American/European Americans, and 81% of American Indian/European Americans changed their racial identification (Doyle & Kao, 2007a; Hitlin, Brown, & Elder, 2006). Changes among persons with African American and Asian American ancestry were toward their minority race, whereas changes among those with American Indian ancestry were toward their European American identity. Data on those who identified as Latino or Hispanic were not analyzed because Latino/a and Hispanic are not racial categories and include persons of all racial groups.

In one study, higher self-esteem and socioeconomic status were associated with a lower likelihood of changing racial identification (Hitlin et al., 2006). High self-esteem may be associated with satisfaction with one's racial identity. High socioeconomic status in this study usually also meant living in a predominantly European American neighborhood in which racial contrasts were salient and possibly perceived as relatively unchangeable. On the other hand, higher intelligence was also associated with changing racial identification, which suggests that those who change racial identification are cognitively flexible.

Among monoracial adolescents, only 3% of monoracial European Americans, 3% of monoracial African Americans, and 7% of monoracial Asian Americans changed their racial identification (Doyle & Kao, 2007a). Among monoracial American Indians, 30% changed their racial identification, and these changes were inconsistent and included identification as European American, African American, and Asian American. This inconsistency among American Indians may be because, similar to Latino and Hispanic, American Indian is not a racial category.

Multiracial persons may have different perspectives on race than monoracial persons (Shih, Bonam, Sanchez, & Peck, 2007). Multiracial persons are more comfortable than monoracial persons in marrying someone or adopting a child from a different racial background. The performance of multiracial persons on quantitative tasks is less influenced by an emphasis on their race before the task than is the performance of monoracial persons. These findings suggest that multiracial persons perceive the meaning of race as socially constructed and may be therefore less concerned about racial boundaries and less influenced by racial stereotypes (Shih et al., 2007).

Does a biracial identity create social advantages with more than one racial group? Recall from Chapter 3 that people are better at recognizing same-race than different-race faces (Golby et al., 2001). For multiracial persons, does this mean that they are skilled at recognizing faces in more than one racial group? Biracial (African American/European American) adults were generally better at recognizing African American faces than European American faces (Chiao, Heck, Nakayama, & Ambady, 2006). However, after writing an essay about their European American parent's ethnic identity, biracial adults were better at recognizing European American faces. Similarly, they were better at recognizing African American faces after writing an essay about their African American parent's ethnic identity. These results suggest that biracial individuals are able to identify with more than one racial group and may develop cognitive flexibility that allows them to adjust to the demands of different racial group contexts. Such adaptability among multiracial persons has been characterized as a chameleon experience (Miville, Constantine, Baysden, & So-Lloyd, 2005).

Who are the best friends of multiracial persons? The best friends of monoracial persons are primarily members of their own racial group (Doyle & Kao, 2007b). Does it follow that the best friends of multiracial persons will be other multiracial persons? In a sample of adolescents, the answer appears to be "no" (Doyle & Kao, 2007b). Less than 11% of African

American/European Americans, Asian American/European Americans, American Indian/European Americans, American Indian/African Americans, or Asian American/African Americans reported having multiracial best friends. In general, having European American ancestry made it more likely for biracial persons to have monoracial European American best friends and having African American ancestry made it more likely to have monoracial African American best friends. The best friends of African American/European Americans were approximately equally divided between monoracial African Americans and monoracial European Americans. It could be contended that there were few multiracial best friends because of lack of availability. However, biracial persons had fewer multiracial than monoracial best friends even after controlling for availability. These data suggest that multiracial adolescents perceive themselves as part of monoracial communities. However, most monoracial African Americans and European Americans in this study did not report that their best friends were multiracial. Thus, perceptions of who is one's best friend may not be mutual. It is probable that a monoracial person who is perceived as a best friend by a multiracial person often does not perceive the multiracial person as his or her best friend.

In summary, most multiracial persons identify themselves as multiracial. The second most common identity is with a monoracial minority group. Identification as multiracial is influenced by physical appearance, cultural access, and community acceptance. Racial and ethnic identification tend to be more flexible among multiracial persons compared to monoracial persons, particularly among those having American Indian ancestry. Multiracial persons may be skilled at facial recognition in more than one racial/ethnic community. Their best friends tend to be monoracial, although it is unclear if multiracial persons are perceived as best friends by monoracial persons.

FAMILY ISSUES

Patterns of interracial marriage correspond with societal stereotypes. Asian Americans are more likely to marry a partner of a different racial background than are African Americans (Cheng & Powell, 2007). Such differences may be associated with positive stereotypes associated with Asian Americans and negative ones associated with African Americans. Thus, Black-White color barriers still remain in marriage. With respect to European American intermarriages, men are more likely to marry Asian American women than Latina American or African American women, and women are more likely to marry Latino American men than Asian American or African American men. Gender stereotypes portray Asian American women as more desirable than Asian American men. Conversely, African American men may be stereotyped as more desirable than African American women, as African American men are more likely to marry European American women than African American women are to marry European American men.

Parents' racial designation of their children depends on the parents' races. Interracial couples with a European American parent are more likely than interracial couples without a European American parent to designate their kindergarten children as multiracial (Brunsma, 2005). Interracial couples without a European American parent are more likely to designate their kindergarten child as monoracial. Interracial couples in which one parent was European American and neither parent was African American were more likely to designate their kindergarten children as European American than European American/African American couples. Conversely, interracial couples with a Latino/a American parent are least likely to designate their children as multiracial and commonly designate their kindergarten children as Hispanic. A Hispanic person can be from any racial group, which may be why in Brunsma Latino/a

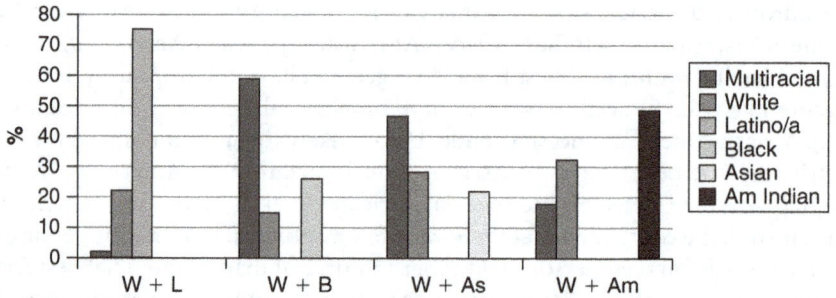

FIGURE 10.1   Parents' Racial Designation of Their Multiracial Children

American parents referred to their multiracial children as Hispanic. See Figure 10.1 for interracial parents' (including a European American parent) racial designations of their children and Figure 10.2 for interracial parents' (not including a European American parent) racial designations of their children.

Consistent with the Brunsma (2005) results, over half of parents in African American/European American and in Asian American/European American couples designated their children as biracial, and nearly half of American Indian/European American parents designated their children as American Indians (Roth, 2005). Roth studied children of all ages and found that older children with a European American parent were more likely to be designated by their parents as European American than younger children, possibly because a European American identity is more desirable for parents of adolescents than a minority identity. Parents with higher education levels were also more likely to designate their children as biracial, which may suggest that more educated persons are more aware of racial options for their children. Moreover, parents who resided in areas with relatively large biracial communities were more likely to designate their children as biracial.

Data are conflicting on whether parents of multiracial children versus monoracial children are more likely to engage in racial/ethnic socialization. Multiracial college students reported that their parents emphasized race significantly less compared to monoracial college students of color or monoracial European American college students (Shih et al., 2007). The difference in this study on parental emphasis on race between monoracial college students of color and monoracial European American college students was small, which is at odds with other research that suggests that parents of college students of color emphasize race more than parents of European American

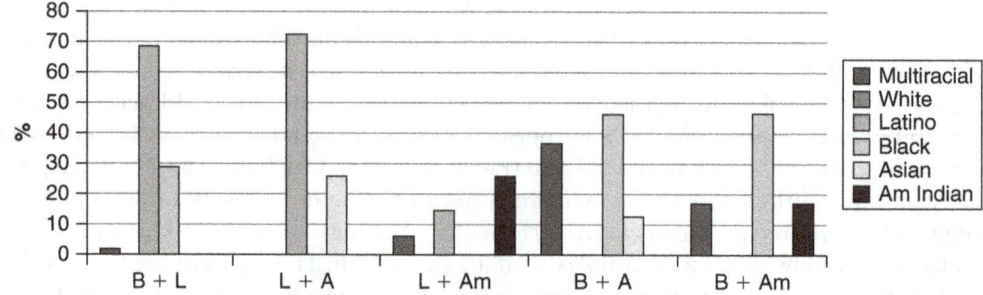

FIGURE 10.2   Parents' Racial Designation of Their Multiracial Children

college students (e.g., Schwartz et al., 2007). Shih and colleagues (2007) acknowledged that it may have been socially desirable to indicate that one's parents de-emphasized race, regardless of one's parents' actual behavior. In contrast to the Shih et al. (2007) results, monoracial parents of multiracial kindergarteners indicated that they discussed their child's racial/ethnic heritage as much as other parents of monoracial kindergartners of color, and more than parents of European American kindergartners (T. N. Brown, Tanner-Smith, Lesane-Brown, & Ezell, 2007).

In summary, patterns of interracial marriage reflect ethnic and gender stereotypes. Among interracial couples, those with a European American member were likely to designate their child as multiracial or European American, whereas those without a European American member were more likely to designate their child as monoracial. Interracial couples having a Latino/a American member are likely to designate their children as Hispanic, and those having an American Indian member are likely to designate their child as American Indian, probably because Latino/a Americans and American Indians are not considered racial groups and encompass multiple racial groups. Parental racial/ethnic designation of their multiracial children is also a function of the child's age, parental education, and access to multiracial communities. Evidence is mixed on how much racial/ethnic socialization that parents of multiracial children engage in relative to parents of monoracial children.

MENTAL HEALTH

Because multiracial persons are members of more than one racial or ethnic group, it has been assumed that they experience identity confusion and that such confusion leads to mental health problems. However, multiracial persons are as well adjusted as their monoracial peers on most psychological outcomes (Shih & Sanchez, 2005). Within clinical populations, multiracial individuals experience racial identity development difficulties, such as rejection by others and confusion about belonging. Multiracial persons in clinical populations also experience greater depression, lower self-esteem, behavior problems (e.g., delinquency, alcohol use), and lower school performance relative to European Americans in clinical populations. Differences on these problems in clinical populations are less pronounced between multiracial persons and monoracial persons of color, with multiracial persons faring better on some dimensions (e.g., school performance).

As with the monoracial groups of color discussed in this book, minority status may influence the mental health of multiracial persons. In a low-income community in which 95% of the residents were monoracial African Americans, mixed-race adolescents reported higher levels of hopelessness, marijuana use, and violent behavior than did monoracial African American or European American adolescents (Bolland et al., 2007). Although it is unclear whether these problems were a direct result of minority status, multiracial adolescents had a lower sense of community than did the monoracial adolescents.

Discrimination may have a greater impact on multiracial than monoracial persons. As discussed above, the standpoint theory predicts that multiracial persons are more sensitive to discrimination than monoracial ethnic minority persons. In a study of adolescents, perceived discrimination was more strongly associated with substance abuse among multiracial than among monoracial ethnic minority youth (Choi, Harachi, Gillmore, & Catalano, 2006). Choi et al. did not report whether multiracial youth experienced more discrimination than did monoracial ethnic minority youth. However, based on other evidence that multiracial persons experience greater levels of discrimination (Brackett et al., 2006; M. Herman, 2004), the stronger effects of discrimination on substance abuse among multiracial youth may have been because they experienced discrimination more frequently.

In summary, multiracial persons in nonclinical populations do not experience greater levels of psychological problems than their monoracial peers. However, in clinical populations, multiracial persons appear to experience greater levels of psychological problems than European Americans and slightly greater levels of psychological problems than monoracial persons of color. Minority status and perceived discrimination are also associated with psychological problems among multiracial persons.

ACADEMIC ACHIEVEMENT AND CAREER DEVELOPMENT

There is extremely limited psychological research on academic achievement or career development among multiracial Americans. Indicating more than a single racial or ethnic group is not an option in most studies. Similar to the data on mental health, multiracial students who are not in clinical populations perform well in school (Shih & Sanchez, 2005). However, multiracial students from clinical populations are characterized by poor academic performance. Among college students, the grade point average of multiracial students was not significantly different than that of monoracial students of color, but it was lower than that of European American students (Ying et al., 2001).

Conclusion

Relative to the monoracial groups reviewed in this book, there is very limited research on multiracial persons. Although conceptual models of multiracial identity have been proposed, there is limited empirical research on multiracial identity development. There traditionally has been an emphasis on the adjustment problems of multiracial persons. However, evidence from nonclinical samples suggests that the adjustment of multiracial persons does not differ from monoracial persons. It appears that many of the difficulties that multiracial persons experience are more a result of being members of ethnic minority groups than of being multiracial per se. There is a need for work on variability among multiracial persons. For example, more work on similarities and differences among multiracial persons having European American ancestry (e.g., Asian/European American, African/European American, Latino/European American) and differences between those having European American ancestry and only minority ancestry (e.g., Latino/Asian American, African/Asian American, Latino/African American) could be investigated.

As with other groups discussed in this book, there is a need for research on the resources and strengths of multiracial persons. Across all research topics on multiracial Americans, most studies have focused on adolescents. More research across the life span is needed, as well as longitudinal research to track development and changes within cohorts of people (Shih & Sanchez, 2005).

I began this chapter with a quote from President Barack Obama. A multiracial, multicultural person is now the leader and the face of the United States. People of color and multicultural issues can no longer be relegated to the margins of society. Although 55% of European Americans did not vote for Obama in the presidential election, the majority of people of color did, which offset the European American majority (CNN, 2008). These data suggest that groups must collaborate to succeed, as the European American minority that voted for Obama could not have elected him without the votes of people of color, nor could people of color have elected Obama without the votes of European Americans.

The election of Barack Obama will not end racism nor will it immediately cause all Americans to embrace multiculturalism. His election is but a first step on the path toward the more perfect union that Obama spoke about in his speech on race. Much of the research reviewed in this book can guide us on this path. I am hopeful that psychology will not continue to marginalize multicultural issues but will embrace them and, rather than react to change, become a proactive influence in society.

Discussion Questions

1. What might motivate someone to ask a complete stranger who is multiracial, "What are you?" Are there situations in which a multiracial person might interpret such a question as benign or even positive? When is such a question a microaggression?

2. Monoracial parents of biracial children may have difficulty knowing how to socialize their child in a biracial manner. Even if a child is racially socialized by each monoracial parent, each form of socialization could be monoracial. What would motivate monoracial parents to biracially socialize their child, and how could this be accomplished?

3. Does Barack Obama having a European American mother make him more appealing than if his mother had been of African ancestry? Is he likely to be viewed as a role model by all multiracial Americans or primarily by biracial African American/European Americans?

REFERENCES

Abe-Kim, J., Okazaki, S., & Goto, S. G. (2001). Unidimensional versus multidimensional approaches to the assessment of acculturation for Asian American populations. *Cultural Diversity and Ethnic Minority Psychology, 7,* 232–246.

Abe-Kim, J., Takeuchi, D. T., Hong, S., Zane, N., Sue, S., Spencer, M. S., Appel, H., Nicdao, E., & Alegria, M. (2007). Use of mental health-related services among immigrant and US-born Asian Americans: Results from the National Latino and Asian American study. *American Journal of Public Health, 97,* 91–98.

Abed, R. T. (1998). The sexual competition hypothesis for eating disorders. *British Journal of Medical Psychology, 71,* 525–547.

Aboud, F. E. (1988). *Children and prejudice.* Oxford, England: Blackwell.

Aboud, F. E., Mendelson, M. J., & Purdy, K. T. (2003). Cross-race peer relations and friendship quality. *International Journal of Behavioral Development, 27,* 165–173.

Abraído-Lanza, A. F., Armbrister, A. N., Flórez, K. R.., & Aguirre, A. N. (2006). Toward a theory-driven model of acculturation in public health research. *American Journal of Public Health, 96,* 1342–1346.

Agbayani-Siewert, P., & Revilla, L. (1995). Filipino Americans. In P. G. Min (Ed.), *Asian Americans: Contemporary trends and issues* (pp. 134–168). Thousand Oaks, CA: Sage.

AhnAllen, J. M., Suyemoto, K. L., & Carter, A. S. (2006). Relationship between physical appearance, sense of belonging and exclusion, and racial/ethnic self-identification among multiracial Japanese European Americans. *Cultural Diversity and Ethnic Minority Psychology, 12,* 673–686.

Alegria, M., Mulvaney-Day, N., Woo, M., Torres, M., Gao, S., & Oddo, V. (2007). Correlates of past-year mental health service use among Latinos: Results from the National Latino and Asian American Study. *American Journal of Public Health, 97,* 76–83.

Alexander, M. G., Brewer, M. B., & Livingston, R. W. (2005). Putting stereotype content in context: Image theory and interethnic stereotypes. *Personality and Social Psychology Bulletin, 31,* 781–794.

Allport, G. W. (1954). *The nature of prejudice.* Reading, MA: Addison-Wesley.

Altschul, I., Oyserman, D., & Bybee, D. (2006). Racial-ethnic identity in mid-adolescence: Content and change as predictors of academic achievement. *Child Development, 77,* 1155–1169.

Alvarez, A. N., Juang, L., & Liang, C. T. H. (2006). Asian Americans and racism: When bad things happen to "model minorities." *Cultural Diversity and Ethnic Minority Psychology, 12,* 477–492.

Alvarez, L. (2007). Derecho u obligación?: Parents' and youths' understanding of parental legitimacy in a Mexican origin familial context. *Hispanic Journal of Behavioral Sciences, 29,* 192–208.

American Psychiatric Association. (2000). *Diagnostic and statistical manual of mental disorders* (4th ed., text revision). Arlington, VA: American Psychiatric Association.

Anglin, D. M., & Wade, J. C. (2007). Racial socialization, racial identity, and Black students' adjustment to college. *Cultural Diversity and Ethnic Minority Psychology, 13,* 207–215.

Antonio, A., Chang, M., Hakuta, K., Kenny, D., Levin, S., & Milem, J. (2004). Effects of racial diversity on complex thinking in college students. *Psychological Science, 15,* 507–510.

Arias, E., MacDorman, M. F., Strobino, D. M., & Guyer, B. (2003). Annual summary of vital statistics—2002. *Pediatrics, 112,* 1215–1230.

Arnett, J. J. (2008). The neglected 95%: Why American psychology needs to become less American. *American Psychologist, 63,* 602–614.

Aronson, J., Quinn, D. M., & Spencer, S. J. (1998). Stereotype threat and the academic underperformance of minorities and women. In J. K. Swim & C. Stangor (Eds.), *Prejudice: The target's perspective* (pp. 83–103). San Diego, CA: Academic Press.

Asante, M. K. (1987). *The Afrocentric idea.* Philadelphia: Temple University Press.

Baer, J. C., & Schmitz, M. F. (2007). Ethnic differences in trajectories of family cohesion for Mexican American and Non-Hispanic White adolescents. *Journal of Youth and Adolescence, 36,* 583–592

Banks, K. H., & Kohn-Wood, L. P. (2007). The influence of racial identity profiles on the relationship between racial discrimination and depressive symptoms. *Journal of Black Psychology, 33,* 331–354.

Bar-Haim, Y., Ziv, T., Lamy, D., & Hodes, R. M. (2006). Nature and nurture in own-race face processing. *Psychological Science, 17,* 159–163.

Baron, R. M., & Kenny, D. A. (1986). The moderator–mediator variable distinction in social psychological research: Conceptual, strategic, and statistical considerations. *Journal of Personality and Social Psychology, 52,* 1173–1182.

Baumrind, D. (1991). Parenting styles and adolescent development. In R. Lerner, A. C. Peterson, & J. Brooks-Gunn (Eds.), *The encyclopedia on adolescence* (pp. 746–758). New York: Garland Press.

Bay-Cheng, L. Y., Zucker, A. N., Stewart, A. J., & Pomerleau, C. S. (2002). Linking femininity, weight concern, and mental health among Latina, Black, and White women. *Psychology of Women Quarterly, 26,* 36–45.

Bazargan, S., Sherkat, D. E., & Bazargan, M. (2004). Religion and alcohol use among African American and Hispanic inner-city emergency care patients. *Journal for the Scientific Study of Religion, 43,* 419–428.

Beach, S. R. H., Kogan, S. M., Brody, G. H., Chen, Y., Lei, M., & Murry, V. M. (2008). Change in caregiver depression as a function of the Strong African American Families Program. *Journal of Family Psychology, 22,* 241–252.

Beals, J., Belcourt-Dittloff, A., Freedenthal, S., Kaufman, C., Mitchell, C., Whitesell, N., Albright, K., Beauvais, F., Belcourt, G., Duran, B., Fleming, C., Floersch, N., Foley, K., Jervis, L., Kipp, B. J., Mail, P., Manson, S., May, P., Mohatt, G., Morse, B., Novins, D., O'Connell, J., Parker, T., Quintero, G., Spicer, P., Stiffman, A., Stone, J., Trimble, J., Venner, K., & Walters, K. (2009). Reflections on a proposed theory of reservation-dwelling American Indian alcohol use: Comment on Spillane and Smith (2007). *Psychological Bulletin, 135,* 339–343.

Beals, J., Novins, D., Whitesell, N., Spicer, P., Mitchell, C., & Manson, S. (2005). Prevalence of mental disorders and utilization of mental health services in two American Indian reservation populations: Mental health disparities in a national context. *American Journal of Psychiatry, 162,* 1723–1732.

Beauvais, F. (1998). American Indians and alcohol. *Alcohol Health & Research World, 22,* 253–259.

Benet-Martinez, V., & John, O.P. (1998). Los Cincos Grandes across cultures and ethnic groups: Multitrait-multimethod analyses of the Big Five in Spanish and English. *Journal of Personality and Social Psychology, 75,* 729–750.

Bernal, G., & Enchautegui-de-Jesús, N. (1994). Latinos and Latinas in community psychology: A review of the literature. *American Journal of Community Psychology, 22,* 531–557.

Bernal, G., & Shapiro, E. (1996). Cuban families. In M. McGoldrick, J. Giordano, & J. K. Pearce (Eds.), *Ethnicity and family therapy* (2nd ed., pp. 155–168). New York: Guilford.

Bernstein, M. (2005). Identity politics. *Annual Review of Sociology, 31,* 47–74.

Berry, J., Phinney, J., Sam, D., & Vedder, P. (2006). *Immigrant youth in cultural transition: Acculturation, identity, and adaptation across national contexts.* Mahwah, NJ: Erlbaum.

Berry, J. W. (1974). Psychological aspects of cultural pluralism: Unity and identity reconsidered. *Topics in Cultural Learning, 2,* 17–22.

Berry, J. W. (2003). Conceptual approaches to acculturation. In K. M. Chun, P. B. Organista, & G. Marin (Eds.), *Acculturation: Advances in theory, measurement, and applied research* (pp. 17–37). Washington, DC: American Psychological Association.

Berry, J. W., Poortinga, Y. H., Segall, M. H., & Dasen, P. R. (2002). *Cross-cultural psychology: Research and applications* (2nd ed.). New York: Cambridge University Press.

Bierman, A. (2006). Does religion buffer the effects of discrimination on mental health? Differing effects by race. *Journal for the Scientific Study of Religion, 45,* 551–565.

Bigler, R. S., & Averhart, C. J., Liben, L. S. (2003). Race and the workforce: Occupational status, aspirations, and stereotyping among African American children. *Developmental Psychology, 39*, 572–580.

Bobo, L. D. (1999). Prejudice as group position: Microfoundations of a sociological approach to racism and race relations. *Journal of Social Issues, 55*, 445–472.

Bodas, J., & Ollendick T. H. (2005). Test anxiety: A cross-cultural perspective. *Clinical Child and Family Psychology Review, 8*, 65–88.

Bolland, J. M., Bryant, C. M., Lian, B. E., McCallum, D. M., Vazsonyi, A. T., & Barth, J. M. (2007). Development and risk behavior among African American, Caucasian, and mixed-race adolescents living in high poverty inner-city neighborhoods. *American Journal of Community Psychology, 40*, 230–249.

Bonham, V. L., Warshauer-Baker, E., & Collins, F. S. (2005). Race and ethnicity in the genome era: The complexity of the constructs. *American Psychologist, 60*, 9–15.

Bornstein, M. H., & Cote, L. R. (2004). Mothers' parenting cognitions in cultures of origin, acculturating cultures, and cultures of destination. *Child Development, 75*, 221–235.

Bowen, W., & Bok, D. (1998). *The shape of the river: Long-term consequences of considering race in college and university admissions*. Princeton, NJ: Princeton University Press.

Boykin, A. W. (1994). Harvesting culture and talent: African American children and school reform. In R. Rossi (Ed.), *Schools and students at risk: Context and framework for positive change* (pp. 116–138). New York: Teachers College Press.

Boykin, A. W., Albury, A., Tyler, K. M., Hurley, E. A., Bailey, C. T., & Miller, O. A. (2005). Culture-based perceptions of academic achievement among low-income elementary students. *Cultural Diversity and Ethnic Minority Psychology, 11*, 339–350.

Bracey, J. R., Bámaca, M. Y., & Umaña-Taylor, A. J. (2004). Examining ethnic identity and self-esteem among biracial and monoracial adolescents. *Journal of Youth and Adolescence, 33*, 123–132.

Brackett, K. P., Marcus, A., McKenzie, N. J., Mullins, L. C., Tang, Z., & Allen, A. M. (2006). The effects of multiracial identification on students' perceptions of racism. *Social Science Journal, 43*, 437–444.

Brave Heart, M. Y., & DeBruyn, L. M. (1998). The American Indian holocaust: Healing historical unresolved grief. *American Indian and Alaska Native Mental Health Research, 8*, 56–78.

Bravo, M. (2003). Instrument development: Cultural adaptations for ethnic minority research. In G. Bernal, J. E. Trimble, A. K. Burlew, & F. T. L. Leong (Eds.), *Handbook of racial and ethnic minority psychology* (pp. 220–236). Thousand Oaks, CA: Sage.

Brega, A. G., & Coleman, L. M. (1999). Effects of religiosity and racial socialization on subjective stigmatization in African-American adolescents. *Journal of Adolescence, 22*, 223–242.

Brody, G. H., Chen, Y., Murry, V. M., Ge, X., Simons, R. L., Gibbons, F. X., Gerrard, M., & Cutrona, C. E. (2006a). Perceived discrimination and the adjustment of African American youths: A five-year longitudinal analysis with contextual moderation effects. *Child Development, 77*, 1170–1189.

Brody, G. H., Murry, V. M., Gerrard, M., Gibbons, F. X., Molgaard, V., McNair, L., Brown, A. C., Wills, T. A., Spoth, R. L., Luo, Z., Chen, Y., & Neubaum-Carlan, E. (2004). The Strong African American Families Program: Translating research into prevention programming. *Child Development, 75*, 900–917.

Brody, G. H., Murry, V. M., Kogan, S. M., Gerrard, M., Gibbons, F. X., Molgaard, V., Brown, A. C., Anderson, T., Chen, Y., Luo, Z., Wills, T. A. (2006b). The Strong African American Families Program: A cluster-randomized prevention trial of long-term effects and a mediational model. *Journal of Consulting and Clinical Psychology, 74*, 356–366.

Brody, G. H., Murry, V. M., McNair, L., Chen, Y., Gibbons, F. X., Gerrard, M., & Wills, T. A. (2005). Linking changes in parenting to parent-child relationship quality and youth self-control: The Strong African American Families Program. *Journal of Research on Adolescence, 15*, 47–69.

Brondolo, E., Brady, N., Thompson, S., Tobin, J. N., Cassells, A., Sweeney, M., Mcfarlane, D., & Contrada, R. J. (2008). Perceived racism and negative affect: Analyses of trait and state measures of affect in a community sample. *Journal of Social and Clinical Psychology, 27*, 150–173.

Brown, C., & Lavish, L. A. (2006). Career assessment with Native Americans: Role salience and career decision-making self-efficacy. *Journal of Career Assessment, 14*, 116–129.

Brown, C. S., & Bigler, R. S. (2005). Children's perceptions of discrimination: A developmental model. *Child Development, 76*, 533–553.

Brown, C. S., Mistry, R. S., & Bigler, R. S. (2007). Hurricane Katrina: African American children's perceptions of race, class, and government involvement amid a national crisis. *Analyses of Social Issues and Public Policy, 7,* 191–208.

Brown, T. L., & Krishnakumar, A. (2007). Development and validation of the Adolescent Racial and Ethnic Socialization Scale in African American families. *Journal of Youth and Adolescence, 36,* 1072–1085.

Brown, T. N., Tanner-Smith, E. E., Lesane-Brown, C. L., & Ezell, M. E. (2007). Child, parent, and situational correlates of familial ethnic/race socialization. *Journal of Marriage and Family, 69,* 14–25.

Brucker, P. S., & Perry, B. J. (1998). American Indians: Presenting concerns and considerations for family therapists. *American Journal of Family Therapy, 26,* 307–319.

Bucko, R. A. (2007). Native American families and religion. In D. S. Browning & D. A. Clairmont (Eds.), *American religions and the family: How faith traditions cope with modernization and democracy* (pp. 70–86). New York: Columbia University Press.

Buki, L. P., Ma, T., Strom, R. D., & Strom, S. K. (2003). Chinese immigrant mothers of adolescents: Self-perceptions of acculturation effects on parenting. *Cultural Diversity and Ethnic Minority Psychology, 9,* 127–140.

Brunsma, D. L. (2005). Interracial families and the racial identification of mixed-race children: Evidence from the Early Childhood Longitudinal Study. *Social Forces, 84,* 1131–1157.

Bryant, A., & LaFromboise, T. D. (2005). The racial identity and cultural orientation of Lumbee American Indian High school students. *Cultural Diversity and Ethnic Minority Psychology, 11,* 82–89.

Bureau of Indian Affairs. (2002, July 12). Indian entities recognized and eligible to receive services from the United States Bureau of Indian Affairs. *Federal Register, 67.*

Burlew, A. K. (2003). Research with ethnic minorities: Conceptual, methodological, and analytical issues. In G. Bernal, J. E. Trimble, A. K. Burlew, & F. T. L. Leong (Eds.), *Handbook of racial and ethnic minority psychology* (pp. 179–197). Thousand Oaks, CA: Sage.

Cachelin, F. M., Phinney, J. S., Schug, R. A., & Striegel-Moore, R. H. (2006). Acculturation and eating disorders in a Mexican American community sample. *Psychology of Women Quarterly, 30,* 340–347.

Caetano, R., Ramisetty-Mikler, S., Vaeth, P. A. C., & Harris, T. R. (2007). Acculturation stress, drinking, and intimate partner violence among Hispanic couples in the U.S. *Journal of Interpersonal Violence, 22,* 1431–1447

Caldwell, C. H., Kohn-Wood, L. P., Schmeelk-Cone, K. H., Chavous, T. M., & Zimmerman, M. A. (2004a). Racial discrimination and racial identity as risk or protective factors for violent behaviors in African American young adults. *American Journal of Community Psychology, 33,* 91–105.

Caldwell, C. H., Sellers, R. M., Bernat, D. H., & Zimmerman, M. A. (2004b). Racial identity, parental support, and alcohol use in a sample of academically at-risk African American high school students. *American Journal of Community Psychology, 34,* 71–82.

Caldwell, C. H., Zimmerman, M. A., Bernat, D. H., Sellers, R. M., & Notaro, P. C. (2002). Racial identity, maternal support, and psychological distress among African American adolescents. *Child Development, 73,* 1322–1336.

Cameron, L., Rutland, A., Brown, R., & Douch, R. (2006). Changing children's intergroup attitudes toward refugees: Testing different models of extended contact. *Child Development, 77,* 1208–1219.

Campbell, M. E., & Troyer, L. (2007). The implications of racial misclassification by observers. *American Sociological Review, 72,* 750–765.

Carlson, S. M., & Moses, L. J. (2001). Individual differences in inhibitory control and children's theory of mind. *Child Development, 72,* 1032–1053.

Carpenter, S., Zarate, M. A., & Garza, A. A. (2007). Cultural pluralism and prejudice reduction. *Cultural Diversity and Ethnic Minority Psychology, 13,* 83–93.

Carson, D. K., & Hand, C. (1999). Dilemmas surrounding elder abuse and neglect in Native American communities. In T. Tatara (Ed.), *Understanding elder abuse in minority populations* (pp. 161–184). Philadelphia: Brunner/Mazel.

Casas, J. M., Turner, J. A., & Esparza, C. A. R. (2005). Machismo revisited in a time of crisis: Implications for understanding and counseling Hispanic men. In G. Good, & G. R. Brooks (Eds), *The new handbook of psychotherapy and counseling with men: A comprehensive guide to settings, problems, and treatment approaches* (pp. 337–356). San Francisco: Jossey-Bass.

Castillo, L. G., Conoley, C. W., & Brossart, D. F. (2004). Acculturation, White marginalization, and family support as predictors of perceived distress in Mexican American female college students. *Journal of Counseling Psychology, 51*, 151–157.

Castillo, L. G., Conoley, C. W., Choi-Pearson, C., Archuleta, D. J., Phoummarath, M. J., & Van Landingham, A. (2006). University environment as a mediator of Latino ethnic identity and persistence attitudes. *Journal of Counseling Psychology, 53*, 267–271.

Castro, F. G., Proescholdbell, R. J., Abeita, L., & Rodriguez, D. (1999). Ethnic and cultural minority groups. In B. S. McCrady & E. E. Epstein (Eds.), *Addictions: A comprehensive guide* (pp. 499–526). New York: Oxford University Press.

Caughy, M. O., Nettles, S. M., O'Campo, P. J., & Lohrfink, K. F. (2006). Neighborhood matters: Racial socialization of African American children. *Child Development, 77*, 1220–1236.

Caughy, M. O., O'Campo, P. J., Randolph, S. M., & Nickerson, K. (2002). The influence of racial socialization practices on the cognitive and behavioral competence of African American preschoolers. *Child Development, 73*, 1611–1625.

Cavalli-Sforza, L. L., Menozzi, P., & Piazza, A. (1994). *The history and geography of human genes.* Princeton, NJ: Princeton University Press.

Chao, R. K. (1994). Beyond parental control and authoritarian parenting style: Understanding Chinese parenting through the cultural notion of training. *Child Development, 65*, 1111–1119.

Chao, R. K. (2001). Extending research on the consequences of parenting style for Chinese Americans and European Americans. *Child Development, 72*, 1832–1843.

Charmaz, K. (2000). Grounded theory: Objectivist and constructivist methods. In N. K. Denzin & Y. S. Lincoln (Eds.), *Handbook of qualitative research* (pp. 509–534). Thousand Oaks, CA: Sage.

Chavez, N. R., & French, S. E. (2007). Ethnicity-related stressors and mental health in Latino Americans: The moderating role of racial socialization. *Journal of Applied Social Psychology, 37*, 1974–1998.

Chavous, T. M., Bernat, D. H., Schmeelk-Cone, K., Caldwell, C. H., Kohn-Wood, L., & Zimmerman, M. A. (2003). Racial identity and academic attainment among African American adolescents. *Child Development, 74*, 1076–1090.

Cheng, S., & Powell, B. (2007). Under and beyond constraints: Resource allocation to young children from biracial families. *American Journal of Sociology, 112*, 1044–1094.

Cheryan, S., & Bodenhausen, G. V. (2000). When positive stereotypes threaten intellectual performance: The psychological hazards of "model minority" status. *Psychological Science, 11*, 399–402.

Cheryan, S., & Monin, B. (2005). Where are you really from? Asian Americans and identity denial. *Journal of Personality and Social Psychology, 89*, 717–730.

Chesley, G. L., & Wagner, W. G. (2003). Adults' attitudes toward multiracial children. *Journal of Black Psychology, 29*, 463–480.

Chiao, J. Y., Heck, H. E., Nakayama, K., & Ambady, N. (2006). Priming race in biracial observers affects visual search for Black and White faces. *Psychological Science, 17*, 387–392.

Choi, Y., Harachi, T. W., Gillmore, M. R., & Catalano, R. F. (2006). Are multiracial adolescents at greater risk? Comparisons of rates, patterns, and correlates of substance use and violence between monoracial and multiracial adolescents. *American Journal of Orthopsychiatry, 76*, 86–97.

Choi, Y., He, M., & Harachi, T. W. (2008). Intergenerational cultural dissonance, parent-child conflict and bonding, and youth problem behaviors among Vietnamese and Cambodian immigrant families. *Journal of Youth and Adolescence, 37*, 85–96.

Chun, K. M., Morera, O. F., Andal, J. D., & Skewes, M. C. (2007). Conducting research with diverse Asian American groups. In F. T. L. Leong, A. Ebreo, L. Kinoshita, A. G. Inman, & L. H. Yang (Eds.), *Handbook of Asian American psychology* (2nd ed., pp. 47–65). Thousand Oaks, CA: Sage.

Chun, S. (2007). The "other Hispanics"—What are their national origins?: Estimating the Latino-origin populations in the United States. *Hispanic Journal of Behavioral Sciences, 29*, 133–155.

Chung, R. H. G. (2001). Gender, ethnicity, and acculturation in intergenerational conflict of Asian American college students. *Cultural Diversity and Ethnic Minority Psychology, 7*, 376–386.

Clark, R. (2006a) Interactive but not direct effects of perceived racism and trait anger predict resting systolic and diastolic blood pressure in Black adolescents. *Health Psychology, 25*, 580–585.

Clark, R. (2006b). Perceived racism and vascular reactivity in Black college women: Moderating effects of seeking social support. *Health Psychology, 25*, 20–25.

Clark, R., Anderson, N. B., Clark, V. R., & Williams, D. R. (1999). Racism as a stressor for African Americans: A biosocial model. *American Psychologist, 54*, 805–816.

CNN (2008). *Exit polls.* Retrieved November 5, 2008 from http://www.cnn.com/ELECTION/2008/results/polls/#USP00p1

Coatsworth, J. D., Maldonado-Molina, M., Pantin, H., & Szapocznik, J. (2005). A person-centered and ecological investigation of acculturation strategies in Hispanic immigrant youth. *Journal of Community Psychology, 33*, 157–174.

Cochran, P. A. L., Marshall, C. A., Garcia-Downing, C., Kendall, E., Cook, D., McCubbin, L., & Gover, R. M. S. (2008). Indigenous ways of knowing: Implications for participatory research and community. *American Journal of Public Health, 98*, 22–27.

Cohen, G. L., & Garcia, J. (2005). "I am us": Negative stereotypes as collective threats. *Journal of Personality and Social Psychology, 89*, 566–582.

Cole, E. R., & Yip, T. (2008). Using outgroup comfort to predict Black students' college experiences. *Cultural Diversity and Ethnic Minority Psychology, 14*, 57–66.

Cole, M. (1996). *Cultural psychology: A once and future discipline.* Cambridge, MA: Belknap Press.

Comas-Díaz, L. (2001). Hispanics, Latinos, or Americanos: The evolution of identity. *Cultural Diversity and Ethnic Minority Psychology, 7*, 115–120.

Commission on Wartime Relocation and Internment of Civilians (1982). *Personal justice denied.* Washington, DC: Government Printing Office.

Comas-Díaz, L., Lykes, M. B., & Alarcón, R. D. (1998). Ethnic conflict and the psychology of liberation in Guatemala, Peru, and Puerto Rico. *American Psychologist, 53*, 778–792.

Constantine, M. G., & Blackmon, S. K. (2002). Black adolescents' racial socialization experiences: Their relations to home, school, and peer self-esteem. *Journal of Black Studies, 32*, 322–335.

Cooper, R. S. (2005). Race and IQ: Molecular genetics as deus ex machina. *American Psychologist, 60*, 71–76.

Cosmides, L., Tooby, J., & Kurzban, R. (2003). Perceptions of race. *Trends in Cognitive Sciences, 7*, 173–179.

Costello, D. M., Swendsen, J., Rose, J. S., & Dierker, L. C. (2008). Risk and protective factors associated with trajectories of depressed mood from adolescence to early adulthood. *Journal of Consulting and Clinical Psychology, 76*, 173–183.

Costigan, C. L., & Dokis, D. P. (2006). Relations between parent-child acculturation differences and adjustment within immigrant Chinese families. *Child Development, 77*, 1252–1267.

Crago, M., & Shisslak, C. M. (2003). Ethnic differences in dieting, binge eating, and purging behaviors among American females: A review. *Eating Disorders: The Journal of Treatment and Prevention, 11*, 289–304.

Crockett, L. J., Iturbide, M. I., Stone, R. A. T., McGinley, M., Raffaelli, M., & Carlo, G. (2007). Acculturative stress, social support, and coping: Relations to psychological adjustment among Mexican American college students. *Cultural Diversity and Ethnic Minority Psychology, 13*, 347–355.

Crosby, F. (1984). The denial of personal discrimination. *American Behavioral Scientist, 27*, 371–386.

Crosby, F. J., & Cordova, D. I. (1996). Words worth of wisdom: Toward an understanding of affirmative action. *Journal of Social Issues, 52*, 33–49.

Crosby, F. J., Iyer, A., Clayton, S., & Downing, R. A. (2003). Affirmative action: Psychological data and the policy debates. *American Psychologist, 58*, 93–115.

Crosby, F. J., Iyer, A., & Sincharoen, S. (2006). Understanding affirmative action. *Annual Review of Psychology, 57*, 585–611.

Crosnoe, R. (2005). The diverse experiences of Hispanic students in the American educational system. *Sociological Forum, 20*, 561–588.

Cross, W. E. (1971). Negro-to-Black conversion experience. *Black World, 20*, 13–27.

Cross, W. E. (1991) *Shades of black: Diversity in African American identity.* Philadelphia: Temple University Press.

Cross, W. E., & Fhagen-Smith, P. (2001). Patterns of African American identity development: A life span perspective. In C. L. Wijeyesinghe & B. W. Jackson (Eds.), *New perspectives on racial identity development* (pp. 243–270). New York: New York University Press.

Cross, W. E., & Vandiver, B. J. (2001). Nigrescence theory and measurement: Introducing the Cross Racial Identity Scale (CRIS). In J. G. Ponterotto, J. M. Casas, L. A. Suzuki, & C. M. Alexander (Eds.), *Handbook of multicultural counseling* (2nd ed., pp. 371–393). Thousand Oaks, CA: Sage.

Cuellar, I., Arnold, B., & Maldonado, R. (1995). Acculturation Rating Scale for Mexican Americans-II: A revision of the original ARSMA scale. *Hispanic Journal of Behavioral Sciences, 17,* 275–304.

Cummins, L. H., Simmons, A. M., & Zane, N. W. S. (2005). Eating disorders in Asian populations: A critique of current approaches to the study of culture, ethnicity, and eating disorders. *American Journal of Orthopsychiatry, 75,* 553–574.

Cutrona, C. E., Russell, D. W., Hessling, R. M., Brown, P. A., & Murry, V. (2000). Direct and moderating effects of community context on the psychological well-being of African American women. *Journal of Personality and Social Psychology, 79,* 1088–1101.

Dana, R. H. (1993). *Multicultural assessment perspectives for professional psychology.* Needham Heights, MA: Allyn & Bacon.

D'Andrea, M., Daniels, J., & Heck, R. (1991). Evaluating the impact of multicultural counseling training. *Journal of Counseling and Development, 70,* 143–150.

Daniel, G. R., & Castaneda-Liles, J. M. (2006). Race, multiraciality, and the neoconservative agenda. In D. L. Brunsma (Ed.), *Mixed messages: Multiracial identities in the "color-blind" era* (pp. 117–145). Boulder, CO: Lynne Rienner.

David, E. J. R. (2008). A colonial mentality model of depression for Filipino Americans. *Cultural Diversity and Ethnic Minority Psychology, 14,* 118–127.

David, E. J. R., & Okazaki, S. (2006). Colonial mentality: A review and recommendation for Filipino American psychology. *Cultural Diversity and Ethnic Minority Psychology, 12,* 1–16.

Davis, F. J. (2006). Defining race: Comparative perspectives. In D. L. Brunsma (Ed.), *Mixed messages: Multiracial identities in the "color-blind" era* (pp. 15–31). Boulder, CO: Lynne Rienner.

Davis-Kean, P. E. (2005). The influence of parent education and family income on child achievement: The indirect role of parental expectations and the home environment. *Journal of Family Psychology, 19,* 294–304.

Devos, T., & Banaji, M. R. (2005). American = White. *Journal of Personality and Social Psychology, 88,* 447–466.

Dick, D. M., Rose, R. J., Viken, R. J., Kaprio, J., & Koskenvuo, M. (2001). Exploring gene-environment interactions: Socioregional moderation of alcohol use. *Journal of Abnormal Psychology, 110,* 625–632.

Dickens, W. T., & Flynn, J. R. (2006). Black Americans reduce the racial IQ gap: Evidence from standardization samples. *Psychological Science, 17,* 913–920.

Dixon, S. V., Graber, J. A., & Brooks-Gunn, J. (2008). The roles of respect for parental authority and parenting practices in parent-child conflict among African American, Latino, and European American families. *Journal of Family Psychology, 22,* 1–10.

Dodge, K. A., McLoyd, V. C., & Lansford, J. E. (2005). The cultural context of physically disciplining children. In N. E. Hill & K. A. Dodge (Eds), *African American family life: Ecological and cultural diversity* (pp. 245–263). New York: Guilford.

Dovidio, J. F., & Gaertner, S. L. (1996). Affirmative action, unintentional racial biases, and intergroup relations. *Journal of Social Issues, 52,* 51–75.

Dovidio, J. F., & Gaertner, S. L. (2000). Aversive racism and selective decisions: 1989–1999. *Psychological Science, 11,* 315–319.

Dovidio, J. F., Gaertner, S. L., Kawakami, K., & Hodson, G. (2002). Why can't we all just get along? Interpersonal biases and interracial distrust. *Cultural Diversity and Ethnic Minority Psychology, 8,* 88–102.

Doyle, J. M., & Kao, G. (2007a). Are racial identities of multiracials stable? Changing self-identification among single and multiple race individuals. *Social Psychology Quarterly, 70,* 405–423.

Doyle, J. M., & Kao, G. (2007b). Friendship choices of multiracial adolescents: Racial homophily, blending, or amalgamation? *Social Science Research, 36,* 633–653.

Duarte, C. S., Bird, H. R., Shrout, P. E., Wu, P., Lewis-Fernandéz, R., Shen, S., & Canino, G. (2008). Culture and psychiatric symptoms in Puerto Rican children: Longitudinal results from one ethnic group in two contexts. *Journal of Child Psychology and Psychiatry, 49*, 563–572.

DuBois, D. L., Burk-Braxton, C., Swenson, L. P., Tevendale, H. D., & Hardesty, J. L. (2002). Race and gender influences on adjustment in early adolescence: Investigation of an integrative model. *Child Development, 73*, 1573–1592.

Dudley, N. M., McFarland, L. A., Goodman, S. A., Hunt, S. T., & Sydell, E. J. (2005). Racial differences in socially desirable responding in selection contexts: Magnitude and consequences. *Journal of Personality Assessment, 85*, 50–64.

Dunifon, R., & Kowaleski-Jones, L. (2002). Who's in the house? Race differences in cohabitation, single parenthood, and child development. *Child Development, 73*, 1249–1264.

Duran, B. M., & Duran, E. F. (1999). Assessment, program planning, and evaluation in Indian country: Toward a postcolonial practice. In R. M. Huff & M. V. Kline (Eds.), *Promoting health in multiculutral populations: A handbook for practitioners* (pp. 291–311). Thousand Oaks, CA: Sage.

Duran, E., Duran, B., Brave Heart, M. Y. H., & Yellow Horse-Davis, S. (1998). Healing the American Indian soul wound. In Y. Danieli (Ed.), *International handbook of multigenerational legacies of trauma* (pp. 341–354). New York: Plenum.

Durik, A. M., Hyde, J. S., Marks, A. C., Roy, A. L., Anaya, D., & Schultz, G. (2006). Ethnicity and gender stereotypes of emotion. *Sex Roles, 54*, 429–445.

Eap, S., DeGarmo, D. S., Kawakami, A., Hara, S. N., Hall, G. C. N., & Teten, A. L. (2008). Culture and personality among European American and Asian American men. *Journal of Cross-Cultural Psychology, 39*, 640–643.

Edman, J. L., & Johnson, R. C. (1990). Filipino American and Caucasian American beliefs about the causes and treatment of mental problems. *Cultural Diversity and Ethnic Minority Psychology, 5*, 380–386.

Edwards, L. M., & Lopez, S. J. (2006). Perceived family support, acculturation, and life satisfaction in Mexican American youth: A mixed-methods exploration. *Journal of Counseling Psychology, 53*, 279–287.

Ehlers, C. L., Spence, J. P., Wall, T. L., Gilder, D. A., & Carr, L. G. (2004). Association of ALDH1 promoter polymorphisms with alcohol-related phenotypes in Southwest California Indians. *Alcoholism: Clinical and Experimental Research, 28*, 1481–1486.

Eibach, R. P., & Keegan, T. (2006). Free at last? Social dominance, loss aversion, and White and Black Americans' differing assessments of racial progress. *Journal of Personality and Social Psychology, 90*, 453–467.

Elizondo, E., & Crosby, F. (2004). Attitudes toward affirmative action as a function of the strength of ethnic identity among Latino college students. *Journal of Applied Social Psychology, 34*, 1773–1796.

Enchautegui-de-Jesús, N., Hughes, D., Johnston, K. E., & Oh, H. J. (2006). Well-being in the context of workplace ethnic diversity. *Journal of Community Psychology, 34*, 211–223.

Evans-Campbell, T. (2008). Historical trauma in American Indian/Native Alaska communities: A multilevel framework for exploring impacts on individuals, families, and communities. *Journal of Interpersonal Violence, 23*, 316–338.

Faer, L. M., Hendriks, A., Abed, R. T., & Figueredo, A. J. (2005). The evolutionary psychology of eating disorders: Female competition for mates or for status? *Psychology and Psychotherapy: Theory, Research and Practice, 78*, 397–417.

Fairburn, C. G., & Cooper, Z. (1993). The Eating Disorder Examination (12th ed.). In C. G. Fairburn & G. T. Wilson (Eds.), *Binge eating: Nature, assessment and treatment* (pp. 317–360). New York: Guilford.

Falicov, C. J. (1998). *Latino families in therapy: A guide to multicultural practice.* New York: Guilford.

Farmer, M. M., & Ferraro, K. F. (2005). Are racial disparities in health conditional on socioeconomic status? *Social Science and Medicine, 60*, 191–204.

Farver, J. A. M., Narang, S. K., & Bhadha, B. R. (2002). East meets West: Ethnic identity, acculturation, and conflict in Asian Indian families. *Journal of Family Psychology, 16*, 338–350.

First, M. B., Spitzer, R. L., Gibbon, M., & Williams, J. B. W. (2001). *Structured clinical interview for DSM-IV-TR axis disorders (Research version).* New York: Biometrics Research Department, New York State Psychiatric Institute.

Fishbein, H. D. (1996). *Peer prejudice and discrimination: Evolutionary, cultural, and developmental dynamics.* Boulder, CO: Westview.

Fisher, C. B., Hoagwood, K., Boyce, C., Duster, T., Frank, D. A., Grisso, T., Levine, R. J., Macklin, R., Spencer, M. B., Takanishi, R., Trimble, J. E.., & Zayas, L. H. (2002). Research ethics for mental health science involving ethnic minority children and youths. *American Psychologist, 57,* 1024–1040.

Fisher, P. A., & Ball, T. J. (2003). Tribal participatory research: Mechanisms of a collaborative model. *American Journal of Community Psychology, 32,* 207–216.

Fitzgerald, K. J. (2007). *Beyond White ethnicity: Developing a sociological understanding of Native American identity reclamation.* Lanham, MD: Lexington Books.

Flores, E., Tschann, J. M., Marin, B. V., & Pantoja, P. (2004). Marital conflict and acculturation among Mexican American husbands and wives. *Cultural Diversity and Ethnic Minority Psychology, 10,* 39–52.

Flores, L. Y., Carrubba, M. D., & Good, G. E. (2006a). Feminism and Mexican American adolescent women: Examining the psychometric properties of two measures. *Hispanic Journal of Behavioral Sciences, 28,* 48–64.

Flores, L. Y., Ojeda, L., Huang, Y., Gee, D., & Lee, S. (2006b). The relation of acculturation, problem-solving appraisal, and career decision-making self-efficacy to Mexican American high school students' educational goals. *Journal of Counseling Psychology, 53,* 260–266.

Fong, T. P. (1998). *The contemporary Asian American experience: Beyond the model minority.* Upper Saddle River, NJ: Prentice-Hall.

Forman, T. A., Williams, D. R., & Jackson, J. S. (1997). Race, place, and discrimination. *Perspectives on Social Problems, 9,* 231–261.

Foster, E. M., & Kalil, A. (2007). Living arrangements and children's development in low-income White, Black, and Latino families. *Child Development, 78,* 1657–1674.

Frabutt, J. M., Walker, A. M., & MacKinnon-Lewis, C. (2002). Racial socialization messages and the quality of mother/child interactions in African American families. *Journal of Early Adolescence, 22,* 200–217.

Franklin, A. J. (1999). Invisibility syndrome and racial identity development in psychotherapy and counseling African American men. *The Counseling Psychologist, 27,* 761–793.

Franko, D. L., & Striegel-Moore, R. H. (2002). The role of body dissatisfaction as a risk factor for depression in adolescent girls: Are the differences Black and White? *Journal of Psychosomatic Research, 53,* 975–983.

French, S. E., Seidman, E., Allen, L., & Aber, J. L. (2006). The development of ethnic identity during adolescence. *Developmental Psychology, 42,* 1–10.

Fuligni, A. J., & Pedersen, S. (2002). Family obligation and the transition to young adulthood. *Developmental Psychology, 38,* 856–868.

Fuligni, A. J., Witkow, M., & Garcia, C. (2005). Ethnic identity and the academic adjustment of adolescents from Mexican, Chinese, and European backgrounds. *Developmental Psychology, 41,* 799–811.

Fuligni, A. J., Yip, T., & Tseng, V. (2002). The impact of family obligation on the daily activities and psychological well-being of Chinese American adolescents. *Child Development, 73,* 302–314.

Gaertner, S. L., & Dovidio, J. F. (2000). *Reducing intergroup bias: The common ingroup identity model.* Philadelphia: Psychology Press.

Garcia-Preto, N. (1996a). Latino families: An overview. In McGoldrick, J. Giordano, & J. K. Pearce (Eds.), *Ethnicity and family therapy* (2nd ed., pp. 141–154). New York: Guilford.

Garcia-Preto, N. (1996b). Puerto Rican families. In McGoldrick, J. Giordano, & J. K. Pearce (Eds.), *Ethnicity and family therapy* (2nd ed., pp. 183–199). New York: Guilford.

Garrett, M. T., & Pichette, E. F. (2000). Red as an apple: Native American acculturation and counseling with or without reservation. *Journal of Counseling and Development, 78,* 3–13.

Garroutte, E. M., Goldberg, J., Beals, J., Herrell, R., Manson, S.M., & the AI-SUPERPFP Team. (2003). Spirituality and attempted suicide among American Indians. *Social Science and Medicine, 56,* 1571–1579.

Gee, C. B., & Rhodes, J. E. (2003). Adolescent mothers' relationship with their children's biological fathers: Social support, social strain and relationship continuity. *Journal of Family Psychology, 17,* 370–383.

Gee, G. C., Ryan, A., Laflamme, D. J., & Holt, J. (2006). Self-reported discrimination and mental health status among African descendants, Mexican Americans, and other Latinos in the New Hampshire

REACH 2010 Initiative: The added dimension of immigration. *American Journal of Public Health, 96,* 1821–1828.

Gee, G. C., Spencer, M. S., Chen, J., & Takeuchi, D. (2007). A nationwide study of discrimination and chronic health conditions among Asian Americans. *American Journal of Public Health, 97,* 1275–1282.

Gee, G. C., Spencer, M., Chen, J., Yip, T., & Takeuchi, D. T. (2007). The association between self-reported racial discrimination and 12-month DSM-IV mental disorders among Asian Americans nationwide. *Social Science and Medicine, 64,* 1984–1996.

Geisinger, K. F. (1994). Cross-cultural normative assessment: Translation and adaptation issues influencing the normative interpretation of assessment instruments. *Psychological Assessment, 6,* 304–312.

Gerrard, M., Gibbons, F. X., Brody, G. H., Murry, V. M., Cleveland, M. J., & Wills, T. A. (2006). A theory-based dual-focus alcohol intervention for preadolescents: The Strong African American Families Program. *Psychology of Addictive Behaviors, 20,* 185–195.

Giang, M. T., & Wittig, M. A. (2006). Implications of adolescents' acculturation strategies for personal and collective self-esteem. *Cultural Diversity and Ethnic Minority Psychology, 12,* 725–739.

Gibbons, F. X., Gerrard, M., Cleveland, M. J., Wills, T. A., & Brody, G. (2004). Perceived discrimination and substance use in African American parents and their children: A panel study. *Journal of Personality and Social Psychology, 86,* 517–529.

Gil, A. G., Wagner, E. F., & Vega, W. A. (2000). Acculturation, familism, and alcohol use among Latino adolescent males: Longitudinal relations. *Journal of Community Psychology, 28,* 443–458.

Gilbert, S. C. (2003). Eating disorders in women of color. *Clinical Psychology: Science and Practice, 10,* 444–455.

Giscombé, C. L., & Lobel, M. (2005). Explaining disproportionately high rates of adverse birth outcomes among African Americans: The impact of stress, racism, and related factors in pregnancy. *Psychological Bulletin, 131,* 662–683.

Go, C. G., & Le, T. N. Gender differences in Cambodian delinquency: The role of ethnic identity, parental discipline, and peer delinquency. *Crime and Delinquency, 51,* 220–237.

Goedde, H. W., Agarwal, D. P., Fritze, G., Meier-Tackmann, D., Singh, S., & Beckmann, G., Bhatia, K., Chen, L. Z., Fang , B., Lisker , R., Paik , Y. K., Rothhammer, F., Saha , N., Segal, B., Srivastava, L. M., & Czeizel, A. (1992). Distribution of ADH2 and ALDH2 genotypes in different populations. *Human Genetics, 88,* 344–346.

Golby, A. J., Gabrieli, J. D. E., Chiao, J. Y., & Eberhardt, J. L. (2001). Differential responses in the fusiform region to same-race and other-race faces. *Nature Neuroscience, 4,* 845–850.

Goldston, D. B., Molock, S. D., Whitbeck, L. B., Murakami, J. L., Zayas, L. H., & Hall, G. C. N. (2008). Cultural considerations in adolescent suicide prevention and psychosocial treatment. *American Psychologist, 63,* 14-31.

Gone, J. P. (2006). Research reservations: Response and responsibility in an American Indian community. *American Journal of Community Psychology, 37,* 333–340.

Gonzalez, J. (2000). *Harvest of empire: A history of Latinos in America.* New York: Viking.

Good, C., Aronson, J., & Inzlicht, M. (2003). Improving adolescents' standardized test performance: An intervention to reduce the effects of stereotype threat. *Journal of Applied Developmental Psychology, 24,* 645–662.

Gosling, S. D., Vazire, S., Srivastava, S., & John, O. P. (2004). Should we trust Web-based studies? A comparative analysis of six preconceptions about Internet questionnaires. *American Psychologist, 59,* 93–104.

Greene, M. L., Way, N., & Pahl, K. (2006). Trajectories of perceived adult and peer discrimination among Black, Latino, and Asian American adolescents: Patterns and psychological correlates. *Developmental Psychology, 42,* 218–238.

Grills, C., & Longshore, D. (1996). Africentrism: Psychometric analyses of a self-report measure. *Journal of Black Psychology, 22,* 86–106.

Griner, D., & Smith, T. B. (2006). Culturally adapted mental health intervention: A meta-analytic review. *Psychotherapy: Theory, Research, Practice, Training, 43,* 531–548.

Guarnaccia, P. J., Pincay, I. M., Alegría, M., Shrout, P. E., Lewis-Fernández, R., & Canino, G. J. (2007). Assessing diversity among Latinos: Results from the NLAAS. *Hispanic Journal of Behavioral Sciences, 29,* 510–534.

Gurin, P., Nagda, B.A., & Lopez, G.E. (2004). The benefits of diversity in education for democratic citizenship. *Journal of Social Issues, 60*, 17–34.

Gushue, G. V., & Whitson, M. L. (2006). The relationship of ethnic identity and gender role attitudes to the development of career choice goals among Black and Latina girls. *Journal of Counseling Psychology, 53*, 379–385.

Gutman, L. M., & Eccles, J. S. (2007). Stage-environment fit during adolescence: trajectories of family relations and adolescent outcomes. *Developmental Psychology, 43*, 522–537.

Guzman, M. R., Santiago-Rivera, A. L., & Hasse, R. F. (2005). Understanding academic attitudes and achievement in Mexican-origin youths: Ethnic identity, other-group orientation, and fatalism. *Cultural Diversity and Ethnic Minority Psychology, 11*, 3–15.

Halgunseth, L. C., Ispa, J. M., & Rudy, D. (2006). Parental control in Latino families: An integrated review of the literature. *Child Development, 77*, 1282–1297.

Hall, C. C. I. (1997). Cultural malpractice: The growing obsolescence of psychology with the changing U.S. population. *American Psychologist, 52*, 642–651.

Hall, C. C. I. (2003). Not just Black and White: Interracial relationships and multicultural individuals. In J. S. Mio & G. Y. Iwamasa (Eds.), *Culturally diverse mental health: The challenges of research and resistance* (pp. 231–248). New York; Brunner-Routledge.

Hall, G. C. N. (1996). *Theory-based assessment, treatment, and prevention of sexual aggression.* New York: Oxford University Press.

Hall, G. C. N. (2001). Psychotherapy research with ethnic minorities: Empirical, ethical, and conceptual issues. *Journal of Consulting and Clinical Psychology, 69*, 502–510.

Hall, G. C. N. (2004). Editorial. *Cultural Diversity and Ethnic Minority Psychology, 10*, 3–4.

Hall, G. C. N. (2006). Diversity in clinical psychology. *Clinical Psychology: Science and Practice, 13*, 258–262.

Hall, G. C. N., & Allard, C. B. (in press). Application to graduate psychology programs by undergraduate students of color: The impact of a research training program. *Cultural Diversity and Ethnic Minority Psychology.*

Hall, G. C. N., Bansal, A., & Lopez, I. R. (1999). Ethnicity and psychopathology: A meta-analytic review of 31 years of comparative MMPI/MMPI-2 research. *Psychological Assessment, 11*, 186–197.

Hall, G. C. N., & Barongan, C. (2002). *Multicultural psychology.* Upper Saddle River, NJ: Prentice-Hall.

Hall, G. C. N., & Eap, S. (2007). Empirically-supported therapies for Asian Americans. In F.T.L. Leong, A. Inman, A. Ebreo, L. Yang, L. Kinoshita, & M. Fu (Eds.), *Handbook of Asian American psychology* (2nd ed., pp. 449–467). Thousand Oaks, CA: Sage.

Hall, G. C. N., Iwamasa, G. Y., & Smith, J. N. (2003). Ethical principles of the psychology profession and ethnic minority issues. In W. O'Donohue & K. E. Ferguson (Eds.), *Handbook of professional ethics for psychologists: Issues, questions, and controversies* (pp. 301–318). Thousand Oaks, CA: Sage.

Hall, G. C. N., Lopez, I. R., & Bansal, A. (2001). Academic acculturation: Race, gender, and class issues. In D. Pope-Davis & H. Coleman (Eds.), *The intersection of race, gender, and class: implications for counselor training* (pp. 171–188). Thousand Oaks, CA: Sage.

Hall, G. C. N., & Maramba, G. G. (2001). In search of cultural diversity: Recent literature in cross-cultural and ethnic minority psychology. *Cultural Diversity and Ethnic Minority Psychology, 7*, 12–26.

Hall, G. C. N., Teten, A. L., DeGarmo, D. S., Sue, S., & Stephens, K. A. (2005). Ethnicity, culture, and sexual aggression: Risk and protective factors. *Journal of Consulting and Clinical Psychology, 73*, 830–840.

Hamid, P. N., Lai, J. C. L., & Cheng, S. T. (2001). Response bias and public and private self-consciousness in Chinese. *Social Behavior and Personality, 29*, 733–742.

Hardway, C., & Fuligni, A. J. (2006). Dimensions of family connectedness among adolescents with Mexican, Chinese, and European backgrounds. *Developmental Psychology, 42*, 1246–1258.

Harrell, S. P., & Bond, M. A. (2006). Listening to diversity stories: Principles for practice in community research and action. *American Journal of Community Psychology, 37*, 365–376.

Harrison, D. A., Kravitz, D. A., Mayer, D. M., Leslie, L. M., & Lev-Arey, D. (2006). Understanding attitudes toward affirmative action programs in employment: Summary and meta-analysis of 35 years of research. *Journal of Applied Psychology, 91*, 1013–1036.

Hawkins, E. H., Cummins, L. H., & Marlatt, G. A. (2004). Preventing substance abuse in American Indian and Alaska Native youth: Promising strategies for healthier communities. *Psychological Bulletin, 130,* 304–323.

Haycox, S. (2002). *Alaska: An American colony.* Seattle: University of Washington Press.

Hays, P. A. (2006). Cognitive-behavioral therapy with Alaska Native people. In P. A. Hays & G. Y. Iwamasa (Eds.), *Culturally responsive cognitive-behavioral therapy: Assessment, practice, and supervision* (pp. 47–71). Washington, DC: American Psychological Association.

Heine, S. J., & Norenzayan, A. (2006). Toward a psychological science for a cultural species. *Perspectives on Psychological Science, 1,* 251–269.

Helms, J. E. (1990). *Black and White racial identity: Theory, research, and practice.* New York: Greenwood Press.

Helms, J. E. (2007). Some better practices for measuring racial and ethnic identity constructs. *Journal of Counseling Psychology, 54,* 235–246.

Helms, J. E., & Carter, R. T. (1990). Development of the White Racial Identity Inventory. In J. E. Helms (Ed.), *Black and White racial identity: Theory, research and practice* (pp. 67–80). Westport, CT: Greenwood Press.

Helms, J. E., Jernigan, M., & Mascher, J. (2005). The meaning of race in psychology and how to change it: A methodological perspective. *American Psychologist, 60,* 27–36.

Herman, K. C., Ostrander, R., & Tucker, C. M. (2007). Do family environments and negative cognitions of adolescents with depressive symptoms vary by ethnic group? *Journal of Family Psychology, 21,* 325–330.

Herman, M. (2004). Forced to choose: Some determinants of racial identification in multiracial adolescents. *Child Development, 75,* 730–748.

Hernandez, M. (1996). Central American families. In McGoldrick, J. Giordano, & J. K. Pearce (Eds.), *Ethnicity and family therapy* (2nd ed., pp. 214–224). New York: Guilford.

Herring, R. (1999). Helping Native American Indian and Alsaka Native male youth. In A. M. Horne & M. S. Kiselica (Eds.), *Handbook of counseling boys and adolescent males* (pp. 117–136). Thousand Oaks, CA: Sage.

Herrmann, R. K., & Fischerkeller, M. (1995). Beyond the enemy image and spiral model: Cognitive-strategic research after the Cold War. *International Organization, 49,* 415–450.

Hines, P. M., & Boyd-Franklin, N. (1996). African American families. In M. McGoldrick, J. Giordano, & J. K. Pearce (Eds.), *Ethnicity and family therapy* (2nd ed., pp. 66–84). New York: Guilford.

Hitlin, S., Brown, J. S., & Elder, G. H. (2006). Racial self-categorization in adolescence: Multiracial development and social pathways. *Child Development, 77,* 1298–1308.

Hodge, F. S., & Fredericks, L. (1999). American Indian and Alaska Native populations in the United States: An overview. In R. M. Huff & M. V. Kline (Eds.), *Promoting health in multiculutral populations: A handbook for practitioners* (pp. 269–289). Thousand Oaks, CA: Sage.

Holliday, B. G. (in press). The history and visions of African American psychology: Multiple pathways to place, space, and authority. *Cultural Diversity and Ethnic Minority Psychology.*

Hong, J. J., & Woody, S. R. (2007). Cultural mediators of self-reported social anxiety. *Behaviour Research and Therapy, 45,* 1779–1789.

Hough, R. L., Canino, G. J., Abueg, F. R., & Gusman, F. D. (1996). PTSD and related stress disorders among Hispanics. In A J. Marsella, M. J. Friedman, E. T. Gerrity, & R. M. Scurfield (Eds.), *Ethnocultural aspects of posttraumatic stress disorder: Issues, research, and clinical applications* (pp. 301–338). Washington, DC: American Psychological Association.

Huddy, L., & Virtanen, S. (1995). Subgroup differentiation and subgroup bias among Latinos as a function of familiarity and positive distinctiveness. *Journal of Personality and Social Psychology, 68,* 97–108.

Hughes, D. (2003). Correlates of African American and Latino parents' messages to children about ethnicity and race: A comparative study of racial socialization. *American Journal of Community Psychology, 31,* 15–33.

Hughes, D., & Dodge, M. A. (1997). African American women in the workplace: Relationships between job conditions, racial bias at work, and perceived job quality. *American Journal of Community Psychology, 25,* 581–599.

Hughes, D., Rodriguez, J., Smith, E. P., Johnson, D. J., Stevenson, H. C., & Spicer, P. (2006). Parents' ethnic-racial socialization practices: A review of research and directions for future study. *Developmental Psychology, 42,* 747–770.

Huntsinger, C. S., & Jose, P. E. (2006). A longitudinal investigation of personality and social adjustment among Chinese American and European American adolescents. *Child Development, 77,* 1309–1324.

Huo, Y. J. (2003). Procedural justice and social regulation across group boundaries: Does subgroup identity undermine relationship-based governance. *Personality and Social Psychology Bulletin, 29,* 336–348.

Hurtado, S. (2005). The next generation of diversity and intergroup relations research. *Journal of Social Issues, 61,* 595–610.

Hwang, W. (2006). Acculturative Family Distancing: Theory, research, and clinical practice. *Psychotherapy: Theory, Research, Practice, Training, 43,* 397–409.

Hwang, W., Chun, C., Takeuchi, D. T., Myers, H. F., & Siddarth, P. (2005). Age of first onset major depression in Chinese Americans. *Cultural Diversity and Ethnic Minority Psychology, 11,* 16–27.

Hwang, W., Myers, H. F., Abe-Kim, J., & Ting, J. Y. (2008). A conceptual paradigm for understanding culture's impact on mental health: The cultural influences on mental health (CIMH) model. *Clinical Psychology Review, 28,* 211–227.

Hwang, W., & Ting, J. Y. (2008). Disaggregating the effects of acculturation and acculturative stress on the mental health of Asian Americans. *Cultural Diversity and Ethnic Minority Psychology, 14,* 147–154.

Inclán, J. E., & Herron, D. G. (1998). Puerto Rican adolescents. . In J. T. Gibbs & L. N. Huang (Eds.), *Children of color: Psychological interventions with culturally diverse youth* (2nd ed., pp. 240–263). San Francisco: Jossey Bass.

Iwamasa, G. Y., & Sorocco, K. H. (2002). Aging and Asian Americans: Developing culturally appropriate research methodology. In G. C. N. Hall & S. Okazaki (Eds.), *Asian American psychology: The science of lives in context* (pp. 105–130). Washington, DC: American Psychological Association.

Jackson, M. F., Barth, J. M., Powell, N., & Lochman, J. E. (2006). Classroom contextual effects of race on children's peer nominations. *Child Development, 77,* 1325–1337.

Jackson, Y. (2003). Research in ethnic minority communities: Cultural diversity issues in clinical psychology. In M. C. Roberts & S. S. Ilardi (Eds.), *Handbook of research methods in clinical psychology* (pp. 376–395). Malden, MA: Blackwell.

Jaffee, S. R., Caspi, A., Moffitt, T. E., & Taylor, Alan. (2004). Physical maltreatment victim to antisocial child: Evidence of an environmentally mediated process. *Journal of Abnormal Psychology, 113,* 44–55.

Jagers, R. J., Sydnor, K., Mouttapa, M., & Flay, B. R. (2007). Protective factors associated with preadolescent violence: Preliminary work on a cultural model. *American Journal of Community Psychology, 40,* 138–145.

Jensen, J. M. (1988). *Passage from India: Asian Indian immigrants in North America.* New Haven, CT: Yale University Press.

Jones, B. T., Corbin, W., & Fromme, K. (2001). A review of expectancy theory and alcohol consumption. *Addiction, 96,* 57–72.

Jones, D. J., Zalot, A. A., Foster, S. E., Sterrett, E., & Chester, C. (2007). A review of childrearing in African American single mother families: The relevance of a coparenting framework. *Journal of Child and Family Studies, 16,* 671–683.

Jones, J. M. (1986). Racism: A cultural analysis of the problem. In J. F. Dovidio & S. L. Gaertner (Eds.), *Prejudice, discrimination, and racism* (pp. 279–314). Orlando, FL: Academic Press.

Jones, J. M. (1997). *Prejudice and racism* (2nd ed.). New York: McGraw-Hill.

Jorde, L. B., & Wooding, S. P. (2004). Genetic variation, classification and 'race'. *Nature Genetics, 36,* 28–33.

Juvonen, J., Nishina, A., & Graham, S. (2006). Ethnic diversity and perceptions of safety in urban middle schools. *Psychological Science, 17,* 393–400.

Kaiser, C. R., Dyrenforth, P. S., & Hagiwara, N. (2006). Why are attributions to discrimination interpersonally costly? A test of system- and group-justifying motivations. *Personality and Social Psychology Bulletin, 32,* 1523–1536.

Kane, T. J. (2003). The long road to race-blindness. *Science, 302,* 571–73.

Kao, G., & Vaquera, E. (2006). The salience of racial and ethnic identification in friendship choices among Hispanic adolescents. *Hispanic Journal of Behavioral Sciences, 28*, 23–47.

Kaslow, N. J., Webb Price, A., Wyckoff, S., Bender Grall, M., Sherry, A., Young, S., Scholl, L., Millington Upshaw, V., Rashid, A., Jackson, E. B., & Bethea, K. (2004). Person factors associated with suicidal behavior among African American women and men. *Cultural Diversity and Ethnic Minority Psychology, 10*, 5–22.

Katigbak, M. S., Church, A. T., Guanzon-Lapena, M. A., Carlota, A. J., & del Pilar, G. H. (2002). Are indigenous personality dimensions culture specific? Philippine inventories and the five-factor model. *Journal of Personality and Social Psychology, 82*, 89–101.

Keel, P. K., & Klump, K. L. (2003). Are eating disorders culture-bound syndromes? Implications for conceptualizing their etiology. *Psychological Bulletin, 129*, 747–769.

Kendler, K. S. (2005). "A gene for . . .": The nature of gene action in psychiatric disorders. *American Journal of Psychiatry, 162*, 1243–1252.

Khanna, N. (2004). The role of reflected appraisals in racial identity: The case of multiracial Asians. *Social Psychology Quarterly, 67*, 115–131.

Kiang, L., Yip, T., Gonzales-Backen, M., Witkow, M., & Fuligni, A. J. (2006). Ethnic identity and the daily psychological well-being of adolescents from Mexican and Chinese backgrounds. *Child Development, 77*, 1338–1350.

Kim, B. S. K., Atkinson, D. R., & Yang, P. H. (1999). The Asian Values Scale: Development, factor analysis, validation, and reliability. *Journal of Counseling Psychology, 46*, 342–352.

Kim, B. S. K., & Omizo, M. M. (2005). Asian and European American cultural values, collective self-esteem, acculturative stress, cognitive flexibility, and general self-efficacy among Asian American college students. *Journal of Counseling Psychology, 52*, 412–419.

Kim, B. S. K., & Omizo, M. M. (2006). Behavioral acculturation and enculturation and psychological functioning among Asian American college students. *Cultural Diversity and Ethnic Minority Psychology, 12*, 245–258.

Kim, B. S. K., Yang, P. H., Atkinson, D. R., Wolfe, M. M., & Hong, S. (2001). Cultural value similarities and differences among Asian American ethnic groups. *Cultural Diversity and Ethnic Minority Psychology, 7*, 343–361.

Kim, H. S. (2002). We talk, therefore we think? A cultural analysis of the effect of talking on thinking. *Journal of Personality and Social Psychology, 83*, 828–842.

Kim, H. S., & Sherman, D. K. (2007). "Express yourself": Culture and the effect of self-expression on choice. *Journal of Personality and Social Psychology, 92*, 1–11.

Kim-Ju, G. M., & Liem, R. (2003). Ethnic self-awareness as a function of ethnic group status, group composition, and ethnic identity orientation. *Cultural Diversity and Ethnic Minority Psychology, 9*, 289–302.

King, E. B., Madera, J. M., Hebl, M. R., Knight, J. L., & Mendoza, S. A. (2006). What's in a name? A multiracial investigation of the role of occupational stereotypes in selection decisions. *Journal of Applied Social Psychology, 36*, 1145–1159.

Kistner, J. A., David-Ferdon, C. F., Lopez, C. M., & Dunkel, S. B. (2007). Ethnic and sex difference in children's depressive symptoms. *Journal of Clinical Child and Adolescent Psychology, 36*, 171–181.

Kitano, H. H. L., & Daniels, R. (1995). *Asian Americans: Emerging minorities.* Englewood Cliffs, NJ: Prentice Hall.

Klonoff, E. A., & Landrine, H. (1999). Cross-validation of the Schedule of Racist Events. *Journal of Black Psychology, 25*, 231–254.

Klonoff, E. A., Landrine, H., & Ullman, J. B. (1999). Racial discrimination and psychiatric symptoms among Blacks. *Cultural Diversity and Ethnic Minority Psychology, 5*, 329–339.

Knight, G. P., Bernal, M. E., Cota, M. K., Garza, C. A., & Ocampo, K. A. (1993). Family socialization and Mexican American identity and behavior. In M. E. Bernal & G. P. Knight (Eds.), *Ethnic identity: Formation and transmission among Hispanics and other minorities* (pp. 105–129). Albany: State University of New York Press.

Knight, G. P., Bernal, M. E., Garza, C. A., Cota, M. K., & Ocampo, K. A. (1993). Family socialization and the ethnic identity of Mexican-American children. *Journal of Cross-Cultural Psychology, 24*, 99–114.

Koopmans, J. R., Slutske, W. S., van Baal, G. C. M., & Boomsma, D. I. (1999). The influence of religion on alcohol use initiation: Evidence for genotype X environment interaction. *Behavior Genetics, 29*, 445–453.

Kressin, N. R., Chang, B., Hendricks, A., & Kazis, L. E. (2003). Agreement between administrative data and patients' self-reports of race/ethnicity. *American Journal of Public Health, 93*, 1734–1739.

Kulis, S., Okamoto, S. K., Rayle, A. D., & Sen, S. (2006). Social contexts of drug offers among American Indian youth and their relationship to substance use: An exploratory study. *Cultural Diversity and Ethnic Minority Psychology, 12*, 30–44.

Ladd, G. W., & Burgess, K. B. (2001). Do relational risks and protective factors moderate the linkages between childhood aggression and early psychological and school adjustment? *Child Development, 72*, 1579–1601.

LaFromboise, T. D., Berman, J. S., & Sohi, B. K. (1994). American Indian women. In L. Comas-Diaz & B. Greene (Eds.), *Women of color: Integrating ethnic and gender identities in psychotherapy* (pp. 30–71). New York: Guilford.

LaFromboise, T., & Bigfoot, D. (1988). Cultural and cognitive considerations in the prevention of American Indian adolescent suicide. *Journal of Adolescence, 11*, 139–153.

LaFromboise, T. D., Coleman, H. L. K., & Gerton, J. (1993). Psychological impact of biculturalism: Evidence and theory. *Psychological Bulletin, 114*, 395–412.

LaFromboise, T. D., & Graff Low, K. (1998). American Indian children and adolescents. In J. T. Gibbs & L. N. Huang (Eds.), *Children of color: Psychological interventions with minority youth* (pp. 112–142). San Francisco: Jossey-Bass.

LaFromboise, T. D., Hoyt, D. R., Oliver, L., & Whitbeck, L. B. (2006). Family, community, and school influences on resilience among American Indian adolescents in the upper Midwest. *Journal of Community Psychology, 34*, 193–209.

Landrine, H., & Klonoff, E. A. (1996a). *African American acculturation: Deconstructing race and reviving culture.* Thousand Oaks, CA: Sage.

Landrine, H., & Klonoff, E. A. (1996b). The Schedule of Racist Events: A measure of racial discrimination and a study of its negative physical and mental health consequences. *Journal of Black Psychology, 22*, 144–168.

Lau, A. S., McCabe, K. M., Yeh, M., Garland, A. F., Wood, P. A., & Hough, R. L. (2005). The acculturation gap-distress hypothesis among high-risk Mexican American families. *Journal of Family Psychology, 19*, 367–375.

Lazur, R. F., & Majors, R. (1995). Men of color: Ethnocultural variations of male gender role strain. In R. F. Levant & W. S. Pollack (Eds.), *A new psychology of men* (pp. 337–358). New York: Basic Books.

Le, H., Berenbaum, H., & Raghavan, C. (2002). Culture and alexithymia: Mean levels, correlates and the role of parental socialization of emotions. *Emotion, 2*, 341–360.

Lee, D., & Tracey, T. J. G. (2005). Incorporating idiographic approaches into multicultural counseling research and practice. *Journal of Multicultural Counseling and Development, 33*, 66–80.

Lee, D. C., & Quintana, S. M. (2005). Benefits of cultural exposure and development of Korean perspective-taking ability for transracially adopted Korean children. *Cultural Diversity and Ethnic Minority Psychology, 11*, 130–143.

Lee, E. (1997). Overview: The assessment and treatment of Asian American families. In E. Lee (Ed.), *Working with Asian Americans: A guide for clinicians* (pp. 3–36). New York: Guilford.

Lee, J., & Bean, F. D. (2004). America's changing color lines: Immigration, race/ethnicity, and multiracial identification. *Annual Review of Sociology, 30*, 221–242.

Lee, L. C. (1998). An overview. In L. C. Lee & N. W. S. Zane (Eds.), *Handbook of Asian American psychology* (pp. 1–20). Thousand Oaks, CA: Sage.

Lee, R. M. (2003). Do ethnic identity and other-group orientation protect against discrimination for Asian Americans? *Journal of Counseling Psychology, 50*, 133–141.

Lee, R. M. (2005). Resilience against discrimination: Ethnic identity and other-group orientation as protective factors for Korean Americans. *Journal of Counseling Psychology, 52*, 36–44.

LeMaster, P. L., Connell, C. M., Mitchell, C. M., & Manson, S. M. (2002). Tobacco use among American Indian adolescents: Protective and risk factors. *Journal of Adolescent Health, 30*, 426–432.

Leong, F. T. L. (2001). The role of acculturation in the career adjustment of Asian American workers: A test of Leong and Chou's (1994) formulations. *Cultural Diversity and Ethnic Minority Psychology, 7,* 262–273.

Leong, F. T. L., & Okazaki, S. (in press). History of Asian American psychology. *Cultural Diversity and Ethnic Minority Psychology.*

Leong, F. T. L., Okazaki, S., & Tak, J. (2003). Assessment of depression and anxiety in East Asia. *Psychological Assessment, 15,* 290–305.

Levin, S., Sinclair, S., Veniegas, R. C., & Taylor, P. L. (2002). Perceived discrimination in the context of multiple group memberships. *Psychological Science, 13,* 557–560.

Liang, C. T. H., Alvarez, A. N., Juang, L. P., & Liang, M. X. (2007). The role of coping in the relationship between perceived racism and racism-related stress for Asian Americans: Gender differences. *Journal of Counseling Psychology, 54,* 132–141.

Lickliter, R., & Honeycutt, H. (2003). Developmental dynamics: Toward a biologically plausible evolutionary psychology. *Psychological Bulletin, 129,* 819–835.

Lin, M. H., Kwan, V. S. Y., Cheung, A., & Fiske, S. T. (2005). Stereotype content model explains prejudice for an envied outgroup: Scale of Anti-Asian American stereotypes. *Personality and Social Psychology Bulletin, 31,* 34–47.

Lonner, W., & Ibrahim, F. (2002). Appraisal and assessment in cross-cultural counseling. In P. Pedersen, J. G. Draguns, W. J. Lonner, & J. E. Trimble (Eds.), *Counseling across cultures* (5th ed., pp. 355–379). Thousand Oaks, CA: Sage.

Lopez, E. M., Gallimore, R., Garnier, H., & Reese, L. (2007). Preschool antecedents of mathematics achievement of Latinos: The influence of family resources, early literacy experiences, and preschool attendance. *Hispanic Journal of Behavioral Sciences, 29,* 456–471.

López, S. R., & Guarnaccia, P. J. J. (2000). Cultural psychopathology: Uncovering the social world of mental illness. *Annual Review of Psychology, 51,* 571–598.

López, S. R., Nelson Hipke, K., Polo, A. J., Jenkins, J. H., Karno, M., Vaughn, C., & Snyder, K. S. (2004). Ethnicity, expressed emotion, attributions, and course of schizophrenia: Family warmth matters. *Journal of Abnormal Psychology, 113,* 428–439.

Love, J. A., & Buriel, R. (2007). Language brokering, autonomy, parent-child bonding, biculturalism, and depression: A study of Mexican American adolescents from immigrant families. *Hispanic Journal of Behavioral Sciences, 29,* 472–491.

Luczak, S. E., Glatt, S. J., & Wall, T. L. (2006). Meta-analyses of *ALDH2* and *ADH1B* with alcohol dependence in Asians. *Psychological Bulletin, 132,* 607–621.

Maddux, W. W., Galinsky, A. D., Cuddy, A. J. C., & Polifroni, M. (2008). When being a model minority is good . . . and bad: Realistic threat explains negativity toward Asian Americans. *Personality and Social Psychology Bulletin, 34,* 74–89.

Major, B., Gramzow, R., McCoy, S. K., Levin, S., Schmader, T., & Sidanius, J. (2002). Perceiving personal discrimination: The role of group status and status legitimizing ideology. *Journal of Personality and Social Psychology, 80,* 782–796.

Major, B., Kaiser, C. R., O'Brien, L. T., & McCoy, S. K. (2007). Perceived discrimination as worldview threat or worldview confirmation: Implications for self-esteem. *Journal of Personality and Social Psychology, 92,* 1068–1086.

Malcarne, V. L., Chavira, D. A., Fernandez, S., & Liu, P. (2006). The scale of ethnic experience: Development and psychometric properties. *Journal of Personality Assessment, 86,* 150–161.

Mandara, J., & Murray, C. B. (2002). Development of an empirical typology of African American family functioning. *Journal of Family Psychology, 16,* 318–337.

Marcia, J. (1980). Identity in adolescence. In J. Adelson (Ed.), *Handbook of adolescent psychology* (pp. 159–187). New York: Wiley.

Marks, A. K., & Coll, C. G. (2007). Psychological and demographic correlates of early academic skill development among American Indian and Alaska Native youth: A growth modeling study. *Developmental Psychology, 43,* 663–674.

Marsella, A. J., & Leong, F. T. L. (1995). Cross-cultural issues in personality and career assessment. *Journal of Career Assessment, 3*, 202–218.

Martin, J. K., & Hall, G. C. N. (1992). Thinking Black, thinking internal, thinking feminist. *Journal of Counseling Psychology, 39*, 509–514.

Martinez, C. R., DeGarmo, D. S., & Eddy, J. M. (2004). Promoting academic success among Latino youths. *Hispanic Journal of Behavioral Sciences, 26*, 128–151.

Martinez, C. R., & Eddy, J. M. (2005). Effects of culturally adapted parent management training on Latino youth behavioral health outcomes. *Journal of Consulting and Clinical Psychology, 73*, 841–851.

Masuoka, N. (2006). Together they become one: Examining the predictors of panethnic group consciousness among Asian Americans and Latinos. *Social Science Quarterly, 87*, 993–1011.

Maton, K. I., Kohout, J. L., Wicherski, M., Leary, G. E., & Vinokurov, A. (2006). Minority students of color and the psychology graduate pipeline: Disquieting and encouraging trends, 1989–2003. *American Psychologist, 61*, 117–131.

Mattison, E., & Aber, M. S. (2007). Closing the achievement gap: The association of racial climate with achievement and behavioral outcomes. *American Journal of Community Psychology, 40*, 1–12.

Mays, V. M., Cochran, S. D., & Barnes, N. W. (2007). Race, race-based discrimination, and health outcomes among African Americans. *Annual Review of Psychology, 58*, 201–225.

McConahay, J. B. (1986). Modern racism, ambivalence, and the Modern Racism Scale. In J. F. Dovidio & S. L. Gaertner (Eds.), *Prejudice, discrimination and racism* (pp. 91–126). Orlando, FL: Academic Press.

McDonald, J. D., & Gonzalez, J. (2006). Cognitive-behavioral therapy with American Indians. In P. A. Hays & G. Y. Iwamasa (Eds.), *Culturally responsive cognitive-behavioral therapy: Assessment, practice, and supervision* (pp. 23–45). Washington, DC: American Psychological Association.

McHale, S. M., Crouter, A. C., Kim, J., Burton, L. M., Davis, K. D., Dotterer, A. M., & Swanson, D. P. (2006). Mothers' and fathers' racial socialization in African American families: Implications for youth. *Child Development, 77*, 1387–1402.

McKown, C., & Weinstein, R. S. (2008). Teacher expectations, classroom context, and the achievement gap. *Journal of School Psychology, 46*, 235–261.

Meier, M. H., Slutske, W. S., Arndt, S., & Cadoret, R. J. (2007). Positive alcohol expectancies partially mediate the relation between delinquent behavior and alcohol use: Generalizability across age, sex, and race in a cohort of 85,000 Iowa schoolchildren. *Psychology of Addictive Behaviors, 21*, 25–34.

Mejia-Arauz, R., Rogoff, B., Dexter, A., & Najafi, B. (2007). Cultural variation in children's social organization. *Child Development, 78*, 1001–1014.

Mendes, W. B., Major, B., McCoy, S., & Blascovich, J. (2008). How attributional ambiguity shapes physiological and emotional responses to social rejection and acceptance. *Journal of Personality and Social Psychology, 94*, 278–291.

Mendoza-Denton, R., Downey, G., Purdie, V. J., Davis, A., & Pietrzak, J. (2002). Sensitivity to status-based rejection: Implications for African American students' college experience. *Journal of Personality and Social Psychology, 83*, 896–918.

Merritt, M. M., Bennett, G. G., Williams, R. B., Edwards, C. L., & Sollers, J. J. (2006). Perceived racism and cardiovascular reactivity and recovery to personally relevant stress. *Health Psychology, 25*, 364–369.

Miller, M. J. (2007). A bilinear multidimensional measurement model of Asian American acculturation and enculturation: Implications for counseling interventions. *Journal of Counseling Psychology, 54*, 118–131.

Miville, M. L., Constantine, M. G., Baysden, M. F., & So-Lloyd, G. (2005). Chameleon changes: An exploration of racial identity themes of multiracial people. *Journal of Counseling Psychology, 52*, 507–516.

Moradi, B., & Risco, C. (2006). Perceived discrimination experiences and mental health of Latina/o American persons. *Journal of Counseling Psychology, 53*, 411–421.

Morales, A., & Hanson, W. E. (2005). Language brokering: An integrative review of the literature. *Hispanic Journal of Behavioral Sciences, 27*, 471–503.

Moreno, C. L. (2007). The relationship between culture, gender, structural factors, abuse, trauma, and HIV/AIDS for Latinas. *Qualitative Health Research, 17,* 340–352.

Murry, V. M., Berkel, C., Brody, G. H., Gibbons, M., & Gibbons, F. X. (2007). The Strong African American Families Program: Longitudinal pathways to sexual risk reduction. *Journal of Adolescent Health, 41,* 333–342.

Mutchler, J. E., Baker, L. A., & Lee, S. (2007). Grandparents responsible for grandchildren in Native-American families. *Social Science Quarterly, 88,* 990–1009.

Nagata, D. K. (1998). The assessment and treatment of Japanese American children and adolescents. In J. T. Gibbs & L. N. Huang (Eds.), *Children of color: Psychological interventions with culturally diverse youth* (2nd ed., pp. 68–111). San Francisco: Jossey Bass.

Nagata, D. K., & Cheng, W. J. Y. (2003). Intergenerational communication of race-related trauma by Japanese American former internees. *American Journal of Orthopsychiatry, 73,* 266–278.

Nagel, J. (1995). American Indian ethnic renewal: Politics and the resurgence of identity. *American Sociological Review, 60,* 947–965.

Naglieri, J. A., Rojahn, J., & Matto, H. C. (2007). Hispanic and non-Hispanic children's performance on PASS cognitive processes and achievement. *Intelligence, 35,* 568–579.

Nakanishi, D. T. (1988). Seeking convergence in race relations research: Japanese–Americans and the resurrection of the internment. In P. A. Katz & D. A. Taylor (Eds.), *Eliminating racism: Profiles in controversy* (pp. 159–180). New York: Plenum.

Nakashima, C. L. (2005). Asian American studies through (somewhat) Asian eyes: Integrating "mixed race" into the Asian American discourse. In K. A. Ono (Ed.), *Asian American studies after critical mass* (pp. 111–210). Malden, MA: Blackwell.

National Survey of Latinos (2002). *National survey of Latinos: Summary of findings.* Washington, DC: Pew Hispanic Center.

Nazroo, J. Y. (2003). The structuring of ethnic inequalities in health: Economic position, racial discrimination, and racism. *American Journal of Public Health, 93,* 277–284.

Newman, D. L. (2005). Ego development and ethnic identity formation in rural American Indian adolescents. *Child Development, 76,* 734–746.

Niemann, Y. F., & Dovidio, J. F. (2005). Affirmative action and job satisfaction: Understanding underlying processes. *Journal of Social Issues, 61,* 507–523.

Nisbett, R. E. (2005). Heredity, environment, and race differences in IQ: A commentary on Rushton and Jensen (2005). *Psychology, Public Policy, and Law, 11,* 302–310.

Nishi, S. M. (1995). Japanese Americans. In P. G. Min (Ed.), *Asian Americans: Contemporary trends and issues* (pp. 95–133). Thousand Oaks, CA: Sage.

Nishio, K., & Bilmes, M. Psychotherapy with Southeast Asian American clients. *Professional Psychology: Research and Practice, 18,* 342–346.

Nobles, W. W. (1973). Psychological research and the black self-concept: A critical review. *Journal of Social Issues, 29,* 11–31.

Noh, S., Kaspar, V., & Wickrama, K. A. S. (2007). Overt and subtle racial discrimination and mental health: Preliminary findings for Korean immigrants. *American Journal of Public Health, 97,* 1269–1274.

Norenzayan, A., & Heine, S. J. (2005). Psychological universals: What are they and how can we know? *Psychological Bulletin, 131,* 763–784.

Norton, I. M., & Manson, S. M. (1996). Research in American Indian and Alaska Native communities: Navigating the cultural universe of values and process. *Journal of Consulting and Clinical Psychology, 64,* 856–860.

Nowak, M. A., & Sigmund, K. (2005). Evolution of indirect reciprocity. *Nature, 437,* 1291–1298.

O'Connor, L. A., Brooks-Gunn, J., & Graber, J. (2000). Black and White girls' racial preference in media and peer choices and the role of socialization for Black girls. *Journal of Family Psychology, 14,* 510–521.

O'Neill, S. K. (2003). African American women and eating disturbances: A meta-analysis. *Journal of Black Psychology, 29,* 3–16.

Oberlander, S. E., Black, M. M., & Starr, R. H. (2007). African American adolescent mothers and grandmothers: A multigenerational approach to parenting. *American Journal of Community Psychology, 39,* 37–46.

Ogbu, J. U. (1986). The consequences of the American caste system. In U. Neisser (Ed.), *The school achievement of minority children: New perspectives* (pp. 19–56). Hillsdale, NJ: Erlbaum.

Okazaki, S. (2002). Beyond questionnaires: Conceptual and methodological innovations for Asian American psychology. In G. C. N. Hall & S. Okazaki (Eds.), *Asian American psychology: The science of lives in context* (pp. 13–39). Washington, DC: American Psychological Association.

Okazaki, S., & Sue, S. (1995). Methodological issues in assessment research with ethnic minorities. *Psychological Assessment, 7*, 367–375.

Olson, L. M., & Wahab, S. (2006). American Indians and suicide: A neglected area of research. *Trauma, Violence, and Abuse, 7*, 19–33.

Ong, A. D., Phinney, J. S., & Dennis, J. (2006). Competence under challenge: Exploring the protective influence of parental support and ethnic identity in Latino college students. *Journal of Adolescence, 29*, 961–979.

Orellana, M. F., Dorner, L., & Pulido, L. (2003). Accessing assets: Immigrant youth's work as family translators or "para-phrasers." *Social Problems, 50*, 505–524.

Ota Wang, V., & Sue, S. (2005). In the eye of the storm: Race and genomics in research and practice. *American Psychologist, 60*, 37–45.

Oyserman, D., Coon, H. M., & Kemmelmeier, M. (2002). Rethinking individualism and collectivism: Evaluation of theoretical assumptions and meta-analyses. *Psychological Bulletin, 128*, 3–72.

Oyserman, D., Kemmelmeier, M., Fryberg, S., Brosh, H., & Hart-Johnson, T. (2003). Racial-ethnic self-schemas. *Social Psychology Quarterly, 66*, 333–347.

Padilla, A. (in press). A history of Latino psychology. *Cultural Diversity and Ethnic Minority Psychology.*

Page, J. (2003). *In the hands of the Great Spirit: The 20,000-year history of American Indians.* New York: Free Press.

Pahl, K., & Way, N. (2006). Longitudinal trajectories of ethnic identity among urban Black and Latino adolescents. *Child Development, 77*, 1403–1415.

Parham, T. A. (1989). Cycles of psychological Nigrescence. *The Counseling Psychologist, 17*, 187–226.

Parke, R. D., Coltrane, S., Duffy, S., Buriel, R., Dennis, J., Powers, J., French, S., & Widaman, K. F. (2004). Economic stress, parenting, and child adjustment in Mexican American and European American families. *Child Development, 75*, 1632–1656.

Patterson, M. M., & Bigler, R. S. (2006). Preschool children's attention to environmental messages about groups: Social categorization and the origins of intergroup bias. *Child Development, 77*, 847–860.

Peregrine, P. N., Ember, C. R., & Ember, M. (2003). Cross-cultural evaluation of predicted associations between race and behavior. *Evolution and Human Behavior, 24*, 357–364.

Perez, D. J., Fortuna, L., & Alegria, M. (2008). Prevalence and correlates of everyday discrimination among U. S. Latinos. *Journal of Community Psychology, 36*, 421–433.

Perl, P., Greely, J. Z., & Gray, M. M. (2006). What proportion of adult Hispanics are Catholic? A review of survey data and methodology. *Journal for the Scientific Study of Religion, 45*, 419–436.

Pettigrew, T. F. (1998). Intergroup contact theory. *Annual Review of Psychology, 49*, 65–85.

Pettigrew, T. F. (2004). Justice deferred a half century after *Brown v. Board of Education. American Psychologist, 59*, 521–529.

Pew Internet and American Life Project (2007). *Demographics of Internet users.* Retrieved October 2, 2007 from http://www.pewinternet.org/trends/User_Demo_6.15.07.htm.

Pewewardy, C. (1999). Culturally responsive teaching for American Indian students. In E. R. Hollins & E. I. Oliver (Eds.), *Pathways to success in school* (pp. 85–100). Mahwah, NJ: Erlbaum.

Pfeifer, J. H., Rubble, D. N., Bachman, M. A., Alvarez, J. M., Cameron, J. A., & Fuligni, A. J. (2007). Social identities and intergroup bias in immigrant and nonimmigrant children. *Developmental Psychology, 43*, 496–507.

Phinney, J. S. (1989). Stages of ethnic identity development in minority group adolescents. *The Journal of Early Adolescence, 9*, 34–49.

Phinney, J. (1992). The Multigroup Ethnic Identity Measure: A new scale for use with diverse groups. *Journal of Adolescent Research, 7*, 156–176.

Phinney, J. S. (1996). When we talk about American ethnic groups, what do we mean? *American Psychologist, 51,* 918–927.

Phinney, J. S., Dennis, J., & Osorio, S. (2006). Reasons to attend college among ethnically diverse college students. *Cultural Diversity and Ethnic Minority Psychology, 12,* 347–366.

Phinney, J. S., & Ong, A. D. (2007). Conceptualization and measurement of ethnic identity: Current status and future directions. *Journal of Counseling Psychology, 54,* 271–281.

Piaget, J. (1952). *The origins of intelligence in the child.* New York: Norton.

Pianka, E. R. (1970). On r- and K- selection. *American Naturalist, 104,* 592–597.

Ponterotto, J. G., & Mallinckrodt, B. (2007). Introduction to the special section on racial and ethnic identity in counseling psychology: Conceptual and methodological challenges and proposed solutions. *Journal of Counseling Psychology, 54,* 219–223.

Ponterotto, J. G., & Park-Taylor, J. (2007). Racial and ethnic identity theory, measurement, and research in counseling psychology: Present status and future directions. *Journal of Counseling Psychology, 54,* 282–294.

Ponterotto, J. G., Utsey, S. O., & Pedersen, P. B. (2006). *Preventing prejudice: A guide for counselors, educators, and parents* (2nd ed.). Thousand Oaks, CA: Sage.

Portes, A., & Rumbaut, R. G. (2001). *Legacies: The story of the immigrant second generation.* Berkeley: University of California Press.

Postmes, T., & Branscombe, N. R. (2002). Influence of long-term racial environmental composition on subjective well-being in African Americans. *Journal of Personality and Social Psychology, 83,* 735–751.

Poston, W. S. C. (1990). The biracial identity development model: A needed addition. *Journal of Counseling and Development, 69,* 152–155.

Prentice, D., & Miller, D. (1996). Pluralistic ignorance and the perpetuation of social norms by unwitting actors. *Advances in Experimental Social Psychology, 28,* 161–209.

Purdie-Vaughns, V., Steele, C. M., Davies, P. G., Ditlmann, R., & Crosby, J. R. (2008). Social identity contingencies: How diversity cues signal threat or safety for African Americans in mainstream institutions. *Journal of Personality and Social Psychology, 94,* 615–630.

Pugh, L. A., & Bry, B. H. (2007). The protective effects of ethnic identity for alcohol and marijuana use among Black young adults. *Cultural Diversity and Ethnic Minority Psychology, 13,* 187–193.

Quillian, L., & Campbell, M. E. (2003). Beyond black and white: The present and future of multiracial friendship segregation. *American Sociological Review, 68,* 540–566.

Quinn, K. A., Roese, N. J., Pennington, G. L., & Olson, J. M. (1999). The personal/group discrimination discrepancy: The role of informational complexity. *Personality and Social Psychology Bulletin, 23,* 1430–1440.

Radin, S. M., Neighbors, C., Walker, P. S., Walker, R. D., Marlatt, G. A., & Larimer, M. (2006). The changing influences of self-worth and peer deviance on drinking problems in urban American Indian adolescents. *Psychology of Addictive Behaviors, 20,* 161–170.

Raine, A. (2002). Biosocial studies of antisocial and violent behavior in children and adults: A review. *Journal of Abnormal Child Psychology, 30,* 311–326.

Ramos, B., Jaccard, J., & Guilamo-Ramos, V. (2003). Dual ethnicity and depressive symptoms: Implications of being Black and Latino in the United States. *Hispanic Journal of Behavioral Sciences, 25,* 147–173.

Rees, R. W. (2007). *Shades of difference: A history of ethnicity in America.* New York: Rowman and Littlefield.

Regents of the University of California v. Bakke 438 U.S. 265 (1978).

Ricciardelli, L. A., & McCabe, M. P. (2004). A biopsychosocial model of disordered eating and the pursuit of muscularity in adolescent boys. *Psychological Bulletin, 130,* 179–205.

Ricciardelli, L. A., Mccabe, M. P., Williams, R. J., & Thompson, J. K. (2007). The role of ethnicity and culture in body image and disordered eating among males. *Clinical Psychology Review, 27,* 582–606.

Richardson, K. (1998). *The origins of human potential: Evolution, development, and psychology.* London: Routledge.

Ridley, C. R. (1984). Clinical treatment of the nondisclosing Black client: A therapeutic paradox. *American Psychologist, 39,* 1234–1244.

Rieckmann, T. R., Wadsworth, M. E., & Deyhle, D. (2004). Cultural identity, explanatory style, and depression in Navajo adolescents. *Cultural Diversity and Ethnic Minority Psychology, 10,* 365–382.

Roberts, R. K., Swanson, N. G., & Murphy, L. R. (2004). Discrimination and occupational mental health. *Journal of Mental Health, 13,* 129–142.

Roberts, S. A. (1999). Socioeconomic position and health: The independent contribution of community socioeconomic context. *Annual Review of Sociology, 25,* 489–516.

Rockquemore, K. A. (1999). Being Black and White: Exploring the biracial experience. *Race and Society, 1,* 197–212.

Rockquemore, K. A., & Brunsma, D. L. (2001). *Beyond Black: Biracial identity in America.* Thousand Oaks, CA: Sage.

Rodríguez, M. D., Davis, M. R., Rodríguez, J., & Bates, S. C. (2006). Observed parenting practices of first-generation Latino families. *Journal of Community Psychology, 34,* 133–148.

Rodriguez, N., Mira, C. B., Paez, N. D., & Myers, H. F. (2007). Exploring the complexities of familism and acculturation: Central constructs for people of Mexican origin. *American Journal of Community Psychology, 39,* 61–77.

Romero, A. J., Cuellar, I., & Roberts, R. E. (2000). Ethnocultural variables and attitudes toward cultural socialization of children. *Journal of Community Psychology, 28,* 79–89.

Romero, A. J., & Roberts, R. E. (2003). Stress within a bicultural context for adolescents of Mexican descent. *Cultural Diversity and Ethnic Minority Psychology, 9,* 171–184.

Root, M. P. P. (1992). *Racially mixed people in America.* Newbury Park, CA: Sage.

Root, M. P. P. (1996). *The multiracial experience.* Thousand Oaks, CA: Sage.

Rose, R. J., Dick, D. M., Viken, R. J., & Kaprio, J. (2001). Gene-environment interaction in patterns of adolescent drinking: Regional residency moderates longitudinal influences on alcohol use. *Alcoholism: Clinical and Experimental Research, 25,* 637–643.

Rosenfarb, I. S., Bellack, A. S., & Aziz, N. (2006a). Family interactions and the course of schizophrenia in African American and White patients. *Journal of Abnormal Psychology, 115,* 112–120.

Rosenfarb, I. S., Bellack, A. S., & Aziz, N. (2006b). A sociocultural stress, appraisal, and coping model of subjective burden and family attitudes toward patients with schizophrenia. *Journal of Abnormal Psychology, 115,* 157–165.

Roth, W. D. (2005). The end of the one-drop rule? Labeling of multiracial children in Black intermarriages. *Sociological Forum, 20,* 35–67.

Rumbaut, R. G. (1995). Vietnamese, Laotian, and Cambodian Americans. In P. G. Min (Ed.), *Asian Americans: Contemporary trends and issues* (pp. 232–270). Thousand Oaks, CA: Sage.

Rushton, J. P. (1995a). *Race, evolution & behavior.* New Brunswick, NJ: Transaction.

Rushton, J. P. (1995b). *Race, evolution, and man.* Princeton, NJ: Princeton University Press.

Sack, W. H., & Clarke, G. N. (1996). Multiple forms of stress in Cambodian adolescent refugees. *Child Development, 67,* 107–116.

Sangrigoli, S., Pallier, C., Argenti, A. M., Ventureyra, V. A. G., & de Schonen, S. (2005). Reversibility of the other-race effect in face recognition during childhood. *Psychological Science, 16,* 440–444.

Santiago-Rivera, A., Arredondo, P., & Gallardo-Cooper, M. (2002). *Counseling Latinos and la familia.* Thousand Oaks, CA: Sage.

Schmader, T., & Johns, M. (2003). Converging evidence that stereotype threat reduces working memory capacity. *Journal of Personality and Social Psychology, 85,* 440–452.

Schmerund, A., Sellers, R., Mueller, B., & Crosby, F. (2001). Attitudes toward affirmative action as a function of racial identity among African American college students. *Political Psychology, 22,* 759–774.

Schmitt, D. P. & Pilcher, J. J. (2004). Evaluating evidence of psychological adaptation: How do we know one when we see one? *Psychological Science, 15,* 643–649.

Schwartz, S. J., Zamboanga, B. L., & Jarvis, L. H. (2007). Ethnic identity and acculturation in Hispanic early adolescents: Mediated relationships to academic grades, prosocial behaviors, and externalizing symptoms. *Cultural Diversity and Ethnic Minority Psychology, 13,* 364–373.

Scollon, C. N., Diener, E., Oishi, S., & Biswas-Diener, R. (2004). Emotions across cultures and methods. *Journal of Cross-Cultural Psychology, 35,* 304–326.

Scott, L. D. (2003). The relation of racial identity and racial socialization to coping with discrimination among African Americans. *Journal of Black Studies, 33,* 520–538.

Scribner, R., Hohn, A., & Dwyer, J. (1995). Blood pressure and self-concept among African-American adolescents. *Journal of the National Medical Association, 87,* 417–422.

Sears, D. O. (1988). Symbolic racism. In P. A. Katz & D. A. Taylor (Eds.), *Eliminating racism: Profiles in controversy* (pp. 53–84). New York: Plenum.

Sears, D. O., Citrin, J., Cheleden, S. V., & van Laar, C. (1999). Cultural diversity and multicultural politics: Is ethnic balkanization psychologically inevitable? In D. A. Prentice & D. T. Miller (Eds.), *Cultural divides: Understanding and overcoming group conflict* (pp. 35–79). New York: Russell Sage Foundation.

Seaton, E. K., Scottham, K. M., & Sellers, R. M. (2006). The status model of racial identity development in African American Adolescents: Evidence of structure, trajectories, and well-being. *Child Development, 77,* 1416–1426.

Segall, M. H., Lonner, W. J., & Berry, J. W. (1998). Cross-cultural psychology as a scholarly discipline: On the flowering of culture in behavioral research. *American Psychologist, 53,* 1101–1110.

Sekaquaptewa, D., Waldman, A., & Thompson, M. (2007). Solo status and self-construal: Being distinctive influences racial self-construal and performance apprehension in African American women. *Cultural Diversity and Ethnic Minority Psychology, 13,* 321–327.

Sellers, R. M., Rowley, S. A. J., Chavous, T. M., Shelton, J. N., & Smith, M. A. (1997). Multidimensional inventory of black identity: A preliminary investigation of reliability and construct validity. *Journal of Personality and Social Psychology, 73,* 805–815.

Sellers, R. M., & Shelton, J. N. (2003). The role of racial identity in perceived racial discrimination. *Journal of Personality and Social Psychology, 84,* 1079–1092.

Sellers, R. M., Smith, M. A., Shelton, J. N., Rowley, S. A. J., & Chavous, T. M. (1998). Multidimensional model of racial identity: A reconceptualization of African American racial identity. *Personality and Social Psychology Review, 2,* 18–39.

Shanahan, M. J., & Hofer, S. M. (2005). Social context in gene-environment interactions: retrospect and prospect. *Journals of Gerontology: Series B: Psychological Sciences and Social Sciences, 60B,* 65–76.

Shelton, J. N., & Richeson, J. A. (2005). Intergroup contact and pluralistic ignorance. *Journal of Personality and Social Psychology, 88,* 91–107.

Shelton, J. N., & Sellers, R. M. (2000). Situational stability and variability in African American identity. *Journal of Black Psychology, 26,* 27–50.

Sheth, M. (1995). Asian Indian Americans. In P. G. Min (Ed.), *Asian Americans: Contemporary trends and issues* (pp. 169–198). Thousand Oaks, CA: Sage.

Shih, M., Ambady, N., Richeson, J. A., Fujita, K., & Gray, H. M. (2002). Stereotype performance boosts: The impact of self-relevance and the manner of stereotype activation. *Journal of Personality and Social Psychology, 83,* 638–647.

Shih, M., Bonam, C., Sanchez, D., & Peck, C. (2007). The social construction of race: Biracial identity and vulnerability to stereotypes. *Cultural Diversity and Ethnic Minority Psychology, 13,* 125–133.

Shih, M., Pittinsky, T. L., & Ambady, N. (1999). Stereotype susceptibility: Identity salience and shifts in quantitative performance. *Psychological Science, 10,* 80–83.

Shih, M., Pittinsky, T. L., & Trahan, A. (2006). Domain-specific effects of stereotypes on performance. *Self and Identity, 5,* 1–14.

Shih, M., & Sanchez, D. T. (2005). Perspectives and research on the positive and negative implications of having multiple racial identities. *Psychological Bulletin, 131,* 569–591.

Shweder, R. A. (2000). The psychology of practice and the practice of the three psychologies. *Asian Journal of Social Psychology, 3,* 207–222.

Sidanius, J., & Pratto, F. (1999). *Social dominance: An intergroup theory of social hierarchy and oppression.* Cambridge, UK: Cambridge University Press.

Sidanius, J., Van Laar, C., Levin, S., & Sinclair, S. (2004). Ethnic enclaves and the dynamics of social identity on the college campus: The good, the bad, and the ugly. *Journal of Personality and Social Psychology, 87*, 96–110.

Simon, C. E., Crowther, M., & Higgerson, H. (2007). The stage-specific role of spirituality among African American Christian women throughout the breast cancer experience. *Cultural Diversity and Ethnic Minority Psychology, 13*, 26–34.

Simons, R. L., Murry, V., McLoyd, V., Lin, K., Cutrona, C., & Conger, R. D. (2002). Discrimination, crime, ethnic identity, and parenting as correlates of depressive symptoms among African American children: A multi-level analysis. *Development and Psychopathology, 14*, 371–393.

Smalls, C., White, R., Chavous, T., & Sellers, R. (2007). Racial ideological beliefs and racial discrimination experiences as predictors of academic engagement among African American adolescents. *Journal of Black Psychology, 33*, 299–330.

Smetana, J. G., Campione-Barr, N., & Daddis, C. (2004). Longitudinal development of family decision making: Defining healthy behavioral autonomy for middle-class African American adolescents. *Child Development, 75*, 1418–1434.

Smith, E. P., Atkins, J., & Connell, C. M. (2003). Family, school, and community factors and relationships to racial-ethnic attitudes and academic achievement. *American Journal of Community Psychology, 32*, 159–173.

Smokowski, P. R., & Bacallao, M. L. (2006). Acculturation and aggression in Latino adolescents: A structural model focusing on cultural risk factors and assets. *Journal of Abnormal Child Psychology, 34*, 659–673.

Sommers, S. R. (2006). On racial diversity and group decision making: Identifying multiple effects of racial composition on jury deliberations. *Journal of Personality and Social Psychology, 90*, 597–612.

Spickard, P. (2007). *Almost all aliens.* New York: Routledge.

Spillane, N. S., & Smith, G. T. (2007). A theory of reservation-dwelling American Indian alcohol use risk. *Psychological Bulletin, 133*, 395–418.

Steele, C. M. (1997). A threat in the air: How stereotypes shape the intellectual identities and performance of women and African Americans. *American Psychologist, 52*, 613–629.

Sternberg, R. J., Grigorenko, E. L., & Kidd, K. K. (2005). Intelligence, race, and genetics. *American Psychologist, 60*, 46–59.

Sternberg, R. J., & Williams, W. M. (1997). Does the Graduate Record Examination predict meaningful success in the graduate training of psychologists? A case study. *American Psychologist, 52*, 630–641.

Stevenson, H. C., Herrero-Taylor, T., Cameron, R., & Davis, G. Y. (2002). "Mitigating instigation": Cultural phenomenological influences of anger and fighting among "big-boned" and "baby-faced" African American youth. *Journal of Youth and Adolescence, 31*, 473–485.

Stevenson, H. C., McNeil, J. D., Herrero-Taylor, T., & Davis, G. Y. (2005). Influence of perceived neighborhood diversity and racism experience on the racial socialization of Black youth. *Journal of Black Psychology, 31*, 273–290.

Stone, R. A. T., Whitbeck, L. B., Chen, X., Johnson, K., & Olson, D. M. (2006). Traditional practices, traditional spirituality, and alcohol cessation among American Indians. *Journal of Studies on Alcohol, 67*, 236–244.

Striegel-Moore, R. H., Dohm, F. A., Kraemer, H. C., Taylor, C. B., Daniels, S., Crawford, P. B., & Schreiber, G. B. (2003). Eating disorders in White and Black women. *American Journal of Psychiatry, 160*, 1326–1331.

Sue, D. W. (2001). Multidimensional facets of cultural competence. *The Counseling Psychologist, 29*, 790–821.

Sue, D. W. (2004). Whiteness and ethnocentric monoculturalism: Making the "invisible" visible. *American Psychologist, 59*, 761–769.

Sue, D. W., Bingham, R. P., Porche-Burke, L., & Vasquez, M. (1999). The diversification of psychology: A multicultural revolution. *American Psychologist, 54*, 1061–1069.

Sue, D. W., Capodilupo, C. M., Torino, G. C., Bucceri, J. M., Holder, A. M. B., Nadal, K. L., & Esquilin, M. (2007). Racial microaggressions in everyday life: Implications for clinical practice. *American Psychologist, 62*, 271–286.

Sue, S. (1991). Ethnicity and culture in psychological research and practice. In J. D. Goodchilds (Ed.), *Psychological perspectives on human diversity in America* (pp. 51–85). Washington, DC: American Psychological Association.

Sue, S. (1999). Science, ethnicity, and bias—Where have we gone wrong? *American Psychologist, 54*, 1070–1077.

Sue, S., Fujino, D. C., Hu, L., Takeuchi, D. T., & Zane, N. W. S. (1991). Community mental health services for ethnic minority groups: A test of the cultural responsiveness hypothesis. *Journal of Consulting and Clinical Psychology, 59*, 533–540.

Sue, S., & Okazaki, S. (1990). Asian-American educational achievements: A phenomenon in search of an explanation. *American Psychologist, 45*, 913–920.

Sue, S., & Sue, L. (2003). Ethnic research is good science. In G. Bernal, J. E. Trimble, A. K. Burlew, & F. T. L. Leong (Eds.), *Handbook of racial and ethnic minority psychology* (pp. 198–207). Thousand Oaks, CA: Sage.

Suizzo, M., & Stapleton, L. M. (2007). Home-based parental involvement in young children's education: Examining the effects of maternal education across U.S. ethnic groups. *Educational Psychology, 27*, 533–556.

Supple, A. J., Ghazarian, S. R., Frabutt, J. M., Plunkett, S. W., & Sands, T. (2006). Contextual influences on Latino adolescent ethnic identity and academic outcomes. *Child Development, 77*, 1427–1433.

Sutton, C. T., & Broken Nose, M. A. (2005). American Indian families: An overview. In M. McGoldrick, J. Giordano, & N. Garcia-Preto (Eds.), *Ethnicity and family therapy* (3rd ed., pp. 43–54). New York: Guilford.

Suyemoto, K. L. (2004). Racial/ethnic identities and related attributed experiences of multiracial Japanese European Americans. *Journal of Multicultural Counseling and Development, 32*, 206–221.

Suyemoto, K. L., & Dimas, J. M. (2003). To be included in the multicultural discussion: Check one box only. In J. S. Mio & G. Y. Iwamasa (Eds.), *Culturally diverse mental health: The challenges of research and resistance* (pp. 55–81). New York; Brunner-Routledge.

Suzuki-Crumly, J., & Hyers, L. L. (2004). The relationship among ethnic identity, psychological well-being, and intergroup competence: An investigation of two biracial groups. *Cultural Diversity and Ethnic Minority Psychology, 10*, 137–150.

Sy, S. R. (2006). Family and work influences on the transition to college among Latina adolescents. *Hispanic Journal of Behavioral Sciences, 28*, 368–386.

Tafoya, N., & Del Vecchio, A. (2005). Back to the future: An examination of the Native American holocaust experience. In M. McGoldrick, J. Giordano, & N. Garcia-Preto (Eds.), *Ethnicity and family therapy* (3rd ed., pp. 55–63). New York: Guilford.

Tajfel, H., & Turner, J. C. (1986). The social identity theory of intergroup behaviour. In S. Worchel & W. G. Austin (Eds.), *Psychology of intergroup relations* (pp. 7–24). Chicago: Nelson.

Takaki, R. (1993). *A different mirror: A history of multicultural America.* New York: Little, Brown.

Taylor, G. J. (1984). Alexithymia: Concept, measurement, and implications for treatment. *American Journal of Psychiatry, 141*, 725–732.

Taylor, S. E., Sherman, D. K., Kim, H. S., Jarcho, J., Takagi, K., & Dunagan, M. S. (2004). Culture and social support: Who seeks it and why? *Journal of Personality and Social Psychology, 87*, 354–362.

Teo, T. (2004). The historical problematization of "mixed race" in psychological and human-scientific discourses. In A. S. Winston (Ed.), *Defining difference: Race and racism in the history of psychology* (pp. 79–108). Washington, DC: American Psychological Association.

Thomas, A. J., & Speight, S. L. (1999). Racial identity and racial socialization attitudes of African American parents. *Journal of Black Psychology, 25*, 152–170.

Thomas, D. E., Townsend, T. G., & Belgrave, F. Z. (2003). The influence of cultural and racial identification on the psychosocial adjustment of inner-city African American children in school. *American Journal of Community Psychology, 32*, 217–228.

Thompson, N. L., Hare, D., Sempier, T. T., & Grace, C. (2008). The development of a curriculum toolkit with American Indian and Alaska Native communities. *Early Childhood Education Journal, 35*, 397–404.

Torres, L., & Rollock, D. (2007). Acculturation and depression among Hispanics: The moderating effect of intercultural competence. *Cultural Diversity and Ethnic Minority Psychology, 13*, 10–17.

Triandis, H. C. (1996). The psychological measurement of cultural syndromes. *American Psychologist, 51*, 407–415.

Trickett, E. J., & Jones, C. J. (2007). Adolescent culture brokering and family functioning: A study of families from Vietnam. *Cultural Diversity and Ethnic Minority Psychology, 13*, 143–150.

Trimble, J. E. (2007). Prolegomena for the connotation of construct use in the measurement of ethnic and racial identity. *Journal of Counseling Psychology, 54*, 247–258.

Trimble, J. E., & Dickson, R. (2005). Ethnic identity. In C. B. Fisher & R. M. Lerner (Eds.), *Encyclopedia of applied developmental science* (Vol. 1, pp. 415–420). Thousand Oaks, CA: Sage.

Trimble, J. E., Fleming, C. M., Beauvais, F., & Jumper-Thurman, P. (1996). Essential cultural and social strategies for counseling Native American Indians. In P. B. Pedersen, J. G. Draguns, W. J. Lonner, & J. E. Trimble (Eds.), *Counseling across cultures*, (4th ed., pp. 177–209). Thousand Oaks, CA: Sage.

Trimble, J. E., Helms, J. E., & Root, M. P. P. (2003). Social and psychological perspectives on ethnic and racial identity. In G. Bernal, J. E. Trimble, A. K. Burlew, & F. T. L. Leong (Eds.), *Handbook of racial and ethnic minority psychology* (pp. 239–275.). Thousand Oaks, CA: Sage.

Trimble, J. E., & Thurman, P. J. (2002). Ethnocultural considerations and strategies for providing counseling services to Native American Indians. In P. B. Pedersen, J. G. Draguns, W. J. Lonner, & J. E. Trimble (Eds.), *Counseling across cultures* (5th ed., pp. 53–91). Thousand Oaks, CA: Sage.

Tropp, L. R., & Pettigrew, T. F. (2005). Relationships between intergroup contact and prejudice among minority and majority status groups. *Psychological Science, 16*, 951–957.

Trujillo, A. (2000). Psychotherapy with Native Americans: A view into the role of religion and spirituality. In P. S. Richards & A. E. Bergin (Eds.), *Handbook of psychotherapy and religious diversity* (pp. 445–466). Washington, DC: American Psychological Association.

Tsai, J. L., Chentsova-Dutton, Y., & Wong, Y. (2002). Why and how we should study ethnic identity, acculturation, and cultural orientation. In G. C. N. Hall & S. Okazaki (Eds.), *Asian American psychology: The science of lives in context* (pp. 41–65). Washington, DC: American Psychological Association.

Tsai, J. L., Simeonova, D. I., & Watanabe, J. T. (2004). Somatic and social: Chinese Americans talk about emotion. *Personality and Social Psychology Bulletin, 30*, 1226–1238.

Tsai, J. L., Ying, Y., & Lee, P. A. (2000). The meaning of "being Chinese" and "being American: Variation among Chinese American young adults." *Journal of Cross-Cultural Psychology, 31*, 302–332.

Tsai, J. L., Ying, Y., & Lee, P. A. (2001). Cultural predictors of self-esteem: A study of Chinese American female and male young adults. *Cultural Diversity and Ethnic Minority Psychology, 7*, 284–297.

Tseng, V. (2006). Unpacking immigration in youths' academic and occupational pathways. *Child Development, 77*, 1434–1445.

Tucker, W. H. (2004). "Inharmoniously adapted to each other": Science and racial crosses. In A. S. Winston (Ed.), *Defining difference: Race and racism in the history of psychology* (pp. 109–133). Washington, DC: American Psychological Association.

Tuvblad, C., Grann, M., & Lichtenstein, P. (2006). Heritability for adolescent antisocial behavior differs with socioeconomic status: Gene–environment interaction. *Journal of Child Psychology and Psychiatry, 47*, 734–743.

U.S. Bureau of the Census (2000). Scholars of all ages: School enrollment 2000. Retrieved September 25, 2007 from http://www.census.gov/population/pop-profile/2000/chap08.pdf

U.S. Bureau of the Census (June 2004). *Hispanic and Asian Americans increasing faster than overall population.* Retrieved May 24, 2008, from http://www.census.gov/PressRelease/www/releases/archives/race/001839.html

U.S. Bureau of the Census (December 2004a). *We the people: Asians in the United States: Census 2000 special reports.* Retrieved May 24, 2008 from http://www.census.gov/population/www/cen2000/briefs.html#sr

U.S. Bureau of the Census (December 2004b). *We the people: Hispanics in the United States: Census 2000 special reports.* Retrieved May 24, 2008 from http://www.census.gov/population/www/cen2000/briefs.html#sr

U.S. Bureau of the Census (August 2005). *We the people: Pacific Islanders in the United States: Census 2000 special reports.* Retrieved May 24, 2008 from http://www.census.gov/population/wwwcen2000/briefs .html#sr

U.S. Bureau of the Census (January 2006). *African-American History Month: February 2006.* Retrieved September 19, 2007 from: http://www.census.gov/Press-Release/www/2006/cb06ff01-2.pdf

U.S. Bureau of the Census (February 2006). *We the people: American Indians and Alaska Native in the United States.* Retrieved September 16, 2008 from: http://www.census.gov/population/www/socdemo/race/ censr-28.pdf

U.S. Bureau of the Census (October 2006). *School enrollment—Social and economic characteristics of students: October 2006.* Retrieved November 20, 2008 from http://www.census.gov/population/www/ socdemo/school/cps2006.html

U.S. Bureau of the Census (2007). *Current population survey: Annual social and economic (ASEC) supplement.* Retrieved September 19, 2007 from http://pubdb3.census.gov/macro/032007/pov/new01_100_03.htm

U.S. Bureau of the Census (March 2007). *Asian/Pacific American Heritage Month: May 2007.* Retrieved September 19, 2007 from http://www.census.gov/Press-Release/www/2007/cb07ff-05.pdf

U.S. Bureau of the Census (July 2007). *Hispanic Heritage Month 2007: September 15 to October 15.* Retrieved September 19, 2007 from http://www.census.gov/Press-Release/www/2007/cb07ff-14.pdf

U.S. Bureau of the Census (August 2007). *More Than 300 Counties Now "Majority-Minority" Press release August 9, 2007.* Retrieved September 10, 2007 from http://www.census.gov/Press-Release/www/ releases/archives/population/010482.html

U.S. Bureau of the Census (November 2007). *American Indian and Alaska Native Meritage Month: November 2007.* Retrieved September 16, 2008 from: http://www.census.gov/Press-Release/www/releases/ archives/facts_for_features_special_editions/010849.html

U.S. Department of Education (2004). *National study of postsecondary faculty.* Retrieved July 28, 2008 from http://nces.ed.gov/pubs2005/2005172.pdf

U.S. Department of Health and Human Services. (2006). *Promoting responsible fatherhood: Federal resource site.* Retrieved May 5, 2008, from http://fatherhood.hhs.gov/

Umaña-Taylor, A. J., & Fine, M. A. (2004). Examining ethnic identity among Mexican-origin adolescents living in the United States. *Hispanic Journal of Behavioral Sciences, 26,* 36–59.

Umaña-Taylor, A. J., & Shin, N. (2007). An examination of ethnic identity and self-esteem with diverse populations: Exploring variation by ethnicity and geography. *Cultural Diversity and Ethnic Minority Psychology, 13,* 178–186.

Umaña-Taylor, A. J., & Updegraff, K. A. (2007). Latino adolescents' mental health: Exploring the interrelations among discrimination, ethnic identity, cultural orientation, self-esteem, and depressive symptoms. *Journal of Adolescence, 30,* 549–567.

Updegraff, K. A., McHale, S. M., Whiteman, S. D., Thayer, Shawna M., & Crouter, A. C. (2006). The nature and correlates of Mexican-American adolescents' time with parents and peers. *Child Development, 77,* 1470–1486.

Utsey, S. O., Giesbrecht, N., Hook, J., & Stanard, P. M. (2008). Cultural, sociofamilial, and psychological resources that inhibit psychological distress in African Americans exposed to stressful life events and race-related stress. *Journal of Counseling Psychology, 55,* 49–62.

Van de Vijver, F. J. R., & Leung, K. (2000). Methodological issues in research on culture. *Journal of Cross-Cultural Psychology, 31,* 33–51.

Van Widenfelt, B. M., Treffers, P. D. A., de Beurs, E., Siebelink, B. M., & Koudijs, E. (2005). Translation and cross-cultural adaptation of assessment instruments used in psychological research with children and families. *Clinical Child and Family Psychology Review, 8,* 135–147.

Varela, E. R., Vernberg, E. M., Sanchez-Sosa, J. J., Riveros, A., Mitchell, M., & Mashunkashey, J. (2004). Anxiety reporting and culturally associated interpretation biases and cognitive schemas: A comparison of Mexican, Mexican American, and European families. *Journal of Clinical Child and Adolescent Psychology, 33,* 237–247.

Vasquez, M. J. T., & Jones, J. M. (2006). Increasing the number of psychologists of color: Public policy issues for affirmative diversity. *American Psychologist, 61,* 132–142.

Verkuyten, M., Kinket, B., & van der Weilen, C. (1997). Preadolescents' understanding of ethnic discrimination. *Journal of Genetic Psychology, 158*, 97–112.

Vygotsky, L. S. (1978). *Mind in society: The development of higher psychological processes.* Cambridge, MA: Harvard University Press.

Walker, R. L., Wingate, L. R., Obasi, E. M., & Joiner, T. E. (2008). An empirical investigation of acculturative stress and ethnic identity as moderators for depression and suicidal ideation in college students. *Cultural Diversity and Ethnic Minority Psychology, 14*, 75–82.

Wallace, J. M., Bachman, J. G., O'Malley, P. M., Johnston, J. D., Schulenberg, J. E., & Cooper, S. M. (2002). Tobacco, alcohol, and illicit drug use: Racial and ethnic differences among U.S. high school seniors, 1976-2000. *Public Health Reports, 117*(Suppl. 1), S67–S75.

Walls, M. L., Chapple, C. L., & Johnson, K. D. (2007). Strain, emotion, and suicide among American Indian youth. *Deviant Behavior, 28*, 219–246.

Walton, G. M., & Cohen, G. L. (2007). A question of belonging: Race, social fit, and achievement. *Journal of Personality and Social Psychology, 92*, 82–96.

Waters, M. C. (1990). *Ethnic options: Choosing identities in America.* Berkeley: University of California Press.

Whitbeck, L. B. (2006). Some guiding assumptions and a theoretical model for developing culturally specific preventions with Native American people. *Journal of Community Psychology, 34*, 183–192.

Whitbeck, L., Adams, G., Hoyt, D., & Chen, X. (2004). Conceptualizing and measuring historical trauma among American Indian people. *American Journal of Community Psychology, 33*, 119–130.

Whitesell, N. R., Mitchell, C. M., Kaufman, C. E., & Spicer, P. (2006). Developmental trajectories of personal and collective self-concept among American Indian adolescents. *Child Development, 77*, 1487–1503.

Whitfield, K. E., & McClearn, G. (2005). Genes, environment, and race: Quantitative genetic approaches. *American Psychologist, 60*, 104–114.

Wilkinson, C. (2005). *Blood struggle: The rise of modern Indian nations.* New York: Norton.

Willadsen-Jensen, E. C., & Ito, T. A. (2006). Ambiguity and the timecourse of racial perception. *Social Cognition, 24*, 580–606.

Willadsen-Jensen, E. C., & Ito, T. A. (2008). A foot in both worlds: Asian Americans' perceptions of Asian, White, and racially ambiguous faces. *Group Processes and Intergroup Relations, 11*, 182–200.

Williams, C. L., & Berry, J. W. (1991). Primary prevention of acculturative stress among refugees: Application of psychological theory and practice. *American Psychologist, 46*, 632–641.

Williams, D. R. (1999). Race, socioeconomic status, and health: The added effects of racism and discrimination. In N. Adler & M. Marmot (Eds.), *Socioeconomic status and health in industrial nations: Social, psychological, and biological pathways: Annals of the New York Academy of Sciences* (Vol. 896, pp. 173–188). New York: New York Academy of Sciences.

Williams, D. R., Neighbors, H. W., & Jackson, J. S. (2003). Racial/ethnic discrimination and health: Findings from community studies. *American Journal of Public Health, 93*, 200–208.

Williams, K. M. (2006). *Mark one or more: Civil rights in multiracial America.* Ann Arbor: University of Michigan Press.

Wills, T. A., Murry, V. M., Brody, G. H., Gibbons, F. X., Gerrard, M., Walker, C., & Ainette, M. G. (2007). Ethnic pride and self-control related to protective and risk factors: Test of the theoretical model for the Strong African American Families Program. *Health Psychology, 26*, 50–59.

Wittig, M. A. (1996). Taking affirmative action in education and employment. *Journal of Social Issues, 52*, 145–160.

Wong, S. K. (1999). Acculturation, peer relations, and delinquent behavior of Chinese-Canadian youth. *Adolescence, 34*, 108–119.

Wood, J. T. (1997). *Communication theories in action.* Belmont, CA: Wadsworth.

Xie, H., Li, Y., Boucher, S. M., Hutchins, B. C., & Cairns, B. D. (2006). What makes a girl (or a boy) popular (or unpopular)? African American children's perceptions and developmental differences. *Developmental Psychology, 42*, 599–612.

Yali, A. M., & Revenson, T. A. (2004). How changes in population demographics will impact health psychology: Incorporating a broader notion of cultural competence into the field. *Health Psychology, 23*, 147–155.

Yen, S., Robins, C. J., & Lin, N. (2000). A cross-cultural comparison of depressive symptom manifestation: China and the United States. *Journal of Consulting and Clinical Psychology, 68*, 993–999.

Ying, Y., Lee, P. A., Tsai, J. L., Hung, Y., Lin, M., & Wan, C. T. (2001). Asian American college students as model minorities: An examination of their overall competence. *Cultural Diversity and Ethnic Minority Psychology, 7*, 59–74.

Yip, T., & Cross, W. E. (2004). A daily diary study of mental health and community involvement outcomes for three Chinese American social identities. *Cultural Diversity and Ethnic Minority Psychology, 10*, 394–408.

Yip, T., Gee, G. C., & Takeuchi, D. T. (2008). Racial discrimination and psychological distress: The impact of ethnic identity and age among immigrant and United States–born Asian adults. *Developmental Psychology, 44*, 787–800.

Yip, T., Seaton, E. K., & Sellers, R. M. (2006). African American racial identity across the lifespan: Identity status, identity content, and depressive symptoms. *Child Development, 77*, 1504–1517.

Yoo, H. C., & Lee, R. M. (2005). Ethnic identity and approach-type coping as moderators of the racial discrimination/well-being relation in Asian Americans. *Journal of Counseling Psychology, 52*, 497–506.

Yoon, D. P. (2001). Causal modeling predicting psychological adjustment of Korean-born adolescent adoptees. *Journal of Human Behavior in the Social Environment, 3*, 65–82.

Yoon, D. P. (2004). Intercountry adoption: The importance of ethnic socialization and subjective well-being for Korean-born adopted children. *Journal of Ethnic and Cultural Diversity in Social Work, 13*, 71–89.

Zane, N., Hall, G. C. N., Sue, S., Young, K., & Nunez, J. (2004). Research on psychotherapy with culturally diverse populations. In M. J. Lambert (Ed.), *Handbook of psychotherapy and behavior change*, 5th edition (pp. 767–804). New York: Wiley.

Zane, N., & Mak, W. (2003). Major approaches to the measurement of acculturation among ethnic minority populations: A content analysis and an alternative empirical strategy. In K. M. Chun, P. B. Organista, & G. Marin (Eds.), *Acculturation: Advances in theory, measurement, and applied research* (pp. 39–60). Washington, DC: American Psychological Association.

Zárate, M. A., & Garza, A. A. (2002). In-group distinctiveness and self-affirmation as dual components of prejudice reduction. *Self and Identity, 1*, 235–249.

Zheng, Y., Lin, K., Takeuchi, D., Kurasaki, K. S., Wang, Y., & Cheung, F. (1997). An epidemiological study of neurasthenia in Chinese-Americans in Los Angeles, *Comprehensive Psychiatry, 38*, 240–259.

BIOGRAPHICAL SKETCH

Gordon C. Nagayama Hall is a professor of psychology at the University of Oregon. He received his PhD in clinical psychology from Fuller Theological Seminary. Dr. Hall was previously a professor of psychology at Kent State University and Pennsylvania State University. His research interests are in the cultural context of psychopathology. Dr. Hall is currently investigating cultural moderators of the effectiveness of treatments for depression with Asian Americans. This work is part of the Asian American Center on Disparities Research supported by the National Institute of Mental Health. Dr. Hall was president of the American Psychological Association Society for the Psychological Study of Ethnic Minority Issues (Division 45) and received the Distinguished Contribution Award from the Asian American Psychological Association. He is the editor of *Cultural Diversity and Ethnic Minority Psychology* and the an associate editor of the *Journal of Consulting and Clinical Psychology*.

AUTHOR INDEX

A

Abed, R. T., 42
Abeita, L., 136
Abe-Kim, J., 22, 110, 114, 126
Aber, J. L., 59
Aber, M. S., 72
Aboud, F. E., 54, 71
Abraído-Lanza, A. F., 127
Abueg, F. R., 124
Adams, G., 146
Agbayani-Siewert, P., 103
Aguirre, A. N., 127
AhnAllen, J. M., 157
Alarcón, R. D., 120
Alegria, M., 22, 131
Alexander, M. G., 70
Allard, C. B., 81
Allen, A. M., 59
Allport, G. W., 78
Altschul, I., 59, 62, 133
Alvarez, A. N., 56, 65
Alvarez, L., 66, 125, 126
Ambady, N., 25, 77, 158
Anaya, D., 171
Andal, J. D., 23
Anderson, N. B., 88
Anglin, D. M., 64, 98
Antonio, A., 7, 74, 81
Argenti, A. M., 41
Arias, E., 48
Armbrister, A. N., 127
Arndt, S., 145
Arnett, J. J., 3
Arnold, B., 44
Aronson, J., 75, 132
Asante, M. K., 92
Atkins, J., 57, 97
Atkinson, D. R., 109, 110
Averhart, C. J., 99
Aziz, N., 95

B

Bacallao, M. L., 130
Baer, J. C., 128
Baker, L. A., 143
Ball, T. J., 23
Bámaca, M. Y., 157
Banaji, M. R., 68, 72
Banks, K. H., 96
Bansal, A., 23, 28, 33
Bar-Haim, Y., 41, 42, 51
Barnes, N. W., 45
Baron, R. M., 31
Barongan, C., 2
Barth, J. M., 73
Bates, S. C., 26
Baumrind, D., 116
Bay-Cheng, L. Y., 43
Baysden, M. F., 158
Bazargan, M., 130
Bazargan, S., 130
Beach, S. R. H., 95
Beals, J., 146
Bean, F. D., 151, 157
Beauvais, F., 137
Belgrave, F. Z., 57
Bellack, A. S., 95
Benet-Martinez, V., 28
Bennett, G. G., 46
Berenbaum, H., 26
Berkel, C., 95
Berman, J. S., 139
Bernal, G., 119, 121, 122, 123, 124
Bernal, M. E., 53
Bernat, D. H., 61, 63
Bernstein, M., 10
Berry, J. W., 3, 7, 16, 17, 18, 19, 26, 29,
    33, 63, 154, 156
Bierman, A., 96
Bigfoot, D., 146
Bigler, R. S., 51, 52, 55, 56, 99

SUBJECT INDEX